The Ludic Self in Seventeenth-Century English Literature

SUNY Series, The Margins of Literature

Mihai I. Spariosu, Editor

The Ludic Self in Seventeenth-Century English Literature

Anna K. Nardo

State University of New York Press

Cover illustration from *Annalia Dubrensia* (1636),
showing a player in the Cotswold Games.
By permission of the Folger Shakespeare Library.

Published by
State University of New York Press, Albany

Printed in the United States of America

For information, address State University of New York
Press, State University Plaza, Albany, N.Y. 12246

Production by M. R. Mulholland
Marketing by Theresa A. Swierzowski

Library of Congress Cataloging-in-Publication Data

Nardo, Anna K., 1947–
The ludic self in seventeenth-century English literature / Anna K.
Nardo.
p. cm. — (SUNY series, the margins of literature)
Includes bibliographical references and index.
ISBN 0–7914-0721–7 (acid-free) . — ISBN 0–7914-0722–5 (pbk. : acid
-free)
1. English literature—Early modern, 1500–1700—History and
criticism. 2. Self in literature. 3. Play in literature.
I. Title. II. Series: SUNY series, margins of literature.
PR438.S45N37 1991
820.9'355'09032—dc20

90–44797
CIP

10 9 8 7 6 5 4 3 2 1

To the Memory of Nita L. and John Nardo

Magistra Ludorum et Piscator

Contents

Acknowledgments

Parts of this book first appeared elsewhere, and I would like to thank the following journals and presses for allowing me to reprint revised versions of these essays:

"The Play of and the Play in Literature." In *The Many Faces of Play,* ed. Kendall Blanchard, 124–32. Champaign, Illinois: Human Kinetics, 1986.

"Hamlet, 'A Man to Double Business Bound.'" *Shakespeare Quarterly* 34 (1983): 181–99.

"John Donne at Play in Between." In *The Eagle and the Dove: Reassessing John Donne,* ed. Ted-Larry Pebworth and Claude J. Summers, 157–65. Columbia: Univ. of Missouri Press, 1986.

"The Poetry of John Donne's Liminal Play." In *The Paradoxes of Play,* ed. John W. Loy Jr., 34–41. Champaign, Illinois: Human Kinetics, 1982.

"George Herbert Pulling for Prime." *South Central Review* 3 (1986): 28–42.

"Sir Thomas Browne: *Sub Specie Ludi.*" *The Centennial Review* 21 (1977): 311–20.

"'A Recreation of a Recreation': Reading *The Compleat Angler.*" *South Atlantic Quarterly* 79 (1980), 302–11.

* * *

The ability to play is a gift given to children and by children. I wrote *The Ludic Self,* in part, to understand this strange gift. Those who have taught me about play and literature are many, and I owe them thanks: Robert Hinman, who opened to me the play of seventeenth-century literature; the members of The Association for the Study of Play, especially Brian Sutton-Smith, who introduced me to the wide expanse of play theory; and the staff and fellows of the National Humanities Center, especially Steven Marcus, among whom scholarship became what it should be, play. I also owe thanks to many without whose generous encouragement and careful reading this "playing labour" could not have been published: Sumita Roy, William Aaron Tarver, Michelle Massé, Giuseppe Mazzotta, and Mihai I. Spariosu. Grants from the Southeast Institute for Medieval and Renaissance Studies and from the National Endowment for the Humanities allowed me to study play history and theory. Louisiana State University gave me two sabbatical leaves, a summer research grant, and hundreds of lively students with whom I have played out these ideas over the years.

Some gifts, however, are like grace; the only thanks possible is joy. So I rejoice in the memory of my mother, who gave me the gift of play; in my husband, Neal Cronin, who managed computer and domestic logistics with equal patience, and never lost faith in this project; and in our children, Patrick and Kate, whose play is a lesson and a wonder.

1

Self and Play: Definitions

In the first half of the seventeenth century, England produced an extraordinary array of self-conscious literary players, both fictional and real. At the turn of the century, Hamlet assumed his "antic disposition," and John Donne posed as faithful lover, then libertine, then Platonic idealist in riddling verse. George Herbert followed, composing puzzle poems in which he engaged both God and his readers in sacred games of wit. As political, intellectual, and religious disputes escalated toward civil war and a revolution of consciousness, men of letters continued to play. Despite his Puritan affiliations, Andrew Marvell had a playful streak that sparked him, even during the Interregnum, to write whimsical but enigmatic lyrics. Robert Burton called *The Anatomy of Melancholy,* his voluminous medical treatise, a "playing labour" written to stave off his own melancholy. Sir Thomas Browne, in defending the religion of a doctor, considered the universe his toy globe to "turne . . . round sometimes for [his] recreation." And Izaak Walton composed a fishing manual to be a "recreation of a recreation."[1]

Play, especially its relation to seriousness, fascinated men and women of the era. In "A Treatise on Playe" (1597), John Harington, the translator of Ariosto, attempts what twentieth-century cultural historians, sociologists, psychologists, anthropologists, philosophers, and theologians have labored to formulate: a definition of play. By describing it as "a spending of the tyme eyther in speeche or action, whose only end is delyght of the mynd and speryt," Harington includes devotion as a "kynde of recreation," indeed "absolutely the best." He justifies sacred play by the example of David, who played instruments and, although naked, danced before the Ark of the Covenant. When reproached for acting like a buffoon, King David replied, *"Ludam et fiam vilior"*—in the Douay translation of the Vulgate, "I will both play and make myself meaner than I have done: and I will be little in my own eyes" (2 Kings 6:22).[2] Playing freely in the Lord's loving presence becomes an important motif in much of the poetry and emblem literature of the period, and serious devotional writers frequently associate the Christian life with play.[3] Even the dissolute Thomas Carew, while deprecating his profane verse in comparison to George Sandys's holy poems, hopes to redeem his "unwasht Muse" and imitate King David's play:

> Though nor in tune, nor wing, she reach thy Larke,
> Her Lyrick feet may dance before the Arke.
> Who knowes, but that her wandring eyes that run,
> Now hunting Glow-wormes, may adore the Sun?[4]

Like many of his contemporaries, Carew sees that innocent play may lead to worship.

Naturally not everyone in the seventeenth century (nor today) could believe that play and seriousness are compatible. Puritan conduct books, manuals on sermon writing, and diatribes against dicing, church ales, and stage plays allow only those lawful pastimes that render humans more fit for work, and reject playfulness associated with devotion. Condemning especially "Prayers with strong lines," Daniel Featley mimics these lines to ridicule the man who comes "unto *God,* not *with the soales of his feet, but the feet of his soule,*" because "this is *playing,* not *Praying.*"[5] Even the master of strong lines, John Donne, occasionally doubts that his playful language is appropriate to serious devotion: in "The Litany," he prays for deliverance from "my excess / In seeking secrets, or poeticness" and from being "moved to seem religious / Only to vent wit."[6] Whether or not seventeenth-century writers and readers approved, they recognized much writing on serious issues, even religion, as play.

A puzzling question is why so many writers throughout the Renaissance represented their experience of a divided world in the spirit of play. Acute readers have studied this efflorescence of literary playfulness, which was not limited to England. Mikhail Bakhtin reads Rabelais's use of carnivalesque play as a literary regeneration of the communal grotesque body of the people, in opposition to both the passing medieval hierarchical self and the emerging individualized bourgeois self. Richard Lanham finds the motives for the playful eloquence of representative works from Chaucer to Shakespeare in the education that emphasized rhetoric and thus encouraged writers to assume any role that would persuade. This education, he argues, produced a species of man, *homo rhetoricus,* without a centrally rooted self, who found reality only in the role play of rhetoric. Taking his cue from Lanham, Richard Helgerson defines the serious selves projected by "self-crowned laureates," like Spenser, Jonson, and Milton, in contrast to amateurs like Donne and professionals like Shakespeare, who were detached role players on a world stage.

Leah Sinanoglou Marcus is less concerned with play and self-definition than with play and history. She explains the importance of play to seventeenth-century English poets as sometimes a retreat to the innocence and humility of childhood to escape from political conflicts and social turmoil, and as other times an oblique engagement in those conflicts through allusions to the Stuart policies on merrymaking promulgated in *The Book of Sports*. The broadest of these studies, Frank J. Warnke's survey of seventeenth-century European literature, attributes the period's playfulness to the baroque style and suggests some relationship between play and the confusions of seventeenth-century life: "Possibly there is some connection between the spirit of the seventeenth century, with its incessant conflicts of ideologies, values, and modes of thought, and the characteristic works of art of that century, which consistently express an awareness of the contradictions of experience and resolve those contradictions in the hallowed sphere of play."[7] That connection is one goal of this study: to describe how play offered Hamlet, Donne, Herbert, Marvell, Burton, and Browne a way to live within the contradictions and conflicts of their experience. They found in play a new stance for the self—not some universal body of the people, nor the nonself of *homo rhetoricus,* but a ludic self that allowed them to stand, without retreating, in the midst of difficult dilemmas.

To catch a glimpse of this new self founded in play and to follow its darting through an era of such profound change requires some preparation. Minimal working definitions of *self* and *play* establish my starting point for interpretation. A fictional example from the turn of the century, Hamlet, provides us with a paradigm of the self who finds in play a precarious stance amid maddening contradictions. Then a historical overview surveys the uses of play among real selves ill-equipped for revolutionary change—an overview that must expand and complicate the original working definitions of *self* and *play.* The first three chapters offer these definitions, illustration, overview, and redefinitions. After this preparation, the central chapters analyze distinct versions of the ludic self—from Donne's tense, flashy illusiveness to Browne's assured toying with the cosmos; from Herbert's wrestling with the angel of God to Burton's wrestling with the chaos of knowledge; from Marvell's recreating to Marvell's re-creating the self. My conclusion both backtracks and points ahead—to glance at the antecedent tradition of literary play in works from Rabelais to Cervantes, to preview a new concept of play in Izaak Walton's best seller, *The Compleat Angler,* and thus to locate the literary players of the midseventeenth century in a historical poise between folly and leisure.

I

Selves come into being in every era, and variable child-rearing practices, determined by and inculcating variable cultural codes, delimit the range of available structures for the self in a given era. The earliest events in the process of self-formation, however, seem universal, although timed and negotiated differently. So, when we take account of historically specific child-rearing practices, as we shall later, we can use the research of modern psychoanalysis into these early events to understand a version of self available in seventeenth-century England.

In the current debate over what, if anything, constitutes the self, theorists in various camps agree in locating the origin of subjectivity earlier than the Oedipal period, in the infant's first interactions with the world of objects and caregivers. In its primary narcissism, the infant seems merged with the source of nurture in an omnipotence that perceives no distinction between me and not-me. The inevitable and mysterious absences of the caregiver, however, shatter this illusion. Alone, the infant experiences being, not as a self, but as a flood of stimuli from within and without, as the pressure of impulses over which s/he has no control, and as a body whose movements s/he cannot coordinate. When the caregiver returns, more or less accurately perceives the infant's needs, and responds, then the infant finds in this care a kind of mirror of what s/he is. When mothers and fathers celebrate a spontaneous gesture as a wave or a grimace as a smile, then the infant sees in their response an image of what to be. When placed before an actual mirror (at between six and eighteen months), the infant appears enthralled, even ecstatic at the image of wholeness s/he perceives, so different from the inner experience of uncoordination.

As the caregivers physically hold the infant and arrange through nurture a holding environment, s/he experiences a cohesion of once random sensorimotor discharges. Captivated by the human face that offers an image of a self, the infant begins to identify with that image, composed of some mixture of the caregivers' responses to perceived need and projections from their own desires into an identity for the child. The symbiosis of this period breaks at around eighteen months with a thundering "NO!" as simultaneously the child begins to assert autonomy and to gain language. Entry into linguistic competence gives the child power in the struggle for autonomy from the caregivers' image and also subjects the child to the cultural codes that constitute and are constituted in language. The mastery of language completes the construction of the basic structure for a self—a framework that a life of linguistic and social interaction will continue to elaborate.

So much for fundamental agreement. What happens to the child seems clear, but theorists draw battle lines at what these events mean, particularly at two key points of interpretation: the status of the self, and the significance of the space opened up by separation. Jacques Lacan and his followers, in line with the opposition of current continental philosophy to the concept of a transcendent self, argue that the infant's first image of an "I" is an illusion or attribution. The mirror reflects a unity that does not match the infantile experience of fragmentation, and the caregivers' image projects their own desire; thus the infant identifies with a desire that is "other." Although language frees the child from "captivation" by this image, the codes and laws of language require subjection to a greater "Other," and words are by their nature absence, a substitution for a presence of being to itself, lost forever with primary narcissism. For Lacan, the self is a "subject" position in language, a locus, not an entity, constituted in experiences of alienation; the space opened up by separation is an abyss.[8]

In general, theorists of object relations and theorists of narcissism (the following chapters will detail the findings of D. W. Winnicott, Margaret Mahler, and Heinz Kohut) perceive the same events, although their theories are based on observations of infants and on clinical data rather than on the debates of continental philosophy. The self they describe also originates in separation and is constructed in relation to primary objects. However, they do not assume that, because the self is constructed, it is a void or an illusion. The infant is not born with a self, only with needs, drives, and a genetic potential. When s/he looks in a mirror or gazes at a face, there is no entity yet to be alienated from. When s/he experiences the holding of nurture, identifies with caregivers' images, and internalizes cultural codes, a structure consolidates where only randomness existed before. So Lacanian phrases like the "fictional direction" of the ego, "the armour of alienating identity," or "the primary alienation of the *infans* from 'himself'" seem more like rhetoric than useful theoretical constructs.[9]

Depending on how the infant's earliest experiences are managed, s/he may, in fact, not be able to construct the framework for a viable self. If caregivers' absences are prolonged or traumatic, if caregivers *only* project their own psychic agenda and seldom perceive and respond to the child's spontaneous gestures, if cultural codes are inculcated in ways that confuse the child or warp potential, then s/he may form a self too compliant to external expectations to own internal desire, one too rigid or too weak to sustain conflict, or no self at all. Indeed, there are "false," divided, and wholly fragmented selves.[10] In the Renaissance and today they languish in institutions and wander the streets, and their real sufferings call into question the facile use in literary criticism of phrases like "the dispersion of . . . simultaneous selves" and "the void that constitutes identity" to characterize authors or readers.[11]

Most people, however, do survive the vicissitudes of infancy and childhood with a functional self; they feel a sense of identity, albeit cobbled together, between what they have been and may be, between impulse, thought, and action. The key word here is *functional*. Neither a transcendent ego nor a void, this self may experience tension, at times wrenching conflicts; it will be more or less vulnerable to dissolution; and certainly it will be subject to further construction.[12] Nevertheless, theories of object relations describe the self as a complex, ongoing inner synthesis characterized by a feeling of sameness and continuity.[13]

In regard to the second point of conflict, these theories do not interpret the experience of separation—between image and impulse, caregiver and infant, word and presence—as necessarily an abyss of alienation. D. W. Winnicott sees in these gaps a potential space for the earliest play, where infants and children may negotiate the boundaries between self and other. In this "play space," neither wholly in-here nor wholly out-there, the infant can connect the inner world of impulse and need with the external world that s/he has painfully discovered to be beyond omnipotent control. This play transforms part of the not-me world (a toy, a blanket, nurturing hands) in accord with some fantasy from the me-world (the caregiver's comforting presence, her breast, or her puzzling disappearance and return). Through play as simple as peek-a-boo, the child discovers that s/he is separate from the world of objects s/he manipulates, but that s/he is not alienated, because s/he can transform those objects; the self is neither merged with nor abandoned by the other.[14]

From this perspective, Freud's grandson's famous game (in which he repeated "Fort! Da!" as he reenacted the absence and return of his mother by throwing away and then retrieving a spool on a string) is more than a demonstration of Freud's theory of repetition compulsion or a "myth of origins" for Lacan's theory of the constitution of the subject in absence.[15] It is an example of play at mastery. The child transforms objects in accord with fantasy and thus locates the self in between what is inside and what is other. Winnicott further conjectures that such early play in the space opened by separation is the basis for human culture, the means whereby adults make themselves at home in a world no longer designed to gratify their desires.

As one of the elements of human culture, writing can become, like the earliest play, a self-constituting act. Against those who limit language to a system of differences serving the social system of exchange, Julia Kristeva has asserted that "the science of linguistics has no way of apprehending anything in language which belongs not with the social contract but with play, pleasure or desire." In poetic language, the play of primary process thinking erupts into the secondary process of linguistic structure, creating a dynamic interaction.[16] As the author sorts through these bits of fantasy from the unconscious, perceptions from consciousness, and pressures from the outside world—arranging and rearranging them in a dialogue with linguistic structures—s/he constructs a whole, and in the process may bring a confused or disjointed self into focus. So the entry into language is not simply the loss of presence, not always a deferral; it can be a means to give voice to and synthesize the competing forces that constitute identity. In the resulting text, the author projects a version of self, not necessarily identical with the internal structure, but not wholly unrelated either.

II

'Play' is a no less vexed concept than 'self'. It is such a multidimensional phenomenon that no single discipline can exhaust its complexities. Suppose we seat a varied group of the learned behind a one-way mirror looking into a nursery school class of five-year-olds, some of whom are playing house while others roughhouse. Then let us ask the learned what they see. The ethologist observes the hubbub—squealing, wiggling, and jockeying for position and toys—and then describes its roots in animal evolution toward adaptation strategies more flexible than instinct. "This apparent chaos," adds the psychologist, "also fits into a larger pattern of human development: these preschoolers are moving beyond the sensorimotor play of toddlers into make-believe play; they won't play rule-bound games for two or three years yet." The psychoanalyst interrupts, "But that withdrawn boy in the corner, who is sucking a frayed blanket and rocking back and forth, has too fragile a sense of self to venture it in even the most elementary exploratory play, much less in make-believe."

The sociologist veers off in another direction, pointing out how the two games, roughhouse and house, illustrate the social construction of gender and prepare these children for adult roles. The anthropologist agrees, but questions the psychologist's assumption that there are universal, developmental stages of play; he contrasts these children to those of the Nyansongo of Kenya who almost never play make-believe. Although agreeing with the anthropologist and sociologist, the cultural historian reminds them of the influence that available toys exert on this kind of play; he compares the classroom's elaborate "home-living center" to the single rag doll in the home of a tot in nineteenth-century rural America. At this point, the communications theorist interjects, "Wait a minute. How much of this behavior is actually play? Most of the time these kids are negotiating who will play what in the game that only lasts an instant before new negotiations about the game erupt: 'You be the daddy.' 'No, I'm Batman.' 'You can't be Batman; I'm Batman.'"

While both children and colleagues argue, the philosopher and theologian listen patiently and, after a pause, leave their seats to join the children. When asked later to explain their odd behavior, they reply, in chorus, "I saw in this play the ground of my being." "The joy and innocence of amoral creation and destruction," continues the philosopher. "No, the joy and innocence of living a narrative life," counters the theologian. "But," they muse, "why did the children look at us funny and quit playing when we took their blocks and dolls?"

Albeit playful, this parable is not far from the truth about the state of research on play. Everyone sees something different. Several excellent surveys have tried to bring order to these varied perspectives, obviating the need to rehearse all these theories here.[17] What this project needs now is a working definition of play, to be expanded later by some of the theories oversimplified in our parable. But definitions, like theories, have proliferated. In literary study, two quite diverse conceptions have dominated: those of Johan Huizinga and Jacques Derrida.[18] These two theorists, a historian of culture and a philosopher of language, articulate two opposed concepts of play: play as voluntary, intentional human action, and play as impersonal, involuntary movement.

Huizinga defines play as "an activity which proceeds within certain limits of time and space, in a visible order, according to rules freely accepted, and outside the sphere of necessity or material utility." From this definition, he argues, "All poetry is born of play: the sacred play of worship, the festive play of courtship, the martial play of the contest, the disputatious play of braggadocio, mockery, and invective, the nimble play of wit and readiness." Other cultural institutions that Huizinga believes originated in play—religion, science, law, war, and politics—become less playful as they become more organized, but poetry, he asserts, is always play.[19] Derrida agrees that all culture is played but denies that individuals determine the play. Since he believes that there are no absolute centers—neither subjects like authors and readers, nor objects, like texts, that have stable significations—then all literature and interpretation are "free play." Authors and readers themselves result from the free play of various constituting factors, so the texts authors and literary critics produce come not from selves, but from the free play of language in previous texts.[20]

Both these theories rely on partial definitions that blur distinctions important for literary criticism. Derrida's concept of free play, as Mihai Spariosu has traced it, extends into the domain of language a concept of play employed by Nietzsche and Heidegger. Reacting against the rationalist tradition, these philosophers return to pre-Socratic thought, embracing Heraclitus's dictum, "Lifetime is a child at play, moving pieces in a game, the kingship belongs to the child." Like the philosopher in our playful parable, they see in the play of the child, and by analogy the play of the artist, an amoral creation and destruction that signifies the aimless to-and-fro movement of the cosmos. This conception of play offers little utility for analyzing play in literature for two reasons.[21]

First, it is based on a metaphor that won't work. To image the arbitrariness and aimlessness of becoming and passing, this line of philosophers, although not Derrida himself, compares life to a playing child. But to see child's play as the groundless ground of being is to mystify it. After all, when the philosopher in our parable tried to play this game, the children stopped theirs. Child's play is not arbitrary or aimless. Despite the apparent chaos in the nursery school class, the learned saw nascent selves negotiating their boundaries, roles, and power. Building and smashing block houses is not the amoral joy of aleatory creation and destruction. Both the building and smashing have meaning and follow patterns in the development of intellectual skills, emotions, gender roles, cultural values, and so forth.

Eugen Fink, a disciple of Heidegger, also sees play as a symbol of the world, but draws an important distinction. Although within its world human play has reasons and goals, the world totality itself, within which all means and ends arise, is without reason, goal, value, or plan. Cosmic power, he argues, is the play of becoming and passing, and its totality may shine through in the child's or the artist's sense of freedom, power, and irresponsibility. Still, unlike human play, world play has no intending subject.[22] So, although the spontaneity and ceaseless motion of child's play may help philosophers image a decentered universe without meaning, we cannot take this metaphor as a description of how play functions within the world of culture and use it to interpret other forms of human play like literature. Similarly, the play of the artist, so close to the child at play, may image for philosophers the capricious making and unmaking that moves the cosmos, but their image does not define art as a capricious making and unmaking. For Nietzsche and his successors, the artist creating and the child at play symbolize cosmic becoming and passing, but this metaphor is not an interpretive tool.

Second, even if we dispense with Heraclitus's problematical metaphor of child's play and focus on Derrida's more abstract concept of *free play,* the term still has little utility for analyzing play in literature. Derrida equates *play* with slippage or random movement—as in the sentence "There is too much *play* in this steering wheel." Since everything in his view is free play—language, texts, subjects, objects—Derrida rejects a theory of play that places an initiating subject at its center. If every act is the product, not of an intending self, but of random to-and-fro movement within and between systems with no center, then there are no distinctions to be made between playful and nonplayful acts. But if we return to our parable, we may remember the difference between the withdrawn boy in the corner, who sucks a blanket and rocks, and his romping classmates. In human terms, some movement is play and some is not; some children can play and some cannot. Derrida's concept of free play blurs such distinctions.

Furthermore, to explore, to pretend, and to compete, a child must have a self centered enough to ground any movement into the open space of play. There is no "free play" among children without some center. The same, I would argue, is true for literary critics. If we accede to Derrida's proclamation that the self is an absent center, a stance questionable on psychoanalytic grounds, we are left with universal free play, a concept that cannot help us make distinctions among the rich proliferation of playful acts in literature. We must either abandon criticism altogether or endlessly chart the slippages that destabilize meaning. Like the boy in our parable, we won't be able to play at all, or we will be able to play only one game, rocking back and forth.

Huizinga's definition of play (a rule-governed activity limited in time and space, set apart from what is necessary or useful) is more attentive to human play than Derrida's, but he tries to classify that which itself classifies. Play is so hard to define precisely because it is itself a defining activity: it communicates the definition of a situation to participants. Attempts to delimit play to a category of activities, so that a given action will always be play, are inadequate. Sunday TV viewers know that, when an NFL lineman breaks from the huddle, his mood is more likely to be deadly earnest than playful. Readers of eighteenth-century novels know that *Clarissa* is less playful than *Tristram Shandy.* Not a class of certain kinds of activities (not all football games are play; not all literature is play), play defines a given action in a certain way (punching another player may or may not be play; allusions to sexuality may or may not be playful). Play is a context, a frame, or a stance players adopt toward a source, almost any source—such as an object when toying with a pencil, or a person when teasing a friend, or a role when acting Macbeth, or an activity when playing war. The text produced by this context alludes to, purports to imitate, and transforms the source of the play.[23]

Gregory Bateson first noticed the importance of framing in play while watching otters in a zoo. The otters took their chasing, nipping, and scuffling—behaviors that might signal "This is a fight"—to mean "This is play." Observing this complex communication, Bateson realized that the otter who nips a playfellow gives a double message in a single action. The context message, "This is play, not a bite," frames the situation, redefining and transforming the fact of the bite, the physiological message, "This is a bite." Because of this doubleness of definition, play creates a logical paradox. For the otters, the paradox takes the form "This bite does not signify what a bite signifies." The play frame, Bateson reasoned, resembles the classic self-referential paradox formulated by Epimenides, the Cretan, who claimed, "All Cretans are liars." If the statement is true, then Epimenides, because he is a Cretan, must be lying, but then his statement must be false, and he may be telling the truth. This tangle reduces to the paradox: if Epimenides is telling the truth, then he is lying. Similarly, the otter's playful nip both is and is not a bite.

These self-references create logical paradoxes because the definition of the class of actions is itself one of the actions being defined. Although theoretically invalid, this confusion of logical types—of the defining frame with what is inside the frame—pervades human life and can produce great pleasure. This same paradox frames other forms of cultural play such as drama and ballet: the ballerina who dances *Swan Lake* both is and is not a swan.[24] Furthermore, because play conflates the defining frame with what is inside the frame, a single play action takes place simultaneously on two levels of reality: the player both participates in his action and stands apart framing the action, thereby gaining distance and perspective on himself. Although using different terms, Fulke Greville recognized this doubleness of the play stance; in his *Life of Sir Philip Sidney,* he describes "that hypocriticall figure *Ironia,* wherein men commonly (to keep above their workes) seeme to make toies of the utmost they can doe."[25] The seventeenth century understood the relation between play and perspective.

Following the lead of Bateson, Erving Goffman has classified the frames by which we define our experience. Several of these frames resemble play because they transform one kind of activity into another, which, although patterned on the first activity, is perceived by participants as something else. The frame of "make-believe," which applies to Bateson's otters and ballerinas, includes imitation, playfulness, fantasy, and drama. "Contests" include games and sports, in which clear limits of time and/or space and voluntarily accepted rules define the play frame so clearly that players need not continue to give the metamessage (a message about how to take a message) "This is play." As a result, these limits and rules create a microcosm, a secondary world, which takes on a separate "reality" so compelling that players sometimes forget their paradoxical position. They may feel that their actions are "real," not both real and not real simultaneously (hence the NFL lineman's earnestness when breaking from the huddle).[26]

When art gives form and limits to make-believe and fantasy (the time from the dimming of the lights to the final curtain, the space between the margins on the page), it may create an even more compelling "reality" than do games. Goffman's taxonomy helps clarify why, although literature may originate in play (in the play that generates culture as Winnicott and Huizinga would have it, or the daydreams of the author as Freud would have it), literature occupies its own class, the aesthetic domain. Like any other cultural category, literature may or may not be played.[27]

III

Two well known seventeenth-century lyrics can illustrate this distinction between playful and not-so-playful texts, and preview some moves of the ludic self. In 1652, after interrupting his promising poetic career to serve the revolutionary cause, John Milton was struck totally blind. As a record of anger and frustration, but ultimate submission to God's will, he composed "When I consider how my light is spent."[28] Although no one can be privy to the mind of a long dead poet, we may speculate that Milton played while writing this serious poem. As an Italian sonnet, its rigid meter and rhyme demand masterful skill with language. Yet within this form Milton manipulates its conventions to match his meaning, transcends the sonnet's brevity with allusions, and makes words serve double functions. He ends the thought of the octave in the middle of line 8 to enact the intervention of "patience to prevent" his almost blasphemous murmurings, which rumble through the first seven lines, from controlling the sonnet's first partition. He weaves into the texture of what appears to be spontaneous thought allusions to the parable of the talents and to the distinctions that arcane angelology draws between messenger angels, who "post o're Land and Ocean," and contemplative angels, "who only stand and waite" before God's radiance. And he ends the sonnet with a pun on *wait,* meaning both to attend idly and to serve actively—a quibble that encapsulates the speaker's hard-won realization that passive waiting is active service.

Whether or not this technical virtuosity resulted from Milton's play when he wrote the sonnet, the voice of the poem is not playful. It does not call attention to the use of literary conventions or invite the reader to pit his or her interpretive skills against the poet's cleverness. Rather, Milton uses literary structures and codes to create a miniature drama of a blind man on a spiritual pilgrimage to light, and through sonnet form, allusions, and puns he summons the reader to identify with the poetic voice and journey with him out of spiritual blindness toward submission before God's throne.

Like Milton, John Donne faced mid-life with anxiety, which he tried to allay by submission to God. Probably in 1623 after a serious illness, he recorded one such attempt at submission in "A Hymn to God the Father." As a hymn, this poem tested Donne's composing skills as the sonnet form did Milton's. Its stanzaic pattern, repetitive questions, and refrain, which puns on the speaker's name, suggest that Donne may also have played while composing. But the voice singing this hymn, unlike the well-defined voice of Milton's sonnet, is ambiguous and playful indeed.

Donne's catalogue of sins, his reiterated prayers for forgiveness, and his longing to bask in the radiance of the Son of God characterize him as a rueful penitent working out his salvation in fear and trembling. Yet, behind the penitent dances the irrepressible, slippery sinner, who seems almost gleeful at dredging up sin after sin to exhaust even God's patience. The refrain sounds like the boast of a playful child running from his father, to whom the hymn is explicitly addressed. Teasing "God the Father" to chase and catch him, the impish speaker taunts, "When thou has done [finished], thou hast not done [the man], / For I have more." Here the pun on Donne's name contrasts markedly to Milton's pun on *wait* in the sonnet on his blindness. Whereas Milton's climactic pun compresses the poem's dramatic tension into one word, thereby moving the reader to share the speaker's experience of frustration and submission, Donne's name pun characterizes the speaker, who both seeks and runs away from God, as a ludic self playing catch-me-if-you-can.

Likewise, the voice of the hymn plays hide-and-seek with the reader. At least in part, Donne's hymn is not a solemn musical offering to God, but a game for the reader to test his or her ability to get the joke. Will s/he recognize *done* as *Donne,* and maybe even *more* as *More*—a pun on the family name of Donne's deceased wife, whom he may have loved idolatrously? The refrain implies that God cannot have *done* (finished) and have *Donne* (the man) so long as Donne has *more* sins and his passion for Anne *More*.[29] Instead of increasing the reader's identification with the speaker, as does Milton's pun, Donne's wit both distances and attracts the reader, making him a playmate, even a competitor, challenging her not only to get the joke, but to find the hiding speaker. Is he a sincere penitent terrified that his sins abound more than grace, and that he will "perish on the shore" at his death? Or is he a tease whose insatiable needs demand repeated assurances of love, and who, while pleading to God for these assurances, always has an eye on the reader, whom he also wants to impress with his flashy wit? The self projecting the voice of this poem is an artful dodger who dares the reader to pin him down.

Although both Milton and Donne may have played while writing these poems, and readers may imaginatively share the poets' self-dramatization, the hymn self-consciously frames itself as play and calls for a playful response from its reader, whereas the sonnet does not.[30] These examples generate two related questions to help us identify literary play: (1) What kind of voice does the text project: the voice of a single self who communicates definable (if complex) ideas, emotions, or experiences to the reader, or the voice of an ambiguous, tricky self who plays with the reader? (2) What kind of response does the voice require from the reader: understanding of the communicated ideas and empathy with the emotions or experiences, or countermoves as in a game, solutions as in a puzzle, or a tense anticipation of the next play, a tension that precludes complete empathy?[31]

With these working definitions of *self* and *play,* and this preview of the ludic self, we can now explore the relation between play and contradictions that threaten the self. *Hamlet* appears at the turn of a century of contradictions, and its protagonist offers a paradigm for the other, later players to be studied here. All are emersed in worlds of destructive conflict and paradox, and all play to defend or integrate a self. As complex as *Hamlet* is, it is art, not life; its characters and world, although multifaceted and ambiguous, are circumscribed and formed, as life is not. So in the limited world of a drama, we can clarify the interrelation between play, self, and contradiction, as seen through contemporary eyes, before we turn to the morass of contradiction in seventeenth-century life and to the role of play in history. *Hamlet* dramatizes two families enmeshed in maddening dilemmas and one man's attempt to preserve his self in play.

2

Hamlet, "A Man to Double Business Bound": An Example

Ironically, Claudius, not Hamlet, articulates the paralysis of a man facing a dilemma. Alone in his private chapel, he feels impelled by his guilt to pray. But, he laments,

> Pray can I not,
> Though inclination be as sharp as will:
> My stronger guilt defeats my strong intent;
> And, like a man to double business bound,
> I stand in pause where I shall first begin,
> And both neglect. (3.3.38–43)

Like so many passages in Shakespeare's most ambiguous play, Claudius's words apply less to himself than to Hamlet. In self-pity Claudius feels like the victim of a double bind, when in reality he has a clear moral choice: to renounce "crown . . . ambition and . . . queen" and pray for forgiveness, or to keep "those effects for which [he] did the murder" and live with his guilt. He lacks the courage to choose and tries unsuccessfully to have it both ways, kneeling and hoping lamely, "All may be well." Hamlet, however, is a true victim of double binds. Thrust into a familial situation remarkably similar in its patterns of interaction to families that produce mad children, he confronts contradictory demands from which he cannot escape. Both Hamlet and Ophelia face double binds, and although Hamlet plays to elude and finally to transcend the traps set for him, their struggles within their bonds result in tragedy.[1]

I

The double bind is a pattern of communication, often found in families with a schizophrenic adolescent or young adult, that impedes offspring from forming a functional, separate self. The pattern generally occurs under the following conditions:

1. When the individual is involved in an intense relationship; that is, a relationship in which he feels it is vitally important that he discriminate accurately what sort of message is being communicated so that he may respond appropriately.
2. And, the individual is caught in a situation in which the other person in the relationship is expressing two orders of message and one denies the other.
3. And, the individual is unable to comment on the messages being expressed to correct his discrimination of what order of message to respond to, i.e., he cannot make a metacommunicative statement.[2]

Being caught in a double bind feels like confronting a sign that says, "Don't read this sign." By definition, a sign asks to be read, but the message *on* the sign conflicts with the message *of* the sign qua sign. Although this paradox is comical, double binds experienced repeatedly from infancy, in intimate relationships of mutual dependency, are not; they can enfeeble the self, eventually causing it to disintegrate.

Unfortunately, in human behavior double binds are seldom so clear or countable as verbal paradoxes because they arise out of the whole context of communication in a long-term relationship and cannot be understood outside of the relationship. Nevertheless, the following situation illustrates the double bind:

> A young man who had fairly well recovered from an acute schizophrenic episode was visited in the hospital by his mother. He was glad to see her and impulsively put his arm around her shoulders, whereupon she stiffened. He withdrew his arm and she asked, "Don't you love me any more?" He then blushed, and she said, "Dear, you must not be so easily embarrassed and afraid of your feelings." The patient was able to stay with her only a few minutes more and following her departure he assaulted an aide and was put in the tubs.[3]

While rejecting her son on the level of body communication, the mother in this example verbally demands affection. Drawing the knot of the double bind tight, she prevents him from perceiving the contradiction by blaming him for being afraid and embarrassed at displays of feeling, when clearly she cannot accept such displays. The son is trapped: if he wants to keep his tie to his mother, he must not show her that he loves her, but if he does not show her that he loves her, then he will lose her. In families that communicate in double bind patterns, the individuals' mutual dependency or a specific prohibition blocks escape from the field.[4]

The originators of the double bind theory formulated it to explain the genesis of schizophrenia as a pattern of irrational perception and behavior learned in infancy and perpetuated throughout childhood. Entangled in these paradoxical modes of communication, a family may maintain a relative status quo until maturational and social pressures compel the vulnerable child to become more independent. Typically, the attempted separation produces a schizophrenic episode in the adolescent or young adult. The psychosis may be an unsuccessful attempt to deal with the frustrations and paralysis of double bind situations. More successful ways to untie double binds are recognizing the incongruity of the two messages and giving a double message in reply. Not even these always forestall madness. Bateson, one of the originators of the theory, has observed, "The psychotic patient may make astute, pithy, often metaphorical remarks that reveal an insight into the forces binding him. Contrariwise, he may become rather expert in setting double bind situations himself." Hamlet does both.[5]

II

Because *Hamlet* opens in darkness and confusion with "Who's there?," employs question, doubt, and irony as its most common rhetorical modes, and involves almost everyone in the play in duplicity, it is not surprising to find the characters in double bind situations.[6] From the first moment we see Hamlet, his black clothes implicitly rebuking the mirthful court's disrespect for his dead father, he is evading traps set by Claudius. With hypocritical oxymorons ("mirth in funeral . . . dirge in marriage") and pointed reminders to the courtiers that they approved his hasty marriage to his brother's widow, the king delivers an unctuous speech commencing a public ritual in which all must legitimize his dubious act by their tacit assent. Because Hamlet nonverbally refuses to participate, Claudius tries to force either public sanction of the marriage and his kingship, regardless of Hamlet's personal feelings, or public opposition, in which case Claudius could remove him in the interest of national security, as he does in act 4. When Claudius asks metaphorically why his stepson is still in mourning, Hamlet correctly perceives the real message and translates "How is it that the clouds still hang on you?" (1.2.66) as "Sanction my marriage to your mother by dressing appropriately." He evades the trap by not responding to either the explicit or implicit message; instead, he pretends to take Claudius's cloud metaphor literally and answers with a punning riddle: "Not so, my lord; I am too much in the sun" (1.2.67)—too much out of doors, too much in the sun of Claudius's favor, too much of a son to Claudius. This first exchange clearly demonstrates Hamlet's remarkable ability to recognize and manipulate levels of communication. By shifting to the literal level, he does more than evade Claudius's trap; he delivers a multiple insult that epitomizes his anger and opposition to his stepfather but that Claudius cannot answer. Like his mourning clothes, Hamlet's puns allow him tacitly to oppose Claudius's regime without fear of retribution and without betraying "that within which passeth show" to hypocritical "seems," as, he pointedly hints, Gertrude and the courtiers have already done (1.2.76–86).

Ironically, not the crafty Claudius, but the weak-willed and naive Gertrude traps Hamlet in a double bind. Neither the veiled threats in the insulting terms the king uses to describe Hamlet's grief ("obstinate condolement... impious stubbornness... unmanly grief..."), nor the bribe of being "most immediate to [the] throne" impels Hamlet to stay in Elsinore, "in the cheer and comfort" of Claudius's watchful eye (1.2.87–117). Hamlet assents only to his mother's simple plea, which, in the context of their whole relationship, is anything but simple. When his father died—a father he idealized as "Hyperion"—his mother, instead of leaning on her son for comfort, rejected him by remarrying very hastily indeed. Making her rejection more painful, she chose her husband's brother—a "satyr" by comparison to Hamlet's father. These actions have given her son an unequivocal message: "I am not an asexual madonna, but a carnal woman with desires you cannot fulfill. You must emotionally separate from the family and make your own life." This message might have left Hamlet disillusioned, but not trapped; he could have returned to Wittenberg and resumed his studies. But now Gertrude delivers a verbal message that contradicts the message conveyed by her behavior: "Let not thy mother lose her prayers, Hamlet: / I pray thee, stay with us" (1.2.118–19). In the total context of the court scene, where her husband has staged a public ceremony of assent to his sinful marriage and his new regime, she has asked for much more: "Love me, condone my incest and rejection of your father's memory, and treat this man, whom you seem to despise, as a loving father." Her plea that he stay in Elsinore, markedly contrasting with the leave granted Laertes, springs the trap, because it blocks any escape from the contradiction in her messages.

Eluding Claudius's ploys only to fall into a double bind imposed by his mother, Hamlet reveals how trapped he feels in his first soliloquy. The intense disillusion with Gertrude breaks out in a tirade against her hypocritical tears, her sensuality, and the "weary, stale, flat and unprofitable... uses of this world" (1.2.133–34). But the son's love for his mother surfaces, albeit fleetingly, in the vignette he paints of the love between Gertrude and the father he emulates:

> So excellent a king . . .
> . . . so loving to my mother
> That he might not beteem the winds of heaven
> Visit her face too roughly . . .
> . . . why, she would hang on him,
> As if increase of appetite had grown
> By what it fed on. (1.2.139–45)

Poignantly, his final words expose both his love and his trap. He cries, "But break, my heart," because, despite his disgust, his heart yields to his mother when he promises to obey her wishes, and because he must contain his swelling anger and grief: "for I must hold my tongue" (1.2.159). He cannot leave, he cannot love his mother and accept her husband, he cannot openly condemn her and Claudius, and he cannot, and be true to himself, lie. The only escape he sees is "self-slaughter," against which "the Everlasting . . . [has] fix'd / His canon" (1.2.131–32). He is bound.

Again ironically, Hamlet confronts a second and even more constricting double bind imposed by the father he loves, not the duplicitous stepfather who sets snares for him. The ghost tells his son a story that is probably more shocking than the forbidden secrets of his prison house, which would, he claims,

> harrow up thy soul, freeze thy young blood,
> Make thy two eyes, like stars, start from their spheres,
> Thy knotted and combined locks to part
> And each particular hair to stand an end,
> Like quills upon the fretful porpentine. (1.5.16–20)

By calling Claudius "that adulterate beast," he exposes Gertrude as an adulteress, who sated herself in a celestial bed and now preys on garbage.[7] By cursing Claudius's "traitorous gifts" to her, he implies she is a whore. Without clarifying whether or not she was party to the murder, he describes his death in gruesome detail. Into his ear, Claudius poured a "leperous distilment," whose

> sudden vigour . . . doth posset
> And curd, like eager droppings into milk,
> The thin and wholesome blood,

covering his body "Most lazar-like, with vile and loathsome crust" and sending his soul to torments so horrible that he must leave them to Hamlet's overwrought imagination (1.5.59–80). After this blood-curdling tale, he commands his son,

> Let not the royal bed of Denmark be
> A couch for luxury and damned incest.
> But, howsomever thou pursues this act,
> Taint not thy mind, nor let thy soul contrive
> Against thy mother aught: leave her to heaven. (1.5.82–86)

But, as readers have often puzzled, the ghost demands the impossible.[8]

This complex command is actually two sets of contradictory injunctions: "Avenge my murder and your mother's incest," and "Neither allow your character to become depraved, nor punish your mother." If Hamlet believes the ghost's horrific story and becomes a bloody avenger, he cannot avoid taint: the corruption in his own family, which the ghost has forced him to see so graphically, will have already tainted his mind, and he will defy the Christian prohibition against vengeance and embrace the pagan code of retribution.[9] Furthermore, to avenge the crimes against his father, he must punish Gertrude—if not physically, at least by exposing to the nation her guilt in marrying her husband's murderer, whether or not she was privy to the deed. If Gertrude remains unscathed, Hamlet will not have completely avenged the incest, which she has knowingly committed. His love and respect for his father, his awe before a ghost who has returned from the grave to reveal a buried truth, and the terror of the night conceal from Hamlet the contradictions in his father's impossible demands. To the ghost's superfluous parting words, "remember me," Hamlet cries,

> Remember thee!
> Ay, thou poor ghost, whiles memory holds a seat
> In this distracted globe. Remember thee! (1.5.95–97)

A second double bind has snared Hamlet.

The only escape from a double bind is either to recognize and label the incongruity of the messages or to respond with a double message. Lacking any emotional ties to Claudius that might obscure his stepfather's duplicity, Hamlet easily slips through the king's nets by answering in puns with double and triple messages. But his love for his mother and father blinds the usually quick-witted prince to the contradictions in their demands, and the strain of trying to obey almost breaks him.[10] Before announcing his plan to assume an "antic disposition," he seems on the very brink of madness: he makes tautological jokes ("There's ne'er a villain dwelling in all Denmark / But he's an arrant knave"), mouths chit-chat that Horatio dismisses as "wild and whirling words," and turns the horror of following the ghost's subterranean voice around the battlements into macabre comedy by calling his tormented father's spirit "truepenny," "this fellow in the cellarage," "old mole," and "worthy pioner" (1.5.117–81). But these double binds do not drive Hamlet mad because he plays mad instead.

III

By its nature, play is double, and therefore a possible response to a double bind. As we have seen, play creates a context in which actions both are and are not what they are, both are and are not serious. Put this way, the paradox of play sounds complicated, but we take it for granted daily. Obviously, players of poker and chess, spectators of football and tragedy, prizefighters and stamp collectors are intensely serious, but they can also dismiss their acts as "just play," as somehow set apart from everyday reality. According to the philosopher Eugen Fink, "We play in the so-called real world, but while playing there emerges an enigmatic realm. . . . The play world is not suspended in a purely ideal world. It always has a real setting, and yet it is never a real thing among other real things, although it has an absolute need of real things as a point of departure." We can see this paradoxical quality clearly in drama; Falstaff is "not nothing," but he is "nothing real."[11]

Hamlet knows a great deal about play. He loves drama, rejoices at the arrival of the players despite having "lost all [his] mirth" (2.2.307), begs a speech on the spot (which he half recites), and instructs them wisely in their trade. The tears of the actor who recounts the misery of Hecuba strike him with what every playgoer knows but often takes for granted: how

> this player here,
> But in a fiction, in a dream of passion,
> Could force his soul so to his own conceit
> That from her working all his visage wann'd,
> Tears in his eyes, distraction in 's aspect,
> A broken voice, and his whole function suiting
> With forms to his conceit? and all for nothing!
> For Hecuba!
> What's Hecuba to him, or he to Hecuba,
> That he should weep for her? (2.2.577–86)

The paradox of play, its transcendence of the rigid distinction between illusion and reality, miraculously whisks the player off to the fall of Troy while he displays the skills of his trade thousands of years later far to the north of the Mediterranean.

We have also described the doubleness of play in another way. Because the player simultaneously acts and frames his action as play, he can be in two places at once, inside and outside his action, thereby distancing himself from his immediate situation. Hamlet uses play's benign duplicity when maddening double binds threaten his sanity. By playing mad, he can both be and not be mad.[12] Although he experiences the disintegrating confusions of madness, a part of him remains aloof, framing his "antic disposition" as play. Moreover, playing the madman allows him an even greater freedom to play: to play with words, to play with people's ignorance, to play the part of chorus in "The Murder of Gonzago," to play with others' feelings for him, and so forth. Since not only Claudius, but his henchmen Polonius, Rosencrantz, and Guildenstern, with Ophelia and Gertrude as dupes, all bait traps for him everywhere, he desperately needs the freedom available in play. When his traitorous school fellows chide him for offending Claudius with "The Murder of Gonzago" and reject his riddling response with "Good my lord, put your discourse into some frame" (3.2.320–21), they suggest why Hamlet must play. If he provides stable contexts, frames, for his words and actions, his pursuers may pin him down. But because all his messages are within the paradoxical frame of play, and are, therefore, true and not true, serious and "just play" simultaneously, no one can "pluck out the heart of [his] mystery"—a "mystery" which is both his enigmatic ways and his trade as a player par excellence.

Playing is also how he attempts to escape from the ghost's devastating double bind, which precipitates the tragedy. When confronted with the impossible demand to avenge the murder and incest without tainting his mind or punishing his mother, Hamlet gives, by his actions, a double response: he plays avenger. Under the cloak of madness, he requites his father's murder precisely—by pouring poison into the ears not only of the poisoner himself, but of all who are guilty by association with his regime. With biting sarcasm, salacious puns, brutal satire, and diseased imagery, he assaults his enemies without actually performing the act of vengeance.[13] Netted around with the intrigues of Claudius and company and the double binds imposed by his parents, Hamlet plays for both his life and sanity.[14]

Playing the madman for the benefit of the court and the avenger out of his own need to obey his father, he gleefully attacks Claudius by exposing his minion, Polonius, as an old fool with "eyes purging thick amber and plumtree gum" and "most weak hams" (2.2.198–202), as "so capital a calf" (3.2.110–11), and as a flatterer who will agree that any cloud resembles a camel, a weasel, and a whale in order to ingratiate himself (3.2.390–400). Whereas Rosencrantz and Guildenstern would, says Hamlet, "play upon me; you would seem to know my stops . . . you would sound me from my lowest note to the top of my compass" (3.2.380–83), actually Hamlet plays them as skillfully as a musician plays a recorder. After barely five minutes of greetings and conversation, he has them confessing themselves Claudius's spies. Still, these sallies of wit against unworthy opponents are only practice thrusts to prepare him for the duel with Claudius himself—a duel that is, however, "just play."[15]

After being struck by the power of drama in the player's passion for Hecuba, Hamlet formulates his plan: "the play's the thing / Wherein I'll catch the conscience of the king" (2.2.633–34). But "the play's the thing" in at least two senses. First, Hamlet uses the play to play avenger by tormenting Claudius with the knowledge that Hamlet knows all the details of the crime and by threatening Claudius with death: the king's own nephew boldly announces that the murderer, Lucianus, is the player-king's nephew. Second, Hamlet uses the play to do what he believes the player, who was so moved by the illusory Hecuba, would do if he had Hamlet's real "cue for passion":

> Make mad the guilty and appal the free,
> Confound the ignorant, and amaze indeed
> The very faculties of eyes and ears. (2.2.590–92)

He prepares to madden Claudius and shock the court by mixing art with life.

During the intervening weeks between the ghost's appearance and the players' arrival, Hamlet has been coping with the double bind imposed by the ghost not solely by playing mad and playing avenger; he has discovered another escape route. If the ghost is not his father's spirit at all, but a devil tempting him to perdition, as he fears, or to madness and suicide, as Horatio originally feared, then he is free from its contradictory demands.[16] To determine the truth, he stages an illusion to test Claudius and the ghost. If the ghost's tale, the matter of the play, proves true, then Hamlet will feel bound by his father's impossible commands. But in this case the play itself becomes part of the vengeance his father requires. Like the patient whose years of receiving incongruent messages have made him an expert at setting double binds for others, Hamlet imposes on Claudius a double bind that will torment him for his sins, as Hamlet's father is "confin'd to fast in fires" for his "foul crimes" (1.5.11–12).

When asked the play's title, Hamlet answers, "The Mouse-trap. Marry, how? Tropically," with a pun on "trapically" (3.2.247).[17] The humor of the pun conceals the truth that the play is both a trope, a figurative expression such as metaphor, and a trap. Indeed, Hamlet can turn a play into a trap precisely because it is a trope. Drama is a kind of figurative expression, a metaphor for life, in which the players, as Hamlet says, "hold . . . the mirror up to nature" (3.2.26), and both drama and tropes are inherently double. Just as Falstaff both is and is not real, the poet's lady both is and is not a red, red rose. A play can arouse an audience's deepest emotions because it contains them in the safe context, "This is only a play, a metaphor for life and not life itself." Paradoxically, viewers are moved because the play is not really real. Except for Don Quixote, driven mad by reading chivalric romances, the passions aroused by poetic or dramatic illusion do not ordinarily threaten the everyday world. If they do, the audience withdraws its undefended emotions, for life has usurped art.[18]

When Claudius comes to "The Murder of Gonzago," he expects to enjoy a trope, a kind of pleasurable and innocent duplicity, but he finds a trap instead. By inviting him to a play, Hamlet conveys the message, "This is fiction, a harmless diversion," and he sustains this message as long as possible by dismissing Claudius's suspicions after the opening scene with "No, no, they do but jest, poison in jest; no offense i' the world" (3.2.244–45). That Claudius approaches the play in this context is clear by his joy and relief when he learns that Hamlet is amusing himself with the players. The king will attend the dramatic soiree, he tells Rosencrantz and Guildenstern,

> With all my heart; and it doth much content me
> To hear [Hamlet] so inclin'd.
> Good gentlemen, give him a further edge,
> And drive his purpose into these delights. (3.1.25–28)

But when Claudius sees and hears the precise details of his crime portrayed on stage and narrated by Hamlet's choral asides, he receives another order of message that violently contradicts the first: "This is the truth and a threat to your life." The incongruity of the two messages is so shocking that it cracks the deceitful mask Claudius has successfully worn since the murder.

Although no soliloquy reveals his thoughts at the moment he rises, calls for light, and summarily dismisses the festive gathering, surely he must be perplexed in the extreme: how, on earth, could Hamlet know the details of a murder known only to the murderer and the victim? If Hamlet does not know these details, how could a fiction portray the exact truth? Having no ties of emotional dependency to Hamlet, Claudius physically escapes from the field. But he is bound nevertheless because his flight acknowledges that the paradox of a true illusion has, at least, momentarily maddened him, and his madness reveals his guilt. By recognizing and manipulating the doubleness of drama—so that "The Murder of Gonzago" is not, like most plays, both true and not true, but true and true—Hamlet has cunningly prepared a double bind to "Make mad the guilty."

IV

Unfortunately, he helps make mad the innocent as well. In his callous treatment of Ophelia, he adds to the double binds that drive her not momentarily mad, like Claudius, nor playfully mad, like himself, but mad indeed. Polonius's family, as presented in acts 1 and 2, has created a very confusing atmosphere for a young woman coming of age. Her father always "With windlasses and with assays of bias, / By indirections find[s] directions out" (2.1.65–66), nor does he see any contradiction in outlining the tactical deceptions that produce worldly success (such as "Give thy thoughts no tongue" and "the apparel oft proclaims the man") in the same breath with the counsel,

> This above all: to thine own self be true,
> And it must follow, as the night the day,
> Thou canst not then be false to any man. (1.3.59–80)

With his spying, love of policy, and propensity, he admits, "To cast beyond ourselves in our opinions" (2.1.115), he ensnares his daughter in double binds.

While warning her to beware of Hamlet's "tenders / Of . . . affection," he chides,

> think yourself a baby;
> That you have ta'en these tenders for true pay,
> Which are not sterling. Tender yourself more dearly;
> Or . . . you'll tender me a fool. (1.3.105–109)

Here and throughout this scene, he sends contradictory messages to Ophelia:

1. You are a baby, an innocent, whose virginity must remain undefiled; therefore, you must reject Hamlet's attentions.
2. You are capable of having a baby ("you'll tender me a fool"), of attracting the thirty-year-old heir apparent, and perhaps of winning a queenship if you "Tender yourself more *dearly*" and "Set your entreatments at a *higher rate* / Than a command to parley" (1.3.107, 122–23, emphasis mine).

In his repeated imagery of buying and selling, and in his later willingness to use his daughter as bait to catch Hamlet, Polonius becomes in truth what Hamlet calls him in jest—"a fishmonger," a bawd. His language and actions implicitly instruct Ophelia to be a whore, while at the same time explicitly warning her to remain pure. She cannot comment on the incongruity of her father's messages because, despite the glimmer of perceptiveness she shows in teasing Laertes about following his own advice, her father and brother have usurped her right to think. When Polonius scornfully asks if she believes Hamlet's professions of love, she murmurs, "I do not know, my lord, what I should think" (1.3.104), so Polonius tells her. Unlike her brother, who leaves for France, she cannot escape from the field because in her world daughters must obey fathers, even if—like Jephthah to whom Hamlet compares Polonius—the fathers sacrifice the daughters.

Always the dutiful daughter, she rejects her suitor and allows his enemies to use her. Consequently, she confirms Hamlet's harsh judgment spawned by disgust for his mother: "Frailty, thy name is woman!" (1.2.146).[19] After discovering that Ophelia has betrayed him to the spies behind the arras, he deliberately sets psychological traps for her. Arousing her tender feelings by confessing, "I did love you once" (3.1.115), he then scorns her as false and lewd. Because like all women, he rails, she will deceive men with her "paintings" and will surely cuckold her future husband, he banishes her to a "nunnery"—meaning both a convent, where she will not "be a breeder of sinners" (3.1.123), and a whorehouse, where she can continue the trade she learned from her father. In this pun he telescopes the double messages that assault her: be a virgin; be a whore.

Later at "The Murder of Gonzago," Hamlet sets more vicious traps for Ophelia. In the following exchange, he flirts with her in bawdy language, then condemns her for having salacious thoughts:

> Hamlet: Lady, shall I lie in your lap?
> [Lying down at Ophelia's feet.]
> Ophelia: No, my lord.
> Hamlet: I mean, my head upon your lap?
> Ophelia: Ay, my lord.
> Hamlet: Do you think I meant country matters?
> Ophelia: I think nothing, my lord.
> Hamlet: That's a fair thought to lie between maids' legs.
> Ophelia: What is, my lord?
> Hamlet: Nothing. (3.2.118–28)

After she chastely rejects his initial lewd request, Hamlet ridicules her for mistaking his supposedly innocent question for ribaldry. But if she had not understood his remark and answered, "Yes," he could have embarrassed her by treating her reply as a sexual proposition. He punishes her for understanding his meaning, and may punish her regardless of her answer. When she tries to escape from the dilemma by refusing to understand ("I think nothing, my lord"), he makes even her retreat an insulting sexual innuendo: "thing" and "nothing" often refer to the genitalia that "lie between maids' legs." Throughout "The Murder of Gonzago," Hamlet acts madly to divert the court spies from his real intent, and he vents his anxiety over the plan to test

Claudius and the ghost by using Ophelia, whom he now considers a traitoress, as the straight man in his comedy routine. Although the game he stalks is Claudius, the results for Ophelia of his diversionary tactics and high-strung nerves are jarring double messages, which simultaneously arouse and damn her budding sexuality. Her pitiful attempts to laugh away his cruel jests reveal her confusion. Both her father and her former lover have prepared her for madness by demanding that she be virginal, treating her like a whore, and discouraging her from thinking for herself, which might lead her to see their demands as incongruous.

The vehemence of Hamlet's assault on Ophelia indicates that his interim solutions to the double bind he faces have failed. Playing mad to preserve his sanity, playing avenger to satisfy his obligation, and directing a play to test the ghost and punish Claudius have not fulfilled his father's impossible demands. First—despite his exultation over the success of "The Mousetrap," which, he brags, will "get me a fellowship in a cry of players" (3.2.288–89) —when he comes upon his enemy alone and defenseless in the chapel, he shirks the command to avenge in earnest, not play, the murder and incest. (And in the next scene, he kills the wrong man instead.) Second, his longing for death, his insulting treatment of Ophelia, and the foul imagery he uses to condemn his mother's lust reveal his thoughts to be as "rank and gross" as the "unweeded garden" of the world around him, despite his father's injunction, "Taint not thy mind."[20] And finally, he does punish Gertrude. Answering the summons to her closet, he physically restrains her; makes her call out in fear lest he become a matricide like Nero, whose soul he must consciously expel from his bosom; forces her to compare her two husbands; and appalls her with the filthiness of her sin:

> Nay, but to live
> In the rank sweat of an enseamed bed,
> Stew'd in corruption, honeying and making love
> Over the nasty sty. (3.4.91–94)

Instead of leaving her to heaven, he pours these poisonous words into her ears, until she begs, "No more, sweet Hamlet!" for his words feel like daggers (3.4.95–96). Emphasizing what this and the two previous scenes have shown—Hamlet's failure to obey any of his father's commands—the ghost reappears and reiterates their contradictory nature: do not forget your "almost blunted purpose" of revenge, and have pity on your mother's weakness (3.4.110–15).

Even in the midst of playing avenger, however, Hamlet earlier has glimpsed the truth. An aficianado of the drama, he knows that he has merely been acting the part of the stock Elizabethan/Jacobean stage avenger. After seeing the passion of the player for Hecuba, he whips himself into a frenzied speech that might have won applause for Kyd's Hieronimo or Marston's Malevole or Tourneur's Vindice:[21]

> I should have fatted all the region kites
> With this slave's offal: bloody, bawdy villain!
> Remorseless, treacherous, lecherous, kindless villain!
> O, vengeance! (2.2.607–10)

But immediately he steps down from the stage, becoming the audience and critic of his own performance: "This is most brave, / That I . . . Must, like a whore, unpack my heart with words" (2.2.611–12, 14). Instead of doing the deed, which he cannot do because the ghost's commands are contradictory, he continues, despite his self-realization, to play the role of the doer, an expedient that provides only fleeting moments of relief.

Perhaps his posturing as a ruthless avenger best explains his excuse for not killing Claudius in the chapel. Right after staging an abortive revenge tragedy and just before finding Claudius alone, Hamlet meditates,

> 'Tis now the very witching time of night,
> When churchyards yawn and hell itself breathes out
> Contagion to this world: now could I drink hot blood,
> And do such bitter business as the day
> Would quake to look on. (3.2.406–10)

Here he seems more like a stage character—Lucianus or the brutal Pyrrhus on his way to slaughter Priam—than the intelligent but deeply disillusioned prince who speaks his other soliloquies. Elation over his successful revenge play has encouraged him to bring to life the attitudes of art. Of course, when confronted with Claudius's real throat to cut, he balks. But he turns even his hesitation into a sentiment worthy of the most sinister stage avenger:

> Up, sword; and know thou a more horrid hent:
> When he is . . . about some act
> That has no relish of salvation in 't;
> Then trip him, that his heels may kick at heaven,
> And that his soul may be as damn'd and black
> As hell, whereto it goes. (3.3.88–95)

Hamlet both surpasses his father's command and avoids obeying it by planning to kill Claudius's soul with his body—at some unspecified future date. Once again, playing the remorseless avenger frees him from the double bind—momentarily.

Soon all his evasions fail, and when he is arrested in act 4, his behavior becomes careless and chaotic. This act resembles a *danse macabre* because it presents Ophelia's poignant lunacy and Hamlet's most bizarre antics since his frenzy after meeting the ghost on the battlements. The strain of the double binds in which their families have ensnared them has finally pushed Hamlet to and Ophelia beyond the breaking point. After failing to discharge his duty, Hamlet is cornered by his father, and after inadvertently killing Polonius, he is cornered by Claudius. Unable to play his way out of these corners, he drops all disguises, threatening Claudius with the story of "how a king may go a progress through the guts of a beggar" (4.3.32–33), and telling him cleverly, but clearly, to go to hell. Hamlet's grisly jokes about the odor of decay and the "politic worms" that will fatten themselves on Claudius's minister of policy are no longer merely feigned madness; they resemble the astute perceptions often found, by Shakespeare's contemporaries and modern psychoanalysts, in the truly mad.

In fact, double binds do not finally madden Hamlet because he is forced into the escape he could not choose for himself. Claudius, fearing for his life, banishes Hamlet from his "prison," as he once called Denmark. Ophelia, however, can only retreat into madness. But why now? Everyone who had assaulted her with contradictory messages is gone: her father is dead, her brother has not yet returned from France, and her erstwhile lover is banished. Why is she not now free to grow into a sexual woman, neither a child nor a whore? Because her family has so stunted her self that it is too weak to cope with this forced separation from those who have always defined her. Having formed a self in a confusing and destructive but stable family system built around Polonius's self-aggrandizement, she has learned not to think, only to collude in preserving the homeostasis. The loss of its center is, in fact, the loss of her self.

The overtly sexual references in her mad ramblings strike even the amateur Freudian as the result of repressions imposed by her father and her society. Less obvious, but no less significant, the no-win position of the heroine in her valentine song epitomizes the double binds fostered by Ophelia's almost exclusively male world. The naive lass in the song (4.5.47–66) wants to be sure to be her lad's valentine. So, counting on the belief that he must choose the first girl he sees on Valentine's morning, she innocently goes to his window. With a proposal of marriage, he seduces her, then rejects her as unfit to be his wife because she is no longer a virgin. If she refuses his sexual offer, she will jeopardize her marriage proposal, but because she accepts the offer, he withdraws the proposal. Like Ophelia, the lass is simultaneously treated like a whore and told to be a virgin; she is tempted and then damned as lewd. Ironically, the narrator in the song, like the audience to Ophelia's plight, perceives the incongruity in the demands of such young men: "By cock, they are to blame." But even though her song recalls and clarifies her situation, Ophelia has lost all clarity, and her mad actions dramatize her paralysis between childlike innocence and adult sexual knowledge. Gently singing and smilingly passing out flowers, "She turns," says her brother, "Thought and affliction, passion, hell itself . . . to favour and to prettiness" (4.5.188–89). But each flower accurately characterizes the vice of its recipient, and the garland she chooses for herself is made of

> long purples
> That liberal shepherds give a grosser name,
> But our cold maids do dead men's fingers call them. (4.7.170–72)

Instead of being "tumbled" in her lad's bed like the lass in her song, Ophelia, along with her coronet of penile flowers, tumbles into a brook to become a cold maid indeed. The gravedigger may have correctly labelled her death self-defense: it defends her from the intolerable contradictions of her life.

V

Hamlet's defense is, for a time, more fortunate. Banishment forestalls true madness by removing him from the scene of his contradictory obligations long enough to achieve a new perspective on them. Although the audience does not see the events that precipitate this change, a different man approaches the graveyard in act 5. For the first time in the play, Hamlet, once the master of repartee, loses a game of wits, and to a "clown," a worldly wise gravedigger. Now Hamlet, once the mordant court jester to Claudius, sees in the skull of Yorick that not even the "gibes," "gambols," and "infinite jest" of such madcap rogues can elude death. And Hamlet, once the actors' actor, so disdains Laertes's histrionic rendition of the grief-stricken brother that he parodies the extravagant mourning. In the face of death, he has discovered the futility of his past playing—playing with words, playing the fool, and playing the avenger.

Later, when he tells Horatio of his adventures, we learn what has jolted him into this new perspective. By the guiding hand of Providence, he believes, he could not sleep at sea, rashly stole his captors' letters, and thereby discovered Claudius's plot against his life. The genesis of his counterplot was likewise providential:

> Being thus be-netted round with villanies,—
> Ere I could make a prologue to my brains,
> They had begun the play. (5.2.29–31)

Hamlet no longer considers himself an actor who avoids real action by unpacking his heart with words; nevertheless, he remains a player. Before "some craven scruple / Of thinking too precisely on the event" (4.4.40–41) can intervene, his brains begin to enact a drama not of his own devising. His providential waking and the coincidences of his voyage—having with him his father's signet ring to seal the execution order for Rosencrantz and Guildenstern, and escaping on a pirate ship whose brigands willingly serve him instead of slitting his throat—convince him that "a divinity . . . shapes our ends, / Rough-hew them how we will" (5.2.10–11). He will be a player who waits in the wings for Providence to give him his cue: "The readiness is all" (5.2.233). This shift in perspective releases him from both the fear of Claudius's traps and the double bind of his father's contradictory commands because a higher power than either an earthly king or even an apparition from beyond the grave has written the play, determining whom to punish, whom to spare, who will play the role of avenger, and when the catastrophe will come.

No longer needing to play the madman or avenger to defend his life or sanity, Hamlet goes calmly to the duel, telling Laertes that he "will this brother's wager frankly play" (5.2.264). But he is unaware that the fencing match and its accompanying wager are a deadly game he cannot win: because of Laertes's unbated, poisoned sword and Claudius's poisoned congratulatory cup, Hamlet will die by the sword if he loses the match, and by the cup if he wins. The duel recalls the double bind patterns that have snared him and Ophelia throughout the drama. To insure justice, however, Providence reverses the bind. Claudius's clever game stages a fitting vengeance in which he enacts his own punishment in the last scene of Providence's larger play. As Hamlet and Laertes "play" (a word the stage directions use four times), Claudius unwittingly prepares the very setting that Hamlet had hoped would damn the murderer's soul: amid a carousal with drink, drums, trumpets, and cannons like the one Hamlet earlier blamed for soiling Denmark's reputation, and "At game . . . about some act / That has no relish of salvation in 't" (3.3.91–92). Perhaps even in the hesitation to murder the king in his chapel, Hamlet had been an unknowing player in a revenge drama that supersedes the bloody one he had planned for the future. Sparing Claudius's body then has allowed the king to damn his own soul now. Laertes and Claudius arrange a game that Hamlet cannot win, but Providence directs a play that binds Laertes, Claudius, and Gertrude to their sins. As Hamlet realizes before he agrees "to play" the fatal wager, death will eventually net one and all: "If it be now, 'tis not to come; if it be not to come, it will be now; if it be not now, yet it will come" (5.2.231–33).[22] But, in death, what is the state of those souls less guilty than Claudius's?

The play repeatedly raises the question: What results do actions performed in this world produce in the next? But the play gives no answers, portraying the realm beyond the grave as unknowable. The ghost is "forbid / To tell the secrets of [his] prison-house" (1.5.13–14). This initiator of the play's action is itself a "questionable shape"—either "a spirit of health or goblin damn'd" (1.4.43, 40)—but the play never confirms which. The Mousetrap fails to prove the ghost's nature, for, as in *Macbeth,* devils may tell truths to damn souls.[23] Hamlet's meditation on the results of human action, "To be, or not to be," confronts the blank wall of "something after death, / The undiscover'd country" (3.1.78–79). The state of Ophelia's soul is as "doubtful" as her death. Is she a damned suicide, as the skeptical gravediggers and legalistic priest believe, or a "minist'ring angel" (5.1.250, 264), as her loving brother prophesies?[24] Even the eternal fate of Rosencrantz and Guildenstern is ambiguous. Although for their part in Claudius's murder plot Hamlet sends them to their deaths, "Not shriving-time allow'd" (5.2.47), do they die in mortal sin? Did they knowingly conspire with Claudius, or have they been dupes to the end?

These questions about human action and the world beyond, climax at Hamlet's death. In accomplishing the providential revenge, is he God's approved "minister" or His "scourge," an already damned soul used to accomplish divine retribution?[25] When he doubts the ghost, Hamlet fears damnation if he does kill Claudius (2.2.627–32), but when he returns from his voyage, he fears damnation if he does not (5.2.67–70). Will the accidental murders of Polonius and Laertes, the contrived execution of Rosencrantz and Guildenstern, his indirect part in Ophelia's death, and his revenge against Claudius send him to hell? Although literary critics answer this question yes or no, the play is significantly silent.[26] And Hamlet knows the eternal unknowableness of what lies beyond the grave: "since no man of aught he leaves knows, what is 't to leave betimes?" (5.2.233–35).

Despite its fatalism, this final perspective releases Hamlet from the ghost's crippling double bind. For sixteenth- and seventeenth-century English Protestants trying to live with the hard doctrines of Calvinism, life itself imposed something like a double bind. God's commandments required them, in a world of deceptive appearances, to take moral responsibility for their actions, the results of which they could not know; but faith dictated that God's omnipotence would shape these actions to His own inscrutable ends no matter what choices they made; and no one could escape from the field, even through "self-slaughter."[27] In act 1, Horatio and Marcellus unknowingly articulate the poles of this paradox: the scholar counsels patient nonaction in response to the ghost's revelation of rottenness in Denmark—"Heaven will direct it"—but the soldier urges immediate, responsible action—"Nay, let's follow" the desperate Hamlet and the silent ghost (1.4.91). Later, the player king conflates these two poles into an apt epigram, "Our thoughts are ours, their ends none of our own" (3.2.223). For three acts, maddening confusion plagues Hamlet, and only when he returns in act 5, does he transcend the original double binds by recognizing—in his philosophy, if not in his family—this basic incongruity at the heart of human life.

As psychologists document, literary critics explain, and theologians believe, paradoxes and double binds may provoke creative leaps to higher levels of insight as well as psychotic episodes.[28] Hamlet takes one of these creative leaps beyond the double bind when he learns to play his role in God's drama without assurances. He accepts that he must act in "perfect conscience" and quickly ("the interim is mine"), that Providence will shape his rough hewing ("Let be"), and that he cannot know what judgment his actions will merit after death (5.2.67, 73, 235). Dying, he begs Horatio to tell his story and gives his voice to Fortinbras—acts that secure the future of his "name" and country in this world. He does not, however, like Horatio, prophesy about "flights of angels" singing him to a reward in the next. He has learned that "The rest is silence" (5.2.371, 369).

VI

Whatever else it is about, *Hamlet* is about contradiction. It raises questions about taking moral responsibility for action in a bewildering world ruled by an unknowable God. When assaulted by contradictory demands, Hamlet adopts two stances: play that defends a threatened self, and play that integrates the self with a trusted absolute. In acts 2 through 4, the doubleness of play helps Hamlet defend his life from Claudius's traps and his sanity from the double binds imposed by Gertrude and the ghost, which threaten to fragment his sense of self. In act 5, Hamlet's play gives him a perspective on these dilemmas and renews his self. Upon returning from his fateful sea voyage, he no longer bases his self on confusing, parental demands, but on the absolute authority of a superior Father whose providence, he trusts, will insure justice—no matter what his individual fate will be. Having accepted his role in God's drama, he dies with self intact; his salvation or damnation he leaves to higher powers. Despite potentially devastating contradictions, he has learned through play to live and die in ambiguity.

Hamlet's successors adopted similar stances when confronted with conflict and paradox. The contradictions facing the poets and prose writers of the seventeenth century were even less visible to those experiencing them than are the double messages inflicted within families. The victims of double binds, emersed in the strong emotions of family life, lack the perspective to label their situation as impossible paradox. Defined by cultural codes so basic as to be invisible and jostled by historical forces far beyond their control, the participants in a moment of revolutionary change are even more blind. Only rare visionaries can step out of their skins to define the contradictions in competing economic systems, structures of knowledge, political organizations, and modes of belief that threaten to dissolve any sense of a coherent self. From a distance, however, we can look back at seventeenth-century life, with Hamlet's dilemma in mind, to outline the conflicts that bind his contemporaries and to analyze how play can loosen social as well as psychic constraints, thereby enabling a new stance for the self.

3

Play and Historical Process

Although not classic double binds, the contradictions constituting seventeenth-century life threatened psychic stability no less than the binds assaulting Hamlet. The conflicts that he faced extended to politics and theology but originated in the family. The seventeenth-century social, religious, and economic conflicts that escalated into revolution precipitated the era's most profoundly felt contradiction, which also originated in the family: the clash between a conservative ideology inculcated by child-rearing practices and an incongruent historical reality. At every level of this complex historical process—social, familial, individual—play mediates the contradictions that accompany fast-paced change.

I

Compared with the whirl of modernity, the pace of cultural and technological change in medieval Europe was slow. Feudalism remained the dominant political system for centuries, and although the technologies men and women used to plough, harvest, mine, sail, and trade were not static, innovations were infrequent, and influence spread slowly.[1] As in most traditional societies, institutions such as lineage, education, and the polity commanded awe at the communal life and meaning gathered into these systems—an awe enhanced by ritual and ceremony, which channeled the flow of supernatural power and human energy necessary to preserve the culture.[2] Coronation conveyed divine power to the head of state. Investiture of bishops continued the lineage of keepers of the holy kingdom from Christ, to Peter, to future shepherds. Guilds received guild members with no less solemnity than towns installed lord mayors. And all wore appropriate clothing to indicate their status in the nexus: the knight had his coat of arms, the clerk had his gown, there were white friars and black friars, and guilds punished apprentices for deviations from their dress code. Rituals and ceremonies ordered the transitions in political, ecclesiastical, and economic life, marking them as legitimate transfers of power and status. Since order was precious and rare after Rome's collapse, preserving it was essential, and people distrusted innovation, which might threaten stability. Cultural change came slowly, almost imperceptibly.

No human order, however, can encompass all times, all places, all people, and all contingencies. There were times at the interstices of the seasons—like the winter solstice and the coming of spring, marked by riotous festivities between Christmas and Epiphany and before Lent. There were places on the margins of society—like Bartholomew Fair, an annual trade fair held on the outskirts of London, notorious for the sale of vice as well as cloth. And there were people whose deformities or errant lifestyles made their status ambiguous—like "natural" fools, traveling players, and goliards. Although valued as entertainers, often gaining access to the great, they were nobodies without a fixed place in the hierarchy. At liminal times (*limen* = threshold), in marginal places, and among fringe people, folly arose to turn order upside down. During the Feast of Fools, a boy bishop burlesqued the Mass. At Bartholomew Fair all ranks rubbed elbows to buy hobby horses or see the freaks. Even the pious enjoyed the goliards' parodic hymns to carnality, and the "natural" wielded his bauble as a mock scepter in the royal court, where his deformity made him seem touched by God. Extraordinary times, places, and people that fell in between or outside the slots of the social order unleashed the folly that could scramble the order and level the hierarchy—temporarily.[3]

Paradoxically, they also helped preserve the social order. By releasing pent-up emotion under controlled conditions, they protected institutions, serving as safety valves that allowed power structures to marginalize and contain dissidence without accommodating its critique. Furthermore, when carnal appetites are indulged instead of restrained, when fools or children rule instead of being ruled, energy is freed. This energy may be frightening because it tends toward the chaos from which society slowly and painstakingly wrested order. Thus authority can legitimate its power as control over elements deemed harmful to the commonweal. But random energy may also invigorate power by reinfusing it with the vitality that enables it to create order. Without periodic contacts with its primal sources of energy, society stagnates, choked by the structures it has created to channel the potentially destructive and creative power.[4]

So these unbuttoned times, places, and people had two complementary functions: one conservative and the other progressive. Folly could spark change because, although it might be temporary and marginalized, its effects were never wholly contained. As Victor Turner has shown, the spontaneous vitality enjoyed during liminal periods, on the fringes, or by fools shakes up the elements of the culture, playfully rearranging its structure: male becomes female, sacred becomes profane, and words are liberated from sense into joyful nonsense. As cultural symbols combine in shocking ways and revelers experiment with unheard-of behaviors, the society discovers the arbitrariness of its structure and plays with even bizarre alternatives. Out of ludic disorder may come the potential for social change.[5] For example, throughout the early modern period in France, England, Ireland, Wales, and Scotland, dissident men, rioting against oppressive authority, disguised themselves as women, as men often did at carnival time. With their women's garb, they also appropriated for political rebellion the carnival licence allowed members of "the unruly sex," assumed to be enslaved to passion and not responsible for their actions.[6] Thus folly reinforced the social order by flaunting the chaos over which order once triumphed and to which few would want to return. But it also freed energy to prevent stagnation; engendered a subsystem of new ways of seeing, thinking, and being that prepared minds for change; and sometimes provoked action.

This dialectic between order and anarchic play, structure and anti-structure, can only accommodate a slow pace of cultural evolution. During the Middle Ages, the potential for innovation came more from communally sanctioned, periodic, and temporary reversals of the social structure and less from individual innovators. Since occasional folly was a time-honored tradition, individuals generally retained a conservative outlook, their sense of self unperturbed despite the unleashed forces for change.

Beginning in the fourteenth century in Europe and climaxing for England in the sixteenth and seventeenth centuries, the pace of change accelerated, and social mechanisms for regulating tensions could not keep up. Changes both expanded and threatened men's and women's sense of who they were. The Renaissance seemed to burst upon the scene as the great age of self-assertion: financial capitalism was dissolving feudal and communal obligations; the lavish self-display of Italian magnificoes became fashionable among European monarchs, like Henry VIII, eager to consolidate power; the fame of the singular genius like Michaelangelo replaced the anonymity of medieval cathedral sculptors; and writers like Montaigne explored all the cracks and crannies of the self. Stephen Greenblatt has shown that prominent sixteenth-century Englishmen deliberately and artfully fashioned their selves.[7] But as horizons widened socially, intellectually, and geographically, powerful forces were undermining the ritually enhanced structures of life and thought that had supported people's sense of self. The Reformation, political revolution, imperial expansion, economic dislocation, and intellectual dissension heightened by the fast spread of new ideas through printing—these and other forces propelled much of Western Europe toward the modern world whose law and gospel is change.

What transformed medieval man, adapted to a hierarchical order that changed imperceptibly, to modern man, adapted to a world in constant flux? One answer is surprisingly simple: a prolonged youth of play. Whereas medieval society depended on periodic intervals of folly and play to release the potential for innovation, the modern Western world devotes much time in infancy, childhood, and adolescence to play. In these years—sometimes extending into early adulthood—youths spend hours, even while in school, just fooling around: playing with mobiles and their unswaddled bodies in their cribs, roughhousing and playing games (structured and unstructured, sanctioned and covert) at recess, trying on different selves and experimenting with aberrant behavior in high school and college. Since play requires flexibility, the ability to evaluate changing situations and to adapt to the moment's demands, these years of play foster a mobile self adapted to a complex world that changes unpredictably.[8]

English child-rearing practices in the sixteenth and seventeenth centuries produced a very different kind of self. Tudor and Stuart households bore little resemblance to the later child-centered family. For one thing, the practice of hiring wet nurses could separate infant from mother for one and possibly two years, although evidence is mixed on the extent and management of this practice. Wealthy, landed fathers in need of heirs, who were told that sexual relations corrupted mother's milk, insisted on their conjugal rights, not wanting to limit fertility through their wife's lactation. Thus nobles, gentry, and the aspiring urban elite frequently employed wet nurses. The working wives of the "middling sort" also had reason to pay for freedom from child-care duties as they labored alongside their husbands in shops or farms. Some could afford to keep a nurse in the household or nearby, but others had to send their infants to a village nurse. In pious Christian households and among the poor, mothers tended to nurse their children, but poor mothers had to apportion their milk and time between their own children and their nurslings. Despite these class variations, the repeated advice against wet nursing by churchmen and doctors in the family manuals of the day suggests that the practice was widespread enough to prompt reproach.[9]

Mercenary, incompetent, or overworked nurses may have contributed to a mortality rate of 20 to 30 percent in the first year of life. Some historians have theorized that, in the face of these appalling odds, a vicious cycle developed: high infant mortality may have made parents, at least fathers, disinterested in their infants, but disinterest, in turn, contributed to infant mortality by separating mothers and infants. In the 1750s, when the new fashion of domesticity encouraged aristocratic mothers to spend more time with their children, the mortality rate among upper-class infants began to decline substantially—even though maternal breast feeding was not widely practiced until the 1760s. Although apparently maternal attention alone, without improvement in nutrition, could have increased an infant's chances of survival, conventions regulating interaction between parents and infants in the sixteenth and seventeenth centuries seldom encouraged intimacy.[10]

Infants who were fortunate enough to have competent nurses were gratified orally but physically restrained. Handbooks encouraged feeding infants on demand, allowing them to sleep on their own schedule, and not weaning them before two, although in practice most were weaned between one and two. Snugly swaddled for up to a year, infants enjoyed security and warmth, if not maximum cleanliness, but swaddling restricted their freedom to explore the limits of their bodies, and thus of their selves.[11]

Having survived the dangers of weaning—malnutrition and dysentery caused by impure water—children of all ranks often lived with their parents for only a few years. Parents sent boys and girls between seven and eleven away—to other families where, depending on class, they served as domestic help or learned deportment, to grammar schools, or to masters who trained them as apprentices. If apprenticed in his home town, a boy still resided with his master, not his parents. The "cruelty" of English parents who sent their children away, even when no financial need forced the separation, shocked foreign visitors. As an adult, Robert Boyle (b. 1627) speculated on the reason he was sent away at eight: "great men's children at home tempts [sic] them to nicety, to pride, and idleness." Contemporary advice books repeatedly remind parents that children are enslaved to original sin, that saving them requires breaking their will, and that spoiling damns them. This advice, coupled with the regularity with which the English sent their children away, suggests that they did not trust themselves to maintain the discipline deemed necessary to socialize children properly.[12]

In the brief period between being the charge of nurses and being the charge of employers, tutors, schoolmasters, or masters of a trade, children played. Extant toys, Bruegel's 1560 painting overflowing with 250 children playing at least 75 games, and Puritan preachers' warnings that children who "play . . . at sermons [will] have the devil for a play-fellow"—such evidence suggests that sixteenth- and seventeenth-century children played much as ours do, only not for so long. Sir Thomas More allegorizes "Childhood" in the voice of a scamp who desires to play forever:

> I am called Childhood, in play is all my mind,
> To cast a quoit, a cockshy, and a ball.
> A top can I set, and drive it in his kind.
> But would to god these hateful books all,
> Were in a fire burnt to powder small.
> Then might I lead my life always in play:
> Which life god send me to mine ending day.

Although More was an indulgent teacher in the little academy into which he turned his home, play ended and education began for son, daughters, and wards at an early age. Parents probably indulged their children's play between weaning and formal training because they agreed with the physician who wrote, "this age can scarce do anything seriously." On the eve of his son's ninth birthday, however, Lord Chesterfield warned, "No more levity. Childish toys and playthings must be thrown aside, and your mind directed to serious objects."[13] A child's holiday from the pressures of work or social responsibility was brief.

Predictably, the play of schoolboys and apprentices was severely curtailed. In an all-male world isolated from female nurture, grammar school boys endured the initiation ritual of learning Latin, the language of men in society, not the "mother tongue" taught by women. Once they had mastered grammar, boys as young as nine practiced debate, verbal combat that was to determine truth and prepare them for life. The rod discouraged lapses in learning and any play at all. Although some humanists condemned indiscriminate flogging, in practice corporal discipline was brutal.[14] Apprentices enjoyed no more freedom than scholars. Extant court orders and guild statutes record severe punishments for apprentices who tried to kick up their heels. Forbidden pastimes include football, dancing, mumming, frequenting music or fencing schools, playing dice or cards, and wearing extravagant dress or long hair.[15] Neither schoolmasters nor masters of trades considered play a part of training for adult life.

What can be deduced about the self fostered by this pattern of child rearing? One conclusion seems apparent: the self was conformed to a patriarchal absolute. Parents were aloof authorities, not intimate caregivers. Children were expected to stand bareheaded before parents and to kneel for their blessing. The social system turned this obedience to parental authority into obedience to masters of schools and trades, to social superiors, to the opinions of authorities, to the monarch, and to God. Lady Jane Grey's description of parental rigor attests to this hierarchy: "When I am in presence either of father or mother, whether I speak, keep silence, sit, stand, or go, eat, drink, be merry or sad, be sewing, playing, dancing, or doing any thing else, I must do it, as it were, in such weight, measure, and number, even so perfectly as God made the world, else I am so sharply taunted, so cruelly threatened, yea presently sometimes with pinches, nippes, and bobs, and some ways which I will not name for the honour I bear them, so without measure misordered, that I think myself in hell."[16] Jane's parents insisted that her deportment, like every note in the music of creation, must conform to divine harmony in measure, weight, and number.

To instill obedience to authority from birth, permissive nursing encouraged dependency, and swaddling checked the drive toward autonomy. Hurried into rigorous training for adulthood after only a brief interlude of play, these children were socialized not for flexibility and adaptation to change, but for taking their defined position in a hierarchical society. Perhaps schoolboys received some training in flexibility as they learned to try on different selves in imitative Latin compositions and in debates where they took now one, now the other side. Nevertheless, the goal in debate was to develop the skill that would lead to absolute truth, and the roles students played were classical authorities.[17] The narrow dialectic between conformity and role play left little room within the structure of formal education for innovation.[18]

By the seventeenth century, however, the hierarchy of English society was being substantially realigned, and absolute truth and molothic authority were only nostalgic myths. Empiricism questioned the efficacy of verbal debate for finding truth. Skepticism questioned the prospects for finding truth at all. Public wrangling between Catholics, Anglicans, and Puritans undermined religious authority. And the Stuarts' claim to be "divine right" monarchs was self-defense. When rulers, religions, and epistemologies are uncertain, an identity conformed to a fixed authority could become a liability.

More immediately, economic and social changes, which may appear gradual from a historical perspective, seemed to contemporaries to endanger the social structure that grounded their identities. In the sixteenth and seventeenth centuries England's population doubled, and between the early years of each century inflation increased sixfold. Whereas gentry, merchant middlemen, and yeoman landholders could profit from high prices, abundant labor, and low wages, husbandmen and laborers suffered. These new opportunities to be grasped in individualistic agrarian capitalism, clashing with the old system of communal rights and obligations, tended to polarize society. The "middling sort" often realigned themselves away from "neighborliness" and toward the state's desire for "good order" as the lower ranks declined into a permanent proletariat. These changes produced visible and frightening consequences: increased vagrancy and poverty, significant urbanization of a population in search of work (London rose from 50,000 in the 1520s to 400,000 in 1650), a rising crime rate, increased persecutions for witchcraft, and riots for food and against enclosures.[19]

Simultaneous with these social and economic tensions, England experienced a genuine cultural split. As the number of schools and the rate of literacy increased, new ideas and alternatives to custom became more widely available, promoting a degree of cultural diversity hitherto unknown. The growing differences in beliefs, values, and their symbolic expressions are most evident in the conflicts over worship that divided once homogeneous communities in the Civil War.[20] Although these changes were scattered over a century and their magnitude varied with location, they strained the fabric of society.

II

Simply put, the bind confronting the English in the first half of the seventeenth century was the necessity to confront accelerating change with selves nurtured in an ideology of stasis. Of course, some were oblivious, and others waited out the storm, tending to daily affairs. But those more sensitive to the magnitude of the changes and those whose lives and/or livelihoods were jeopardized responded more dramatically. Responses tended to range along two continua—one political, one individual.

Some tried to halt change by retreating to an earlier era, when the social hierarchy kept everyone in a designated place, and to an earlier culture in rhythm with local agrarian economies, not the expanding national economy of trade, manufacture, and agriculture. In the longed-for past, periodic indulgence of folly and licence had regulated social tensions and the slow pace of change. The Stuart kings tried this response, with spectacular lack of success. When Puritan zealots began to criticize defamers of the Sabbath, who attended stage plays or bear baiting, played games, and held festivals on Sunday in defiance of the fourth commandment, James I correctly perceived their criticism not as an isolated sectarian squabble but as an attack on an entire worldview. Rural sports were the remnants of that earlier age—hierarchical, agrarian, and measured by periods of work and holiday in seasonal rhythms. James wanted to sustain this world against the onslaughts of social mobility, the growth of urban society, and a work ethic based on the parable of the talents, not seasonal rhythms. To counter the Puritans' attacks he issued in 1618 *'The Kinges' Majesties Declaration Concerning Lawfull Sports* (most often referred to as *The Book of Sports*), in which he authorized certain recreations on Sundays after services: dancing, archery, leaping, vaulting, May games, Whitsun ales, morris dances, and processions of women carrying rushes for church decorations.[21]

Confronted by an angry Parliament, James withdrew the declaration but continued to encourage rural pastimes. In 1622 he issued an edict requiring nobles to remain in the country at Christmas because the old hospitality had "exceedingly decayed."[22] And in *Basilikon Doron,* his advice to his son and heir Henry, he describes the political uses of play in the section on how to handle the common people. After counseling no freedom of speech, severity to those who complain about royal rule, and rewards to the obedient, he adds, "Therewith also the more to allure them to a common amitie among themselves, certaine dayes in the yeare would be appointed, for delighting the people with publike spectacles of all honest games, and exercise of armes: as also for conveening of neighbours, for entertaining friendship and heartlinesse, by honest feasting and merrinesse."[23] James followed his own advice for keeping nobles and commons too entertained to criticize royal policies. When Robert

Dover, a sportsman of anti-Puritan sympathies, applied for a royal charter to establish yearly national games in the Cotswolds meadows, James granted not only the charter, but also some royal hand-me-downs, which Dover proudly wore at the opening ceremonies each year. Continuing until the Puritans disbanded them in 1644, the games drew commons and gentry from a wide area and were extravagantly praised in a volume of tributary poetry, *Annalia Dubrensia* (1636), by, among others, Ben Jonson, Michael Drayton, Owen Feltham, and Thomas Heywood.[24]

Three years earlier, Charles I had reissued, at the instigation of Archbishop Laud, James's *Book of Sports*. Many ministers, in open defiance of the archbishop, had refused to read the declaration from their pulpits and had been excommunicated. In this atmosphere, the poems of *Annalia Dubrensia* assume a defensive tone.[25] Several condemn "melancholly Swaines," "Hipocrites," and "Zealous Brother[s]" who "teach that Dauncing is a *Jeza-bell, /* And Barley-breake, the ready way to Hell." In opposition to the Puritan "new men," who, according to one poem, would have young limbs "numb'd to every thing, but flaile, and Plowe," the *Annalia* exalts the games as a return to the "Glories of our blessed Jeames" (Ben Jonson), to the era of Camelot and King Arthur's tournaments (Robert Griffin), to the first Olympic games begun in honor of Hercules (Michael Drayton), and to the golden age of Arcadia and Tempe (William Bass).[26] This yearning for the good old days (of increasingly distant locale and ever receding time) reveals that play had become a compelling political symbol, a symbol whose significance Leah Marcus has explored in detail.

To these poets and their sympathizers, like Robert Herrick, traditional sports and holidays bound to the cycle of the liturgical year (mumming at Christmas, cockfights and football at Shrovetide, church ales on Whitsunday, plays on Corpus Christi Day, souling on All Saints Eve) represented the more medieval and ritualistic conception of time that had prevailed before the seventeenth-century crises.[27] Other poets, most prominently Ben Jonson, supported Stuart policies on play while exposing courtly excesses. Although Jonson offered a revisionist and corrective view of mirth, the Stuarts tolerated criticism in masques because, like folly, it was safely contained within a framework that upheld authority.[28] Still other poets tried to retreat from political dissension altogether. The Cavalier poets often sought solace in Stoicism, pastoralism, eroticism, or the Horatian exaltation of a noble community of like-minded friends set apart from a hostile world. As Marcus has also shown, Herrick, Crashaw, Vaughan, and Traherne idealized childhood as a state of innocence and humility removed from the complexities and strife of contemporary life.[29]

The opposite political response to the accelerated pace of change was to speed it up. The demands of extreme Puritans, who wanted more religious reform, and of the radical army, who wanted social and economic reform, pushed moderate parliamentarians toward revolution. This deadly earnest response to political crisis seems far from the Stuarts' hope to regulate social tensions in communal play. But the revolutionaries were unwitting players too.

The social functions of play, as we have seen, are dialectical. Games, sports, and festivals promote social stability by channeling tensions into contest and periodic indulgence of excess and by displaying under controlled conditions the frightening anarchy that a complete release of tensions might unleash. But the experimentation, inversions, and foolery that festivals, games, and sports encourage may also generate newness and prepare the culture to accommodate change. The conservative pole of the dialectic links play to ritual, which orders transitions—from newborn to baptized member of the community, from winter to spring, from heir to king. The innovative pole links play potentially to revolution, in which rituals can no longer contain the thrust for change and violence topples the political structure.

While King James hoped to use the conservative pole of play to sustain the old order and his place in it, Puritan revolutionaries, although ostensibly disdaining play, used the innovative pole to impel social change. The dramatic approach to life and devotion preached by Protestants encouraged men to vivify such Biblical metaphors as Christian warfare by joining the New Model Army and to fulfill in their rebellion against Archbishop Laud's repressive policies such Old Testament types as the exodus of the Chosen People from Egyptian slavery. By enacting holy metaphor and story, these believers lived narrative lives. Similarly, during the Civil War and Interregnum, they repeated in fact events that had only been played during festival games and dramas.

Periods like the English Revolution are liminal; they are gaps between ordered worlds, and almost anything can happen. When basic structures collapse, people in crisis often unconsciously follow what Victor Turner calls "root paradigms," symbols and metaphors at the basis of a culture, kept alive in ritual, folklore, games, and festival customs—in that "latent system of potential alternatives" available in play.[30] Thus when the Puritans killed their king and Charles dramatized his death as a martyrdom, both parties performed in actuality what had in more stable times only been played—the ritual sacrificing of a scapegoat. This pattern underlies not only the Catholic Mass and the devotional literature of the *via crucis*, but also such varied play forms as English sword dancing, in which swords are clashed over dancers' heads, and mummers' plays, in which St. George kills Slasher, whom a braggart doctor then resurrects.[31] In the execution of Charles and in other aspects of Puritan behavior, play broke out of ritual into history. Biblical metaphors such as Christian warfare, types such as the journey to the Promised Land,

and symbolic actions such as sacrificing a king for the health of the nation came alive in civil war, revolution, and regicide.

While tension mounted between political responses to change, those individuals unhinged by the social and intellectual upheaval responded in two, more personal ways: they went mad, or they realigned their sense of self in relation to those absolutes being undermined by historical process. Citing such indices of social stress as the fascination with death, the widespread use of torture, the persecution of witches, heretics, and Jews, historians have argued that anxiety caused by rapid change made the years between 1300 and 1650 the most psychically disturbed era in European history. If the popularity of *The Anatomy of Melancholy,* the numbers of madmen and melancholy malcontents whom audiences applauded at the playhouses, the fashion of visiting Bedlam to gawk at the lunatics, the increase in prosecutions for witchcraft, and the renewed interest in the occult and demonic possession—if these are reliable indicators of the presence of madness in seventeenth-century England, then Robert Burton's description may not be just hyperbole: "All the world is mad... it is melancholy, dotes.... Never so much cause of laughter as now, never so many fools and madmen" (1:39, 52).[32]

More concrete evidence is hard to find, but the case records of Richard Napier, a doctor who treated approximately 3,000 mentally ill Englishmen between 1597 and 1634, provide first-hand descriptions of madness. According to his notes, psychic misery appeared most often, as is true today, in family disturbances, but economic and religious troubles were contributing causes. Napier's patients repeatedly complained of economic misfortunes, and certain villages where many of his patients lived contained Catholic recusants, militant Puritans in conflict with Laudians, or both. Economic and religious dislocations and disputes exacerbated marital conflicts, courtship woes, fears of damnation, and grief over deaths caused ultimately by poverty—the litany of misery Napier recorded. Furthermore, from 1612 to 1632, the number of his insane patients rose sharply, more sharply than the total number of patients, so the increase is not due to Napier's spreading reputation alone.[33] These case notes offer some evidence that madness was a frequent response of Englishmen spun around as the rate of change quickened.

A less destructive response to the dilemmas posed by change was to relocate the self. Some fastened their identities to one of the ideologies competing in the political and religious struggles. A more flexible response, however, was to adopt a stance that adjusts to volatile and unpredictable situations—the precarious stance of Hamlet. Acutely sensitive to contradictions as confusing as the binds that ensnared their fictional contemporary, Donne, Herbert, Marvell, Burton, and Browne neither tried to retreat to an earlier, less confusing time, nor fomented rebellion, nor went mad. They played to find a locus for the self.[34]

III

In their lyrics, the poets seldom image conflict as social upheaval or even its personal effects, like Donne's conversion and ordination. As the story of Hamlet re-enacts binds that usually thwart infant and child in the process of self-formation, these lyrics evoke powerful emotions that we share from our earliest and most confusing experiences. Chapter 1 outlined these experiences: the self forms by separating from the source of nurture and by internalizing caretakers' more or less accurate responses, their projected desires, and the cultural codes constituting and constituted in language. Now, this outline needs expanding to account for these poets' evocations of loss and contradiction within a context of social and cultural change.

The child experiences the ongoing process of separation (birth trauma, absence of caregivers, castration anxiety) as loss—loss of crucial objects that sustain identity. Simultaneously, the child struggles to assert an autonomous self in the face of all opposition. During these stages, interactions between child and caregivers inevitably produce conflict over closeness and separation, merger and independence. The child internalizes particular experiences of contradiction and develops characteristic modes of perceiving conflict and loss. Maturation and compromise usually resolve the outward conflict, but these experiences and modes of perception remain as the psychic residue of this early period of self-formation.

At any later stage of life, this residue can resurface, especially in times of traumatic conflict or change, not just in the family, but also in social and political spheres. Radical historical change intensifies the conflict always present between residual, dominant, and emergent ideologies into an open struggle. Since internalized cultural codes form and continue to sustain identity, tremors in the system of codes shake the self. The self will then perceive these tremors as it did the earliest conflicts of life. Some adults may experience change as an intolerable contradiction between competing systems that divides the self, or even as a devastating loss of the cultural codes in which the self originated. Others may welcome change as an opportunity for exploration or self-assertion against authority. Many more will feel ambivalent, exulting in liberated possibilities but fearing the loss of an assured identity. To summarize this complex process: if political dissention escalates precipitously, collapsing the social structures (such as church and state) that articulate cultural codes that in turn support psychic structures, then adults will perceive the crisis in terms of the losses and contradictions faced in early childhood. Crises for the adult self recall the crises of the nascent self.[35]

Perception, of course, influences response, and the panorama of responses to the seventeenth-century crises, just outlined, reflects the perceptions of childhood. Responses range from the fragmentation or dispersal of the self in madness to the preservation of identity either through obedience—defending a threatened ideology—or through rebellion—subverting authority with a self grounded in a rival ideology. The ludic selves projected in the texts to be studied here opt for neither pole. Still, the lyrics reawaken emotions felt by the emerging self: fears of being engulfed or abandoned, desires for autonomy, and ambivalence toward an idealized parental figure. Burton and Browne confront social and intellectual conflict more directly than the poets. But all relocate the self by playing in the space opened up by separation and contradiction.

Extending the context of this study into history and culture has required expanding our understanding of the formation and preservation of the self. This wider context also requires expanding the working definition of play hammered out in Chapter 1. There, our parable of the learned watching five-year-olds showed many disciplines looking at play and all seeing something different. Furthermore, five-year-olds are not the only ones who play; play is ubiquitous—among individuals from infancy through adulthood and in every form of social interaction. So, what we need now is a synthesis of theories to describe how play serves both psyche and culture. Bateson's structural definition of play, as a framed activity that redefines itself as what it is not, can provide a base for examining play across its wide spectrum. Key theorists from varied disciplines can build this foundation into a model of how players sustain and modify selves and societies. Subsequent chapters will then flesh out this model as details are needed to interpret texts.

In infancy and childhood, play's protective frame facilitates the separation of infant from mother (Winnicott), ritualizes the aggression between males defining their selves against the maternal sphere of power (Walter J. Ong), and gives the self room to experiment with capacities and identities (Brian Sutton-Smith). For adults, play's self-cancelling frame re-creates the protected state of childhood, thereby freeing them, at least temporarily, from the burden of psychic defense. Because players regulate external constraints by setting limitations and rules, they can relax internal constraints and open self to other as they seldom do in the conflicted everyday world (Freud, Mihaly Csikszentmihalyi). Safely framed, players may also regressively re-experience and resolve infantile conflicts in a process resembling psychoanalysis (Bateson, Winnicott, and Heinz Kohut). As we have already seen, cultures also frame playful licence and inversions of social order. During transitional periods in individuals' lives or in the calendar year, in marginal places, or among marginal people, play helps static cultures validate and expand identities in response to change (Turner).

From their varied perspectives, these theories conduct a fruitful dialogue, generating a synthetic understanding of the relation of play to self: play helps the nascent self separate from its caretakers, offers the growing self a protected way to assert autonomy and practice flexibility, and allows the adult to defend a threatened self, recreate a weary self, re-create an impaired self, and accommodate a changing self. This dialogue also identifies attributes of play that extend its definition. Play is in between, originating in the space between self and other, often occurring during transition periods when identities are unstable, and generating an in-between reality. It is double, allowing the player to stand simultaneously inside and outside his own actions, as both actor and framer of the action. And it is paradoxical, displaying the separateness of players while fostering bonds, imposing limits that release freedom, and defining one action as another. Players are never where or what they are.

4

John Donne at Play in Between

Hamlet's stance of the witty malcontent was a popular one at the turn of the century. John Donne also moped around the fringes of court life, vented his disgust at courtiers and women in satirical jibes, lacerated himself for inaction, and suffered from suicidal melancholy that blackened his vision. Nevertheless, like his fictional contemporary, he played with masterful zest and skill.[1] Whereas Hamlet played to live for a while on the edge of madness, Donne played to live always on the edge.

Even in such a self-consciously witty age as the seventeenth century, Donne's poetry and prose stand out as exceptionally playful. The wordplay of his puns, equivocations, and paradoxes, the role play of his mercurial personae, the sacred play in his fanciful use of typology and analogy, and the metaphysical play of his conceits—all this fooling around at every level of technique and content is Donne's trademark, and critics have long acknowledged its power to puzzle and move readers.[2] Some evaluate Donne's play as frivolous, aimed at cocky self-display or at debunking conventions.[3] Others argue that it accomplishes serious poetic or religious goals.[4] And a few find it sometimes frivolous (and thus to be criticized) and other times serious (and thus to be praised).[5] Donne ruefully acknowledged his almost obsessive playing: in a letter, he confessed to having "a ridling disposition"[6] and in a sermon, to punning involuntarily even while praying (10:1, 56). Acutely self-conscious though he was, he never said why he played nor what he gained. Donne played, I think, because play is always in between—the precise location he needed to occupy as private, public, and historical man.

I

Donne defined his self in response to a radical contradiction in his inner life: simultaneous fears of separation from and possession by the beloved—whether a woman or God.[7] To find this contradiction dramatized in his art, we need not assume that Donne's personae speak for Donne, the man. That he creates compelling voices for these fears;[8] that poems, letters, and prose works whose voices speak more directly manifest the same fears; and that he returns to themes of desiring and fleeing union again and again—such evidence shows that this contradiction moved him profoundly. The speakers of his love poems often seek union with the beloved, body and soul: the couple becomes two hemispheres of one globe ("The Good Morrow"), pictures in one another's eyes ("The Ecstasy"), even a phoenix, the "one neutral thing [to which] both sexes fit" during intercourse ("The Canonization"). Almost one-fifth of the *Songs and Sonnets* (not to mention the elegies and several sermon and poetic farewells to earthly life) are valedictions—good-bye poems in which the poet probes and salves the wounds of breaking union with his beloved. On the other hand, many of Donne's love poems are mock-serious paeans to promiscuity ("Confined Love"), cynical justifications for the rake's life ("Community"), or disillusioned renunciations of love ("Love's Alchemy"). Here, the antifeminist or Ovidian speakers seek escape from a stifling union that threatens either to possess them and their means or to trap them into fidelity.[9]

Less distanced personae voice these contradictory fears of separation and union in poems about Donne's relationship to God. The Holy Sonnets argue God's property rights to him ("As due by many titles"), ask God to be the adamant to draw his iron heart ("Thou hast made me"), and even command God to imprison, enthrall, and ravish him because he is powerless to overcome his separation from divine unity ("Batter my heart"). The last (and most grave) sin he confesses in "A Hymn to God the Father" is the fear of eternal separation from God. But just as frequently in the divine poems as in the love lyrics, the speaker willfully runs away from love and grace abounding. The perverse traveler of "Good Friday, 1613. Riding Westward" turns his back on the cross, the source of God's love and grace to man. He both fears to look on "God's face," whose "self life" would annihilate him, and longs to be restored to God's image. Like the equally perverse speakers of "A Hymn to God the Father" and "Batter my heart," who doubt the efficacy of the shining Son, the speaker of "Good Friday" both does and does not want the fulfillment of the blessing God commended to Aaron: "The Lord make his face shine upon thee . . . The Lord lift up his countenance upon thee" (Num. 6:25–26, emphasis mine). He both does and does not want God's shining countenance to "burn" him into newness ("Good Friday," "Batter my heart").

Theories have been offered to explain Donne's fear of separation (although not of union): a mother, widowed and hastily remarried, who was so concerned with her embattled religion and endangered Jesuit relatives that her elder son felt disillusioned and abandoned; an apostasy from the mother (and his mother's) church that led him to project his own desertion onto others whom he feared would desert him.[10] Although intriguing, such biographical scenarios may seem specious to contemporary critics who look for origins, not in the particulars of individual experience, but in historical and social contexts or in the modes of discourse available in a culture. Undoubtedly, the plight of the alienated intellectual in Jacobean England, the patronage system, the coteries that seventeenth-century poets so often addressed, and the absolutist discourse fostered by James I—all these external forces and more impinged on the linguistic choices Donne made when he wrote.[11] They cannot, however, completely account for a theme and style so persistent throughout Donne's canon. If social context or modes of discourse alone determined poetry, then Ben Jonson, for instance, would have written like Donne. But he didn't.

Both Donne and Jonson had to contend with a patronage system that required them to sue for favors from powerful women in court circles; both inherited a conventional language of address to high-born ladies, Petrarchism; and both composed verse letters to Lucy Countess of Bedford that, while exalting their benefactress as far beyond them, assert the poet's own integrity and worth. In his letter "at New Year's Tide," Donne assumes the traditional posture of an abject admirer who would praise and, therefore, preserve the fame of his lady's virtue. Characterizing himself as neither "Debtor to th' old, nor creditor to the new" year, and as reluctant to trust the new year "with hopes," Donne alludes to the financial dependence that underlies his Petrarchan stance of self-abasement before a powerful lady. But he devotes the majority of the poem to voicing God's instructions on how Lucy may preserve her virtue amid the moral ambiguity, lies, spying, and need for secrecy at court:

> God . . . will best teach you, how you should lay out
> His stock of beauty, learning, favour, blood. . . .
> He will teach you, that good and bad have not
> One latitude in cloisters, and in Court,
> Indifferent there the greatest space hath got,
> Some pity is not good there, some vain disport,
> On this side sin, with that place may comport. . . .
> He will make you speak truths, and credibly,
> And make you doubt, that others do not so:
> He will provide you keys, and locks, to spy,
> And 'scape spies, to good ends, and he will show
> What you may not acknowledge, what not know.

Although he claims to be only "One corn of one low anthill's dust, and less" in contrast to Lucy, a "miracle . . . a thing so high . . . infinity," he also assumes the superior position of the exposer of worldly dangers.

Jonson likewise conventionally idealizes the countess as "faire, and free, and wise, / Of greatest bloud, and yet more good then great," and as "curteous, facile, sweet, / Hating that solemne vice of greatnesse, pride."[12] In praising her "influence," which surpasses the day star's, and her "powers" to control destiny, Jonson also alludes to the patronage system that locates him as a conventional Petrarchan admirer of his benefactress. Her mere name, he concludes, supplants his poem; her reality replaces his imagined creation. Nevertheless, this replacement only occurs in the last two lines of the poem, and Jonson devotes the previous sixteen lines to the poet's power "to forme... What kinde of creature I could most desire, / To honor, serve, and love; as *Poets* use." Although in the end he yields his power of feigning an ideal image to the name *"Bedford,"* with all the authority a noble name can command, the poet's imagining dominates the poem. This power to "forme" perfection recalls Jonson's frequent strategy to instill virtue at court, where its perfection was far from complete, through praise.

Donne's and Jonson's poems arise from a shared social context, the patronage system of the Jacobean court; they speak in one of the dominant modes of cultural discourse, the conventions of Petrarchan praise; and they assert the poet's autonomy within his role of financial and social dependence. But the voices of the two poems differ markedly. Donne perceives the court, the source of all benefits, in the same contradictory patterns evident in his sacred and profane lyrics. He obliquely sues for the court's recognition and preferment by depicting the desperate nonbeing of his exclusion: "If I should call me anything, should miss." Here, and in other letters to the countess, only the "tincture" of such a highly placed lady's name can alchemically create or refine him or his verse into being.[13] But, while he seeks incorporation into the courtly circle that alone ensures his identity, he distances himself with his pointed exposure of its treacherous ambiguities. Jonson does not voice this particularly Donnean impulse to simultaneously implore and flee union with the other.

Donne obsessively perceived relationships in this contradictory way, before and after the marriage that seemed to end his career, in a wide variety of contexts and discourses—when dramatizing the vicissitudes of libertine, conjugal, and Platonic love; or the yearnings and fears of a sinner; or, as here in his letter to Bedford, the plight of a seeker after worldly advancement. Thus social and linguistic context alone did not determine his perception; rather, an individualized pattern of perception seems to have determined his responses to varying social and linguistic contexts. What is the source of this pattern? Although specific biographical scenarios about Donne's mother or the effects of his apostasy are too speculative, we can identify the typical source of conflicting fears of separation and merger. Donne's fascination with looking into (or avoiding) the face of the beloved, a key image in his poems of sacred and profane love, alludes to this typical source.

The need for face-to-face encounters recalls the earliest and most important face to a child, the mother's (or nurse's). As mother and child look at each other, exchanging mutual smiles that confirm the other's self and communicating joint need and gratification, this reflexive recognition substitutes for the union from which the child was separated at birth and marks the first step toward forming an identity.[14] Eventually, this face-to-face union is broken as the child unwillingly confronts the mother's absence and later begins to desire independence. In both cases, the child realizes that s/he is not one with the source of nurture, that the self is separate from the other, that there is a world beyond omnipotent merger. This experience typically causes conflict because the child wants the security and immediate gratification of union with the mother, but at the same time s/he wants to explore the world, independent of the mother's presence or control.[15] This ambivalence frequently survives in adults—in some more than others, depending on factors of nature and nurture. Whatever these factors may have been for Donne, the contradictory desires and fears of this period marked his conception of intimacy throughout his life.

To mediate this conflict, Donne needed a way to live in between separation and union. He found it in play—always in between. We have located the earliest play of infants in a potential space between self and other. Infants often fill this space of separation with a blanket, a stuffed monkey, a rag—"transition objects" invested with the nurturant presence, which become neither wholly external like the world beyond infantile omnipotence nor wholly internal like hallucinations. At play in between, the child discovers that likewise the nascent self is neither abandoned (s/he has a substitute for the nurturant presence) nor merged with the other (the favored toy is a portable, manipulable object).

Play is in between in another sense. Because it is a framed activity, play both connects the self to others and sustains a certain distance between them. When the player frames his punch to your midsection as play, his action is a punch, but not a real punch; the play frame has conferred upon his punch a kind of in-between reality. Furthermore, the player has punched you, but he has also stood aside, framing his punch as play; he is simultaneously present and distant. As a result, players need never fear engulfment in relationships of the play world. Because part of the player remains aloof and because play relationships occur between play selves put on for the limited time and space of the play world, no lasting consequences need occur. Kisses during a game of spin-the-bottle are not exactly kisses, nor is the kisser wholly present in the kiss, but they are not nonkisses either, and the kisser is not wholly absent. The defining frame, "This is just play," engages and disengages selves.

Because of its in-between reality, play became Donne's characteristic way to mediate the conflict he felt so keenly between separation and union:

he adopted the ludic self.[16] To assert unity despite apparent disunity, he plays with witty images: a departing lover's tears, which reflect his beloved's face, become whole worlds and seas like those through which he must sail ("A Valediction: of Weeping"); a "ragged bony name" scratched in a window will bring the muscle and sinew of its body home again ("A Valediction: of my Name in the Window"); and the two movable feet that make a single compass represent lovers who, although "two souls," "are one," joined at a point above the fixed foot ("A Valediction: forbidding Mourning"). Readers have described as almost sacramental the images and objects Donne uses in the valedictions to deny the separation of the lovers.[17] Psychoanalysts might compare them to "transition objects"—those portable substitutes for the nurturing presence that allow the child to be physically separate, but not cut off from that presence. In these and other similar poems, Donne's play yokes self to others. Still, the union only lasts in the fragile play world of his wit, and he knows it. Whether exalting union or fleeing it, he is always self-consciously playing. The tone in apparently serious pleas for union and in distanced performances alike is uncertain.

Three examples will suffice. By the end of "The Sun Rising," the arrogant speaker has forestalled the inevitable separation from his beloved that morning threatens by transforming himself into all princes; his lady into both the Indies, then all states; and their humble bedroom into the whole world to which the sun owes service. But does this usurper of the heavens' ruler actually expect the "unruly sun," as he calls it, to obey his solipsistic command to revolve for eternity around his bed while the rest of the world, which rolls on despite his boasts, freezes? Should lady and reader be swept away by the imaginative power of his passion or laugh with a man who is laughing at his own extravagance?

In a second example, the nimble-witted speaker of "Elegy 9: The Autumnal" hammers out a series of clever couplets into what one manuscript entitles "A Paradox of an old woman," a favorite joke in male coteries.[18] Loving her is not shame, but reverence; although past her Golden Age, "now she's gold oft tried, and ever new"; if graves, her wrinkles are only graves for love; and so forth. Yet, when he turns from autumnal to "winter-faces, whose skin's slack . . . Whose mouths are holes . . . ," he beholds his own *memento mori,* and ends what began as a witty paradox by directing his affections to

> descend, and journey down the hill,
> Not panting after growing beauties, so,
> I shall ebb out with them, who homeword go.

Turning from distanced drollery to active engagement with the woman whose ebbing he shares, the speaker may after all have thought the elegy a fitting tribute, as another manuscript would have it, to the sophisticated "Lady Herbert afterwards Danvers."

In a third example, the devout speaker of "Good Friday," through memory and meditation, unites himself with the moment of Christ's crucifixion despite his perverse "Riding Westward" almost 1,600 years later. Still, isn't there something waggish and coy about a penitent who so cleverly transforms turning his back on God into a submission to correction and who offers to face God only if assured of acceptance? All the while these ingenious speakers find ways to transcend separation or to distance themselves, their ambiguous tone moves them both toward and away from their object. By placing his poems in the paradoxical play frame (by its nature, in between), Donne mediates the desire for and fear of union.

Poems like these, whose speakers frame their utterances as play, resemble self-referential paradoxes. Just as the statement by Epimenides, the Cretan, that all Cretans are liars will vacillate forever (being true only if it is false), so a player who claims to be playing will forever perform actions that are and are not themselves (such as the punch to the midsection that conveys the message "This punch does not signify what a punch signifies"). For this reason, some readers feel that Donne's poems are "virtually impossible to see clearly: they will not stay still." Others have tried to grasp in prose the elusive poise between distance and union that Donne achieves in poetry through the self-referential play frame. In "The Sun Rising," says Arnold Stein, "The mind of the poet is at once engaged in its imagining and detached in its knowledge of what it is doing; it is both beholder and partaker as it acts and contemplates itself acting." In "A Hymn to God the Father," says Wilbur Sanders, Donne recognizes "that his congenital addiction to irony has imprisoned him in a . . . fear of relationship (relationship even with God . . .), and perpetual defensive role-playing. . . . But he has also lived long enough with himself to have developed a rough affection for his *alter ego*"—"the slippery ironist in himself, the one who can never be pinned down."[19] So Donne plays on, knowing he is playing, and in his play balancing precariously between closeness and distance.

Understanding how play straddles the poles of true and not true, real and not real, can also help readers who wonder if Donne is "serious" (and about what?) or "flippant."[20] A reader of "The Canonization," moved by the vision of transcendent love for which it argues, may be troubled on a second reading by its rather comical situation: the defensive speaker, who at the beginning of the poem fights the outside world for the right to love, transforms himself and his beloved (through sheer wit and will) into saints, whom by the end of the poem the outside world invokes for couples' counseling. The critic of love, whom the speaker barrages with a rapid fire of images, is left wondering, "What happened?" And the amused but confused reader may ask, "Is this a serious poem about the power of love, a seriously ironic poem about the folly of love, or a bravura display of the power of Donne's sophistry?" Because it is play, it is all and none. Its playfulness neither invalidates its claims about love's mystery nor exalts the lovers to actual sainthood. Perhaps we should take the speaker all the more seriously because, within the play frame, he takes himself so very seriously—a frame that means he does not take himself so seriously after all.[21] This tangle of self-referentiality illustrates why terms like *flippant, serious,* even *ironic* are too crude to describe many of Donne's poems. Like "The Canonization," they enjoy the in-between reality of play, which is neither dream nor fact, which is both true and not, where questions about sincerity are simplistic.

That Donne's lyrics hold opposites in tension has become a critical commonplace: emotion and reason, the concrete and the abstract, flesh and spirit, time and eternity, earth and heaven. Samuel Johnson calls this quality *discordia concors;* T. S. Eliot, the unified sensibility; and others, casuistry or mannerism or what distinguishes metaphysical from baroque or *précieux* poetry.[22] Frank Warnke, however, has gone beyond commonplace to relate Donne's play to this line of criticism. Donne captures, says Warnke, "the imaginative experience of the validity of contradictory truths" that exists "in the sphere of play, with all the connotations of jest, mask, and make-believe contained within that word."[23]

The same causes that made play Donne's characteristic mode also led him to favor themes that capture the experience of being in between. He always felt himself to be a body, to be in the flesh; in order to reach beyond the self to another (whether to a lady or God), he had to experience the other with his flesh. So the peak moments of in-betweenness that he records occur during sex, sickness, and suffering. Beds provide settings for these moments in many *Songs and Sonnets,* three elegies, all his epithalamions, "Holy Sonnet 6" ("This is my play's last scene"), "Hymn to God my God, in my Sickness," the *Devotions Upon Emergent Occasions,* and a sermon on David's penitence, "I am weary with my groaning; all the night make I my bed to swim, I water my couch with my teares . . ." (Ps. 6:6–7).[24] These beds are the locus for multiple mergers: dreaming glides imperceptibly into waking ("The Dream"), body unites with body ("Epithalamion . . . on the Lady Elizabeth and Count Palatine"), bodies metamorphose into souls that interinanimate ("The Ecstasy"), earthly life meets life everlasting ("Hymn . . . in my Sickness," the sermon on penitence, 8: 8, 203), and human flesh falls into the hand of God (*Devotions,* 41).

As the threshold between multiple realities, these beds of joy and affliction become, oddly enough, playgrounds where Donne indulges his "antic disposition." In "The Ecstasy" he conjures up whimsical, incongruous metaphors to connect the reclining but still chaste lovers: sweating palms become "a fast balm" to cement their hands, loving gazes become twisted eye-beams threaded on a double string, and faces reflected in one another's eyes become a peculiar form of asexual "propagation." The convoluted and perplexing argument spoken, presumably in chorus, by the lovers' souls to "unperplex" the nature of human love appeals to metaphysics (already mixed souls mix again in love), horticulture (transplanted violets multiply), cosmology (souls own bodies as angels control spheres), metallurgy (bodies are alloy, not dross), and medicine (blood begets vital spirits comparable to souls). What was announced first as a negotiation "'twixt two equal armies," then as a love duet, has become a whirlwind course through the university. Despite its Neoplatonic sources, it sounds more like a persuasion to love than a "dialogue of one," as the optimistic speaker, who seems to have forgotten that he is negotiating with the enemy, calls it.[25] Here in this outdoor bedroom, "Where, like a pillow on a bed, / A pregnant bank swelled up," the speaker's play mediates several oppositions: lover and beloved, body and soul, total union and amused distance. Playing at legalistic argument, he persuades his beloved to merge their bodies in sex as well as their souls in ecstasy; playing with snippets of learned lore, he argues for the oneness of body and soul; and playfully inverting the conventions of love poetry by, as Dryden accused, perplexing "the minds of the fair sex with nice speculations of philosophy," the speaker maintains his medial position between surrendering himself to the beloved and entertaining her with an elaborate joke.[26]

In the *Devotions Upon Emergent Occasions*, Donne continues to play even while prone on the sick bed that he calls the threshold between earth and heaven: "in the door of the grave, this sick bed," he says, "as yet God suspends me between heaven and earth, as a meteor; and I am not in heaven because an earthly body clogs me, and I am not in the earth because a heavenly soul sustains me" (20–21). For Donne the agony of sickness proves paradoxically that he is not separated from God, that God's hand is upon his flesh and soul (41), that God has branded him as His own with the spots of disease:[27]

> These heats, O Lord, which thou hast brought upon this body, are but thy chafing of the wax, that thou mightst seal me to thee: these spots are but the letters in which thou hast written thine own name and conveyed thyself to me; whether for a present possession, by taking me now, or for a future reversion, by glorifying thyself in my stay here, I limit not, I condition not, I choose not. . . . Only be thou ever present to me, O my God, and this bedchamber and thy bedchamber shall be all one room, and the closing of these bodily eyes here, and the opening of the eyes of my soul there, all one act. (87–88)

Like the beds of Donne's profane love, the sick bed is an in-between place where man in his flesh meets the other in the passage to a transcendent experience that will make "one little room, an every where" ("The Good Morrow").

In between life and death, in the suffering of sickness, Donne engages in what eighteenth-century men-about-town called "deep play"—gambling for stakes so high and at risks so great that Jeremy Bentham later urged its banishment from rational society.[28] Neither an eighteenth-century spark nor a nineteenth-century utilitarian, but a seventeenth-century divine, Donne risks everything to reach from the corrupt flesh of a man ("Meditation 1") who is isolated from friends ("Meditation 5") and centered on annihilation ("Meditation 10"), to the immortality of God ("Meditation 1"), who is a "plurality of persons" ("Meditation 5, 30") and the center of His own emanating light ("Meditation 10"). Donne can bridge this abyss of separation through the wordplay of metaphor, analogy, and typology because God uses these ways with man. As he marvels, "My God, my God . . . thou art a figurative, a metaphorical God too; a God in whose words there is such a height of figures, such voyages, such peregrinations to fetch remote and precious metaphors, such extensions, such spreadings, such curtains of allegories, such third heavens of hyperboles" that men may "make their accesses to thee in such a kind of language as thou wast pleased to speak to them" (124, 126). Because God communicates to man through semiotic play, man reaches toward God first by learning to read His puzzling verbal and living texts and then by playfully transforming his life into a divine text.

In the emergent occasions of his sickness, Donne tries to read God's messages—in the sudden onset of the disease, in the arrival of the physician, in the cordials and pigeons and purgings of his physic, in the sounds from the street.[29] The missives can be read only if Donne translates them by a key, the Bible, and his translation must be as playfully metaphoric as the signs sent from such a "metaphorical God." If he can transform events of his life into Biblical events, then he can meet God in the pages of His text, taking part in the divine story written from all times. In his early lament that his "senses . . . change and fail" (12), Donne prays,

> O my God, who madest thyself a light in a bush, in the midst of these brambles and thorns of a sharp sickness, appear unto me so that I may see thee, and know thee to be my God, applying thyself to me, even in these sharp and thorny passages. Do this, O Lord, for his sake, who was not the less the King of heaven for thy suffering him to be crowned with thorns in this world. (16)

In the words of his text, Donne tries to conform his life to that trace of the divine presence God left on earth, His Word. Donne reads the thorns of his sickness as both the brambles of the bush in which God appeared to Moses and the crown Christ wore to redeem the sickness of sin, thereby uniting Old Testament type, New Testament fulfillment, and modern antitype in the play space of the sickbed. Donne comprehends God's message written in his sickness by translating the events of his suffering into a continuation of God's story told in the Bible. He plays out the Biblical text in his life. Such playful translations re-enact the Incarnation, making the Biblical Word flesh again in the emergent occasions of Donne's sickness.[30]

Yet the union between Word and flesh in Donne's *Devotions* is never complete precisely because the translations are often playful. After transforming his bed into an altar and his body into a sacrificial offering, he suddenly remembers the spots of his disease and worries, "wilt thou accept no spotted sacrifice?" This setback does not detain his fertile wit for long. In the succeeding expostulation, spots of fleshly sin become spots of voluntary confession, then spots of Christ's earthly body, and finally "the constellations of the firmament, to direct my contemplation to that place where thy Son is, thy right hand" (85–87). Donne's worry about his spotted sacrifice is comical, and the spots' progressive metamorphosis into stars is so incongruous that it calls attention more to the play of Donne's wit than to the conformity of his life with the several Biblical texts about spots that he quotes.[31] Even in an ostensibly more serious passage, Donne plays as coyly and self-consciously with God as he does at the end of "Good Friday." Describing his sickness as God's correction, he wheedles,

> Let me think no degree of this thy correction casual, or without signification; but yet when I have read it in that language, as a correction, let me translate it into another, and read it as a mercy; and which of these is the original, and which is the translation; whether thy mercy or thy correction were thy primary and original intention in this sickness, I cannot conclude, though death conclude me; for as it must necessarily appear to be a correction, so I can have no greater argument of thy mercy, than to die in thee and by that death to be united to him who died for me. (50)

The plea to let him retranslate God's message from correction to mercy, the equivocation on *conclude,* and the artful retranslation that he effects, with or without divine permission, casts Donne more in the role of God's playmate than His creature and supplicant.

In private colloquies—whether with a beloved woman or with God—the play relationship sustains for Donne and his personae a middle distance where he balances precariously on the edge.

II

When Donne moved from private colloquies to public performances as a man of God and preacher of the Word, his essential self was not changed, only refocused, and he knew it. In an early sermon a few months after his wife's death, he considers how the prophets—bred in courts and cities, or laboring as shepherds and fishers—understood their new calling in terms of their old. Likewise, he argues, the convert refocuses his compelling passion away from its sinful object onto God, but the passion itself does not change:

> that soul, that hath been transported upon any particular worldly pleasure, when it is intirely turn'd upon God, and the contemplation of his all-sufficiency and abundance, doth find in God fit subject, and just occasion to exercise the same affection piously, and religiously, which had before so sinfully transported, and possest it.
>
> A covetous person, who is now truly converted to God, he will exercise a spiritual covetousness still, he will desire to have him all.... So will a voluptuous man, who is turned to God, find plenty and deliciousnes enough in him. (1:5, 236–37)

So will a man haunted by the desire and fear of union with the beloved, who is turned to God, find in Him a perfect and terrifying closeness. Donne was that man, but his ruling passion, unlike the prophets', was not wholly transformed into virtue. Thus as a preacher he understood the needs of his sinful congregation, indeed of all fallen mankind, in terms of the contradictory desires that had marked his own life.

No theme (not the horror of corporal dissolution emphasized in anthology pieces) so fired Donne's preaching as the terror of separation from and the blessedness of union with God.[32] Repeatedly he images this union in the beatific vision, as in the two famous sermons on 2 Corinthians 4:6, "For, God who commanded light to shine out of darkness, hath shined in our hearts, to give the light of the knowledge of the glory of God, in the face of Jesus Christ" (4:3), and on 1 Corinthians 13:12, "For now we see through a glasse darkly, but then face to face" (8:9). As the face-to-face encounters of his love lyrics figure the wholeness he sought in profane love, the sight of God's radiant face described in his sermons defines sacred union. He exults that in heaven

> I shall have an un-interrupted, and un-intermitted, an un-discontinued sight of God; I shall looke, and never looke off; not looke, and looke againe, as here, but looke, and looke still.... my soule shall sleep, not onely without trouble, and startling, but without rocking, without any other help, then that peace, which is in it selfe; My soule shall be thoroughly awake, and thoroughly asleep too.... I shall see this light in his face, who is all face, and yet all hand, all application, and communication, and delivery of all himselfe to all his Saints. (9:4, 128–29)

The images of gazing into a face, of perfect sleep without rocking to ease fretfulness, of waking sleep, and of nurture recall the bond between mother and child. Such union with God requires complete surrender because "Love," says Donne, "delivers over him that loves into the possession of that that he loves . . . it changes him that loves, into the very nature of that that he loves, and he is nothing else" (1:3, 184–85). Both seeking and fearing such an engulfment of the self into the godhead, Donne suspected that his parishioners shared his perverse desire to ride the other way: "we pretend to be sayling homewards, and yet we desire to have the winde against us; we are travelling to the heavenly *Jerusalem,* and yet we are loath to come thither" (3:8, 203). Perhaps because Donne felt this contradiction at the core of his psychic life, he could revivify for his audiences a Christian commonplace: fallen man yearns toward God, but wants Him at a distance.

So Donne preached about life in between because this was man's lot: "I have not body enough for my body, and I have too much body for my soul; not body enough, not bloud enough, not strength enough, to sustain my self in *health,* and yet body enough to destroy my soul, and frustrate the grace of God in that miserable, perplexed, riddling condition of man" (2:1, 63). Caught in his humanity between flesh and spirit, caught between the fear of being separate and the fear of being possessed, caught in time between the kingdom come and the kingdom promised, Donne, the preacher, realized that being human meant being in between. At his ordination he anchored himself to the sign of all men's radical in-betweenness by taking a new impresa: the god-man raised up between two worlds on a cross shaped like an anchor.

The anchor-cross impresa figures two related concerns of Donne's sermons: the need to ground man's riddling self and the discovery of that anchor in the suffering Body of Christ. Donne confesses that even in private prayer, "I am not alwayes I. . . . Passions and affections sometimes, sometimes bodily infirmities, and sometimes a vain desire of being eloquent in prayer, aliens me, withdraws me from my self" (9:9, 219); even in preaching, "I am not all here. . . . I am here speaking to you, and yet I consider by the way, in the same instant, what it is likely you will say to one another, when I have done" (3:3, 110). Being in between means feeling dispersed, and only at the last day will all these scatterings of the self, along with the dust of the body, be recollected. As Job affirms in Donne's sermon text, "though . . . wormes destroy this body, yet in my flesh shall I see God" (19:26), Donne preaches, "at the Resurrection. . . . *Ego,* I, body and soul, soul and faculties, shall say to Christ Jesus, *Ego sum,* Lord, it is I, and hee shall not say, *Nescio te, I know thee not,* but avow me, and place me at his right hand." In the meantime, there is a guarantee that grounds the self (both flesh and spirit)—suffering: "*Ego sum, I am the man that hath seen affliction, by the rod of his wrath; Ego sum,* and I the same man, shall receive the crown of glory which shall not fade" (3:3, 110). As heir to Job, the type, and Christ, the fulfillment, Donne as the antitype anchors his wayward self, while he awaits the final gathering, to the crucified Body of Christ. The very affliction that defines human life, a fickle mind in an infirm body, identifies him with the divine ground of his being.[33]

Furthermore suffering, he preached, is where man can meet God in between:

> This is a way unconceiveable by any, unexpressible to any, but those that have felt that manner of Gods proceeding in themselves . . . they see God better in the dark, then they did in the light; Their tribulation hath brought them to a nearer distance to God, and God to a clearer manifestation to them. (8:1, 53)

Brought closer to God by pain but separated from Him by fleshy selfhood, the suffering man may experience

> a fundamentall joy, a radicall joy, a viscerall, a gremiall joy, that arises out of the bosome and wombe and bowels of the tribulation it selfe. . . . when as cold and dead water, when it comes to the fire, hath a motion and dilatation and a bubling and a kind of dancing in the vessell, so my soule, that lay asleep in prosperity, hath by this fire of Tribulation, a motion, a joy, an exaltation. (3:16, 343)

In suffering, the soul learns to dance, to play in the space between man and God.

Like the covetous or voluptuous convert who refocuses his ruling passion on God, Donne, the playful convert, joins the dance of Wisdom who, for all eternity, has made play before the face of the Father. And like the prophets who brought the ways of their old calling into their new, Donne brought to preaching his skills as a player. The job suited him perfectly for three reasons: it was in between, its traditions justified displays of wit, and it was dramatic.

As an Anglican priest, Donne's public identity was a man who—by his clothes, his position in a raised pulpit, and his Christian life—was conspicuously set apart from this world to lead men to the next. In his poem "To Mr Tilman after he had taken orders," the priest is an "Ambassador to God" from man; he keeps "heaven's door"; in the sacraments he brings "man to heaven, and heaven again to man"; in him "must meet God's graces, men's offences"; and his calling so knits heaven, the begetter, to the mother earth that he is made "a blessed hermaphrodite." Many sermons detail the preacher's mediational role, and some image him as the nurse of God's children:

Donne begs that God not give him "*dry breasts;* that you may always suck pure milk from us" (6:3, 92); and he hopes that through him God will rain upon his congregation the "dew . . . honey . . . Manna . . . Oyle . . . Balsamum" of consolation (7:4, 134). When he feeds them with the milk and manna of consolation, he is amazed that he is fed in return:

> For, when I have given that man comfort, that man hath given me a Sacrament . . . I have received from him, in his receiving from me . . . Lord, when I went, I was sure, that thou who hadst received me to mercy, wouldst also receive him, who could not be so great a sinner as I; And now, when I come away, I am sure, that thou who art returned to him . . . wilt never depart from mee. (8:10, 249)

In between pulpit and pew, heaven and earth, male and female, the preacher conveys God's presence, receives it, and by his reception returns it to the giver, thereby multiplying that presence into a holy interchange of selves. Donne could preach this union because he came to ground his self in his vocation; he was bound to the Body of Christ manifest not only in his own suffering body, but also in the communal body of his suffering congregation.[34]

The second reason Donne's job suited him was that the mediating presence that he fed to his flock was the Word, the perfect medium for his wit. The *ars praedicandi* (art of discourse) of the Church Fathers offered a tradition congenial to Donne's skills as a player. Augustine's justification of finding multiple transferred meanings in Biblical texts, so long as they conduce to faith, and the emphasis on memory as the key to salvation produced a sermon style in which the preacher played out the significations of his text, weaving an intricate, often fanciful, network of associations. One word of the text might bring to mind other Biblical texts, which might lead to still other allegorized meanings, so that several facets of the Word were polished and revolved in the memory of listeners. Playing thus with the Word, the preacher brought the congregation into his sacred game, which one reader of Donne's sermons has called "play that is delightful and redemptive."[35]

A typical example of Donne's play with the *"diverse senses,"* which, he rejoices, "present the plenty, and abundance of the *holy Ghost* in the *Scriptures,* who satisfies us as with marrow, and with fatnesse" (3:17, 353), is the first half of his 1619 sermon on Matthew 21:44: "Whosoever shall fall on this stone, shall be broken; but on whomsoever it shall fall, it will grinde him to powder" (2:8, 179–96). Because Biblical metaphor suggests that God dwells with man and "builds upon" him, Donne concludes that the stone in the text is Christ. He is the foundation stone on which man builds his life (1 Cor. 3:11), the cornerstone that unites and reconciles (Isa. 28:16), the stone of rest that Jacob used for a pillow when he dreamed of the ladder to heaven

(Gen. 28:10–12), the stone in David's sling that killed Goliath (1 Sam. 17:40–45), and the rock that both gave the Israelites water in the desert (Num. 20:11) and is a dwelling place unmoved by tempests (Isa. 42:11). Donne plays out each of these significations, using allegory (Jacob's ladder becomes the steps toward holy rest), typology (David's sling prefigures the cross by which Christ slew the true giant, sin), and metaphoric associations that circle back upon themselves. (The rock that gave the Israelites water and in which Christians dwell reminds Donne that the father whose son asks for bread will not give him a stone [Luke 11:11]; yet, he adds, all Christians pray for "daily bread" [Matt. 6:11], which is Christ in the sacrament of the Church, which is the stone that both nourishes and provides a safe dwelling.) The same fertile wit that animates this lively sermon once produced so many far-fetched associations on a name scratched in a window pane that the reader wonders, "How long can the fellow keep it up?" Only now the fellow has found a tradition and a God that redeem his compelling passion to play.

The third reason that his job suited him was its potential for high drama. Since in the *ars praedicandi* tradition the Christian was a neotype, reenacting Christ's fulfillment of the Old Testament types, Donne could preach a life of play. By training the hearer's memory to revolve the multifaceted Word in his mind, the preacher showed him the Christ within.[36] Donne tells the listener that he has the Bible without book:

> He hath a *Genesis* in his *memory;* he cannot forget his *Creation;* he hath an *Exodus* in his memory; he cannot forget that God hath delivered him, from some kind of *Egypt,* from some oppression; He hath a *Leviticus* in his memory; hee cannot forget, that God hath proposed to him some Law, some rules to be observed. (2:2, 74)

But the Word must not remain in the memory alone; the hearer must write it in his life. At the end of an allegorization of the aspects (called "characters") of Simeon's life, Donne reminds his hearers to become actors: "I shall onely have time to name the rest of those characters; you must spell them, and put them into their syllables . . . words . . . their Syntaxis, and sentences; that is, you must pursue the imitation" (7:11, 289). Donne's congregation must enact the script written first in the Bible, then in their memories, then in their lives in order to effect a new incarnation—the Word made flesh again in human lives lived as a theatre staged by Christ for the angels (3:9, 218).

For all his skill at using the traditional *ars praedicandi* to join preacher, hearer, and Word into a triple presence, Donne's wit confirms man's distance from that union. His wordplay often takes the same arresting forms in his sermons as in his poetry. Sometimes a pun may broaden and deepen his meaning, as in a comparison of the righteous man at the moment of death to a picture that may require months to engrave on copper but only a moment to print from the press: "when this Picture comes to the Presse, this Man to the streights and agonies of Death," a lifetime of goodness is stamped in his present trust that death is only a sleep (8:7,190). The association of the press that prints with the press of mortal agony may also recall the common trope of Christ's cross as the winepress, the mortal agony that renders death no more than a sleep to the righteous partakers of His body and blood. Here the wit sharpens the point.

At other times, however, the wit's sharpness may be the point. In a Lenten sermon on penance, a simple paradox becomes a comic cadenza: "I must not be alone with my selfe; for I am as apt to take, as to give infection; I am a reciprocall plague; passively and actively contagious; I breath corruption, and breath it upon my selfe; and I am the Babylon that I must goe out of, or I perish" (9:13, 311). Doesn't his wit qualify his penitence? Nor can he resist, even at a funeral, an equivocation worthy of Hamlet on the legal language of divorce bills: "For, though [the soul and body] be separated *à Thoro & Mensa,* from Bed and Board, they are not divorced; Though the soule be at the *Table of the Lambe,* in Glory, and the body but at the table of *the Serpent, in dust*" (7:10, 257). Were Sir Aston Cokayne's grieving friends amused? Finally, his logic can be more clever than convincing. Somewhat altering the proverb, "Truth and oyle are ever above," he proves that, in tribulations (often symbolized by water), God's mercy (imaged as oil) triumphs because "oyl will get to the top" (7:14, 355).[37] Donne's sermon play is as complex as his poetic play; it both brings the congregation to the Word and distances them by his own witty words.

Donne's flair for the dramatic further emphasizes the distance. Despite his frequent warnings against "ostentation, and vain glory . . . and self-pleasing" (4:3, 119) in preaching,[38] his own theatricality impressed his contemporaries and later readers. According to Walton's description, he often wept and carried his hearers aloft with him in "holy raptures." According to the author of one funeral elegy, parishioners might "take notes, from [his] looke, and hand"; his "carriage" and "gesture" were so eloquent that one "might see / An errour vanquish'd by delivery." But according to T. S. Eliot, his preaching smacks of an evangelist's camp meeting.[39] In such personal references as those to his distractions in private prayer (7:10, 264–65), to preaching as a calling not to be undertaken out of melancholy, discontent, or poverty (4:3, 109), to the congregation comparing his sermon to a better one they heard on the same text (3:3, 110), and to the hourglass visibly counting off the minutes of his sermon and their sinful lives (7:14, 368–69; 8:7, 190), Donne turns his life and sermons into high drama. Significantly, he considered those other players across the river at Bankside as his competitors for an audience. He compares spectators "whom lighter affections carry to Shewes, and Masks, and Comedies" to his parishioners, "whom better dispositions bring to these Exercises." Both, he tells them, "conceive some contentment, and some kinde of Joy, in that you are well and commodiously placed, they to see the Shew, you to heare the Sermon" (5:14, 294). Obviously, Donne was a spellbinder; consequently, other readers besides Eliot have questioned his motives as a preacher of the Word.[40]

Yet Donne may not have intended to lead men all the way to faith; other more holy men might do that. But, by his play, he could lead them so far as "wonder," which, he says, "stands as in the midst, betweene knowledge and faith, and hath an eye towards both." He muses, "If I know a thing, or beleeve a thing, I do no longer wonder: but when I finde that I have reason to stop upon the consideration of a thing, so, as that I see enough to induce admiration, to make me wonder, I come by that step . . . to a faith" (6:13, 265).[41] Through the play of allegory, typology, metaphor, paradox (sometimes called the "wonder" by rhetoricians), equivocation, conceit, and drama, Donne charmed his hearers into wonder, leading them out of mere knowledge, but only halfway to faith.

Anglican communicants expressed their faith at least four times a year at the altar, where they joined each other and God in a holy meal. In between their separate pews and the act of union at the altar, in between reading the first collect and feeding them the sacrament, Donne preached his witty sermons, spatially and temporally mediating his hearers' reception of grace. At play in between, he opened their minds to wonder, preparing them for the grace of faith that only God could give.[42]

Long before he became the most celebrated preacher of his age, Donne was acutely aware of a watching public. His most seemingly private colloquies often turn out to be public spectacles as he transforms the bed of love or sickness into a pulpit, a stage, or a scene of martyrdom or sacrifice. The choral argument of "The Ecstasy" is performed for a Neoplatonic voyeur placed "Within convenient distance" to mark how the lovers' "dialogue of one" continues when the ecstatic souls return to their sexual bodies. The disquisition on love, which the nearby novice hears, and the revealed mysteries of love, which he will soon witness, present a sermon and promise a drama to instruct and purify him in the religion of love. In other love poems, the speakers not only preach or act to a named or implied audience (as in "The Indifferent" and "The Sun Rising"), but they also seek public martyrdom for love. Like moths to flame, the lovers of "The Canonization" willingly risk sexual and literal death to become love's saints; the dead lovers of "The Funeral" and "The Relic" contemplate with amusement what public devotion to a love token, "A bracelet of bright hair about the bone," their martyrdom will evoke.

Similarly, Donne's solitary meditations, expostulations, and prayers from his sick bed are a public performance. While still recovering, he published them; even as the spots of disease appeared and as the bell tolled for the unknown dead, he felt the watching presence of his future readers.[43] A meditation on the illusory nature of present time reveals his self-consciousness: "that which you call present, is not now the same that it was when you began to call it so in this line (before you sound that word present, or that monosyllable now, the present and the now is past)" (89). Ever aware of his audience, Donne calls attention to the reader's reading time to prove his point. Not solely a man in private meditation, the speaker of the *Devotions* casts himself in the roles of preacher, actor, and martyr—all for the edification of his public. He prays that his death may be a sermon, that God will aid his physicians "in that measure, as may most glorify thee, and most edify those who observe the issues of thy servants, to their own spiritual benefit" (29). He hopes that he may enact a holy dying (118) and prays that the unknown sufferer for whom the bell tolls will also resemble the "virtuous men" of "A Valediction: forbidding Mourning," who "pass mildly away" as their "sad friends" watch. "Breathe inward comforts," he prays, "to his heart, and afford him the power of giving such outward testimonies thereof, as all that are about him may derive comforts from thence, and have . . . edification, even in this dissolution" (113). While dying for an audience, Donne transforms the pains of his sickness into the stripes (28) and thorns (22) of Christian martyrdom, and his fevers into a sacrificial fire that consumes his altar/bed (21–22).

As a preacher who is also an actor, Donne chooses martyrdom as a favorite subject and role—preaching eloquently on the blessings of martyrdom (8:7, 185), confessing his hopes to die as a consequence of preaching,[44] and even performing a martyr's death. The dying man who preached "Death's Duel" on the first Friday in Lent, then took to his bed, and finally posed in his shroud for his own *memento mori,* sought to edify his parishioners and friends by the spectacle of a public martyrdom. In defining himself as preacher/ actor and martyr, Donne assumed public identities in the traditions of his most illustrious ancestors—John Heywood, the writer of interludes, and St. Thomas More, the Christian humanist and martyr. Perhaps he needed to live up to his family's luminaries despite having rejected their religion.[45] In any case, the public identities he chose locate him in between: in the medial position of a priest, which became for him the play space of drama, and on the cross between earthly degradation and heavenly exaltation. As the private man found in play a way to mediate fears of separation and union, the public man found in drama a way to lead his audience toward the transcendent author of his drama. When the *Devotions* present Donne enacting in his flesh the Biblical texts with which his wit plays, and when his religious poetry, meditations, sermons, and especially his dramatic death recall the *via crucis,* Donne dramatizes the divine story for his reading and watching audience.

Because, however, his mode of presentation is drama, his enactments create a marginal reality. What occurs on a stage may genuinely move audiences; therefore, drama is somehow real, although not real. As Hamlet realizes, Hecuba is not nothing, but is nothing real; she comes to life in the player's passionate fiction. Did Donne then have any public identity at all? Are actor and martyr identities to live by? An actor is a kind of no-thing. He has no single identity, and whatever role he plays at any given moment—be it the antitype of Moses, who hopes to see God in the burning bush of the fevers and thorns of sickness, or the new Paul or Augustine, who has turned from his sinful youth to preach the Word—that role exists somewhere in between truth and fiction. Similarly, becoming a martyr, a key role in Donne's repertoire, annihilates the self. So the startling truth is that Donne defined himself publicly in forms of nonbeing—a not unpredictable choice for a man who once wrote a treatise on suicide.[46] If Walton's story is true, as a youth Donne may have telescoped this odd self-definition in the doggerel rhyme composed after his elopement: "John Donne, Anne Donne, undone." Punning on his name to capture his sense of ambiguity and self-annihilation, he speaks in his characteristic mode, play.

All his life Donne shied away from a defined identity, both lamenting and courting a fringe existence that made him a nobody. As a Catholic in virulently anti-Catholic England, he grew up on the margins of society, unable to take a university degree. As a young adult, he publicly conformed in religion, while privately remaining ambivalent. In "Satire 3," after surveying the competing claims of Rome, Geneva, Erastianism, indifference, and unthinking tolerance, the speaker advocates an undecided poise: "in strange way / To stand inquiring right, is not to stray." Although public religious conformity opened the way to court preferment, he bitterly ridicules courtiers in the satires of these years. And by his rash and secret marriage, which cut him off from all advancement for fourteen years, he seems almost to have deliberately thrown away his career and prolonged his marginality.

In letters of this period, Donne describes himself as stuck in between. Exiled to Mitcham while assiduously seeking preferment, sick but not unto death, he writes, "I shall be in this world, like a porter in a great house, ever nearest the door, but seldomest abroad." He repeatedly confides his sense of nonbeing to his friend Henry Goodyear, closing one letter with a revealing conceit: "Sir, if I were anything, my love to you might multiply it, and dignify it: but infinite nothings are but one such; yet since even chimeras have some name and titles, I am also Yours."[47] He is either a nothing or a hybrid like the mythical chimera (part lion, part goat, part serpent).

His modest success as a propagandist hired to win wavering Catholics to Anglicanism helped sustain his fringe status. Although he clung to worldly ambitions, James I saw in him a much needed spokesman for the national church and barred his way to secular preferment. Still pursuing his ambitions and resisting the royal nudge, Donne sought the patronage of Sir Robert Drury. Whatever Donne's conscious motivations, this choice served in practice to advance him no further than the outskirts of high society, for the ambitious but rash Drury was unlikely to succeed in James's court.[48] Donne's next choice, the Earl of Somerset was worse. Somerset's scandalous marriage (for which Donne wrote an epithalamion) eventually landed the earl and his bride in the Tower for murdering their go-between.[49] So in 1615 Donne accepted the fate he had, at least partially, made for himself: he took orders as an Anglican priest, a calling to be set apart. Performing this office for sixteen years, he left, as the public image he wanted his survivors to retain of his life, an emblem of in-betweenness. The statue in St. Paul's, modeled on his deathbed portrait, depicts an emaciated man in his shroud rising from a funeral urn facing east on the Day of Judgment, a man captured in a moment of time on the threshold between earth and heaven.[50]

III

This discussion of the private and public Donne has yielded rather queer results; then again, readers have always found him one of the most peculiar in Renaissance England's gallery of characters. Critics and literary historians have, however, described his oddities as merely exaggerations of the experiences of his fellows. The accidents of his birth and background, combined with his acute sensitivity to all that occurred around him, made Donne a kind of barometer on which the temper of intellectuals in late Renaissance England was registered—their skepticism, their interest in the "new philosophy," their political and religious malaise.[51] The popularity of Donne's poetry, circulated and copied almost solely in manuscript, and of his sermons, attended by tradesman and king, attests to his ability to strike a resonant chord in his readers and hearers. Consequently, his fascination with in-betweenness marks him not only as private and public man, but also as historical man. He dramatizes the experience of an age on the threshold, and his play not only mediated his private crisis of separation and helped him find a public identity; it may also, in a small way, have prepared his age to cross the threshold.

According to Victor Turner, threshold experiences have common characteristics. From tribal rites of passage, Turner has developed a broad theory of liminality with applications to such varied domains as religious pilgrimages, carnival in Rio, science fiction literature, and (as I argued earlier) medieval folly and the English Civil War. These rites proceed in three phases—separation, transition, reincorporation—and Turner sees the transition phase as a model of experience in between. Physically separated from the larger society and not yet initiated into his new social role, the novice finds himself in a liminal state. Two types of ritual symbols generally dominate this phase: symbols of effacement and of ambiguity and paradox. Because the initiate no longer has his old identity and has not yet assumed a new one, he has no role in the social order: he is either a no-thing or part of two things. Stripped of his name and clothes, he is associated with darkness, shadows, invisibility—nothingness. Simultaneously, he is a living ambiguity or paradox: for example, in some rites the initiators rigidly control the diet of the initiate, who is, at the same time, allowed to steal food from the members of society.[52]

The essence of liminality to Turner is "the analysis of culture into factors and their free or 'ludic' recombination in any and every possible pattern, however weird."[53] This playful inversion, fragmentation, and recombination of cultural elements allow the initiate to defamiliarize the familiar, to loosen rigid boundaries, to experiment with unheard-of juxtapositions, and perhaps to create new unities. In liminal phases the elders of the tribe may display to the initiates the sacred objects of the culture, but these are often fantastically exaggerated monsters—a man's head on a lion's body. Here, cultural elements are withdrawn from their usual settings and recombined in unique configurations in order to isolate those elements for contemplation. When *a* and *b* occur together constantly, they are perceived as the same object. But when *a* is dissociated from *b* and recombined with *x*, the perceiver will discriminate *a* from *b* from *x*. Dissociation and recombination can encourage contemplation in a new light. So when elders, during rites of passage, display an image of a man's head on a lion's body, they prompt initiates to think about the human head in the abstract. It may represent chieftainship, the soul's dominance of the body, the intellect as contrasted with brute force, and so forth. The overly familiar head on a human body cannot engender this thinking about cultural elements; these elements must be inverted, fragmented, or recombined (playfully, even bizarrely) to achieve a kind of rudimentary metaphysical speculation.[54]

Turner believes that this playful realignment of cultural elements can provide an "anti-structure" to the larger society from which the initiate is temporarily excluded. New ideas and possibilities generated in liminal play offer a static culture the potential for creativity and change.[55] Seeing a parallel between the liminal phase in traditional cultures' rites of passage and much play behavior, Brian Sutton-Smith has argued that play can also provide an "anti-structure." Players learn to take variable roles, to experiment with new behaviors, and to develop flexible competencies, and as a result become capable of change and creativity.[56]

But some Marxist cultural theorists have questioned the potential of play to engender new modes of thought. In the symbolic inversions of carnival, for example, a peasant may become king, but the system of low and high, they argue, has not been fundamentally altered. Individuals merely relocate themselves within the structure, thereby calling attention to cultural boundaries and reconfirming the established order.[57] From this perspective the playful vaunt of the extravagant lover in "The Sun Rising," "She'is all states, and all princes, I, / Nothing else is," does not revolutionize the order of the world, as he claims, by creating a transformed universe of love in a bed. Donne's rhetoric remains within the culturally determined confines of absolutism; he has merely crowned a new king.[58]

If, however, cultural elements are not just inverted, but hybridized—removed from their usual structural locus and latched onto other similarly detached fragments—then strange instabilities jar the semiotic system, then the potential arises to shift the terms of the system itself.[59] When the brash speaker of "The Sun Rising" issues peremptory commands to the ruler of the heavens, Donne does more than invert the established relationship between Sun and subject. He removes this absolutist rhetoric from its usual loci, the court and the solar system, and then relocates it—honor and wealth, center and sphere—on a mere bed and one female subject. This relocation of power is equally unstable, for when the braggart speaker so exaggerates his prerogatives with a fantastic boast about the eclipsing power of his mighty wink, his masculine persuasive force looks a little silly. Donne's poetic play jars absolutist rhetoric loose from the structures that supported James and all patriarchal rule, and readers are thus freed to laugh at its arbitrariness and rethink its terms. In whatever context—ritual, festival, or poetry—such play may generate the possibility for psychic and social change.

Always locating himself in between, in identities that are ambiguous, paradoxical, and defined by nonbeing, Donne was a liminal man in a liminal age. In the seventeenth century, as the pace of change accelerated, the social and intellectual structures by which men had defined their identity weakened. Soon after Donne's death, political revolution swept away the monarchy and Anglican establishment, and intellectual ferment released reason from its long service to faith. Donne's generation confronted obstacles to defining oneself unambiguously as a king's man, a church man, or a defender of the faith (Which faith? Donne asks in "Satire 3" and "Show me dear Christ, thy spouse.") And new social and intellectual structures—the parliamentary state, the reign of reason over "enthusiasm"—had not yet evolved to support new self-definitions. As Donne precariously balanced his identity, his poetry and prose dramatized for his contemporaries their experience of liminality: an acute sensitivity to separation; a preference for images of effacement, for paradox and ambiguity; and the playful inversion, fragmentation, and hybridization of cultural elements.

We have seen how Donne's poetry, *Devotions,* and sermons image (sometimes comically, sometimes poignantly) separation from wholeness and the search for reintegration. Although the desire for wholeness is common, it is perhaps more intense in periods of social and political crisis. Donne's experience mirrors, at least in part, the pattern of separation and return that structures Shakespeare's last plays, the longings of Crashaw and Vaughan for union with the divine, and the Cavalier attempts to reintegrate the shattered courtly order within communities of noble friends.

Donne also felt that to be separated from wholeness or to be in between is to be a dark or shadowy nothing. In his love lyrics the fascination with nothingness transcends mere conventional Petrarchism. His faithful lovers feel literally annihilated at parting ("Sweetest love, I do not go..."). In "A Nocturnal upon S. Lucy's Day," the speaker has become, because of his beloved's death, a quintessential nothing: "Study me then," he tells next spring's lovers,

> For I am every dead thing,
> In whom love wrought new alchemy.
> For his art did express
> A quintessence even from nothingness,
> From dull privations, and lean emptiness
> He ruined me, and I am re-begot
> Of absence, darkness, death; things which are not.

Similarly, during his years of virtual unemployment, Donne compares himself in the New Year's verse epistle to the Countess of Bedford to the moment between two years:

> This twilight of two years, not past nor next,
> Some emblem is of me, or I of this,
> Who (meteor-like, of stuff and form perplexed,
> Whose what, and where, in disputation is,)
> If I should call me anything, should miss.

Here, because he has no fixed social status, he sees himself as a confused, twilight nothing. Symbols of effacement were often adopted in the fashionable cult of melancholy gentlemen, and they pervade contemporary drama, most notably Shakespeare's tragedies. Lear's cruel words to Cordelia, "Nothing will come of nothing," return to haunt him in his own unwitting reply to the fool's banter, and the fool describes the erstwhile king as now only "Lear's shadow." Similarly, Hamlet, no longer a youth but not yet a man, wears an "inky cloak" and ruminates on suicide and oblivion.

Even more prominent than these images of effacement are the ambiguity and paradox that we have found at the core of Donne's self-definition. But again, his ambivalent attitude toward union and the ambiguous tone of his lyrics, both manifested in the paradoxical frame in which he locates his life and art, are matched by the virtual epidemic of paradox in the Renaissance that Rosalie Colie has diagnosed, an epidemic that also seized Herbert, Marvell, Burton, and Browne, to name only a few.[60] Paradox shows a formal system's insufficiency to map reality, and it exerts pressure toward formulating a new system.[61] As such, it became a tool of skepticism and empiricism to undermine scholastic thought, which had failed to accommodate, among other changes, new stars, the radically different cultures of the new world, and a heliocentric universe.

If ludic inversion, fragmentation, and hybridization form the true test of liminality, then Donne's verse passes without question. His contemporaries admired his inversions of poetic convention in replacing adoring Petrarchan lovers with cynical Ovidian rakes, and they laughed at his turning his considerable dialectical skills, trained in ponderous scholastic logic, to the task of proving, for example, "Why doth the Poxe so much affect to undermine the nose?"[62] The hallmark of Donne's style, which Crashaw, Marvell, Cowley, Cleveland, King, and others adopted with varying success, is his use of conceits—comparisons of disproportionate objects, symbols, or experiences that shock the reader into a new perspective. In these elaborate metaphors, Donne refracts the spectrum of contemporary culture (alchemy, medicine, cosmology, theology, numismatics, romantic love, physiology, astrology, sex, geography, physics, friendship, etc.) into items, which he then recombines in startling ways. This dissection of "a sun-beam with a prism" into an "exility of particles" is what annoyed Johnson about the metaphysical poets: "Their attempts," he sniffs, "were always analytick; they broke every image into fragments. . . . and produced combinations of confused magnificence."[63] Eliot, too, in a recantation of his earlier dictum about the unified sensibility, describes Donne's use of images as "a puzzled and humorous shuffling of the pieces," a phrase that suggests playing with a kaleidoscope or with counters in a game.[64]

Donne opens "Of the Progress of the Soul: The Second Anniversary" with a group of such shuffled pieces to explain the world's lingering between life and death after the loss of its soul, Elizabeth Drury:

> But as a ship which hath struck sail, doth run
> By force of that force which before, it won:
> Or as sometimes in a beheaded man,
> Though at those two red seas, which freely ran,
> One from the trunk, another from the head,
> His soul be sailed, to her eternal bed,
> His eyes will twinkle, and his tongue will roll,
> As though he beckoned, and called back his soul,

He grasps his hands, and he pulls up his feet,
And seems to reach, and to step forth to meet
His soul; when all these motions which we saw,
Are but as ice, which crackles at a thaw:
Or as a lute, which in moist weather, rings
Her knell alone, by cracking of her strings:
So struggles this dead world, now she is gone;
For there is motion in corruption. (7–22)

In these conceits Donne has isolated and juxtaposed images taken from the physics of inertia (a ship's continued movement without sails); the Old Testament (the parting of the Red Sea on the journey to the Promised Land); public beheadings witnessed by Londoners; the physiology of reflexes (the grotesque twitchings of a body severed from its head); the physics of temperature, moisture, and sound (cracking ice and lute strings); and the physiology of decomposition ("motion in corruption"). In this grouping of images to describe the world's in-between status, Donne illustrates the essence of liminality—the fragmentation and bizarre hybridization of cultural elements.

Such conceits may appear to be a mere jumble—and when we consider the conceits of his entire canon together, they seem even more so—because Donne follows no system consistently. Sometimes he uses images from the old cosmology, sometimes the new; alchemical figures in one poem explain the body's transformation to spirit, but in another they show love to be a hoax; angelology provides a few images, modern theories of magnetism some others. Without respect to their original context, Donne isolates and appropriates snippets of learning from heterogeneous sources to suit his diverse poetic needs,[65] thereby loosening fragments from the monolithic medieval structure that had once ordered and given them meaning. He then plays with them like counters in a game, and in the next game he might play with them differently.

Once Donne had isolated, then intermixed diverse doctrines from cosmology, physiology, theology, and so forth, the reader could look at the pieces in a new light. Just as the dissociation and hybridization of cultural elements that Turner finds in rites of passage encourage initiates to think about culture in the abstract, so the juxtaposition of dissociated images in poems like "Of the Progress of the Soul" (ships moving without sails, the twitchings of decapitated bodies, thawing ice, cracking lute strings, the apparent life in decaying matter) encourages Donne's readers to think metaphysically about the nature of movement, entropy, and the blurred line between life and death. In this way, his conceits and those of his imitators may have served as an anti-structure to the lingering medieval worldview.[66]

From a wider perspective, we can see Donne's poetic canon as an anti-structure in the transition from the medieval to the modern world. His paradoxical rhetoric and the quick-change artistry of his ambiguous personae dramatize the flexibility of mind demanded by a world questioning the old verities. And the playful juxtapositions of the conceits demonstrate the experimental outlook necessary for scientific research.[67] Although some critics have attributed to Donne the outlook of a scientist while others have emphasized his dissatisfaction with contemporary scientism, he probably viewed science as he viewed numerology or the Pythagorean doctrine of the soul's transmigration—as an amusing diversion.[68] Neither incipient scientist nor antiscientist, Donne was a player. By fragmenting the medieval synthesis and juggling the pieces, he may have helped prepare his readers' minds for the scientific mode of vision. Granted, his skeptical paradoxes were, he claimed, mere "alarums to truth," and the goal of his play was often to reinvigorate tradition.[69] Still, the coming age would expose the fragments he dislodged to the light of empirical evidence to create a new set of cultural elements, and hybridization is not far from the kind of playing around with ideas and substances that generated the early experimentation of the Royal Society. Although ostensibly Donne became a conservative in politics and theology, his poetry of liminal play may have offered his readers an experience in new ways of thinking on the eve of revolutions.

Simultaneously and paradoxically, his play exercised their abilities to order confusion. For example, in lyrics such as "Woman's Constancy," he begins with a frame to order the poetic experience, then playfully shifts from frame to frame with the reader panting to keep up. After "one whole day" of love, the speaker (male or female?) wonders if tomorrow the object of desire will reframe the love vow as invalid because of a supposedly previous promise, or because s/he has become a different person from the one who promised to love. Will s/he reframe the promise as an oath taken under duress, or as a contract invalidated by a minideath, sleep, or as a Jesuitical oath with a mental reservation to be false? Finally, will the speaker reframe the whole poem by planning to invalidate his or her own promise? This playful manipulation of frames, so common to Donne's poetry and prose, may seem to disorder the reader's perception of the world, and some have interpreted it as a sign that Donne and his readers felt their world crumbling: "'Tis all in pieces, all coherence gone."[70]

Donne's contemporaries, however, express a different attitude about these playful frame switches. Jasper Mayne describes a Donne poem as "Indeed so farre above its Reader, good, / That wee are thought wits, when 'tis understood."[71] Because of the poem's complex but not chaotic structure, readers who manage to keep all the frames straight through Donne's play take pride in their wit. Erving Goffman argues further that, when we successfully negotiate frame disjunctions, such as those found in wordplay or in the misalignments of Shakespearean comedy, these confusions actually reaffirm our sense that the world is orderly and understandable.[72] Donne's liminal play, then, served two apparently opposite functions: it offered a jumbled "anti-structure" to the dominant world order, and it allowed the fit reader or listener to reassert a sense of order and control. In play, these seemingly incongruent functions coexist: players control the play frame (or in games and sports, they choose to enter a controlled frame) while at the same time submitting themselves to risky but pleasurable confusion within the frame. Thus Donne's play would naturally appeal to his contemporaries, who needed a sense of order while they dismantled the old order.

Donne's liminality did not end with his ordination; he merely found a stable location for his deeply rooted sense of in-betweenness by relocating it within its original, ritual context. The Anglican order of worship prescribes a ritual enactment similar to a rite of passage. Upon entering the church, sinners and penitents are supposed to separate themselves from the larger society. (Donne tried to insist that his parishioners maintain the sacred time and space of worship during services at St. Paul's. He publicly chided the irreverent who refused to kneel [9:5, 152–53], but the buyers and sellers who conducted business in the back of the church were beyond his control.)[73] After this separation from the everyday world, communal confession prepares the worshipper to hear the Word and sermon, which in turn prepare him for the sacrament, on appointed days. After the liturgy he returns to the larger society enlightened and redeemed. In the midst of this ritual, Donne's sermons mediate the transition to the sacrament and/or to the return to profane time and space on a new basis.

Although critics have attributed sacramental qualities to Donne's sermons (their telescoping of all time into the eternal now of sacred time, their use of the Word as an outward expression of and doorway to grace, their progression from the most literal to the most spiritual sense of the text),[74] they are not themselves the sacrament. They are the liminal phase of a ritual that occurs most often on what Donne calls the liminal day of the week: the sabbath, he says, is "*Limen,* or *Ianua Ecclesiae,* The doore by which we enter into the Church" (8:6, 157). Donne was attuned to the transitional nature of the sermon form, and his sermons evince the distinguishing marks of liminality. He repeatedly reminds his hearers that, whatever their social status, they were once equivalent nothings in the incomprehensible darkness out of which God summoned light (2:11, 247; 4:3, 100–101). He emphasizes their ambiguous position between flesh and spirit, between earth and heaven, between the kingdom inaugurated at the Incarnation and the kingdom anticipated in the Resurrection. He reiterates traditional Christian paradoxes, such as the *verbum infans,* the speechless Word (6:8, 184). Of course, Donne did not create these ancient themes; he merely found in them a way to comprehend his own and his congregation's liminality. Similarly, in his fragmentation of the text in the *divisio* and its ludic recombination in his witty, even at times fanciful, dilations, he found a ritual context that allowed him to attain the order he had sought all his life while continuing to play in between.

Donne eventually came to rest in liminality. Protestant Christianity's focus on man's radical contingency gave him a way to comprehend his personal sense of in-betweenness, and therein a public identity. Nevertheless, as a representative of late Renaissance culture, he registered on his nerve endings the era's response to life on the edge.

5

George Herbert Pulling for Prime

Like Wisdom before the Father and David before the Ark, both John Donne and George Herbert play in God's presence. Creating a space between separation from and union with God, Donne's play is violent, dramatic, and slippery. Not so edgy, Herbert finds his playmate within, the indwelling spirit, and they play games together. It was Donne's nature to fool around; he accepted his "ridling disposition." It was Herbert's to be choleric; he was proud of his warrior ancestors. Consequently, each adopted an appropriate style of play: Donne plays freely, switching frames at will to keep his playfellow off balance; Herbert structures his play into games, contests, combats, and puzzles—agons that can turn agony into joy.

Although a gamester himself, Herbert shared the more sober-minded reformers' distrust of play. In "The Church Porch" of *The Temple* he warns against wasting time on "dressing, mistressing, and complement," calls gambling "a civil gunpowder," and counsels men to pursue vocations and "Fool not."[1] Some of the *Outlandish Proverbs* he collected caution against folly ("Play with a foole at home, and he will play with you in the market," 146) and against gambling ("Gamsters and race-horses never last long," 751). But he also shared the opinion of Erasmus, a less dour reformer who knew the value of folly and play. The proverbs acknowledge the wisdom of Lear's fool ("Better be a foole then a knave," 961)[2] and the riskiness of life ("Without danger we cannot get beyond danger," 1010). Likewise, the moralizer of "The Church Porch" rejoices that "All things are bigge with jest" (239), and as often as he advises prudence and condemns gambling, he describes life as a game (at archery or cards) where risks are inevitable, but prudent play will win: in managing money, "age, if it will hit, / Shoots a bow short, and lessens still his stake" (158–59); in conversation, one should gather a variety of subjects into "a good stock . . . then draw the card / That suites him best, of whom thy speech is heard" (293–94). Prudence actually enhances the play. To the man who would be a wit, Herbert offers precepts known by all good comedians: avoid laughing too much at your own material, choose mirth that does not offend your audience, and do not carry the joke too far, lest you spoil the fun (229–46).[3] In short, Herbert's attitude toward play is complex; play (like life) is risky folly that requires prudence.

His attitude toward work is no less complex. Since he believes that "Life is a businesse, not good cheer" ("Employment II"), he emulates the proverbial worker bees who "bring hony" and "Sting [his] delay" ("Employment I," "Praise I"). But sometimes he perversely prefers the "bubble" and "false embroyderies" of earthly delights above "solid work" ("Vanitie II"), and all he has to show for a day's labor is "fome . . . bubbles, balls of winde" ("Even-song"). Nevertheless, the most productive work he describes in *The Temple* is indistinguishable from play: the floral and musical offerings that he would make his Edenic work in "Employment I" and the worship of the beelike stars in "The Starre." The speaker invites the star to refine and quicken his heart, then "flie home like a laden bee," carrying him to "that hive of beams / And garland-streams" that crowns God's face. There he hopes to "Glitter, and curle, and winde" among the other beams—which also resemble garlands and bees. Flower, bee, star, and the speaker seem to merge in the "winding [that] is their fashion / Of adoration"—a worship in which the "Glitter" resembles play and the "gaining," work. For Herbert, true work, like worship, is play.

Still, to say that he reconciles the prudence and structure of work with the risk and freedom of play is not to say how. That question requires an inquiry into the games he plays with the friend who is at once within and far beyond him. Herbert (or Walton's fictive saint; it matters little which, because both present a seventeenth-century perspective) directs the reader to find in *The Temple* "a picture of the many spiritual conflicts that have passed betwixt God and my soul, before I could subject mine to the will of Jesus my Master: in whose service I have now found perfect freedom."[4] The poems of *The Temple* picture conflicts that Herbert has ordered, thereby gaining freedom; such, we will see, is the essence of game. To paint this picture, Herbert projects, from within, a God—a human conception of the divine, who listens, speaks, or enters the poem silently. Herbert also projects, from within, a self—versions of himself, who engage God in games. Sometimes they bandy wit to outsmart one another; at other times they compete in contests or combat, courteous or violent. Through such games, ordered but risky, Herbert gains greater freedom and integrates, even expands, his self.

Many readers of *The Temple* emphasize the closeness of Herbert's relation to God,[5] some notice God entering his poems,[6] and a few remark that the God who is so present is a character created by Herbert out of himself,[7] as is the speaker of the poems.[8] Almost all readers emphasize Herbert's playfulness,[9] and some notice that he struggles and plays specifically with God,[10] but I believe that he engages aspects of himself in games that produce startling results, experienced as numinous.[11] Not all play is agonistic, but games are: they pit opponents against one another in a limited time and space within the structure of rules, generally producing an unequal outcome. The goal, however, in non-zero-sum games is not to win, but just to keep the game going.[12] In a variety of poetic games, Herbert found a way to define and assert his self.

I

If George's brother, Edward Lord Herbert of Cherbury, is to be believed, no man dared call himself a Herbert unless he had proved himself in combat. Their paternal great, great grandfather "twice past through a Great Army of Northern men alone, with his Poll-ax in his hand, and returned without any mortal hurt," and both their great grandfather and grandfather suppressed rebels and brigands on the Welsh border. Their father—assaulted in a churchyard and cut to the brains—fought off his assailants, walked home, and lived to challenge his attacker to a duel. Dueling was, in fact, a Herbert specialty. Edward's autobiography records innumerable challenges to defend his honor. Their brother Richard bore the scars of twenty-four wounds on his body when he died in the Low Countries, and their brother Henry, the courtier, gave "several proofs of his Courage in Duells." The careers of the other two brothers, William, the soldier, and Thomas, the seaman, include fighting with a broken sword in single combat during the Danish wars, avenging a slain captain, and saving a starving fleet by piracy. Even allowing for the hyperbole of Sir Edward's autobiography, these tales confirm that George was born to a warrior clan. Nor was he, according to Edward, "exempt from passion and Choler, being infirmities to which all our Race is subject."[13]

Magdalen Herbert raised this combative brood with shrewdness and strength. Left a beautiful widow with ten children when George was three, she immediately settled Edward's wardship to secure his financial independence and the maintenance of his younger brothers. The personal overseer of all her children's education, she led her family in daily prayers and Sunday church attendance. Although strong, practical, and pious, she was no dour prude. As a matron in her forties, she fascinated John Donne, perhaps inspiring his tribute to autumnal beauty ("Elegy 9"), and she married the handsome John Danvers, a much admired spark half her age. Clearly, Magdalen was an imposing woman whose control and sophistication matched the fire of her sons' choler.[14]

With such a mother, an absent father, and so many passionate and successful brothers, George faced a struggle to establish a separate identity.

Plagued by periodic illnesses, he could not surpass the court successes of Henry, who became Master of the Revels, or Edward, who served as ambassador to France, nor the seamanship and soldiery of his other brothers. He chose the university. Once there, he declared his separation from women in two sonnets sent to his mother, which, while dedicating his poetic gifts to God, describe female flesh as "*filth*" and "that, which one day Worms may chance refuse" ("Two Sonnets sent to his Mother, New-year 1609/10," 206). Letters of the period picture George as discontent with his dependent position: he had to request money from his stepfather to buy books, and although he thanks Danvers for "*London* helps" in sponsoring his candidacy for the university oratorship, he hopes, "I am able to stand on mine own legs."[15] Nor did two juvenile sonnets secure his separation from Magdalen, who continued to exert a powerful influence over his career decisions until she died in 1627.[16]

The first vocation Herbert chose was actually no less agonistic than his brothers' dueling. As university orator at Cambridge, he combined his mother's sophistication and control with his paternal combativeness in his mastery of the rhetorical tools of scholarly debate. In the Renaissance academy, learning was based on oral presentation, attack, and defense, conducted in a special language taught by men, not mothers—Latin.[17] An all-male world structured around ritualized combat, the university provided Herbert with an outlet to display his agonistic skills within the safe and civilized bounds of rule-governed verbal contests. He excelled, winning the university oratorship. This position—"the finest place in the University," he boasts to Danvers—allowed him to assert himself publicly: orating before "King, Prince, or whatever comes to the University," taking place "next the Doctors . . . above the Proctors," and enjoying "such like Gaynesses, which will please a young man well" (letter 7, 369–70). Within the competitive framework of the male academy, George began to establish an identity.

Soon, however, he saw the limitations of that world and self. His "finest" position required him to compose official university thanks for bequests and elegant flattery for dignitaries. One incident suggests his dissatisfaction with the job. When Charles Stuart returned from his abortive attempt to woo the Spanish infanta, he felt insulted and urged war. In an impolitic move, Herbert took the occasion of the heir's visit to Cambridge to lace his complimentary oration with a lengthy praise of peace.[18] Peace continued to be an issue that engaged his energies. His long Latin poem, *Triumphus Mortis,* includes a graphic description of war's carnage, and he probably debated war against Spain during his term in Parliament.[19] Combative by nature and eager to establish a self in the world, but constrained to perform trivial tasks and disgusted by the results of man's aggression, Herbert had come to a crisis. In a rare specifically autobiographical moment in *The Temple,* he laments to God,

Whereas my birth and spirit rather took
The way that takes the town;
Thou didst betray me to a lingring book,
And wrap me in a gown.
I was entangled in the world of strife,
Before I had the power to change my life.

Yet, for I threatned oft the siege to raise,
Not simpring all mine age,
Thou often didst with Academick praise
Melt and dissolve my rage.
I took thy sweetned pill, till I came where
I could not go away, nor persevere. ("Affliction I")

Obscure as the lines are, they describe a man of "spirit" (even "rage") eager for "power" over his own life, but "wrap[ped]" and "entangled" in the academy and a "world of strife" where he wastes his time "simpring." Less confessional, but no less personal, the rest of the poems of "The Church" record his struggling beyond this impasse toward selfhood.

Gaining a self requires some degree of aggression—for the young child, aggression against the source of nurture in order to separate, and for older children and adults, aggression against peers in order to establish a position. Toddlers dart away from their mothers, play rambunctiously, and squeal, "No . . . me . . . mine," as they explore the limits of their separateness. Later, according to Walter Ong, boys and men compete in games, sports, contests, and ritualized combat to display their separation from the feminine and maternal sphere of power and to test the strength of their separate selves against other separate selves. In oral cultures these contests frequently take the form of verbal duels. Whenever young toughs on street corners in Philadelphia ritually insult each other's mothers or Mercutio sharpens his ribald wits at the expense of Romeo's philandering, the contestants are flaunting their separateness.[20]

But games also promote closeness: to play with an other, one must have an other within. A player has to imagine the attitudes and range of behaviors of the other player(s) and gauge his actions in response to his internal player(s). For the shortstop to field a ground ball and initiate a double play, he must imagine the roles (and preferably the individual playing styles) of the man on first, the batter, the first and second basemen, and the umpire. By the same token, for Joe to poetically insult Ralph's mother, he must understand Ralph's personality, Ralph's relation to his mother, as well as the conventions of "playing the dozens" on the street corners of African-American neighborhoods in Philadelphia. We gain this ability to empathize with an other while forming a separate identity—a self apart from the other. We can separate precisely because we can carry within ourselves a "good internal object"—a trustworthy "internal environment," constructed from parental images, that survives separation from the source of nurture. By gaining an other within, the player gains a basis for comprehending the other without.[21] Paradoxically, the play that asserts the separateness of the self from others depends on and strengthens the presence of an internal other. Thus in agons of all kinds—games, contests, combats—contestants display separate selves, which in their play establish interior, sometimes intimate, bonds.

In poems that record the "spiritual conflicts that have passed betwixt God and [his] soul," Herbert stages such agons, in which an aspect of himself, the speaker, encounters within the frame of poetic games a projection of his interior other, a nurturing, ordering Presence.[22] Because Herbert was a Christian in a wholly Christian culture, he understood what psychoanalysts would call "an internalization of parental imagos" in traditional terms—as *"My Lord"* in "The Collar," the eucharistic and welcoming host in "Love III," the whispering "friend" in "Jordan II," the "Deare Friend" and counselor in "Love Unknown," the echoing voice in "Heaven," and the silent Presence in "Deniall." He is the "image of God" gained at creation (Gen. 1:27) and lost at the fall, the "new" or "inward" man renewed in God's image by the second covenant of Christ, who left His spirit to dwell in man (2 Cor. 4:16, Rom. 7:22, Eph. 3:16, Col. 3:9–10).[23] One aspect of Herbert's self meets this inward other in poetic and ludic self-encounters, and in these encounters he gains a new integrity from joining the two selves.

Meeting the internal other can be risky, even deadly, but it can also enlarge the self in an experience sometimes experienced as numinous. What has been denied or unknown is summoned, and the encounter offers a fragmented self a chance to become whole. Psychologist Carl Gustav Jung explains this experience as the achievement of "Self" after the trials of "individuation" and the "integration of the archetypes of the collective unconscious." Theologian Martin Buber describes it as the presence of a greater "Thou" who comes whenever "I" meets not "it," but "thou."[24] And Christ Himself promised, "where two or three are gathered together in my name, there am I in the midst of them" (Matt. 18:20). In whatever terms we choose to understand it (Herbert, of course, knew the third), the meeting of dispersed selves can evoke an experience of wholeness, even Presence.

Games, contests, and combat foster such open meetings between selves because they are structured but risky exchanges. As the play theorist Mihaly Csikszentmihalyi has observed, the structure of games permits players a more open interchange with the environment than is possible in everyday life. Freely chosen rules and limits define the play world, protecting players from unpredictable pressures from their environment or psyche. In Freudian terms, the frame of play reins the id and pacifies the super-ego (the game's rules establish what is prohibited, what ideal), and the frame orders the environment (players choose activities within the manageable limits of their ability). As a result, they may relax everyday defenses and open themselves more fully to the others with whom they play. Of course, games pose risks (or else they would not offer the desired challenge to the assertive self), but the risks are controlled, freely chosen, and manageable, unlike the unpredictable risks of day-to-day life, which make us too fearful to expose our selves.[25] Because of their framework, games can promote the free and open exchange between usually isolated selves that fosters integration.[26]

Herbert's frequently overlooked poem, "Submission," may begin (but only begin) to clarify these complexities:

But that thou art my wisdome, Lord,
　　And both mine eyes are thine,
My minde would be extreamly stirr'd
　　For missing my designe.

Were it not better to bestow
　　Some place and power on me?
Then should thy praises with me grow,
　　And share in my degree.

But when I thus dispute and grieve,
　　I do resume my sight,
And pilfring what I once did give,
　　Disseize thee of thy right.

How know I, if thou shouldst me raise,
　　That I should then raise thee?
Perhaps great places and thy praise
　　Do not so well agree.

Wherefore unto my gift I stand;
　　I will no more advise:
Onely do thou lend me a hand,
　　Since thou hast both mine eyes.

The poet creates two characters: a voice representing an aspect of himself and the "Lord" representing his conception of the divine. The speaker engages the Lord in an agon to win, he says, "my designe. . . . Some place and power," but the poet orders the conflict by rhyme, rhythm, and other elements of poetic structure, and frames it as cajolery and wheedling. It is the controlled agon of a game, not all-out war. The speaker's agonistic strategy is subtle: in stanza 1, he raises a dispute (albeit in the conditional mood) by claiming that he does not dispute; in stanza 2, he tries bribery; in stanza 4, he deflects his opponent's argument by anticipating it with comic and self-deprecating understatement; and in the final stanza, he promises to stop wheedling, then wheedlingly claims reciprocation for his gift of submitting his eyes and wisdom, his all, to God. How did eyes and wisdom become his to give? In stanza 1, his wisdom *is* his Lord, and his eyes belong to Him; in stanza 3, he says he gave them to God; and in stanza 5, he makes claims on the basis of the gift. A clever bit of sophistry by a creature who can give his creator nothing.

In the midst of his cajolery, however (and at the midpoint of the poem), the speaker discovers that ludic combat with his internal other has enlarged his self. After arguing with the second self, he realizes suddenly, "But when I thus dispute and grieve, / I do resume my sight." In combat, he regains his true self ("resume *my* sight," emphasis mine), but since his eyes are his Lord's, his true self sees with God's vision. His true sight is God's sight; he is both self and other. In the end, when he makes claims on his second self ("Onely do thou lend me a hand, / Since thou hast both mine eyes"), the poem opens out to accommodate a more ample self. The speaker deserves, he believes, God's "hand" (both the helping hand of the colloquial phrase and the hand that symbolizes divine might) because God has both his I's, as well as his "eyes" (both the "I" who stands by his putative gift of submission and the "I" who continues to "advise" even after he promises to stop). The last lines create a composite body of divine hand and human eyes, a greater self made of two, who sees himself clearly as a wheedler with His eyes but can forgive him with His might, who sees the imperfect submission of his I's and can help it with His hand.

The Presence of the greater self experienced in "Submission" does not, as some critics have argued, annihilate Herbert's or the speaker's self.[27] The poetic voice is still wheedling with the internal other in the last line of the poem; he still considers his eyes "mine" and the hand God's. Instead of surrendering his self to God, the speaker plans a reciprocal exchange between them. Certainly, God is All, and Herbert cannot advise Him or give Him anything, but he keeps trying because in such attempts he meets his other. One day, Herbert believed, he would be dissolved into that All, but the poem does not record the dissolution. Rather, it records the give and take of a game in which Herbert's self is expanded by meeting his internal other, a meeting that invokes Presence.[28]

II

Like "Submission," other poems of "The Church" picture Herbert's search for a self[29]—not merely the scion of a noble family presided over by an imposing matriarch, nor an exalted functionary in a male academic hierarchy, but a self capable of psychological separation because, paradoxically, he is not separate, because he has an other within. "The Dedication" to *The Temple* announces his agonistic plan. After acknowledging that his "first fruits" are God's, not his own, he sets up a contest between himself and his/God's work: "Accept of them and me, / And make us strive, who shall sing best thy name." The terms of the striving are announced in the first movement of "The Church," the poems from "The Altar" to "Easter Wings," which confront the problem of how man can compete with God.[30]

In "The Sacrifice," the voice of Christ from the cross reiterates in sixty-three stanzas that the answer to the questioning refrain "Was ever grief like mine?" can only be "Never." In "The Thanksgiving," the speaker, who plans to "revenge me on thy love, / And trie who shall victorious prove," thinks he has a topper for all God's blessings: he will turn them back on the giver. Rattling on until he comes to Christ's sacrifice, he sputters finally into silent helplessness: "Then for thy passion—I will do for that— / Alas, my God, I know not what." Checkmated by the cross, he realizes in "The Reprisall," "There is no dealing with thy mighty passion." Christ's "vict'ries overthrow" him, not even allowing "griefs sad conquests." Nor can he win in contests of joy. In "Easter," Christ anticipates Herbert's early rising to gather festal flowers: "But thou wast up by break of day, / And brought'st thy sweets along with thee."

Despite repeated failures and the hopeless odds against him, Herbert devises a strategy to achieve "Victorie!" ("The Thanksgiving," 48). He divides himself into three: a sinning self, often described as stonyhearted; a confessing self; and the interior other, the "Lord" taken into his heart ("Good Friday"). Then he realigns the opponents in the contest: the confessing self and the interior other team up against the sinning self. In "The Altar," God's "servant" confesses that part of him, his hard heart, is recalcitrant and likely to withhold future praise. The servant, however, defeats the stony heart by seeking, and presumably receiving, the Lord's "pow'r" to cut and frame the heart into an altar. While he confesses his sin and God's power, the sinful stones of his broken heart frame themselves into a visible altar, so that the sinning self becomes, before our eyes, a witness to God's Presence, whether or not he wants to. Two selves together, the confessing servant and the Lord, outwit the third, the sinful stony heart—now become an altar.

More discursive than the hieroglyph that opens "The Church," "The Reprisall" articulates the strategy enacted in "The Altar." Realizing that as a sinner he cannot compete with Christ's passion, the speaker asks to be freed from sin so that he may die for God. Then realizing that the passion is what frees him to compete with the passion, he discovers the circularity of his argument: "For by thy death I die for thee." Only after he despairs of victory does the path to victory open before him:

Yet by confession will I come
Into thy conquest: though I can do nought
Against thee, in thee I will overcome
The man, who once against thee fought.

The confessor joins forces with God to beat the sinner. The agon remains, and Herbert can, at the same time, play on the inevitably sinning team by opposing God, and on the inevitably winning team by joining God. The speaking self and two sides of the second self—the sinner and the image of God within—meet in combat that can become joyous, mirthful play.[31]

Herbert's confessions also enact sin—within the safe limits of play. By framing many of his poems as play, he can express with impunity all aspects of his self, including the sinning self, in contests and games that he cannot lose and dramas that expand his self. The opening series of agonistic poems ends in "Easter Wings" with a visual enactment of Herbert's successful competitive strategy. The contraction and expansion that form the poem's wings characterize the actions of both the sinful self and the image of God within. The "Lord" he addresses watches the sinning Everyman (stanza 1) and Herbert's speaker (stanza 2) "Decaying more and more" in the decreasing line lengths. But joined spiritually to the Easter resurrection of Christ, the speaker portrays, in the lengthening lines, the answer to his prayer to "let me rise . . . And sing" (7, 9) and "feel" (18) Christ's "victorie(s)" (9, 18). The confessing self has included all his selves in an emblem that shows how man can win the conflict between sinner and God—by joining the other side. If he imps his wing on Christ, whom he summons in the expanding lines of the poem, then his sinful self, who caused the fall and affliction so visible in the contracting lines, will actually advance his flight. As the cross must precede the resurrection to complete Christ's victory, so contraction must precede expansion to form wings. The agon between sinner and God that results in the fortunate fall reconciles all selves.

Herbert has more than one way to join the other side. In "Easter Wings" he not only pictures the agon between two sides of his self; he also retells the Easter story in his falling and rising. He can unite his self to the internal other by reliving the divine story in typological poetry. What he at first rejects in "The Thanksgiving" ("'Tis but to tell the tale is told") becomes a way to imp his wing on Christ. In a life played as a dramatic reenactment of Christ's life, he meets the image of God within, and from this meeting a greater self emerges.

This first movement of "The Church" (from "The Altar" to "Easter Wings") announces the agonistic themes which the poems that follow expand. Herbert engages God in contests ("The Sacrifice," "The Thanksgiving," "The Reprisall," "Easter") and finds strategies for victory in dramatized, witty confessions ("The Altar," "Easter Wings"), which describe, picture, and reenact confrontations between the sinful self and the image of God within.

Two examples must suffice to show these strategies at work in subsequent poems of "The Church." "The Quip" is a comic masque that personifies acutely the voices of the "merrie world" that Herbert, the proud, witty orator who admired beauty, fine clothes, and music, heard within.[32] Beauty, being ignored, questions the speaker's manly independence: "Whose hands are those?" Money's "chinking" mocks the poor man's "Musick." Glory, "puffing by" in whistling silks, snubs him. And Wit, of course, makes "an Oration." The patient speaker, however, anticipates the day when the "Lord" will answer these jeering voices of the sinful self: "say, I am thine: / And then they have their answer home." Because it lacks quotation marks, however, the answer is ambiguous (Herbert is God's; God is Herbert's), and the ambiguity signifies both that the speaker has joined forces with God against the sinful self (first meaning) and that he has a powerful internal ally to defend him (second meaning). In this one-sided battle of wits, a single, but double-edged "quip" acknowledging Presence ends the "sport."

Freed from the jeering voices of the world, the speaker of "The Crosse" claims all the very best intentions of Herbert's good self: to sing and serve God as His priest, to devote his wealth and family to His honor, to study His renown. Still, the voice that dominates the poem is his whining, carping self, whose complaining proves that the "Much wrastling, many a combate" of his past struggles with God are not over yet. Herbert characterizes the cross, and crossed, speaker as somewhat comic in his petulance ("Besides, things sort not to my will") and indignation ("ev'n in Paradise to be a weed"). Only in the last stanza does the speaker see that these "contrarieties . . . crosse actions . . . contradictions" are precisely the cross he must bear to perform the true service of a priest—*imitatio Christi*.

The realization immediately realigns the selves of the poem: the whining self yields place in the last three lines to a voice that addresses his Father with Christ's words to His Father at Gethsemane: "With but foure words, my words, *Thy will be done*." Through an agon of complaint about the agony of being crossed, Herbert's better self discovers Christ's Presence in his own experience. The sinful whiner feels the cross, allowing the confessing self to recognize his internal other, the Christ within, and to relive His experience and speak, as his own ("*my* words," emphasis mine), Christ's words of acceptance. The self attained in these last lines is not a dissolution of Herbert into Christ, but the greater self that comes when all selves meet.[33] Here Herbert has become the Christian neotype. As in "Aaron," "The Bunch of Grapes," and other typological poems, he achieves "Victorie," an integral self, and the experience of Presence by living out the Bible, whose "words," he says, "do finde me out, & parallels bring, / And in another make me understood" ("The H. Scriptures II").[34]

Not all the agons in "The Church" include the sinful self. Frequently, God and man are friendly contestants, even though the texture of the verse in which they play has an almost muscular force.[35] Every morning, Herbert says, he awakes to a game of catch with God:

> I cannot ope mine eyes,
> But thou art ready there to catch
> My morning-soul and sacrifice:
> Then we must needs for that day make a match.[36] ("Mattens")

Such matches take three related ludic forms in "The Church": games, contests, and combats.

Sometimes Herbert seems to disdain games as trivial. In "Miserie" he characterizes man as singing a drinking song while his house burns because "Folly and Sinne play all his game." In "Love I" he laments to God the narcissism of secular love poetry, in which wit and beauty fancy and arouse only each other, ignoring their source: "they two play out the game, / Thou standing by." And in "Jordan I" he dismisses the riddling love poetry of ambitious poets with a satirical allusion to the card game Primero: "Riddle who list, for me, and pull for Prime." In each case the game itself is not condemned, only the players, particularly those who leave out the most important contestant, *"My God, My King"* with whom poetry should be played.

In fact, Herbert frequently plays Primero with God. A relative of ombre and an ancestor of poker, Primero was a fashionable card game at Renaissance courts throughout Europe. Local variants aside, it generally took this form. Stakes are laid, two cards are dealt, and players examine their cards. They may "pass" or continue to play by "setting" their "rest," betting a second stake agreed on before the game. Those betting may keep their cards or discard and "pull" for better ones; then all players are dealt more to complete a four-card hand. Betting or vying begins, and players may "pass" or "encounter" each other by vying and revying. When the betting ceases, players "show" their hands, one of the highest being a "Prime," four cards in four suits. The best hand takes the entire pool, giving rise to the proverbial expression "Most take all" and its modern variant "Winner take all."[37]

Because several terms from Primero—*rest, pass, set, show,* and *encounter*—have more common meanings, readers may miss Herbert's allusions to the card game or deem them insignificant. In "The Church Porch," he uses these terms to advise caution sometimes, and sometimes risk: the slandered man, who would defend his honor, should pass when the stake is trivial (227–28), but the ignorant man, who "will lose his rest, / Rather then shew his cards," should overcome his pride and risk exposure to learn from conversation with the more knowledgeable (297–98). In "The Church Militant," Herbert uses terms from Primero to describe Christ's battle against Roman luxury: "our Saviour did destroy the game . . . Setting affliction to encounter pleasure" (146–48). Most significantly in "The Church," his subliminal allusions to Primero image a high-stakes game with God in which he risks everything and wins by losing.

The controlling image in "The Pulley" is, of course, the mechanical engine used for hauling, which figures God's stratagem for drawing man to Him, but this image does not preclude allusions to Primero. The multiple puns on *rest,* the title's reference to pulling, and words like *riches, treasure,* and *losers* suggest that the poem has the "laminar" structure of imagery that critics have found in so many poems of "The Church"—two tissues of imagery, one on top of the other.[38] While dramatizing what God might have said to Himself at creation, Herbert projects an interior other who initiates a game between creature and creator. God pours on man a glass of blessings, "the worlds riches" and almost "all his treasure," until He realizes that if He bestows what is left in the glass—the "rest" (noun, *remainder*), which is the gift of "rest" (noun, *repose*)—man will "rest" (verb, *repose* or *remain*) with the gifts, not the Giver. God muses, "So both should losers be." The creation has become, as God contemplates His actions, a game in which He stakes man with "riches" and "treasure" but keeps one stake in reserve—"rest."

"Rest" in Primero refers to "the stakes kept in reserve, which were agreed upon at the beginning of the game, and upon the loss of which the game terminated" (*Oxford English Dictionary,* sb 2, 6). Eager to keep the game going and therefore loth to lose His "rest" (*stake*), God must withhold "rest" (*repose*) in order to keep in contact with man. His opponent, however, should not lack the necessary stakes to play, so God decides, "let him keep the rest," the remainder of his "riches" and "treasure" that constitute his "rest" (*stake*). The goal of this imbalanced game, in which one contestant stakes the other and controls the play, is that "both should [winners] be." Man, although "rich," plays on in "repining restlesnesse," gambling to win God's "rest," His stake of divine repose. God, however, plays a game that resembles the action of a pulley in order to win his opponent, as He says, "to my breast." In such a game with the Maker of the game, God always wins, but so does man. He may lose his stake, "the rest" of his earthly "riches," but he wins God's stake, the "rest" of divine repose. Both man and God risk what they have in order to gain more; they "pull for Prime"—God to "pulley" his cherished creature to Him, and man to gain God's final blessing.[39] Meanwhile, until the end of time, when man will rest in God's breast, playing is winning. The game keeps man from adoring nature and ignoring God, by sustaining contact—albeit agonistic and wearying—between these loving opponents.

Less pervasive, but no less significant, subliminal allusions to Primero in "The Forerunners" and "The Quidditie" remind the reader of the paradoxes in man's agonistic relationship to God. In the end, losing to Him is winning, but in the meantime, merely to play is to win. The harbingers of the king's coming are Herbert's first gray hairs, "The Forerunners" of death, which will usher him into the presence of Christ the King. Not looking toward heaven, however, the speaker keenly feels the loss of those blessings given by God in "The Pulley"—especially "beautie" and "wisdome," which produced his "sparkling notions" and "enchanting language." These were his stake that he now risks losing. Nevertheless, he says, "I passe not, I, what of the rest become, / So *Thou art still my God,* be out of fear" (*pass,* meaning *to care* and *to forego one's turn at cards; rest,* meaning *remainder* and *stakes in Primero*). He will not "passe," thereby dropping out of the game, even though he may lose the "rest," the remainder of his blessings that constitute his stake. After three lamenting stanzas addressed to his losses, he reiterates his intention to play to the death: "Yet if you go, I passe not. . . . let winter have his fee." The only stake requisite to sustain the game is the assurance of Presence, and he will retain *"Thou art still my God"* so long as he continues to play. The circularity is intentional. Merely playing this losing game will win him more blessings than his original stakes of "sweet phrases, lovely metaphors"—the blessings of a Presence "within" that will "be livelier then before." Surely these stakes are more than sufficient to keep him in the game.

"The Quidditie," called "Poetry" in its first version,[40] climaxes with an allusion to Primero that defines a "verse" as a game with God in which the experience of Presence is victory. Pursuing the *via negativa,* Herbert searches for poetry's *quidditas,* its essential whatness, by enumerating what it is not: it is not "a crown" or a "point of honour" (measures of courtly status), it "cannot vault, or dance, or play" (courtly amusements), and it is not "the Exchange, or busie Hall" (middle-class workplaces). Instead, he concludes, "a verse . . . is that which while I use / I am with thee, and *most take all.*" A quiddity is both a trifling subtlety and the essence of a thing, so when Herbert pointedly contrasts both courtly play and courtly and bourgeois business to meeting God in a poem, he exposes the worldly man's "hawk" and "office" as the trifles while he represents the sacred game of poetry as essential. His precise definition, which some might dismiss as mere scholastic hairsplitting, distills the essence of his art: a game with God played by the rule of winner take all. Since, while he writes poetry, he is in the presence of the all-in-all, he wins by being won by an omnipotent god.[41] The poets of "Love I" and "Jordan I," who allow wit and beauty to "play out the game" without God, and who riddle or "pull for Prime" in courtly lyrics, will never win because they risk too little in playing with the wrong opponent. In poetic games with God, Herbert wagers all his "rest" to win the Presence of the All.

Sometimes Herbert stages agons between God and man as contests arising in casual conversation rather than as formal games. "Love-joy" presents two characters gazing presumably at a stained-glass window. The "One standing by" is Herbert's inner friend, who is always close enough at hand to enter his poetic musings, and the speaker is an aspect of Herbert, comically characterized as "never loth / To spend [his] judgement." When asked to interpret the hieroglyph in the window, a grapevine "with *J* and *C* / Anneal'd on every bunch," the know-it-all speaker gives a wrong answer ("*Joy* and *Charitie*"), which his other self understands as the right answer (*"Jesus Christ"*), since Christ is the true vine whose *caritas* offered His blood of suffering to become man's wine of joy. Herbert wins clearer understanding by letting his speaking self lose the interpretation contest to his inner friend.

The most famous contest that Herbert wins by losing is recounted in "Love III," a masterpiece of understatement whose riches this partial analysis can only finger. In the final poem of "The Church," which dramatizes the soul's timorous reception of the eucharist and reluctant entrance into the marriage feast of the Lamb, one aspect of Herbert engages the Bridegroom in what Arnold Stein has called "a contest in courtesy and humility."[42] All the guest's hemming and hawing are merely a ploy to retain his separateness from the host, who moves ever closer. When his "soul drew back," the host "Drew nearer" to him. When he looked away, "Love took [his] hand" and reminded him, with a pun, that He made everyone's separate self, all the I's as well as "eyes." When he argues that his unworthiness deserves a place in hell, as far away as he can get from Love, the host counters that He "bore the blame"—that He suffered for man's sin in man's flesh, making the guest a part of the body of Christ. When the guest makes one final plea for separateness—to serve at the feast, not to eat it—Love sits him down and feeds him with His meat, the eucharistic host who has all along been the welcoming Love.

In this humbler-than-thou contest, the guest, so comical in his reluctance, reveals the true motive for competition—the desire to assert a self separate from the source of nurture. Since the poem takes place at the end of time, when all will be reunited in God, separation is an inappropriate response, to say the least. So man and God finally merge in the last line, awesome in its simplicity: "So I did sit and eat." Still, for Herbert and the reader, who live in the days before the end of time, such total mergers are impossible. They can, however, be prefigured in the eucharist and in the sense of wholeness gained when we reconcile all our competing selves.[43] "Love III" dramatizes the competition and reconciliation between a guilty, confessing self and a loving, accepting internal other. Love inevitably wins the contest by becoming one with the contestant, and Herbert wins a sense of wholeness by losing the contest—by allowing his reluctant self to be won by the image of God within. By being won, he may become one.

Herbert's various selves—sinful, weary, aging, know-it-all, reluctant—oppose the internal friend in games and contests. They also assault Him in combats—ritualized and controlled, but no less fierce for all their ludic spirit. "The Storm" warns God that man's "throbbing conscience . . . Hath a strange force: / It . . . Dares to assault thee, and beseige thy doore." Yet more militant, prayer to Herbert is an "Engine against th' Almightie, sinners towre, / Reversed thunder, Christ-side-piercing spear" ("Prayer I"). Even when hostile, these armed assaults insure access to God: the cruel soldier who thrusts a spear into Christ's side opens a mailbag guaranteed not only to deliver, but to second those militant prayers ("The Bag"). So long as man fights with God, he cannot lose, because, like Job, he does not foresake Him. Herbert calls those Old Testament days "Sweet" when God did "Struggle with Jacob . . . Encounter Moses strong complaints and mone" ("Decay"), and he believes the New Testament temple of the heart can sound "musick for a King" only when the temple/heart becomes a battlefield, and embellishment and pomp become groans. In the "frame and fabrick . . . within," he tells God,

> There thou art struggling with a peevish heart,
> Which sometimes crosseth thee, thou sometimes it:
> The fight is hard on either part.
> Great God doth fight, he doth submit.
> All Solomons sea of brasse and world of stone
> Is not so deare to thee as one good grone. ("Sion")

God enjoys the fight.

Man sometimes does not. In "The Temper I," Herbert's persona feels stretched to the breaking point by alternating moods of spiritual exhaltation and despair. God racks him over the vast expanse of the cosmos, and he complains that his arms are not so long nor his stature so great as God's. The complaint also images his torture as a trial by combat: "Wilt thou meet arms with man . . . ? Will great God measure with a wretch?" Comically characterizing himself as a stretched "crumme of dust," Herbert emphasizes the ludicrous incongruity of creature meeting creator in a contest of arms and of their measuring foils before a fencing match.[44] Despite his desire to "roost and nestle" hidden in heaven's "roof," the speaker comes to realize that God's "way" is openness and contingency, not enclosure and security. He must risk everything in combat of cosmic dimensions to win Presence: "Whether I flie with angels, fall with dust, / Thy hands made both, and I am there." Furthermore, the experience of Presence transforms "one place," the "breast," where his earthly self struggles against the image of God within, into "ev'ry where." No retreat is possible, and the end of the poem leaves the speaker contingent, open to the abyss between "fourtie heav'ns" and "hell," because that is where God is—in risk. Still, because he joins his "love and trust" to God's "power and love," risky combat can become a secure hug, for

God has several ways to "meet arms with man": to measure ("mete") their weapons, to join battle, and to embrace him.[45]

An enlargement of self occurs in "The Temper I" when the complaining self meets the internal other in arms. Similarly, in "Artillerie," a dialogue between a shooting star and an aspect of Herbert becomes a fire fight between God and man that leads to internal wholeness and a glimpse of infinity. What comes from without in this poem really comes from within: the star that unceremoniously drops "one ev'ning" into the speaker's lap is actually *"good motions from* [his] *breast, / Which have the face of fire, but end in rest."* In retaliation, the speaker aims his artillery at the prime mover of these internal motions, returning the fire of his divine opponent, who, he says,

> dost deigne
> To enter combate with us, and contest
> With thine own clay.

Although combative, the speaker is a prudent, even prosaic man—careful about sparks "as knowing well, / That from small fires comes oft no small mishap"; bemused by talking stars; eager to "do or suffer what [he] ought"; and mindful of obligations, promises, and laws (21–24). In his comic primness, he admonishes God to fight fair, reminding Him, "Thy promise now hath ev'n set thee thy laws." He wants his omnipotent opponent to limit Himself to a rule-governed agon, complete with truces for "parley."

Yet the negotiations produce a settlement unforeseen by the nearsighted speaker:

> But I would parley fain:
> Shunne not my arrows, and behold my breast.
> Yet if thou shunnest, I am thine:
> I must be so, if I am mine.
> There is no articling with thee:
> I am but finite, yet thine infinitely.

He begins by requesting his opponent to cease defending Himself and to aim better. Then while parleying, he gradually comprehends the terms of this rather odd combat: that, whether or not his artillery hits the mark, God has won him, that he wins his self by being his opponent's captive, that the combat has no rules he can understand, but that it stretches his finitude toward infinity. The prudent man who, in the opening of the poem, brushed aside divine fire has become, by the end, a player in an agon with unknowable rules who risks his self ("I am thine") to gain a greater self ("I am mine.... yet thine infinitely"). Combat has precipitated a self-encounter that brings wholeness to a man who at first could not recognize his own inner "*motions,*" and that enlightens a rather dim-witted, if well-intentioned, aspect of Herbert.[46]

III

In these poetic games, contests, and combats, Herbert has presented his divine opponent as the speaker ("The Pulley"), a character in a dramatized agon ("Love III"), and the silent presence whom he addresses ("The Temper I"). In other poems (for example, "Jordan II" and "The Pilgrimage"), he characterizes God as a disembodied voice that seems to enter the poem from without but, like the shooting star of "Artillerie," actually comes from within. "Love Unknown" makes the internal source of this voice explicit when the speaker, addressing his "Deare Friend," merges the characters in the poem by describing his Lord's servant as one who

did know his [master's] eye
Better then you know me, or (which is one)
Then I my self.

The speaker's friend is his second self, the indwelling Christ, the servant of God the master, who throws the speaker's heart into the bloody fountain and the boiling caldron, who slips His blood into the eucharistic cup to be "taken inwardly," who stuffs his bed with thorny thoughts, and who delivers the final interpretation of His own actions.

Frequently, the second self enters Herbert's agonistic poems—as a voice or a silent, controlling Presence—to untangle the knots into which the speaker has tied himself. In "A true Hymne," Herbert characterizes Him by His prevenient actions: "when th' heart sayes (sighing to be approved) / *O, could I love!* and stops: God writeth, *Loved.*" Herbert figures a God who interprets even the most blasphemous rebellion generously. For example, He reads the wild raving of "The Collar" as a "sighing to be approved," and many readers have noticed that He silently enters the poem, even before His final calling, to write the proof of His love in the double meanings of the speaker's words of rebellion.[47] The "board" the speaker strikes, his "harvest" of "a thorn," "cordiall fruit," "wine," and "corn" all represent the eucharistic feast that offers him the "double pleasures" (and more) that he would seek abroad. As he grows fiercer "At every word," the inner voice is "calling" at almost every word by writing "*Loved*" in his unintentional allusions.

Because, however, the speaker's ravings are so loud that they deafen him to the internal call, he fragments himself into near oblivion. His "I" remembers a past rebellious "I"; then the rebel remembers a past foolishly obedient "I." As his rage builds, the rebel further splits himself into a complaining voice, a voice that urges action, and a self-justifying voice. Because these "I's" argue only among themselves, not (as in other complaints like "Artillerie") confronting the divine opponent, the second self, in a fruitful agon, they disperse rather than integrate the self. When the Father turns from His strategy of silence to call aloud, *"Child!"* the squabbling "I's" all come together and recognize their name. The final answer of the reunified "I" voices his acceptance of a stable identity as child of a lordly father. For all his blasphemy, the speaker has only been playing at rebellion; he pulls up short at the first hint of admonition. Likewise, Herbert's characterization of God plays with the speaker by manipulating his words, toying with him as one might tease a child out of a temper tantrum.

Other poems in which the second self enters as a silent Presence also suggest that God plays with man. This suggestion need not be so fearsome as it is for Gloucester in *King Lear,* who fears that the gods "kill us for their sport" (4.1.39), but it does entail risk. Some ancients, such as Heraclitus, and moderns, such as Jürgen Moltmann, who have conceived of God as *deus ludens* and man as His plaything, stress divine freedom from necessity and the groundlessness, from a human perspective, of being. No less free, but more predictable, Herbert's version of God at play is more like that of Catholic theologian Hugo Rahner: God is a benevolent, if sometimes whimsical, inner Presence who plays with the speaker's words as he utters them.[48] He is free to stretch or contract man throughout the universe, yet He comes to Herbert most often in the controlled risks of a game, the agonistic poems in which the poet can feel, "I am with thee, and *most take all.*"

Although readers have often noted God's entrance into the last line of "Deniall" to regularize the speaker's "broken . . . verse" and "mend [his] ryme,"[49] the divine intervention in "A Wreath" appears even more miraculous and humorous. The speaker, eager to praise God, sets out to compose a poetic wreath for Him. As he begins to interweave his lines into a wreath (repeating the end of each line early in the next), his verse abandons praise and enacts sin instead. Crestfallen in midpoem, he realizes that, for all his worshipful intentions, his sinful self has usurped the poem, making it a hieroglyph of his "crooked winding wayes." Although he believes that "life is straight, / Straight as a line, and ever tends to thee" and calls his artful crookedness "deceit" that leads to death, he seems powerless to halt the downward spiral. The rhymes ("praise / give / wayes / live / straight / thee / deceit / simplicitie") show no sign of turning upward to close the circle of a wreath.

Then a miracle occurs—or rather Herbert stages a silent entrance of *deus ex machina* to rescue his sinful self. Unlike the rueful but static speaker of "Sinnes Round," who can only confess the circularity of his self-generating sin, the speaker of "A Wreath" discovers his sin while he speaks, and cries out to God for help against the powers of deceit and crookedness. Since Herbert's God is far above man's deceitful cleverness, as soon as the speaker begs, "Give me simplicitie," God answers his prayer silently by entering the poem and using his own crookedness to bring him back to the beginning.[50] Repeating in reverse order the first four rhymes ("live / wayes / give / praise"), the last four lines reascend in the same serpentine pattern back to life ("that I may live," cf. l. 4), to the knowledge and practice of God's straight ways ("that I may know . . . and practice them," cf. l. 3), and finally to a "crown," not merely a garland of praise for God (cf. ll. 1–2). Despite (and in part because of) the speaker's deceitful crookedness, God gains a wreath of praise. As intricate as a puzzle, "A Wreath" portrays the action of a silent inner Presence, more clever even than Herbert's witty self—a friend who answers prayers immediately. By picturing an encounter between a poet too clever for his own good and a second self who redeems the poet's deceitful art, Herbert demonstrates the reconciliation between "simplicitie" and poetic invention that he seeks in the more discursive poems, "The Forerunners" and "Jordan I and II." As an aspect of himself plays with words, he imagines a second self playing with him; he wins a sense of wholeness, and God wins the praise.

The silent Presence visibly enters "Deniall" and "A Wreath" only in response to a final prayer, and He remains concealed beneath double entendres in "The Collar" until His climactic exclamation. From beginning to end, however, "Paradise" displays the Presence of "the sweetest FREND," whose "sharpnes" the speaker requests to "prune and PARE" and make him "more fruitfull." Even before the prayer is uttered, Herbert's inner friend answers it as a gardener, snipping off the initial letter of the second and third rhyming words in each triplet. Such prunings as Herbert figures so gently here are nevertheless the "sharp and TART . . . cuttings" that he feels as afflictions and crosses in "Affliction I." Here Herbert reenacts in play the disciplines of God that he lamented in the prior poem in "The Church." Once God had afflicted him with sickness and bereavement so that he felt "thinne and lean without a fence or friend," then debilitated him with a sense of worthlessness so that he wished, he says,

> I were a tree;
> For sure then I should grow
> To fruit or shade. ("Affliction I")

In "Paradise," by playing the God who plays with the speaker's words, Herbert takes possession of his suffering; it becomes what he chooses from within, not what befalls him from without, and thus he no longer feels diminishment as affliction. Instead of lacking "fence or friend," he feels safe in the "inclosure" of his "sweetest FREND"; instead of wishing he were a fruitful tree, he has become one, growing "Among thy trees," he rejoices to God, "which in a ROW / To thee both fruit and order OW." So long as he can project in play the healing Presence that prunes him, he will enjoy the "fruit," "order," and "inclosure" of paradise regained, feeling the fall, and his own fall into the diminishment of sickness and self-loathing, as fortunate.

This projection of God from the self—whether as a visual or vocal Presence with which Herbert plays in his poems—is problematical. With what, precisely, does he play? Freudians would answer that Herbert addresses the imagos of the absent father, who died when he was three and from whom he seeks unfaltering paternal love, and of the lost mother, for whose nurture the Church and eucharist substitute.[51] But the specific biographical sources for Herbert's internal other are hidden from us in the past. These imagos can only be embodied now in language, and that is fundamentally what the poet plays with—sound, rhythm, convention, pattern—in order to experience a measure of integration. When Herbert brings his various sinful, passionate, weary, confused, and dim-witted selves to metrical language, he sets up an interplay between his waywardness and patterns that he believed mirrored divine order.[52] So Lacanians would answer that Herbert engages "the name of the Father," the linguistic structures and codes of his culture, which are both beyond and within the subject. Once internalized, these structures free the subject from captivation to parental imagos but subject it to textuality.[53]

In part, I agree. In manipulative play with language that creates dramatized agons between versions of self and an internal other, Herbert plays with those cultural codes and ideals that are internalized in the process of self-formation. His poems, however, do not portray a self that has been dissolved, either into Christ or textuality. As we have seen repeatedly, the self becomes whole and expands in fruitful agons between its once dispersed parts.

In what terms did Herbert, a seventeenth-century divine, understand this mysterious experience of wholeness that comes from uniting the self with the internal other embodied in language, an experience that I have used the terms of twentieth-century psychoanalysis to understand? We may find an answer to this question in "Heaven," the penultimate poem of "The Church" in which the echo of the speaker's voice describes what he cannot yet know, the joys of heaven. The echo has a double status: it repeats the speaker's words, transforming them into answers to his questions, but it also claims to repeat the voice of heaven, describing its source as the unfading leaves of holy scriptures, which are themselves "the Echo . . . of blisse." If man finds himself echoed in the Bible, and if heaven is also echoed in the Bible, then in Biblical words a projection of man becomes divine; man's words become God's words; what is within is also without.[54] How can this interpenetration of man and God occur? Only through the incarnation. The Word became flesh and dwelt among men, fulfilling all the Old Testament types, and when He departed, He left Himself as the new man in believers' hearts. As neotypes of Christ, they will find, says Herbert, that Biblical "storie pennes and sets us down" ("The Bunch of Grapes"). Consequently, when believers project the internal other out of the self—whether as a silent Presence visible in playful poems or as an echo—this second self can be the image of God. And when the poetic speaker meets or hears this Presence, he gains a glimpse of bliss. Prefigured in the mundane poetic play of "Heaven," heaven will be a kingdom of "Leisure" without "cares and businesse" where light, joy, and pleasure will persevere ever—a kingdom of play.

The miracle of the incarnation renders Herbert's poetic games, contests, and combats with his second self exceedingly complex. As he frequently reminds the reader (for example, in "Man" and "The Familie"), the creator of the universe has chosen to dwell in man; thus the container of all is itself contained. This paradox strikes Herbert forcefully when he contemplates his priestly office: he marvels that priests' "hands convey him, who conveys their hands" ("The Priesthood") and that, when Christ brings His head, breast, and music to live *in His priests,* they become well dressed *in Christ* ("Aaron"). Because of the incarnation, when Herbert projects a God out of himself who engages him in play, he finds that the playmate he once contained actually contains him. The poetic games, like "Heaven," which he cannot lose because he, as poet, controls them, mirror the cosmic game that a benevolent, providential God plays with him.

Although not agons between the self and the second self, several other poems play with these complexities. The witty tangle of possessive pronouns, which ties the reader of "Clasping of hands" in knots, represents the speaker's attempt to untangle the paradox of the incarnation. He vacillates between the two poles of human opposition—"mine" and "thine"—because neither alone suffices to express the greater self that is won when the self loses to the image of God within: "to be thine, doth me restore,." or, as he claims in "The Holdfast," "all things [are] more ours by being his." Similarly, in "Coloss. 3.3" Herbert adopts two strategies to picture the containment of the container. He significantly alters the Biblical text of his title when embedding it obliquely in the poem. The diagonal motto, "My Life is Hid in Him That Is My Treasure," places the speaker inside that which he holds. Also, while the verse asserts his containment in God, he literally contains the verse in his poem. In the verbal and visual tricks of "Clasping of Hands" and "Coloss. 3.3," Herbert plays with the paradox that underlies his agonistic poems such as "Artillerie" and "The Quidditie": in play with his second self, who is both within and beyond, he can hold fast to, clasp hands with, and hold while hiding in God.

From the first to the last poem in "The Church," in games, contests, and combats, with a visible, vocal, or silent opponent, Herbert has shown himself to be a Jacob, wrestling with God and not letting go until he receives a blessing. The story of Jacob, from whom Herbert took his personal motto, *"Lesse then the least / Of all Gods mercies"* ("The Posie," Gen. 32:10), is in many ways Herbert's story.

> Jacob was left alone; and there wrestled a man with him until the breaking of the day.... And [the man] said, Let me go, for the day breaketh. And [Jacob] said, I will not let thee go, except thou bless me.... And [the man] said, Thy name shall be called no more Jacob, but Israel [meaning "He who strives with God"]: for as a prince hast thou power with God and with men, and hast prevailed.... And Jacob called the name of the place Peniel: for I have seen God face to face, and my life is preserved. (Gen. 32: 24–30)

As Jacob's agon with God wins for him a blessing and a new name signifying a new self, Herbert's poetic agons with the indwelling spirit win for him the blessing of a felt Presence and the experience of a whole self.[55] As Jacob sees God face to face and lives, Herbert sees, hears, and plays with a God whom he can encounter face to face, without Donne's fear of annihilation, because he finds that face in the mirror. Herbert achieved an identity, not as his brothers did, in contests with men, but as Israel did, by striving with God.

IV

Herbert strives not only with versions of his self, but also with the reader in puzzle poems that offer the challenge of pitting one's wits against the poet's. What he says in praise of his divine playmate applies equally well to his lyrics: "The *beauty* lies in the *discovery*" (second sonnet to his mother). Herbert's avowed goal as a "Verser," proclaimed to the reader in the opening lines of "The Church Porch," is to "Rhyme thee to good, and make a bait of pleasure.... And turn delight into a sacrifice." This goal raises two critical problems.

Taking their cue from Herbert's own distrust of the cleverness and wit that weave the self into the sense, readers have asked if his poetic ingenuity draws too much attention to the craft of the poetry and thereby evinces pride, not piety.[56] Although aware of this risk, the Verser offers his artfulness to tantalize readers into interpretation, engaging them in hermeneutic agons that may draw them from their stance outside the poem into its experience.[57] George Wither pursued a similar strategy. Appending to his *Collections of Emblemes, Ancient and Moderne* (1635) a game of chance by which readers could select emblems, he offered both this game and the wit of the pictures as enticements: "I... am not ashamed to set forth a *Game at Lots*, or (as it were) a *Puppet-play* in *Pictures,* to allure men to the more serious observation of the profitable *Morals,* couched in these *Emblems*.... For, when levitie, or a childish delight, in trifling Objects, hath allured them to looke on the Pictures; Curiositie may urge them to peepe further, that they might seeke out also their *Meanings,* in our annexed *Illustrations*."[58] The readers' "pleasure" in their own interpretive play, not their admiration for Herbert's wit, is the Verser's "bait" to catch the soul.

Other readers have questioned the place of readers presented with poems to enjoy as an aesthetic experience that purport to be intimate colloquies between a soul and God.[59] If readers are an audience enjoying a closet drama, are the colloquies prayer or staged play? The Verser answers that he would turn their aesthetic "delight into a sacrifice," an offering whose purpose is to summon God's presence into human life. In play with his internal other, Herbert experiences Presence, and in play with the reader he extends the opportunity to share the experience. To this end, he offers God his tools for creating delight: "then shall our brain / All her invention on thine Altar lay" ("Love II"). Like the juggler before the Virgin, Herbert asks that the cleverness and wit he so frequently distrusts be redeemed as a sacrifice to bring God, Herbert, and the reader into each other's presence, releasing the joy and exhilaration that accompany play.

Reading many of the lyrics of "The Church" is like solving a series of puzzles. Whereas Donne dazzles readers with the twists and turns of arguments in which he can hide, keeping us always engaged but at a distance, Herbert challenges readers to games in which we must match our powers of discovery to the poet's clues.[60] Donne eludes readers with mocking arguments like "Woman's Constancy"; Herbert meets us in puzzles like "Coloss. 3.3," "Clasping of hands," "A Wreath," "Trinitie Sunday," "Jesu," and "Ana—{MARY / ARMY}gram." Tightly structured, frequently employing visual as well as verbal techniques, many of them even look like puzzles. To solve them, readers must know the Bible, typology, church doctrine, liturgy, and iconography—as Rosemond Tuve and others have proved.[61] Then we must use our wits to discover how Herbert plays with convention and tradition by, for example, burying an unstated pun on *host* in the dramatic situation of "Love III," or alluding obliquely to one or more aspects of the Trinity in every line of "Trinitie Sunday," or concretizing Biblical references in "The Altar" so that language from Exodus 20:25, Deuteronomy 27:2–6, Luke 19:40, and 2 Corinthians 3:3 becomes what it describes.

By creating poetic puzzles, Herbert invites readers to engage in a game that the poet wins only when we discover the solution. No learning occurs, no "delight" is shared, and nobody wins if we are stumped. Of course, Herbert's fit audience would not have been stumped (and is not now, thanks to scholarship) because his visual and verbal clues employ accepted conventions. So again he wins by losing, since the real object of his play is the play itself. Just as Herbert wins his agons with God by meeting the Presence that the game invokes, he wins his games with readers by engrossing our wit so that we meet his mind in the poem. To sustain active play, opponents must have roughly equivalent abilities lest players become discouraged or bored and leave the game.[62] Thus Herbert projects a God who "deigne[s] / To enter combate with us, and contest / With thine own clay" ("Artillerie"), who limits Himself to enter Herbert's poems. Similarly, he creates solvable puzzles for his readers, poems whose riches are not readily exhausted, but which are not so radically ambiguous as Donne's or Marvell's lyrics; they do not leave readers fundamentally unsure of our playmate's position.

The opportunities for the play of discovery offered in each lyric are multiplied exponentially when *The Temple* is read as a whole. As poem follows poem, image patterns interweave (all the "sweets" lost in "Vertue" are magnified in "The Odour"); solutions anticipate problems ("The Starre" glories in the proper use of the curling and winding condemned in "Jordan II"); solutions to previous problems appear (the obedient prayer pictured in the tight structure of "The Call" replaces the rebellious raging pictured in the loose form of "The Collar"); and a single theme plays in different keys (while "Church-monuments" is a sober meditation on man's dissolution into dust, and "Mortification" preaches Herbert's version of "Death's Duel," "Death" mocks death's skeletal appearance with lighthearted humor). As these interconnections proliferate, the entire volume becomes a puzzle, which teases readers to discover its underlying patterns of organization.[63] Perhaps, as many have remarked, Herbert intended to create a book with "configurations" and "constellations" like those in the Bible, for "The H. Scriptures II" describes *The Temple* as accurately as Scripture: "This verse marks that, and both do make a motion / Unto a third, that ten leaves off doth lie."

Although there is courtly elegance in Herbert's games with God and the reader, there is toughness as well. His poetic play sustains an aristocratic refinement and decorum reminiscent of Sir Philip Sidney,[64] an intensity of religious fervor comparable to Milton's, and spiritual combat between aspects of the self bordering at times on blasphemy. He waged a civil war within the temple of his heart and reenacted that war in a temple of poetry. Never denying the conflicts he felt, but always bringing poetic order out of internal confusion, Herbert contained in the play frame of his lyrics many of the struggles that marked the inner lives of the English in the seventeenth century.

"The Church-Porch" offers a young aristocrat advice on handling money, gambling, dueling, conversing with the great, and other pitfalls of worldly society; and lyrics like "The Pearl" reject "the wayes of Honour... The quick returns of courtesie... the wayes of Pleasure... mirth and musick... love and wit." While advising and modelling virtue, these poems expose the essential emptiness of the Jacobean and Caroline court. Similarly, "The Church Militant" and lyrics like "Church-rents and schismes" lament the failures of the contemporary institutional church to build a temple to house Christ. Thus framed by warnings against courtly vice and by the history and prophesy of ecclesiastical degeneration, "The Church" portrays a cross-biassed and fragmented speaker. According to Marion White Singleton, the subjects (for example, "Giddinesse"), images (for example, "Dooms-day"), and syntax (for example, "Dotage") of this conflicted speaker reflect his contemporaries' experience of the dissolution of values and structures, such as court and church, by which they once defined their identity.[65]

Throughout the middle years of the century, as outlined earlier, competing ways of defining the self were threatening psychological as well as political stability. Nevertheless, in *The Temple* Herbert's readers could play with a self in the process of integration, who reconciled an acknowledgment of personal turmoil with a desire for fit order. In the violent years after Herbert's death, however, the play frame could no longer contain in fruitful dialectic courtly decorum and reforming zeal. The world that had defined the self primarily by its place in a familial and social hierarchy was yielding to a world that would increasingly define the self by individual achievement. The inner war that led Herbert through psychological separation toward selfhood in Christ gave place to a real Civil War that separated England irrevocably from the remnants of medieval kingship and thrust it into the modern, parliamentary state.

6

Andrew Marvell Recreating the Self

Hamlet's constricting family would deny him a self, Donne's contradictory fears crowd his self in between, and the burden of Herbert's intimidating ancestry impels him to compete for a separate self. Although threatened by forces that would fragment or engulf him, each man finds in play a *modus vivendi*. Similarly, Andrew Marvell plays to defend and re-create the self. His lyrics tell a variety of stories about the self endangered by separation from nurture and by contradictory demands. But in speaking of the self, Marvell, like Donne and Herbert, also speaks to the world beyond. Their singular responses to a culture in crisis image their contemporaries' experience in universal terms. When Donne evokes the child's ambivalent desires for union and separation, he dramatizes the felt liminality of his contemporaries. When Herbert reenacts the child's agon of separation from the source he internalizes, he reflects his contemporaries' struggle, at a time of institutional decline, toward identities less dependent on social and familial status. And when Marvell recalls the perils and contradictions in the child's experience of separation, he articulates his contemporaries' loss of mythic structures that had for centuries defined identity, and their perplexity amid competing versions of truth. To describe Marvell's self-representations is, however, a tricky business because he seems to have had virtually no self at all.[1]

A more private man would be hard to imagine. His whereabouts for several years, shifting political allegiances, means of financial support, clandestine spying, marital status, the authorship and dates of his poems, and (most maddeningly) his personality are all in doubt. This enigma, who wrote letters about himself in the third person, candidly confessed, "I am naturally . . . inclined to keep my thoughts private."[2] An attempt, then, to discover the self behind Marvell's lyrics seems doomed from the outset. Coolly detached, Marvell, the man, does not speak undisguised in these poems. Nevertheless, heed-ing wise caveats that poetry is not autobiography and that the personae Marvell creates are various,[3] I can hear, behind the naive personae or the speaker's ambiguity, a consistent voice. The voice may or may not speak directly for the man, who has been called an "alchemical ventriloquist," but the preoccupations of that voice can reveal much about the man.[4] The voice of Marvell's lyrics is preoccupied with threats to primary narcissism and with play as a counter to those threats and a way to integrate the self.

Readers have, in passing, remarked on narcissism in Marvell's lyrics;[5] more frequently his playfulness has attracted notice. In the nineteenth century, as soon as the lyrics emerged as an object of critical attention from the obscurity to which Marvell's fame as a satirist had relegated them, critics attributed their wit, fancy, elegance, and humor to "playing," even "trifling."[6] In the twentieth century, Eliot's description of Marvellian wit as an "alliance of levity and seriousness (by which the seriousness is intensified)" refocused critical attention on the sophistication of Marvell's play,[7] although some still objected that it produced dazzling surfaces with no depths.[8] In opposition to the excesses of new critical readings, scholars emphasizing Marvell's use of tradition often ignored or denied his playfulness,[9] and other critics opposed what they deemed scholarly excesses.[10] More recently, attempts to reconcile play and traditionalism have produced studies of Marvell's baroque or mannerist sensibility and of his play with received genres.[11] Although almost everyone agrees cursorily that Marvell plays in his lyrics, few concentrate on this play or define its significance for the poet.[12] Play, I will argue, offered Marvell both an interim defense and a way to restructure the self in lyrics that dramatize dangers to the emerging self.[13]

I

Confronted with separation from the source of nurture, the infant learns that it is not the omnipotent satisfaction of its own desires. This self-perception as the weak recipient of others' care shatters the infant's primary narcissism. Yet in their care it can see its separate self mirrored for the first time—a something, not its mother, that has needs but is weak. Perceiving its helplessness, the nascent self may desire to merge with the source of gratification or to idealize its caregivers, deeming them omnipotent to assure itself that they will meet all needs. As they sometimes satisfy but inevitably fail to meet these inflated expectations, the child gradually internalizes their roles as mirrors and ideals, building key structures that form the self. In childhood these internal structures are weak and unrealistic, requiring the support of caregivers who will mirror the child's grandiosity, allow themselves to be idealized, but also insure that life's normal frustrations modify, without severe trauma, the emergent self.[14]

This growth into selfhood is not always completed because traumatic and protracted frustrations can stunt the self. If, instead of accurately mirroring the child, the parent gives contradictory messages (as in the earlier instance of the mother who stiffens when embraced, all the while verbally demanding affection), the child will be unable to see a self-reflection and, therefore, to form a coherent internal self. As Ophelia's plight demonstrates, prolonged exposure to such double binds may cause the self to fragment entirely or may teach the child to perceive the world in double-bind patterns. Likewise, if frustrations in early care have been intolerable, finding a locus for the self may seem impossible. The weak self may seek to merge with a stronger other, but then it will be dissolved and be no self at all. The weak self may desire to engulf the stronger other, but then the stronger other will no longer exist to provide strength. The weak self may try to strengthen itself by pursuing an ideal so rarified as to be unattainable on earth; it must then become a not-self to become a strong self. Any lesser ideal lacks the perfection necessary to provide security. So the weak self can never win. Its fear of dissolution or disintegration may be so intense that it defends itself by maintaining rigid barriers against the merger it both desires and fears.[15]

Speakers or characters in Marvell's lyrics repeatedly find themselves in such untenable positions, trapped between destructive alternatives. Remarking on the prevalence of dialectic in his poems, critics have contrasted his use of antithesis, which polarizes opposites, to Donne's preference for paradox, which joins opposites in one figure.[16] Whereas Donne locates himself in between, Marvell often leaves the self no place to stand. Sometimes it is trapped in double binds, sometimes it defends itself futilely against the annihilation threatened by merger, and sometimes it faces intolerable alternations between being bountifully fed and being devoured.

In "A Dialogue between the Soul and Body," we hear two voices—the soul lamenting its enslavement to the body and the body complaining about torments inflicted by the soul—but no word from the self whom these elements should constitute. In the reality created by the poem, no self exists, only carping fragments who refer to each other (except once, l. 32) in the third person: the body's eyes and ears, claims the soul, are blinding and deafening; the soul's spirit of life, claims the body, "Has made me live to let me dye." No human self can exist without both: a body without a soul is dead, and a soul without a body is no longer human. Still, each desires what would destroy the other and thus the self. The soul longs to gain "the Port" of bodily death and complains of being "Shipwrackt into Health." The body, more contradictory in its complaints than the soul, wants to stifle the soul's force, preferring a "Fever" (hazardous to the body) to the animating spirit of physical life, and the lumpish "rest" of unconsciousness to emotional life. This morass of contradictions silences the self.

Other poems threaten the self with a similar fate. To defend against this threat, Marvell often describes rigid barriers against unions that would dissolve the self—barriers that only engender new contradictions. In "The Definition of Love," if the "Two perfect Loves . . . close," the universe will be nullified: Fate ruined, "the giddy Heaven" collapsed, the earth convulsed, and "the World . . . cramp'd into a *Planisphere*"—a mere map of what once existed. If, in fact, perfect lovers could ever merge in perfect love, thereby eliminating the movement generated by desire and the space created by separation, then man's original wholeness would be restored, a motionless, timeless union (not unlike prenatal bliss) that would depose Fate from its rule over time and motion, and collapse the space between heaven and earth. No motion (so no time), no space (so no world), consequently no lovers (so no self)—this state of oblivion is what Fate so rigidly "debarrs" with "Iron wedges" and "Decrees of Steel." Although Marvell's speaker insures his selfhood by setting his ideal love so high that Fate marshalls all its might to prevent consummation, the price is as high as his ideal—eternal frustration. Forever bound to "Conjunction" by love, but debarred in "Opposition" by Fate, he cannot abandon his love and he cannot have her.[17]

In "Daphnis and Chloe," Chloe tries to bind Daphnis in a similar stasis. With coy refusals that change to yielding when Daphnis begins to leave, Chloe "neither knew t'enjoy, / Nor yet let her Lover go." Daphnis faces the trap—"Sudden Parting closer glews." In order to keep him, Chloe thinks she must refuse him, and in order to win her, Daphnis, who has been pursuing the wrong strategy, must leave her, and (if these contradictions were not enough) her yielding may be a tease to lure him back to the original stalemate. Daphnis appears to experience her offer not as a harmless tease but as a threat to his self. Although the narrator conventionally compares the departure from the beloved to death (X, XXV), Daphnis says that to mix gratification with departure is to torture the dying, and he describes the contradiction in four unconventional images of annihilation: a meal being fattened for a cannibal, sex with a freshly dead corpse, the Jews who lusted after flesh struck dead in midbite, and a witch made invisible by the fern seed he waked at midnight to find. The pain of departure is tolerable, but the coquette's practiced mixture of *come hither* and *begone* would leave his self "undone, / Between Joy and Sorrow rent." Wisely, he prefers to pine in "manly stubborness" with a self at least intact enough to choose the moment of his own execution/parting.

In "The Definition of Love" and "Daphnis and Chloe," barriers between lovers or between denial and gratification counter threats to the self posed by intolerable contradictions. Daphnis's fear of being fattened up for a cannibal previews another danger to the self—the archaic fear of being indulgently fed by what will turn and feed on you. This confusion of eating and being eaten is one way the weak self, enfeebled by inconsistent caretaking during infancy when feeding dominates perceptions, imagines its relation to the stronger self with whom it desires to merge: if I eat you to sustain my self, then you might eat me, and I would have no self. "The unfortunate Lover," whose story recounts the life cycle of man,[18] faces such a trap.

Before birth into the life of passion, the lover "yet playes" with "the Infant Love" in a garden world of "Fountains cool, and Shadows green." Like the child playing in a protected environment, the innocent lover has not yet faced the loss of Eden, the rude shock of separation and entry into the world where the self futilely tries "To make impression upon Time." This second (psychological) birth of separation—as important to the formation of the self as physical birth[19]—is described in violent and lurid terms: shipwrecked in a storm, the unfortunate's mother is "split against the Stone, / In a *Cesarian Section*." This cruel and unnatural birth throws the lover into a chaos of roaring seas, wind, and "ratling Thunder," which mirrors his internal confusion as "The Orphan of the *Hurricane*." Instead of a mother to nurture and mirror his nascent self, the lover has the "cruel Care" of "Corm'rants" and "quarrelling Elements." His surrogate mothers, most ravenous birds of prey, simultaneously feed him "up with Hopes and Air" and devour his heart. Marvell emphasizes the disastrous contradictions in the lover's earliest nurture:

> Thus while they famish him, and feast,
> He both consumed, and increast:
> And languished with doubtful Breath,
> Th' *Amphibium* of Life and Death.

Like the cormorants, the chaotic storm does more than mirror his internal confusion; it torments him with more.

Trapped between love's "Flames" and fortune's "Waves," with "Thunder" above and the "stubborn Rock" below, the lover proudly defines his self in combat with the contradictions that will inevitably destroy him: "all he saies" is "a Lover drest / In his own Blood does relish best." But his self-definition is ambiguous and self-defeating. Dressed like a bird for dinner in a sauce of his life's blood, does the lover relish (transitive verb, *to be pleased by, enjoy the taste of*) himself, or does he relish (intransitive verb, *have an appetizing taste*) as the maternal cormorants and elements butcher and devour him?[20] In one case, he enjoys his narcissistic posturing as the doomed lover who "e're brought forth, was cast away"; in the other, he has willingly accepted his lot as a martyr devoured by love and fate. In either case, the poem recounts the self's annihilation in nightmarish images recalling the genesis of madness: early and violent separation from the mother and intolerably contradictory care.

Whether fragmented by internal contradictions ("The Dialogue between the Soul and Body"), threatened with annihilation by fulfilled love ("The Definition of Love"), or tormented by gratifications that turn into their opposites ("Daphnis and Chloe" and "The unfortunate Lover"), the self in Marvell's lyrics is frequently endangered. Likewise, in "The Coronet" a contrary and sinful nature threatens to shatter poet as well as poem, in "The Match" fulfilled love might result in annihilation of the lovers, and in "The Gallery" the lover seems caught between devouring and bountiful images of his beloved. Other lyrics trace the self's placement in untenable positions to unfulfilled needs for a mirror and a realistic ideal to sustain the self. Since the pastoral portrays an ideal world at one with the poet's desires, it lends itself to dramas about the growth and/or stunting of the self.[21] As with other genres, Marvell stretches the pastoral beyond its usual limits, describing not merely harmony, but mergers between man and nature. Still, his dramas seldom end happily, as mirrors and ideals fail.

Some of Marvell's lyrics are veritable halls of mirrors: tears and eyes mutually reflect each other ("Eyes and Tears," XIIII; "Mourning," II), dewdrops reflect heaven ("On a Drop of Dew," 5–8; "Ros," 35–36), a prospect seems a "Landskip drawen in Looking-Glass," a river becomes a *"Chrystal Mirrour"* ("Upon Appleton House," 458, 636–40), and Cromwell mirrors his dying daughter, who is his image in wax ("A Poem upon the Death of O. C.," 53–54, 73–78). Marvell's fascination with self-reflections also leads him to create mirror images in which things resemble themselves (the dewdrop shining "Like its own Tear,"13), and to write Latin and English poems that mirror (not merely translate) one another.[22] Predictably, he gravitates to the pastoral, in which nature reflects man.

In the Mower poems, the naive Damon assumes that nature should always reflect his psychological state and fulfill his needs. On this assumption he divides the world into what mirrors him and what does not; the latter shocks and appalls him. "Damon the Mower" dramatizes his childish grandiosity and the self-destructive quality of his narcissism. Because he feels himself to be the object of nature's parental ministrations, no false modesty restrains his childlike, singsong boast: "I am the Mower *Damon* known / Through all the Meadows I have mown." By his report, the feminine morning showers him with dew before "her darling Daffadils," the masculine sun licks off his noon sweat, the evening bathes his feet in flower water, the immortal fairies choose him to "lead" their dances, and they gather around when he sings. Nature even seems to mirror his sorrow when Juliana rejects him: "ev'ry thing did seem to paint / The Scene more fit for his complaint." That dew, sun, and wet vegetation would serve anyone as it does him; that the day would still be fair and scorching, his scythe sharp, and the grass withered regardless of Juliana's eyes, his "am'rous Care," sorrow, and dashed hopes—these are facts that have not yet intruded on his primary narcissism.

Damon defines his grandiose self by his job, more especially by his tool: the "Sharp... Sythe" (7) with which he discovers more ground than the rival shepherd's flock covers (51–52), in which he admires his image, "As in a crescent Moon the Sun" (57–60), with whose sharpening he tunes his lovelorn sighs (71–72), and with which he mows himself (75–78). Its phallic quality—signaled not only by its shape (cf. "Upon an Eunuch; a Poet," 2), but also by Damon's unabashed pride in it, identification with it, and resort to it when rejected—emphasizes his narcissism. He has founded an ideal self-image on one body part. In selecting presents for Juliana that mirror this grandiose self—the snake of phallic desire, tamed to please her; the equally phallic chameleon, a lizard capable of amazing metamorphoses; and oak leaves sacred to no less than the king of the gods—he hopes that Juliana, like adoring nature, will accept and reflect his inflated self-appraisal. If Juliana had rejected his presents, she would have at least noticed his existence, but she utterly ignores them and him, to Damon's dismay: "Yet Thou ungrateful hast not sought / Nor what they are, nor who them brought." Failing to find his self acknowedged in heterosexual love,[23] he resorts to his original mirror, nature, and to his ideal self as a wielder of a scythe.

Damon's scythe defines him in more than phallic terms: he is a mower like the Grim Reaper, and the last words of "Damon the Mower" are "Death thou art a Mower too." Here and elsewhere, Marvell portrays narcissism as leading to death, often self-inflicted. Either the weakness of the self places it in untenable positions where it can find no place to stand, or its need for reliable mirrors and perfect ideals with which it can merge makes genuine love impossible. Without object love, there can be no self, only retreat into infantile mergers or the terminal self-reflexive act, suicide. Here, after Juliana refuses to mirror his grandiosity, Damon throws himself into frenzied work to compensate for the wound to his narcissism: "thus he threw his Elbow round, / Depopulating all the Ground," and cutting his own ankle. As the victim of his sterile self-reflexiveness, he becomes "the Mower mown." Still, he confidently expects nature's herbs to heal his wound because infantile merger remains a possibility in the pastoral world of "Damon the Mower."

Not so in "The Mower to the Glo-Worms," where passion expels him, as it did the unfortunate lover, from an Edenic world. In the first three stanzas, nature's representatives, the fireflies, minister to Damon and his avatars. As "living Lamps," the fireflies light the studies of the nightingale, whose songs represent the lyrics of poets like Damon.[24] As "Country Comets," instead of warning the exalted world of war and royal deaths, they "presage the Grasses fall," and thus announce Damon's work. As "courteous Lights," they guide wandering mowers, Damon's fellows whom the "foolish Fires" of marsh gas have deluded, safely home. Unlike the ministering fireflies, Juliana has distracted Damon from his essential self as a child of nature.

More like the foolish fires, "She my Mind hath so displac'd," he laments, "That I shall never find my home." By displacing his mind instead of reflecting it, she has rendered the fireflies' courtesy "vain," obscuring the mirror that nature once offered Damon, his true "home."

Damon loses that home forever when he discovers in "The Mower's Song" that nature, like Juliana, has betrayed him. Once, he thought his mind was "the true survey" of the meadows, and he saw his hopes reflected "in the greenness of the grass . . . as in a Glass." Now he sees what his narcissism concealed in "Damon the Mower"—that he may perceive nature as mirroring and ministering to him, but she is indiscriminate. Although sorrow has replaced his hopes, the grass grows "more luxuriant still and fine"; and "gawdy May-games" continue whether or not he leads the fairies. Berating "Unthankful" nature, he gives vent to narcissistic rage.[25] In "Revenge," he vows that "Flow'rs, and Grass, and I and all, / Will in one common Ruine fall"—a Lear-like threat that only threatens him, since his job is to mow the grass anyway. In fact, Damon's job makes him, not nature, the "Unthankful" one: he repays her ministrations by "Depopulating all the Ground."[26]

Dangers to the self and its projections, such as those Damon faces, often produce heightened assertions of grandiosity. A not uncommon response to fears of being unmanned is some such reversal as this: "My prized possession cannot be cut off. It cuts off others'." (Shakespeare comically renders phallic compensation for low status in the opening dialogue of *Romeo and Juliet,* 1.1.1–60.) Damon's pride in his profession seems to stem from this reversed logic, a latent motive that becomes evident only when he feels mown by Juliana. The refrain of his song—"When (For) *Juliana* came (comes), and She / What I do to the Grass, does to My Thoughts and Me"—identifies the cause of his violent cutting: Juliana's cutting of him, both thoughts and self. Of course, his phallic revenge against the meadows (which he implies are male comrades, "Companions" of "fellowship so true") cannot restore the self unmirrored by Juliana and nature, and again we see that the weak self of the narcissist courts death. According to Isaiah (40:6), grass and flesh are one, so Damon's tomb is appropriately adorned with the "Heraldry" of mown grass, a trophy that represents not only his revenge, but also his wound.

Like Damon, the naif in "The Nymph complaining for the death of her Faun" cannot live without a mirror. Betrayed by Sylvio, she forsakes the dangers of heterosexual love and retreats to that haven from which the unfortunate lover is born into the hurricane of passion, her garden, where she nurses and plays with wild Sylvio's tame gift, the pure white fawn. The mutuality of their play, which eases the "Smart" of rejection, teaches the wary nymph to love again. In their game, she says, "it seem'd to bless / Its self in me": its love for her overcomes her reluctance to return its love. "O I cannot be," she admits, "Unkind, t' a Beast that loveth me"—neither ungentle to the fawn, nor unlike it. Each reflects and sustains the other, and their closeness increases as the nymph feeds it milk and sugar. Soon, the soft, white fawn becomes indistinguishable from the soft, white fingers, offering soft, white food, at which it nurses. It even blends into the nymph's garden, lying hidden by its whiteness among the lilies and feeding its reddening lips upon the roses until it might have one day become "Lillies without, Roses within."[27] For its whiteness fostered by the nymph's nurture, the fawn returns to her the redness of her roses by printing them on her lips. Their relationship resembles blissful oral fusion, as the fawn assumes the qualities of the nymph, who feeds it, and of her garden, which it ingests and whose beauty it returns to her in kisses to redden her lips.

As the fragile mirror of the nymph's weak self, which seeks merger with a safe environment, the fawn cannot survive the intrusion of the world outside the garden—the "wanton Troopers riding by" out of the real Civil War into this enacted fantasy of infantile nurture. Its death crushes the nymph, and the white stone of her weeping statue figures the internal deadness the narcissist fears.[28]

But, more than the nymph's fragile mirror, the fawn is her unrealistic ideal: more loving than "false and cruel men," more soft and white than the hands of "any Ladies of the Land," a more perfect offering for the troopers' sin than any "in / The World," and a lover comparable to the Bridegroom of the Canticles (cf. 71–92, Song of Solomon 5–6). Faced with these hyperboles, some readers try to identify the faun in a consistent allegory based on the poem's Biblical and classical allusions. Others read these references as furthering the characterization of a girl who would so excessively idealize her pet. In any case, the narrative of "The Nymph complaining for the death of her Faun" recounts the retreat of the self from heterosexual love to a merger with a mirror and an ideal, and from the loss of these to the coldness of stone.[29]

II

So the self in Marvell's lyrics frequently has nowhere to stand. Marvell, however, distances himself from his narcissistic speakers—from some more than others. Whether or not he ever shared the dangers to selfhood he vividly dramatizes, he finds a vantage point for his self beyond the tangled problems of the squabbling soul and body, Daphnis confused by Chloe's yielding, the lacerated unfortunate lover, lovelorn Damon, and the naive nymph. Play provides a safe locus for the self. Playing with words, syntax, narrative commentary, literary convention, and allusions, Marvell characterizes these narcissists comically. The voice that toys, albeit sympathetically, with threats to selfhood has not succumbed to these threats, because the play frame divides the player's self in two. While one part of the self experiences, the other frames the experience as play, so that even if the experiencing self falls into traps or faces devastating losses, the framing self remains free and whole.[30]

Standing outside the irreconcilable opposition between the soul and body, Marvell invites us to laugh at both, although at the body more than the soul. The soul is a sophisticate. He opens his complaint with an allusion to Romans 7:24, "O wretched man that I am! who shall deliver me from the body of this death?" and its widely known emblem.[31] He speaks in etymological puns ("fetter'd . . . / In Feet"), literalizes metaphors ("Deaf with the drumming of an Ear"), and revels in strings of artfully phrased paradoxes ("I feel, that cannot feel, the pain . . . ," 24–30). Yet his plight—as a character of such wit and refinement enchained in his own "Nerves, and Arteries, and Veins"—is as humorous as pitiful, and the body punctures his pomposity by pointing out that his "wit" has served only "To build me up for Sin so fit." More broadly comic, the body might prefer to be a tree. Except for his parting jab at the soul, his reasoning is full of contradictions, condemning the source of his life for not letting him "rest" in vegetable unconsciousness. The picture of him, longing for brutish lassitude but "stretcht upright," impaled by the soul, himself the "Precipice" down which he would plunge into oblivion, is laughable. Despite man's potentially tragic division between spirit and flesh, Marvell comes to terms with both by playing with the dilemma.

Unlike "A Dialogue between the Soul and Body," in which no narrator speaks, "Daphnis and Chloe" has a narrative frame. From this vantage point, Marvell views the untenable positions of Chloe, betrayed by nature who taught her to be coy, and Daphnis, squirming under Chloe's coquetry. Although Chloe's shock at being overtrumped in the love game by Daphnis is amusing, the gradual revelation of Daphnis's character gives Marvell the greatest scope to play with framed and framing speeches.

In the opening narrative, he characterizes Daphnis, with a witty turn of phrase, as inexperienced in the ways of courtship: "He . . . Knew not that the Fort to gain / Better 'twas the Siege to raise." Still slow on the uptake, Daphnis does not sense Chloe's changed attitude until she tells him; then he tears his "disorder'd Locks" and glares "with rouling Eyes." Warned by the histrionics of his grief, the reader soon hears in Daphnis's farewell speech a false note. In his specious reasons for leaving (XVI–XVII) and the lengths to which he goes to conjure up five witty conceits to support his decision (XVIII–XXII), Daphnis contradicts the narrator's characterization of him in the opening frame as unskilled in the game of love. He is a match for Chloe. In the closing narrative, by recounting Daphnis's subsequent philandering, the narrator confirms what the reader suspects: that Daphnis has not been as devastated by Chloe's double messages as he seemed. As the poet has removed himself into the narrative frame to play with the gradual revelation of Daphnis's sophistication, Daphnis has turned the tables on Chloe to play the sad departing lover in order to play the field.

In descriptive narrative with no persona, Marvell distances himself from the unfortunate lover through play with the outworn conventions of Petrarchan love. Locating themselves at the center of nature, poetic lovers for centuries had called their sighs winds, their tears seas, their passion tempests or flames, and had traded clichés about the shipwreck of love, airy hopes, and hearts devoured by unrequited love. Marvell merely exaggerates and literalizes their metaphors, creating a comic and cosmic emblem that reverses the formulae. Instead of the lover's sighs becoming winds and tears becoming seas, the literalized storm of passion lends the lover water for his tears and wind for his sighs. Marvell further plays with convention by excluding any mention of the beloved and by mocking the lover, so self-absorbed in heroically cuffing the thunder and grappling with the rock. Lacking any object for his love, he seems to "relish" only his own image "drest / In his own Blood."

In some measure, the narcissistic lover transcends the oppositions that kill him by relocating his identity in another order of being, art: "he in Story only rules, / In a Field *Sable* a Lover *Gules*." For persisting in his losing battle, he dies in an odor of perfume like a knight out of Malory, becoming Love's *"Banneret."* Like Damon, emblematized by his tomb adorned with grassy "Heraldry" as "the Mower mown" by love, and like the nymph, sculpted in marble as another Niobe, the lover gains an identity only when he no longer has a self. Marvell, of course, avoids the traps that annihilate his creations because he also, although less destructively, removes himself to another level of reality by playing with their self-absorption.[32]

Poor Damon and the nymph are perhaps Marvell's most endearing creations. He plays with their naiveté, but so sympathetically that the reader enjoys playing at narcissism while smiling at the play with these narcissists. While we empathize with the aggrieved mower, whose self-referential gifts Juliana ignores, we laugh, knowing what Damon does not, that a "fair Shepheardess," or any daughter of Eve, is unlikely to be pleased with a snake, with or without teeth. The image of an innocent rustic bathed in dew, licked by the sun, pampered by flowers and fairies, gazing at his reflection in his scythe, is both lovely and ludicrous. This mixture of comedy and pathos climaxes when, in a Chaplinesque gesture, he mows himself, then allegorizes, rather convincingly, his fall.

Although not broadly comic like Damon, the nymph is characterized somewhat playfully. So innocent in accepting a deer as a surrogate for a male lover, so fragile in responding to a pet's death with her own, and so simple in forgiving its slayers—the nymph seems to be a naif like Damon. Sometimes, however, she does not sound like one. In her diction (*Deodands*), in her puns (*Sylvio/wild* [*silva* = forest], *Faun/Heart*, 33–36), and in allusions comparing the fawn to Christ (23–24) and to the Bridegroom of the Canticles (71–92), the reader hears the voice of the poet behind the nymph's. Toying with her speech, he disengages himself and the reader from her weak self. From this stance, we observe that she loves the fawn primarily because it loves her (43–46), and is ever wary to avoid another narcissistic wound (47–50). Still, she is enchanting. The portraits of her nursing the fawn, of its coy racing style, and of their playing hide-and-seek among the lilies, although slightly precious, entice the reader into the merger they describe. Having outgrown yet still charmed by such child's play, reader and poet can approach but not succumb to it by playing with the nymph's and fawn's play.

The preferred term for Marvell's attitude toward poetic subjects like the nymph is *irony*. But I have deliberately avoided this term in describing his simultaneous engagement and disengagement with the frustrated soul and body, Daphnis and Chloe at cross-purposes, the unfortunate lover, and the doomed naifs, Damon and the nymph. Irony and play share a common structure: both frame messages that redefine themselves. If said ironically, "What a lovely day" redefines itself as "What a terrible day." In play the redefined message is more complex. If said playfully, "What a day to take off your clothes and roll in the grass" may both be and not be a sexual proposition. Although frequently used to describe Marvell's lyrical voice, *irony* seems too limiting a category to define the doubleness of his stance. While the ironic stance distances the poet from what he says or describes, the playing stance gives him greater freedom to stand apart and simultaneously to experience what he represents. An ironic stance toward the nymph would have tended toward ridicule and parody, whereas Marvell's playful stance evokes a more sublte mixture of smiles and empathy.

And Marvell is a subtle player indeed. The doubleness of play not only defends him from the situations that menace his narcissists; it also provides him a way to reintegrate the self. The question of how, precisely, recreation can foster re-creation will redirect our attention toward the potential healing power of play.[33]

III

Adult play revives the protected state of childhood, when caregivers monitor the environment so that children can experiment freely with their capacities and world. As the parent protects the infant's first excursions into the world, the frame of play and the structure of games control the environment for adults so that they are free to regress to archaic modes of thought and to regain something approaching the infant's experience of omnipotence.

In one sense, we are born into a kingdom of play, and reality is always a second home. Even though inner imperatives urge us to grow up and separate from parental protection (our original sin in abandoning Eden), we reluctantly endure our exile. By separating from the source of nurture, the child wins a self, but that self must sustain the burden of living in an unprotected world. It must protect itself. Occasional recreative retreats into play allow the self to relax without risking a return to infantile dependence. Play can also help to re-create the self. Players loosen everyday constraints, try out different roles, and risk freeing repressed impulses—experimenting with ways of being that might change their everyday selves.

This kind of play animates the voices of Marvell's "The Garden" and "Upon Appleton House." The play frame provides these speakers with more than a defensive stance beyond the untenable positions and self-loss threatening the narcissist. Instead of dramatizing the plight of the weak self in the abstract, as in "A Dialogue between the Soul and Body," or portraying a narcissistic persona, like Damon or the nymph, Marvell speaks as an experiencing "I" in "The Garden" and "Upon Appleton House." In recreative reenactments of the journey from primary narcissism to selfhood, he re-creates a whole and more realistic self-representation.

One year after the beheading of Charles I, Lord Thomas Fairfax, once commander in chief of the parliamentary army, retreated from the turmoil of political life to his country estate. He took Marvell with him as tutor to his adolescent daughter and companion in his literary pursuits. Between 1650 and 1653, Marvell shared the leisure and rural isolation of Nun Appleton House and the stimulating presence of a soldier, fellow poet, and translator. Here his poetic genius seems to have flourished, and editors assume that he wrote "The Garden" and "Upon Appleton House" during these years.[34] While the poet enjoyed the companionship of General Fairfax, the speaker of "Upon Appleton House" both idealizes Fairfax's military prowess and moral conscience, and questions his decision to abandon public life. Similarly, while the speaker of "The Garden" enjoys the safety and leisure of pastoral retreat, the garden becomes his ideal and a nurturing environment that mirrors his sense of omnipotence and then disillusions him. As we shall see, both these interchanges—between speaker, patron, and estate, and between speaker and garden—are set apart from the work-a-day world, both replay the emergence of the self from primary narcissism, and both reorient the speakers. We can never define the precise relationship between Andrew Marvell the man and the "I" of "The Garden" and "Upon Appleton House," but we can describe how one aspect of the poetic speaker regresses through an idealization of the "happy Garden-state" and "Heaven's Center" to a merger with nature, and then confronts the limitations of the garden and his patron's world. Meanwhile, another aspect of the poetic speaker wryly observes and plays with his regression, idealization, merger, and disillusionment.[35]

"The Garden" is one of Marvell's most enigmatic poems, prompting scholars to trace its sources in classical poems of Epicurean or Stoic retirement, in the medieval interpretations of God's Book of Nature, in the syncretist philosophies of Renaissance Neoplatonism and Hermeticism, and in the conventions of pastoral poems in general and of garden poems in particular.[36] Although providing the necessary contexts for an informed historical reading of this allusive lyric, these learned source studies do not account for its recreative power.[37] To begin such an account requires separating the inseparable: the speaker's regressive experience of the garden and his play with the experience.

In the two opening stanzas, the speaker abandons the everyday world of ambition, where busy men seek with "uncessant Labours" to win acclaim, symbolized by crowns of "the Palm, the Oke, or Bayes." He enters a garden world of the mind, where the garlands are "repose" and the inhabitants are "quiet" and "Solitude." In stanzas 3 and 4, he rejects the cruelty, fire, and importunity potential in heterosexual passion, preferring instead the love of plants. The speaker has retreated from the world of action and its consequences to an interior realm symbolized by the garden. Once there, he begins to regress, preferring subhuman, vegetative life to humans and the greenness of trees to the red and white in a lady's cheeks. He literally falls in love with the garden.

This regression reanimates two key aspects of infantile experience. First, the speaker begins to idealize the garden, whose perfect bounty and "Innocence" contrast markedly to the "Society . . . all but rude" outside the garden and whose "Beauties . . . exceed" those of all mortal mistresses, even the nymphs chased by gods. Second, the garden—having become, in his comparisons, feminine—mirrors its lover. In the ancient tradition of the *hortus conclusus,* the garden represents the female body, and in the archetypal dream symbolism found by Freud and Jung, it frequently represents, with its womblike enclosure and bountiful food, the mother's body.[38] The speaker describes this body in stanza 4 as not wholly separate from that of its poet-lover. Apollo and Pan, he claims, chased nymphs merely to gain trees, but the trees they gained represent themselves: the laurel and reed symbolizing Apollo's and Pan's deity as gods of poetry. Halfway through the poem, having retreated to interior experience and having regressed from heterosexual passion, the speaker idealizes the garden and perceives it as a feminine mirror.

At the poem's center, the garden's fruits come alive to fulfill the speaker's desires. Luscious grapes crush themselves upon his mouth; fruits, exotic for England's climate, extend themselves into his hands; and a soft bed of grass and flowers cushions, even invites, his fall to the prone position of an infant at the mother's breast. The joy of achieved desire neutralizes any lingering fear of being "Insnar'd" by an engulfing maternal garden. Like the infant cocooned in a nurturing world that meets needs with satisfactions as soon as the infant wills them, Marvell's speaker finds his desires so perfectly mirrored and gratified that he reexperiences the infant's sense of omnipotence. At the same time ("Mean while," he says) as the speaker regresses into a fantasy of perfect physical fulfillment, his mind withdraws into a solipsistic universe like an intrauterine "Ocean" where all things find their "own resemblance." Omnipotent as God, he annihilates all objects separate from himself ("all that's made") and re-creates them in his own image. As the "greenness of the Grass" images his "Hopes" to Damon ("The Mower's Song," 3–4), the "green Thought in a green Shade" of the sojourner in "The Garden" images an ideal world ("Far other Worlds, and other Seas") created out of the speaker's hopes and desires.[39] In psychoanalytic terms, he has repudiated "true objects" and replaced them with "self objects."[40]

As the speaker meditates, the garden has undergone a number of transformations. Beginning as a rural retreat from ambition and passion, it becomes a preferred interior landscape, a representation of the bountiful mother's body, a disembodied mental fulfillment of desire, and finally, in stanza 7, a spiritual state preparative to the joy of heaven. This progressive ascent to ever higher levels of idealization parallels the garden's ever more perfect mirroring of the speaker's desires. When, he muses, "My Soul into the boughs does glide," he merges with the transcendent garden created out of his own omnipotence. Like the preening bird whose shimmering, multicolored plumes reflect "the various Light" above, he approaches divine perfection.

After this climactic relocation of his narcissistic needs onto the garden, stanza 8 drops the speaker with a thud into paradise lost. The "happy Garden-state" existed only in the past and is now lost because of a woman, Eve. In Marvell's lyrics, two related events repeatedly disrupt man's relationship with nature: the arrival of a woman and the intrusion of sexuality. For the unfortunate lover, storms of passion succeed play in the garden with "the Infant Love." Juliana's presence exiles Damon from his "home" as nature's darling. In "The Mower against Gardens," man's quasi-sexual tamperings have turned "willing Nature," which "does to all dispence / . . . Innocence," into a "*Seraglio*": he has taught the flowers to "paint" like alluring women, grafted "Forbidden mixtures" by dealing like a pander between illicit lovers, and created "adult'rate fruit" and "Eunuchs." Either the bounty and nurture of a feminine nature has betrayed man, or man has defiled nature. Here and elsewhere Marvell's lyrics reenact the disillusionment a male child typically experiences in his mother. The boy's demand for a perfect mirror and ideal are so unrealistic that the mother must fail; and later when she becomes the focus of his early sexuality, his prohibited desires projected onto her, coupled with her sexual bond to his father, taint her image as the near divine presence in his world (cf.

"The Mower against Gardens," 35–40). These early experiences of betrayal and taint in the source of nurture and protection may become unbearable. To preserve his ideal, the child, as in fairy tales, or the adult, as in "The Gallery," may split his perception of women in two: the devouring witch and the bountiful goddess—or, as in "The Garden," the woman who first betrayed man in a garden and the nurturing garden herself.[41]

The speaker of "The Garden" projects his disillusionment with the feminine—the child's inevitable disappointment with the source of nurture—onto one representative woman. Eve bears the blame for mankind's loss of that "Place so pure, and sweet." Although disillusioned, the speaker is not devastated. Frustration within tolerable limits leads him in the final stanza to a more realistic perspective not only on the garden, but also on life outside its safe confines.

No longer merged with an ideal garden of the mind, the speaker stands apart, contemplating an English formal garden, planted by a "skilful Gardner" with real "flow'rs and herbes." Confronted with an object beyond his supposed omnipotence, the speaker describes the garden, for the first time, as an actual place. The gardener's skill reminds the speaker of work—now, however, redeemed by his garden experience. Instead of retreating from "uncessant Labours. . . . In busie Companies of Men" and regressing into merger with an interior timeless world, now he images work in "th' industrious Bee," who lives separate from, but in harmony with, the natural world subject to time. Although his final exclamation is poignant, it realistically acknowledges that "such sweet and wholsome Hours" as he has experienced are unavailable outside the world of "herbs and flow'rs." The speaker ends his mental perambulation through the garden knowing that the world outside is not ideal, that it seldom mirrors and gratifies desire, but that work within time and nature is possible.

So far in this partial analysis, the speaker's stay in the garden has evoked a protected space and time, permitting a controlled regression to unrealistic idealizations, to mirroring by a nurturing environment, to infantile omnipotence, and to archaic fantasies of merger. Frustration of these narcissistic needs has resulted in a more realistic perception of objects and a potential for work. If, however, this description were exhaustive, "The Garden" would be a somber case history, not a whimsical, ambiguous lyric. Such a description is obviously incomplete because it ignores the poem's tone. Marvell frames "The Garden" as play, not a clinical report.

Within this safe frame, the speaker regresses in his modes of thinking as well as in the content of his thoughts. He relaxes the logical processes and univocality that dominate adult communication—what Freud called secondary process thought. And he allows flashes of the illogical, ambiguous, imagistic thinking predominant in dreams, psychoses, and childhood—what

Freud called primary process thought—to break through to conscious expression in wordplay and fluid associations that produce comical reversals and odd juxtapositions.[42] So the speaker of "The Garden," by framing his experience as play and thereby separating an observing self from an experiencing self, gives the impression of putting the reader on. He puns freely, concretizes metaphors, blurs levels of discourse, and toys with his literary heritage, with philosophy, and even with theology.

From the opening stanza, we begin to wonder if the speaker is serious. Does he really believe that ambitious men, who compete for the palm, oak, and bays, want shade for their brows, so that he can tempt them with a whole garden full of trees in place of the "narrow verged Shade" of their crowns? In stanza 3, should we believe that he actually prefers trees to pretty girls, and might he carve on a favorite tree "A. M. loves OAK"? By the time we reach stanza 4, we smile at his rewritten mythology, in which lusty gods intend all along to get trees by chasing nymphs. And finally at midpoem, the plight of the helpless speaker assaulted by aggressive and amorous fruit is laughable indeed. All the while the participating aspect of the speaker regresses into an infantile relationship with the garden, the observing aspect frames his regression by illogic, exaggeration, and humor as not quite real.

In the garden of regression, words just will not stand still. From its second word (*vainly,* meaning both "unsuccessfully" and "in a conceited manner"), the poem erupts into a riot of puns. In the first stanza alone, the speaker puns on *amaze* (both "bewilder" and "trap in a maze," such as those often found in seventeenth-century mannerist gardens), *single* (both "individual" and "unmated"), *Toyles* (both "labors" and "snares"), *upbraid* (both "reproach" and "plait together"), and *close* (both "come together" and "embrace"), not to mention later, key puns on *rude, heat, race, curious,* and other words.[43] The semantic univocality of secondary process thought, with which we order our world by keeping concepts separate, has yielded to the language play of primary process thought, in which infinite metamorphoses of objects, concepts, and words are possible.

Nor will levels of reality remain distinct in "The Garden." The speaker mixes symbols (leafy crowns representing achievement) with physical reality (shade from trees) in a process that Rosalie Colie has aptly labeled "unmetaphoring."[44] Instead of carving an inscription to proclaim his love, the speaker considers carving an inscription on his beloved, thereby conflating the symbolic representation of his love with its object, besides threatening his beloved with bodily harm. Similarly, the gods who chase nymphs to get trees also get symbols of themselves, the laurel of Apollonian poetry and the reed of Pan's pastoral songs. But are we to understand the speaker's version of the myths as stories about gods loving plants, one kind of metamorphosis, or about the sublimation of passion into art, another kind of metamorphosis? The speaker has so blurred planes of being that immortal gods chase "mortal Beauty" intending to get physical trees, or symbols of the immortal poetry associated with the gods themselves, or both.

Psychotics, who are trapped in archaic modes of thought, and children, who have not yet matured to the logic of secondary process thought, frequently "unmetaphor" symbolic communications in this manner, but so do joke tellers, who choose to regress temporarily to primary process thinking. Like the joker, the speaker of "The Garden" safely and deliberately regresses to illogical juxtapositions and language play at the same time as he regresses into experiencing the garden as a mirror and ideal. His puns and odd conflations help frame the regressive experience, making it play, not psychosis.

With subtlety and sophistication, the speaker also plays with literary conventions, philosophical doctrines, and theological dogma. Deeply imbued with classical, medieval, and Renaissance culture, Marvell packs his lyrics with allusions, playing with a vast cultural heritage, as three examples will illustrate. By falling in love with the garden and sensually enjoying her favors as a lover as well as an infant, the speaker parodies the genre of libertine garden poems that exalt the naturalness of promiscuous sexuality, a genre with classical antecedents, popular among Marvell's French and English contemporaries.[45] By preferring to live in paradise alone, the speaker plays with both the Neoplatonic doctrine that primal man was a hermaphrodite and with the Biblical story of Eve's creation.[46] Appealing to Renaissance syncretic thought and the tradition of medieval antifeminism, he inverts Christian dogma, exclaiming about the one-person garden, "What other Help could yet be meet!" Since God Himself, seeing Adam alone in Eden, said, "It is not good that the man should be alone; I will make him an help meet for him" (Gen. 2:18), the speaker of "The Garden" is playing fast and loose with holy writ.

In the final stanza, as the speaker's participating self returns from his interior landscape to a real English garden, the observing self also abandons his play in the gardens of French libertine poetry, in the classical golden age, in the Biblical paradise, and in the metamorphic world of primary process thought. Drawn by a "skilful" worker, this real garden is a "Dial," a clock that "works" by replicating the orderliness of cosmic time-keeping, and in which "th' industrious Bee / Computes its time."[47] In detail and diction, the last stanza returns to the logic and order of secondary process thought, as the speaker ends his regression by describing the garden as a place outside the self.

Throughout "The Garden" the willing reader has journeyed with the speaker through interior levels of labyrinthine complexity. Both retire to an enclosed garden of the mind defended by illogic, exaggeration, and humor, which protect a regression into a narcissistic search for mirrors and ideals. Thus defended, both can reintegrate the self in the freedom of playful regression and return.

Marvell's healing sojourn in the garden may not be a case study, but it anticipates with remarkable precision the twentieth century's prescription for the self at risk, the play of psychoanalysis. Although it is a serious and often painful technique for dissolving and reforming the self on a new basis, psychoanalysis structurally resembles play—as Gregory Bateson, D. W. Winnicott, Heinz Kohut, and others have observed.[48] It is part monologue, part verbal interchange between analysand and analyst within the limited time and space of the fifty-minute session in the analyst's office. The analysand establishes with the analyst an intense relationship called transference, in which infantile mental states reemerge, repressed needs and conflicts are freed, and the analysand relates to the analyst out of these past needs, conflicts, and ways of thinking. The analysand feels real and intense emotions, but simultaneously, for the analysis to be successful, s/he must stand with the analyst outside of the experience. With the help of the analyst, the adult, seeing self tries to understand the emotions of the infantile, feeling self and to strengthen the mature self in its mastery over the infantile self.[49] Hence the analysand experiences emotions as both real and not real. Framing all communications within the safe walls and time limit of the analytic appointment, protected from any real consequences by the analyst's rules of confidentiality and nonintervention, the successful analysand plays out needs, fears, and conflicts—all the time observing the play.

More specifically for narcissistic analysands, whose selves are fragmented or weak, the play generally follows this pattern: in the transference relationship, the analysand perceives the analyst as a mirror and/or ideal, and the analyst inevitably fails to measure up. Safely contained as psychoanalytic play, infantile grandiosity and idealizations are gradually transformed into more realistic internal structures. Without either analyst or fees, however, the speaker of "The Garden" also finds an empathetic, idealized object that in the end fails to be perfect.[50] During his rural, meditative retreat—as in the urban "talking cure"—the mirrors, ideals, and frustrations of childhood resurface and yield, through play, to a mature sense of self and world.

IV

The experiencing "I" of "Upon Appleton House" also plays to reintegrate his self. The opening praise of Fairfax's modest home (I–X) announces the playful tone; it is queer praise that conflates levels of reality, describes fantastical metamorphoses, marks humorous incongruities, and transforms the ordinary into the marvelous. The foreign architect's vaulted brain becomes the blueprint for his proud houses that "arch the Brows" of gazers; here the distinctions between maker, thing made, and observer blur. In another confusion of levels, humans become inanimate objects in the

"Frontispice of Poor" and *"Furniture of Friends"* at Appleton House. Contrariwise, the inanimate house comes alive, metamorphosing from square to sphere to accommodate its master. The comic incongruity of winds getting lost in hollow palaces contrasts to the neat congruity between tortoises and their shells—a natural "fit" made to seem marvelous because seventeenth-century craftsmen carved such delicate and intricate "cases . . . of Tortoise-shell." These witty tricks, while ushering the reader into the Appleton estate, also lead him into the play that frames the whole poem.

Although "Upon Appleton House" follows in an impressive line of country house poems, employs Neoplatonic and Hermetic doctrines, hints at events of the Civil War, and alludes to many rich traditions that Marvell knew, the speaker does not sink under the weight of his learning or the burden of history.[51] The poem becomes a playground where Marvell juggles and juxtaposes elements of his culture, its modes of perceiving reality, and the events of its recent past in apparent helter-skelter fashion. Out of this confusion comes a new order, and out of this recreation comes a re-created self, in a process parallel to the speaker's journey through "The Garden": retreat in search of mirrors and ideals with which to merge, and return to a more realistically perceived world. Play, this time within the bounds of the Fairfax estate, both frees and contains the regression to archaic fantasies and ways of thinking.

The poem recounts a series of retreats. In his first words, the speaker invites the reader to enter "Within this sober Frame," Fairfax's humble house. Soon, however, the house expands to the spacious estate through which speaker and reader wander, a stroll toward yet more retreats that metamorphose into expansions, proving the paradox "Things greater are in less contain'd" (VI). The garden fort hints at its owner's retreat from military duties, but it expands toward heaven, because in pastoral seclusion Fairfax also tends "*Conscience*, that Heaven-nursed Plant" that adorns the "Crowns of Saints" (XLV). Beyond the floral *"Bastions"* lies the threatening ambition of prelates, from which the speaker, like his master, retreats further to the meadows (XLVI). Again his retreat expands—into an abyss of grass and into a reenactment of the Biblical exodus and flood and of the English Civil War. From this chaos, he retires once more, taking "Sanctuary in the Wood" (LXI), which in turn opens before him a vision of time from the ancient past ("What *Rome, Greece, Palestine,* ere said") to the future ("Out of these scatter'd *Sibyls* Leaves / Strange *Prophecies* my Phancy weaves") (LXXIII). Perhaps the final "Let's in" is one more expansion, but that is to anticipate a lengthy argument.

In any case, these retreats open toward new possibilities. Safely contained, impulses once repressed now bubble up, restrictions against infantile thinking relax, and the self may dissolve to reconstitute itself anew. Since players stand aside watching themselves play, the dissolution prerequisite to reintegration need not threaten self-loss.

Quite the contrary, everywhere the speaker of "Upon Appleton House" turns in his mental perambulation of the estate, he finds mirrors for the self. Fairfax's house accurately measures his moral stature in its humble design, and his garden embodies his profession. The "Pure, Sweet, Streight, and Fair" Maria, Fairfax's daughter and Marvell's pupil, perfects the estate, which then reflects and returns her perfections: the pure river gives her a looking glass; the sweet meadows, a carpet; the straight woods, a screen for her modesty; and the fair garden, a floral crown (LXXXVII–LXXXVIII).

But unfailing mirrors that ignore intransigent reality may stifle the self. The male voice of Maria's tutor uses the interpolated tale of her ancestor Isabella Thwaites, at least in part, as a warning against such mirrors. The anti-Catholic portrait of the nunnery, of course, ridicules religious retreat, but the episode supports the patriarchal as well as the Protestant elements of the poem's ideology. A place where women, apart from the world of men, work with other women would pose a threat to patriarchal culture. So, in the nun's enticement of Isabella, the speaker portrays the cloistered life as a narcissist's paradise, where infantile fantasies of grandiosity can come true:

> I see the *Angels* in a Crown
> On you the Lillies show'ring down:
> And round about you Glory breaks,
> That something more then humane speaks. (XVIII)

The nuns would mirror Isabella throughout Christendom, using her visage as their model for the stitched images of saints, even the Virgin, that will adorn a thousand shrines (XVII). Once a nun, she might keep Fairfax, the general's heroic ancestor, as her *"Devoto,"* not husband, an adoring worshipper who would reflect her beauty in constant praise (XIX). Thus she might sidestep her obligation to enter history, to bear the son who will continue the Fairfax lineage. Instead of sharing her bed with a man, her opposite, she would have each night a lovely female partner. These matched pearls need never look beyond their reflection in each other's sex to the familial and national destiny that requires their participation (XXIV).

Of course, the nun's persuasion is an ideologically charged negative example intended to point toward Maria's proper role in the world of generation and time. What if, instead of bearing "Offspring fierce," some women working with other women engaged history with no less "Valour" than the Fairfax warriors (XXXI)? That possibility is beyond the ideological vision of the poem. As portrayed by Maria's tutor, the mirrors "the *Suttle Nunns*" offer her ancestor are mere temptations to girlish vanity. Instead of fostering the growth of a realistic self, the nuns would intentionally stunt Isabella, seducing her with childish fantasies in order to devour her estate. Like the devouring maternal cormorants of "The unfortunate Lover," they almost succeed in engulfing her: "The *Nuns* smooth Tongue has suckt her in" (XXV).

Although distancing himself from these treacherous mirrors by the humor of the nun's self-damnation in her precious and sensuous persuasion, the speaker seeks his own reflection in Fairfax's estate. The search is necessary because—having left the protective enclosures of the house, which so neatly fits its master; of its history, in which a valiant hero purges it of corruption perceived as feminine; and of its fortress garden aimed against ambition—the speaker plunges into a phantasmagoric world in which anything can become anything else.[52] "The Abbyss . . . / Of that unfathomable Grass" is wholly unpredictable. Men become dwarfish insects, while giant grasshoppers squeak and laugh at them from precipices of grass (XLVII). As in the ocean's depths, men lose their sense of autonomous motion, and may lose their lives as well (XLVIII). Humility provides no protection from the massacres of mowing or war (L, LII). Although the mowing begins as a neotypological account of the Israelites' exodus and wandering in the desert, soon inconsistent but tantalizing hints about Charles's execution, Civil War battlefields, pillaging, and Leveller agitation complicate the picture.

If this physical, moral, and historical confusion were not enough, levels of reality blur, and widely disparate perspectives succeed each other with dizzying speed. The mowers' greedy cook, Thestylis, always on the lookout for a meal, even subsumes her creator, the poet, by responding to his words, which speak the fiction of her reality (LI). A river drowns itself so that boats sail over bridges and fish climb stables (LIX–LX). And the speaker looks at cattle from a bewildering variety of angles: as if they were in an epic poem's description of a painting or in a looking glass, as if they were moles on faces, fleas before being viewed through a microscope, or constellations perhaps seen through a telescope (LVII–LVIII). Ontologically disoriented, the speaker envisions an uncreated world—the earth an empty blankness, like a canvas or a bull ring, yet threatened by future "stain" and violent death (LVI). Where in this spreading chaos and destruction can the self find a place to stand? One kind of creature metamorphoses into another, events of recent and ancient history jostle randomly, and the ways to make meaning make none.

A psychoanalyst might describe the state of the speaker's self in the meadow and flood sequences as disintegrated, lacking "object constancy," lost in the morass of primary process thought that overwhelms the psychotic.[53] Of course, the speaker is not truly mad; like Hamlet, he is "but mad north-north-west" (2.2.396). Since he is playing in the grassy and watery abyss, he enjoys his regression to archaic modes of thought, and sports with these grotesqueries. Although he ventures beyond the protective house and gardens, the boundaries of the estate contain the meadows. Within this physical enclosure, the speaker makes sense of his bizarre experience of the metamorphic meadow and flood by framing it as a masque, a "Scene that turns with Engines strange" (XLIX). Even the potential terror in the mowers' massacre and the flood's chaos turns into a mere quibble, as the "careless Victors play, / Dancing the Triumphs of the Hay"—hay as both mown grass and a country dance (LIV).[54]

Threatened with disintegration but defended by play, the speaker seeks to strengthen himself by merging with a strong, nurturing environment. Retreating to the "double Wood" joined like the *"Pedigrees"* of Fairfax and his wife (LXII), the speaker finds there loving married couples—the stock doves whose sad song contrasts to their nuptial bliss (LXVI)—and careful parents—the "hatching *Thrastles,"* the heron who entrusts its eldest to the estate's paternal lord (LXVII), and the hewell who fells trees to feed its young (LXVIII-LXX).[55] The speaker feels protected once again by the presence of Lord and Lady Fairfax, and his poetic avatar, the nightingale, sings, confident that the wood will respond appreciatively to her song:

> But highest Oakes stoop down to hear,
> And listning Elders prick the Ear.
> The Thorn, lest it should hurt her, draws
> Within the Skin its shrunken claws. (LXV)

Perhaps the speaker's own "Elders" of the *"Fairfacian Oak,"* the general and his wife, will similarly appreciate this poem and other "Tryals of [his] Voice."

Since the wood so gratifyingly acknowledges poetic self-display, and since its inhabitants so carefully nurture their young, the speaker gradually becomes one with these caretakers: "little now to make me, wants / Or of the *Fowles,* or of the *Plants*" (LXXI). He calls himself an inverted tree, discourses with rapturously attentive birds, and reads history and prophecy in the scattered leaves. In response, leaves, caterpillars, and ivy come alive, like the maternal fruits of "The Garden," to dress him as their *"Prelate,"* while mossy banks offer him rest and the winds cool his brow and refresh his mind (LXXI–LXXV). This progression toward merger with the wood reawakens infantile fantasies of power. Safely "incamp'd" behind the trees, he disdains fear and boasts about the world beyond the wood, "But I on it securely play, / And gaul its Horsemen all the Day" (LXXVI). Earlier, as his imagination wandered through the meadow, he played with the world's assaults in witty allusions to the Civil War; now he acknowledges that he plays for defense.

So necessary is this defense that he begs for a more secure oneness with the wood—to be chained, staked down, even crucified, "That," he says, "I may never leave this Place" (LXXVII–LXXVIII). The hysterical tone, however, and his queer self-characterization as half Christ, half tied-up animal identify this passage as whimsy. Here the speaker openly voices his longing for protection because his play defends him against real self-loss in merger. By playing at having "courteous *Briars* nail [him] through," he can both experience merger with the wood and smile at his experience.

Thus defended, the speaker begins to reintegrate his self. Confused and dispersed by the fantasies arising from the mowers' carnage and the flood, he recollects himself in the sylvan retreat. Despite his pleas, however, he does not remain fettered to the safe wood. Surveying the "newly washt" meadows, he finds in the river, now returned to its banks, a mirror that reflects his emerging self. The river, meadow, and sun have been restored to a loving mutuality after the flood:

> See in what wanton harmless folds
> It [the river] ev'ry where the Meadow holds;
> And its [the river's or the Meadow's?] yet muddy back doth lick,
> Till as a *Chrystal Mirrour* slick;
> Where all things gaze themselves, and doubt
> If they be in it or without.
> And for his shade which therein shines,
> *Narcissus* like, the *Sun* too pines. (LXXX)

At least momentarily, the ambiguous referent of *its* makes the reader wonder what holds and licks what, thereby adding to the portrait of mutual harmony between river and meadow. This portrait is enhanced as "all things" find themselves reflected in the river, and as the sun, like Narcissus, gazes at its image in the water. Instead of threatening dispersal, the river now offers the speaker the same nurture that it offers the banks and the same mirror that it offers the sun. He eagerly responds by donning marsh grass, balancing himself over the water on willow roots and branches, and becoming a river bank—"Abandoning [his] lazy Side, / Stretcht as a Bank unto the Tide" (LXXXI)—to be held, licked, and mirrored.[56]

This recumbent, infantile posture holds him no longer than did his imagined bondage to the nurturing woods. Upon the entrance of his pupil Maria, he hastens to put away all childish things—not just "such Toyes" as "Hooks . . . Quills / And Angles, idle Utensils," but also his blurring of boundaries between self and other, his need for perfect nurture and mirroring, and his regression into the metamorphoses of primary process thought. As her tutor, he is in part responsible for nurturing her, teaching and leading her into adulthood. In the secondary process thought that orders adult consciousness, boundaries between self and other do not usually blur, as they do in the speaker's woodland retreat, and fluid metamorphoses, such as he describes in the meadow and flood, are constrained. As the entrance of Maria signals the return of mature vision to her tutor, his perception of nature alters.

What was "loose" now seems to "recollect" itself in her presence, and her arrival summons evening, as does the halcyon, which "benum[s]" nature with "an horror calm and dumb," which makes the air "viscous," and which compacts the "gellying Stream" where shadows and fish are fixed "As *Flies* in *Chrystal* overt'ane." To the awed speaker, the world seems hushed, and "*Nature* is wholly *vitrifi'd*" (LXXXIII–LXXXVI). As objects become rigid, suddenly and clearly he recognizes boundaries that blurred during his regressive experience of the meadow and flood and during his merger with the wood and river.[57] As he startles from his infantile orientation to nature, the spreading darkness and fixity signal a death of sorts, a loss of childhood as he enters the world in which we never really feel at home. Although primary process thought can be terrifying, we only reluctantly outgrow grandiose desires to metamorphose objects at will.

What the speaker gains in compensation for his loss is a more realistic self that can lead him out of pastoral retreat into history. He finds a mirror and careful nurture in the Appleton estate to help reconstitute his self, then leaves them behind as remnants of childhood. Similarly, he idealizes General Fairfax and his estate, then considers their imperfections. The opening stanzas of the poem, amidst their playfulness, name Fairfax "the *Master* great," a modern saint to whose humble home "the after Age / Shall hither come in *Pilgrimage*" (V, VII). In the historical interlude, his ancestor rescues Isabella Thwaites from the corrupt nuns to become the progenitor of "the great Race" that produced the conquering general himself (XXXI). And while describing the floral fort, the speaker praises the general's weeding ambition and tilling conscience as preludes to gaining a saintly crown (XLV).

But during his mental rambles, the speaker progressively qualifies this idealization of Fairfax and his ancestors. Despite possessing masculine prowess and "the lawful Form," the elder Fairfax looks as silly as the dithering nuns when he mounts an armed attack against women defending their treasure with wailing, *"Wooden Saints,"* an "old *Holy-Water Brush,"* and ineffectual mutterings over *"Beads"* (XXXII). He was right to think "Small Honour would be in the Storm" (XXX)—small dignity as well. Also his descendant, Marvell's patron, appears less than perfect when he, who might have restored England to its proper place as "Garden of the World" (XLI), relegates that "Pow'r which the Ocean might command" to "five imaginary Forts" of flowers (XLIV). The speaker's view of the general is neither simple idealization nor simple disillusionment, but a maturing awareness both of his honorableness, in preferring *"Conscience"* to breaking a treaty and invading Scotland, and of his willingness to sacrifice public need to private scruples. For all his personal integrity in retreating from the corrupting reality of politics and war—broken covenants, pillaging after victories, Leveller rebellion in the ranks, even regicide—he cannot prevent these realities from impinging on life. They intrude into his own home in his employee's playful reveries about mowing and woodpeckers.[58]

Although aware of the general's imperfection and of the tumult and death that have trespassed on Nun Appleton's borders, the speaker has not lost his ideals. At the end of the poem, he relocates them onto Maria, who has been "In a *Domestick Heaven* nurst" (LXXXXI) not only by Fairfax and his wife, but also by her tutor. He may characterize himself as a "trifling Youth" hiding his "Toyes" at her appearance; nevertheless, he, at least in part, instills in her the ascending scale of values for which he praises her: from natural beauty, to the acquired beauty of conversing in "all the Languages," to the *"Wisdome"* beneath the words, to the divinity that generates the wisdom (LXXXIX). Perhaps his praise is, in its exaggeration, a playful lesson to his pupil as well. In any case, the "Maria" of the poem carries with her a part of him. She is his internal ideal projected onto his patron's daughter, not the external ideal, the strong warrior and his Edenic estate, to which the poem is dedicated. Earlier the speaker sought merger with Fairfax's wood and reflection in his river in order to strengthen a self weakened by the violence and confusion of history. Now he praises a self that he has helped foster and that can thrive beyond a protective family circle.

Like the speaker, Maria must grow beyond a world of self-reflections. Although the brook offers her "a Glass . . . / Where *She* may all *her* Beautyes look," the wood accedes to her modesty and "about *her* draws a Skreen" (LXXXVIII). Nor will she, her tutor predicts (and perhaps exhorts), succumb to vanity, as do others of her "fond Sex that on your Face / Do all your useless Study place" (LXXXXII). Instead of gazing at her "Graces" in mirrors, she spends them and "Supplies beyond her *Sex* the *Line*" (LXXXXIII) of Fairfax descendants in "the great Race" (XXXI). Unlike the nun who would lead Isabella Thwaites into a narcissist's paradise of static mirrors for her beauty, the tutor would lead his ideal "Maria" away from the flattering glass into the contingencies of history. And by leading her, he leads himself from temporary regression into maturity.

The speaker describes Maria's, and thus in part his own, entrance into history as a severance: "The *Priest* shall cut the sacred Bud" of mistletoe from the *"Fairfacian Oak"* (LXXXXIII). As earlier he experiences the renunciation of childish fantasies as a deathlike numbness, here he images growth into adult responsibilities as a wound of separation. To face the fallen world, the "rude heap together hurl'd" beyond Nun Appleton's borders, the speaker and his young charge will carry with them an image of a sustaining and idealized past spent in *"Nature's Lap. / And Paradice's only Map."* Still, for all its "decent Order tame," Nun Appleton "contains the same" harsh stuff as the rude world—"Gulfes, Deserts, Precipices, Stone"—and it is only a map of Paradise (LXXXXVI). Like the sojourner in "The Garden," the speaker ends

"Upon Appleton House" with a more realistic vision of his pastoral retreat. He feels a sense of loss, but he knows that the estate never was Eden.

The tone and imagery of the last stanza suggest how the speaker will face life outside this protective enclosure: he will take it with him. Out of the play of mind and memory while gazing on the scene of approaching evening, the speaker finds an image for his *modus vivendi.* Observing the *"Salmon-Fishers"* carrying *"Leathern Boats"* on their heads, chuckling over their resemblance to "*Antipodes* in Shoes" and to the "dark *Hemisphere*" above his head, and perhaps remembering his earlier witticism about the neat fit between the tortoise and its house, the speaker calls men *"Tortoise* like . . . rational *Amphibii."* These final images remind the reader of life's mutability and confusion: darkness follows daylight, salmon swim upstream, fishermen go on land as well as water, people on the far side of the world do things upside down. Still, humans must live and work within flux and reversals. And these images of movement under rounded coverings—fishermen carrying boats, upside-down people wearing shoes on their heads, the speaker encircled by the darkening sky—picture how they may live: tortoiselike. Humans can separate from their original, protective environment because they have incorporated it as part of themselves. Like a tortoise who carries his home with him, the speaker now carries with him into the world of time and chance the integrated self he has gained through his relationship with Nun Appleton and its master. In the slippery playfulness of the last lines, Marvell pictures both the impermanent, perplexing world beyond safe nurture and the self defended but versatile enough to maneuver through life's unpredictability. His parting "Let's in" is only a prelude to one more expansion—this time into history.

V

Here, in the world of flesh and time, the speakers of "To his Coy Mistress" and "An Horatian Ode upon Cromwel's Return from Ireland" take their precarious stands. The voices of these poems do not play to escape untenable positions, as does the speaker of "A Dialogue between the Soul and Body"; they do not play with narcissistic personae like Damon or the nymph; they do not retreat to pastoral worlds in order to reconstitute the self in play. Thrust into history, the lover of a reluctant lady and the praiser of a ruthless conqueror confront time's primal realities: sex and power. These poems are no less playful than Marvell's other lyrics, yet their play neither defends nor helps to reintegrate the self. Their speakers engage history's vicissitudes agonistically with little hope of victory, but with a glint in their eyes.

Their confrontations with sex and power are not blunted by attempts to find mirrors or to merge with ideals of absolute perfection. In fantasizing eons of praise for his coy mistress, the lover twits her narcissism; and in prophesying their inevitable future, he holds up a glass reflecting the grisly reality of her appearance in the grave. The citizen laces his accolades of Cromwell's "Courage," strength, "wiser Art," and restraint with pointed references to the general's violence against "his own Side," his ruination of "Justice" and "antient Rights," Charles's noble death, the Irish massacres, and the uncertain future of a man who lives by the sword. Flattering mirrors will not preserve the lovers from dust and ashes, and Cromwell, imperfectly just, can only depend on the vagaries of power and fate.

Both speakers see traps in time and history. If the lover deliciously cultivates his "vegetable Love" for ages, he and his beloved will merely "languish in [Time's] slow-chapt pow'r"; if they, "like am'rous birds of prey, / Rather at once [their] Time devour," their "sweetness" will still be relished by "Worms." Their option is not eat or be eaten, but eat and be eaten anyway.[59] Similarly, the speaker of "An Horatian Ode" portrays Charles as an ideal king only at the moment when he is unkinged (53–64), and Cromwell as "the Wars and Fortunes Son" whom war and fate may destroy. Not only did Cromwell inflict more pain than any Civil War general, but he also sustained more: "What Field of all the Civil Wars, / Where his were not the deepest Scars?" Fate may impel him toward further conquests as Caesar to Gaul or Hannibal to Italy, but also toward indefatigable marching with "Sword erect" until "greater Spirits come," also impelled by fate, to replace him.[60] Since Charles's nobility is impotent, and Cromwell's potency is less than noble and also uncertain, allegiance to either side leaves the speaker without the assured sustenance of a perfect ideal.

Still, the lover and the citizen do not lose their selves in these no-win situations. Unlike the stalemate in "A Dialogue between the Soul and Body," the eternal frustration in "The Definition of Love," or the intolerable alternations that rend "The unfortunate Lover," the predicaments in "To his Coy Mistress" and "An Horatian Ode" do not leave their speakers unable to accommodate the demands of the body in time. Whereas the dialogue silences the whole self, the definition prohibits physical love as a threat to time and space, and the unfortunate lover only rules outside of time in story, the lover of a coy lady and the supporter of Cromwell face dilemmas and make choices with consequences in time. The lover realizes that he cannot have eternal, ideal love, and the citizen realizes that he cannot have an ideal leader, but both can have something, perhaps enough, before time eats them or a greater power arises. (Such honest appraisals of reality are what analysts hope their narcissistic patients can gain.[61])

The lover chooses to "tear our Pleasures with rough strife, / Thorough the Iron gates of Life," and the citizen chooses to support a man as violent as "the three-fork'd Lightning, first / Breaking the Clouds where it was nurst." They see their choices as violent births that shatter enclosures. Retreat—either to exotic *otium* "by the *Indian Ganges* side" or homely complaints "by the Tide / Of

Humber"—cannot appeal to this lover, as it has to so many of Marvell's pastoral characters threatened by passion.[62] For the headstrong lover, as well as the "restless *Cromwel*," "To inclose / Is more then to oppose." Both speakers counsel emergence from "private Gardens" of courtship, poetry, or husbandry, in full knowledge that the birth of the self into history is violent and death is inevitable.

Neither removed from time by abstractions and pastoral fictions, nor distanced by a naive persona, nor enclosed in a garden, the speakers of "To his Coy Mistress" and "An Horatian Ode" describe life as sport. The lover invites his mistress to "sport us while we may," to roll their life "into one Ball," and to run a chariot race against the sun. In contrast to Charles, "the *Royal Actor*," who creates a "memorable Scene" and "memorable Hour" to preserve his image in a drama outside of time, Cromwell is a sportsman who wages agons in time. He "wove a Net" to catch Charles (49–52), tames the Irish (73–74), hunts the Scots (109–112), and becomes the tame falcon "in the *Republick's* hand," who hunts, then submits to the "lure" of the falconer (81–96).[63] All these sports are as violent as the births that make them necessary. Born into time, the self can confront history's contingencies, impose a measure of order on its unpredictability, and make a place for itself by perceiving life as an agon. While they sport themselves, the lovers and the warrior live in time's trials, accepting victory and defeat, but simultaneously an aspect of them stands apart, freely choosing to enter the struggle, observing the play, and ordering history by imposing upon its vicissitudes an agonistic structure.

Moreover, each speaker approaches his subject in the ludic spirit; he frames his utterance as play, displaying a wit versatile enough to counter threats to the self until death wins. The lover mocks the posturing of courtly love, speculates jokingly about the privacy of graves as trysting spots, and gleefully proposes to speed up time. He will live in time that will eat him, and he will play with that life to craft a self for as long as he can. The citizen begins his poem with the contrary counsel to forsake poetry, deflates exalted praise of Cromwell with smiling understatement (27–28), describes the befuddled king as chasing himself into a trap (51–52), has the massacred Irish praising their conqueror (73–80), and puns at the expense of the treacherous Scots (105–108). The speaker's barbed wit spares no one—neither self, general, king, nor enemy. Whereas in "Upon Appleton House" he encamps his mind behind a tree, galling the world's horsemen with defensive play, here he engages history's uncertainties without the security of a perfect ideal. He takes sides with Cromwell and yet plays with that engagement to stand as a separate self.

VI

The apparent division in Marvell's poetry between lyrics and satires may lead readers to assume that the earlier poems do not engage the issues of his turbulent times. And we have, so far, approached them as play with the perils and processes of individual self-formation. But in these poems the contradictory experiences of early life image a cultural as well as individual separation.[64]

Medieval thought embedded man in his universe—a microcosm to the macrocosm, whose humours paralleled the elements, whose divine intellect could read *"Natures mystick Book,"* whose commonwealth ascended hierarchically and was to be cultivated like a garden. In the seventeenth century this vision, which had lingered in the commonplaces of English Renaissance literature, dimmed. Calvinist theology and skeptical fideism distanced sinful man from an inscrutable God. Baconian empiricism and Cartesian dualism separated man from the nature he was to observe objectively. Machiavellian and Hobbesian political theory uprooted the state from its organic myth and toppled the ladder leading from king to God. Confronted with a waning myth that could no longer support identity, Marvell reframed his identity as a ludic self, and this frame offered his culture (especially select and fit readers like perhaps General Fairfax) a perspective on their relation to nature and on the conflicts that troubled them.

Traditional cultures define themselves and their members by erecting structures and borders. But they also need ways to negotiate with what these limits exclude—historical process, proximate cultures, competing modes of vision, and so forth. Marginal figures, like the ubiquitous fool and trickster, who elude structural definition often accomplish these mediations by playing out the two sides of the conflict. A modern example, with surprising relevance to Marvell's England, illustrates how fool's play can help a culture both sustain and cross its boundaries.

One evening around a fire, a group of Sinai Bedouins complain about the young American vagabonds who sunbathe nude, urinate, and perform sexual acts publicly on the nearby beaches. The Bedouins, however, sell the youths strong tobacco as hashish and the famous "Arab hospitality" in a jerry-built village constructed for the purpose. Although disdaining the Americans, the Bedouins profit from them, and the conversation soon turns to malaise over how these decadent, alien ways have tainted Bedouin culture, vitiating their identity. Spontaneously, a man who owns several huts in the fake village and whom his companions call the "fool," begins an exaggerated, comic performance mocking the vagabonds' methods of urination (the Bedouins urinate squatting to avoid pollution) and sexual foreplay (these Arabs court in poetry and song, barely embracing in intercourse). After his play, which the spectators enjoy, the malaise dissipates and the audience disperses for evening prayers.

In this episode, the play of the fool, a liminal figure who stands socially in between the Bedouins and the Americans, accomplishes two, much needed mediations for himself and his society. First, by mocking alien decadence, he calls attention to the differences between the two cultures. By playing an American, he shows that, even though he has assumed American ways enough to mimic them, he is not after all an American; the Bedouin self remains whole and untainted as it frames the mimicking self. Second, his play allows him and his audience to sustain their profitable relations with the Americans without losing their identity. They need neither separate totally to avoid taint, nor feel submerged in western decadence, because such play as the fool's maintains their awareness of cultural identity despite their proximity to and commercial relations with the Americans. In such instances of cultural conflict, the play of liminal figures, who participate in two realities, allows players and spectators to make and comprehend metacommunicative statements (communications about how to take communications) about their predicaments. Thus they gain a measure of perspective while living within the conflict.[65]

What this illustrative fool does for his culture, Marvell did for his.[66] Both negotiate conflicts at the borders of their cultures, but they perform their mediations differently. Whereas the Bedouin fool plays with the alien and new, thereby preserving his culture's old identity while allowing it to engage alien newness (a more conservative folly), Marvell plays with the myths of the old vision, thereby loosening but not separating his reader's identity from the structures of medieval thought (a more radical folly). For example, by playing at merger, he fosters an awareness of separation. When his speakers comically yield to the importunity of amorous fruit or become the *"Prelate of the Grove"* licked and clasped by ivy; when they wittily conflate levels of reality so that a river is the snake that it, by flooding, breeds; when they blur perspectives so that cattle resemble facial moles, then fleas prepared for magnification, then stars seen through telescopes ("Upon Appleton House," LXXIV, LXXIX, LVIII)—the reader realizes that man is not wholly one with nature. Paradoxically, play in which infinite metamorphoses are possible reveals that the analogical principle, which structured medieval cosmology, has limits. Everything is not part of a single whole, and infinite analogies are not possible. The nymph may describe her fawn as one with the garden, "Lillies without, Roses within," but Marvell is playing with the nymph. From his play, the reader gains a perspective of disengagement, but not alienation from the natural world. An era that was beginning to substitute a modern scientific view of lilies and roses for medieval sacramentalism would need a ludic self to mediate this clash, thereby allowing a reader to have his lilies and roses both ways in play and to achieve a perspective on the conflict.[67]

Marvell plays with man's relationship not only to nature, but also to spirit and politics. "A Dialogue between the Soul and Body" does not answer the vexed theological question of how to reconcile spirit and flesh, but it does offer the reader a playful stance that prevents paralysis between mutually contradictory halves of the self. In "An Horatian Ode," the opposing claims of Cromwell's fated strength and of the "Justice" and "antient Rights" of Charles do not daunt the speaker. His play shows the reader a way to make choices in history while sustaining a perspective on conflicting alternatives. Literary historians frequently classify Marvell as a transitional poet who sums up the traditions of the Renaissance and points toward the satire of the Augustan age.[68] In a small way, his lyric play may have smoothed the transition, helping his readers endure and understand their separation from a world that had seen nature, spirit, and the state as parts of a divinely ordered whole.

In his panegyrics and satires, Marvell does not assume the playful stance that makes his lyrics so enigmatic. Adopting the ludic self can be a defense because players, in their doubleness, are so slippery that one is never quite sure where they stand. The panegyrist and the satirist, however, take a firm stand at some distance from their material in order to praise the virtue one would foster or to expose the folly and vice the other would eliminate. They want the reader to know their position so that s/he may stand with them on the single side of truth, not in the double frame of play. In "Tom May's Death," Marvell proclaims the duty of the public poet in the face of ignominious wavering:

> When the Sword glitters ore the Judges head,
> And fear has Coward Churchmen silenced,
> Then is the Poets time, 'tis then he drawes,
> And single fights forsaken Vertues cause. (63–66)

In "The First Anniversary of the Government under O. C.," he plans a Miltonic career of fighting for virtue, even against foreign kings:

> If gracious Heaven to my Life give length,
> Leisure to Time, and to my Weakness Strength,
> Then shall I once with graver Accents shake
> Your Regal sloth, and your long Slumbers wake. (119–22)

And in "The last Instructions to a Painter," he compares the satirist to a peasant leading a king lost in his own country (959–60). Although Marvell exercises wit, humor, and irony in his satires (and to a lesser degree in his panegyrics), and although his loyalties may shift from poem to poem as the political situation changes, his public voice does not project the ludic self. To fight for virtue, shake foreign kings, or lead one's own requires, within each individual poem, a single, committed stance, not a double, playing stance.[69]

In his last years as part of a controversy with the Anglican Samuel Parker over freedom of conscience, Marvell printed on the title page of the second part of *The Rehearsal Transpros'd* this quotation from a letter he had received: "If thou darest to Print or Publish any Lie or Libel against Doctor *Parker*, By the Eternal God I will cut thy Throat." Directly beneath the threat, Marvell signed his pamphlet, more rancorous and personal than the anonymous first part, "Answered by Andrew Marvel."[70] Forsaking anonymity, he stood forth publicly. Although some may feel that his ludic self produced better poetry, his committed self became a dutiful parliamentarian, courageous defender of religious self-determination, and outspoken critic of government by "Drunkards, Pimps, and Fools" ("Last Instructions," 12).

7

Robert Burton's Play Therapy for a Melancholy Age

Neither Donne nor Herbert nor Marvell published his poetry (with the exception, regrettable to Donne, of his "Anniversaries"). Although Marvell intended his occasional satires for public consumption, these poets shared their lyrics, if at all, only with friends and patrons such as the Countess of Bedford, Nicholas Ferrar, and Sir Thomas Fairfax. The voices in these poems are personal; the ludic selves they present perform their sleight-of-hand tricks as if in an elegant drawing room, a companion's apartments, or a private closet reserved for meditation. In words carefully chosen to signify much in little, in symbols resonant with meaning, and in subtleties of tone that hinge on the least variation of syntax, these poets paint an inner landscape, albeit in a social context, amenable to vision from a psychoanalytic angle.

By contrast, Robert Burton and Sir Thomas Browne wrote popular prose works in numerous editions: Burton expanded *The Anatomy of Melancholy* five times before he died, and Browne saw nine authorized editions of *Religio Medici*. Although forced by a pirated edition to publish these reflections, which were originally written for a small group of colleagues, Browne deliberately addressed the educated reading public in *Pseudodoxia Epidemica*, which ran through six editions in his lifetime. Burton and Browne presented their works to unknown readers—lots of them.[1] Both men engage issues of general interest, not the particularities of personal experience; their common medium is open-ended, discursive prose, not brief lyric; and their aim is as often expository and didactic as expressive. As a result, the selves presented in these prose texts reveal less about individual inner landscapes than do the selves presented in Donne's, Herbert's, and Marvell's lyrics. These prose voices may, however, reveal more about the binds facing their contemporaries.

To establish a relationship with the reader, Burton and Browne assume personae and offer their readers a role or roles to play in relation to the voice of the text.[2] Since their works became so popular so quickly, these authors must have modeled in their personae and offered to their readers roles for the self that seventeenth-century readers could imaginatively adopt. The average reader between 1620 and 1660—faced with economic and social dislocation, religious dissention, political revolution, even regicide—might have felt that s/he lived in a world like the one described in Burton's anatomy, where "horses ride in a coach, men draw it; dogs devour their masters; towers build masons; children rule; old men go to school; women wear the breeches; sheep demolish towns, devour men . . . the world turned upside downward!"[3] To define the stances amid this confusion that Burton and Browne assume and offer to their readers is the goal of the next two chapters.

I

Burton's *Anatomy of Melancholy* is itself a confusing book. Writing for over twenty years, interlarding new material throughout each of five editions, even leaving additions for a posthumous edition, Burton apologized for presenting a book in disarray. Without editorial assistance, he claims, he was "enforced, as a bear doth her whelps, to bring forth this confused lump; I had not time to lick it into form, as she doth her young ones, but even so to publish it as it was first written . . . in an extemporean style . . . out of a confused company of notes, and writ with as small deliberation as I do ordinarily speak" (1:31). Burton had plenty of time but little inclination for corrections, preferring to add rather than to revise (1:33).

In response to this *copia,* modern readers have both faulted him for an almost comic inability to organize his material and praised him for his efforts to contain the universal confusion through art. Some have tried to find order in the results of Burton's scholarly fiddling by defining his book as a scientific treatise on mental illness—either in the tradition of Renaissance psychology or as a precursor of modern psychoanalytic theory—and as an anatomy of England's social, political, economic, and religious ills. Others argue that Burton deliberately confuses the reader in order to model in his persona the symptoms of the disease he is anatomizing or to distract both melancholy author and reader from their disease. Still other readers account for Burton's heterogeneity by placing *The Anatomy* in the Renaissance tradition of paradoxy, or by comparing it to that quintessential humanist institution, the research library, or by describing Burton's persona as a "cosmic personality" who seeks to gain insight into a rapidly changing world by embracing all the possibilities of human variety.[4]

The confusion of *The Anatomy* mirrors the confusion of the late Renaissance, especially its proliferation of "authorities" in the print explosion that multiplied contradictions and fostered epistemological relativism. But, instead of yielding to skepticism or gloom, Burton's characteristic response to this crisis of knowledge was to play. According to Mihai Spariosu, in his survey of the play concept from the pre-Socratics to the postmoderns, Burton's response to an era of "axiological relativism" is not unique. Whenever "implicit governing assumptions begin to lose their authority and undergo a crisis," as "at the end of the Middle Ages and the beginning of the Renaissance, or at the end of the Baroque and the dawn of the Age of Reason," then "the play concept . . . comes again to the foreground of Western consciousness." In such periods of transition, thinkers often cope with "cognitive nihilism" by constructing texts as playgrounds, where ideas collide in play that can produce new and interesting combinations.[5] Burton did just this: he wrote his vast treatise on melancholy "by being busy to avoid melancholy," and called it a "playing labour" (1:20).

Few readers know quite what to make of Burton's playfulness. Those who emphasize his serious objectives tend to deemphasize, for example, the positively gleeful tone with which he conjures up curative lies to tell a female sufferer from love melancholy about her *inamorato:* "That he is an hermaphrodite, an eunuch . . . his mother was a witch, his father hanged, that he hath a wolf in his bosom, a sore leg, he is a leper . . . he cannot hold his water . . . will stab his bed-fellow . . . his house is haunted with spirits . . ." (3:201). Less interested in cure than in a flight of fancy, Burton is having great fun in this comparatively short example of his justly famous catalogues of comic abuse. Some readers do see Burton at play in his scholarly anatomizing. One calls his book an "enormous labyrinthine joke," others praise him for failing at his serious purpose and entertaining the reader with "delightful irrelevance" instead, and at least one reader feels himself, while reading, becoming Burton's "plaything."[6]

Although these critics respond to Burton's antics, they too often dismiss this aspect of the book, as if, having labeled it play, no more need be said. Burton's play is, however, serious business. In the midst of confusion engendered by change, play gives the melancholy scholar a point of vantage for truth. It also offers the reader an experience in a kind of fertile disorder that can give birth to new ways of seeing.

Burton seems to take quite seriously his task to structure his inherently confusing subject, universal melancholy. Repeatedly acknowledging the difficulties of his quest, he nevertheless girds himself in the armor of a hero and goes forth to subdue his subject to order and method. Facing the "labyrinth of accidental causes" of melancholy, he laments, "the farther I wander, the more intricate I find the passage . . . and new causes as so many by-paths offer themselves to be discussed. To search out all, were an Herculean work, and fitter for Theseus; I will follow mine intended thread" (1:357). Although

"The tower of Babel never yielded such confusion of tongues, as the chaos of melancholy doth variety of symptoms," he resolves doggedly that "howsoever they be diverse, intricate, and hard to be confined, I will adventure yet in such a vast confusion and generality to bring them into some order; and so descend to particulars" (1:397). As a scholarly Hercules, Theseus, or hero of Biblical stature, he battles the chaos. If he can just define, arrange, even diagram the causes, symptoms, and previous cures of melancholy, he seems to feel, then a final cure will be in sight. He mounts a two-pronged attack: inclusion and division.

First, he tries to cover everything remotely relevant to his subject, all arranged in proper partitions, sections, members, and subsections. In three partitions of over 1,300 pages, he nearly succeeds. Even though melancholy Dr. Johnson liked *The Anatomy* so much that he arose early to read it, he might have reserved his comment about *Paradise Lost* for Burton's tome: "None ever wished it longer than it is."[7] Whether citing "preparatives and purgers" or "remedies against discontents," Burton aims at inclusiveness. No matter that he finds "a vast chaos of medicines, a confusion of receipts and magistrals, amongst writers, appropriated to this disease," he promises, "some of the chiefest I will rehearse" (2:238–39). No matter that he has centuries of consolations of philosophy to survey, he "will epitomize and briefly insert some of their divine precepts, reducing their voluminous and vast treatises to my small scale" (2:126). Often his subsections resemble gigantic lists. Nor are his listing tendencies exercised only in the more "scientific" parts; his *consolatio* resembles an encyclopedia where, for example, the victim of slander can find the words of wisdom appropriate to his particular mental anguish, "Doth the moon care for the barking of a dog?" (2:201). Presumably, the melancholiac is to thumb through the section, find the precept for him, and be consoled.

Despite his unflagging industry, Burton fears that maximum inclusiveness and precise arrangement are impossible; anyway, they do not really order the chaos. After fifty pages detailing the symptoms of love melancholy, he throws in the towel: "But I conclude there is no end of love's symptoms, 'tis a bottomless pit. Love is subject to no dimensions; not to be surveyed by any art or engine" (3:184). At times he mocks his own method. He ends his digest of consolations with a jumbled collection of proverbs reminiscent of Polonius's contradictory advice to Laertes: "as a fox on the ice, take heed whom you trust. Live not beyond thy means. Give cheerfully.... Admire not thyself.... Undervalue not thyself.... Love others, to be beloved thyself" (2:204–205). Originally an oral form, the proverb gains its piquancy from a particular context of human interaction. Thus a list of proverbs for all occasions will sooner bore than console the reader. Besides, a truly inclusive list is impossible. Not even Burton can include a remedy for every reader's discontent, and he knows it. With comic self-irony that undercuts the preceding eighty pages of "remedies against discontents," he ends his list of proverbs with instructions to "Look for more in Isocrates, Seneca, Plutarch, Epictetus, etc., and for defect, consult with cheese-trenchers and painted cloths" (2:205). Burton realizes that advice, his included, is as cheap and efficacious as tawdry trinkets with pithy morals.

Elsewhere he begins to make precise lists of list makers of good counsel, then becomes impatient with exactitude and hastily rattles off some of their advice. To avoid jealousy "Patricius prescribes four rules to be observed in choosing of a wife (which whoso will may read); Fonseca the Spaniard... sets down six special cautions for men, four for women; Sam. Neander... five for men, five for women; Anthony Guevara many good lessons; Cleobulus two alone, others otherwise; as first to make a good choice in marriage, to invite Christ to their wedding..." (3:300; cf. 3:410). Although some order has been brought to what matters least, the advice givers and the numbers of their precepts, the sufferer finds what he most needs, the curative advice itself, tumbled out in a heap. The whole performance is a comical demonstration of the limits of achieving order through inclusiveness.

The second prong of Burton's attack on chaos is division. The aim of Ramistic dialectic was to find truth and make it evident by dividing a subject into a hierarchy of dichotomies, and then judging one of the opposed arguments true and the other false. Generally, Ramists assumed, the orderly arrangement of axioms would be sufficient to reveal truth, but when doubts arose, they used syllogisms. Introducing each partition with an enormous Ramistic diagram, Burton sets out to pursue this method. But soon categories multiply from two dichotomies to nine subclasses, explanations of sub-subclasses become so copious as to fill in the space that should visually separate elements in an outline (compare 1:126 to 3:2), and digressions from the structure of the treatise intrude into the outline of the structure.[8]

More importantly, when he turns from the prefatory diagrams to the treatise proper, Burton seldom judges between the legion of dichotomies that he assiduously arranges for the reader. Within one representative excerpt of thirteen pages, the reader is spun around by at least five reversals. He reads that "hot countries are most troubled with melancholy" (1:237), but "Cold air in the other extreme is almost as bad" (239); that desert places choke their inhabitants with sand (238); but populous cities choke them with the putrefaction of carrion in the streets (240); that immoderate exercise is "a most forcible cause of melancholy," but "Nothing begets [melancholy] sooner... than idleness" (242); that solitary wretches degenerate from men to beasts (248–49), but those who seek company in taverns become dissolute (246); that "a melancholy man cannot sleep overmuch... yet in some cases sleep may do more harm than good" (249). What can a reader in search of practical advice about how to avoid melancholy learn from these dichotomies?

In presenting such an array of extremes, Burton seems to advocate moderation. But he does not tell his panting reader what precisely the golden mean in any given case is, because, as he confesses, he does not know: "The extremes being both bad, the medium is to be kept, which cannot easily be determined" (2:34).[9] Since the medium is, in fact, undetermined throughout the treatise, the bewildered reader never learns for sure whether poverty is "a blessed estate" or "a severe torture" (1:346; cf. 2:154–63); whether hawking is to be condemned as the fruits of idleness (2:70) or pursued as "exercise rectified" (2:72); whether study (2:89–93), music (2:116–19), and merry company (2:124) are causes of melancholy or cures; whether antimony is a medicine or a poison (2:227–28); whether fasting produces melancholy hallucinations or divine ecstasy (3:343); or even what side of the seventeenth-century controversies over cosmology Burton takes (2:48–60).[10]

Unable either to find the mean between extremes or to use Ramistic dialectic successfully to judge between opposed sides of a dichotomy, Burton pursues method without obtaining its intended results. Sometimes, his subject resists method entirely because melancholy cannot be divided. "It is a hard matter," he complains, "to distinguish these three species [melancholy proceding from the head, from the whole body, from the hypochondries] one from the other, to express their several causes, symptoms, cures, being that they are so often confounded amongst themselves, having such affinity that they can scarce be discerned by the most accurate physicians, and so often intermixed with other diseases that the best experienced have been plunged" (1:176). No series of dichotomies can order this mess.

Other times, method, despite its neat arrangements, does not prevent Burton from blatantly contradicting himself. One minute he agrees that "Those jealous Italians do very ill to lock up their wives" (3:293); the next he advises, "Virtuous women should keep house; and 'twas well performed and ordered by the Greeks, '*Mulier ne qua in publicum / Spectandam se sine arbitro praebeat viro*' [That a woman should not show herself in public unaccompanied by her husband]" (3:307). One minute he admits, "we bachelors desire to be married" (3:217); the next he recants, "farewell wiving for my part" (3:218). He even introduces his consolation compiled of the wisdom of the ages with the self-defeating claim that melancholy men reject "obsolete sentences and familiar sayings" (2:127), and, although he confesses to being impolitic, he delivers a tirade against physicians in a section advising the melancholiac to seek physic (2:207–12).

Neither prong of Burton's attack on chaos achieves order. Inclusiveness is impossible and tends, despite all attempts at arrangement, to produce jumbles not much different from the original chaos to be ordered. Division, admittedly a hopeless task from the beginning, produces either contradictions or dichotomies with no resolution. A key reason that Burton's attack seems doomed is the self-referentiality of the endeavor, which continually entangles him in paradoxes. After proving humankind to be "a company of brain-sick dizzards," he asks the reader, "are they fools? I refer it to you, though you be likewise fools and madmen yourselves, and I as mad to ask the question" (1:72). If, however, "all the world is melancholy, or mad, dotes, and every member of it" (1:120), then who has the sanity to perform the much needed anatomy of the world's folly? Not the author, or his persona, Democritus Jr., by his own admission. Even if a sane anatomist could be found, readers would be blinded by their folly. So the whole communication process is undermined, and Burton's Democritus Jr. is in the same position as Erasmus's Folly: if their characterizations of themselves as mad are true, then what they say about madness is also madness and therefore untrustworthy.[11] With these self-referential speakers, the assumption of their truthfulness leads to the probability of their falsity.

Such paradoxes are man's lot as a creature with a soul and understanding. As for the soul, Burton quotes approvingly, "'We can understand all things by her, but what she is we cannot apprehend'" (1:154); as for the understanding, it "is a power of the soul, by which we perceive, know, remember, and judge . . . a reflecting action, by which it judgeth of his own doings and examines them" (1:165). Here Burton shows himself keenly aware of the limitations of human self-consciousness: we may examine ourselves, but the only lens we have is also ourselves, and our ability to examine ourselves is what we examine when we examine our humanity. No wonder that Burton's subject, the universal melancholy that he shares, creates so many interlinked paradoxes.

In the seventeenth century, man as a self-conscious creature was assumed to possess a soul, producing consciousness, and a body, connected to the soul through the spirits. Because of this double nature, disturbances in man's soul cause bodily suffering, but this effect in turn becomes itself a cause, afflicting the soul with mental anguish that produces further physiological degeneration and so forth in the kinds of seemingly endless feedback loops that Burton so often describes: sorrow is "'the mother and daughter of melancholy, her epitome, symptom, and chief cause'; as Hippocrates hath it, they beget one another, and tread in a ring, for sorrow is both cause and symptom of this disease" (1:259). Because such paradoxes are inevitable in a creature of flesh and spirit, Burton's goal of accurate classification of causes and symptoms is a chimera, and he puzzles over the task: "In such obscurity, therefore, variety and confused mixture of symptoms, causes, how difficult a thing is it to treat of several kinds apart" (1:177). He is not, however, daunted; he tries to comprehend the confusion by apparently participating in it.

Recognizing that he is trapped in the paradox of human nature, Burton deliberately communicates to the reader in paradoxes. Perturbed by the tangle of melancholy causality and apparently unperturbed by his own illogic, he asserts that "every one [of the causes of melancholy] is more grievous than other" (1:250). This paradox makes sense as exaggeration, emphasizing the seriousness of the disease. The reader must merely think paradoxically to comprehend the meaning. But when Burton gives paradoxical orders to the reader that require response, the reader must perform two contradictory actions simultaneously—a neat trick. Having repeatedly assumed that his reader is a melancholiac who is reading this treatise on melancholy to comprehend and cure his disease (for example, 1:176), Burton nevertheless warns, "I would advise him that is actually melancholy not to read this tract of Symptoms, lest he disquiet or make himself for a time worse, and more melancholy than he was before" (1:388; cf. 1:38).[12] Here Burton presents his reader with a conundrum like the man who says, "Don't listen to me." By speaking, he asks to be heard, but the message of his speech contradicts the fact that he is speaking. Likewise, Burton's injunction not to read part of his book conflicts with the nature of the book, a treatise written to teach the melancholy world about its disease.

Caught in the paradox of being warned not to read a book written for him to read, the reader may wonder if Burton is serious or simply playing with him by posing such puzzles. Plagued by confusion in his struggle to order chaos, why would Burton want to confuse his afflicted reader? Perhaps the answer lies in the special qualities of play. More than once Burton describes his serious intent (his "labour" and "quest") as play or sport. After soaring over the universe in his "Digression of Air," he draws himself back to earth with another paradox: "But my melancholy spaniel's quest, my game, is sprung, and I must suddenly come down and follow" (2:61). His "game" is melancholy, the disease he seeks to understand. His "spaniel" may be the kind suited to hunt melancholy, as a coon dog is suited to hunt coons. But the syntax also suggests that the spaniel is itself melancholy. So both the quester and the quest are melancholy—precisely the paradoxical situation in which Burton finds himself while writing *The Anatomy.* He describes this quest as a hunt, a recreation, a "playing labour." And play becomes for Burton a more effective method than Ramistic dialectic for bagging his game. When attacked head-on, melancholy eludes definition by scattering into confusing paradoxes, but perhaps it can be approached obliquely by using its own methods. Fight paradox with paradox.

Play is paradoxical because players are never what or where they are. Play creates self-referential paradoxes (the punch that says, "This is not a punch"), and it locates players in a double position as actors and definers of their actions. So, if the world, seventeenth-century England, seems to present contradictions around every corner, if the subject, universal melancholy, seems so vast that inclusiveness is impossible, so mixed that division only produces conflicting dichotomies with no middle ground, if, in short, Burton seeks to contain the melancholy that contains everyone, then he must find a place to stand outside his world, his affliction, and self-referential paradoxes. Play, as Marvell's lyrics demonstrate, can provide that precarious stance—for a little while. By playing with the colliding worldviews that contributed to Jacobean melancholy, with the irreconcilable dichotomies into which melancholy divides itself, and with deliberate paradoxes, Burton finds a point of vantage outside the mad world, all the while participating in its madness. The part of Burton that frames his play stands aloof, while the other part plays the fool among the rest of the fools. Only in play does he achieve the prospect that he so often seeks (2:34–35, 68–69) and that he imaginatively experiences while soaring above the mad world in the "Digression of Air."

The answer to the question of why Burton, himself afflicted by the confusion he is trying to comprehend, would puzzle his similarly afflicted reader with paradoxes is that, if he can engage the reader in play, then the reader too can find a stance outside the world of conflicting economic, social, political, religious, and intellectual agendas. If a melancholy reader can smile when the symptomology section of the book on melancholy that he is reading says, "Don't read this section on symptomology," then at least for the moment his symptoms may vanish. By yielding to the paradoxes of Burton's play, the reader of *The Anatomy* can escape other paradoxes that afflict him, much as the victim of a double bind can temporarily escape from the double communications that assault him by answering in play, which presents the binder with a double response.[13]

II

Burton, of course, has been at play all along—even while he pursued his two-pronged attack on chaos. In his instructions to look for more proverbs on cheese trenchers and in his hurried list of list makers, he mocks his method of inclusion. In exaggerating the divisions of Ramistic diagrams so as to make his own diagrams virtually unreadable, in refusing to decide between opposed positions, and in contradicting his assertions within a page or two, Burton at times seems to parody logical dialectic. These more subtle examples only hint at the magnitude of Burton's play that fills *The Anatomy* with role play, jokes, and the scholarly play of the virtuoso.

The first words of his preface announce that Burton's book is a stage and he, the player: "Gentle Reader, I presume thou wilt be very inquisitive to know what antic or personate actor this is, that so insolently intrudes upon this common theatre to the world's view" (1:15). In the *theatrum mundi* trope the world is a stage, and roles change constantly, so sometimes Burton recasts his show. The audience to his book takes its place with all mankind as actors on a global stage, and he steps down from the boards to become "A mere spectator of other men's fortunes and adventures, and how they act their parts, which methinks are diversely presented unto me, as from a common theatre or scene" (1:18).[14] As either actor or audience, he sustains a certain distance from the folly enacted by his persona on stage in the text or by the mad world he surveys.

Burton's most sustained role, which has attracted considerable critical attention, is Democritus Jr.[15] In a long preface, Burton plays the seventeenth-century heir to the ancient Greek scientist, Democritus, whom Hippocrates found one day in a garden anatomizing animals to find the seat of melancholy. Behind this mask, Burton plans to satirize the world's madness freely despite readers' censures: even though "some will object, too phantastical," he "will presume to answer . . . 'Tis not I, but Democritus, *Democritus dixit:* you must consider what it is to speak in one's own or another's person . . . and what liberty those old satirists have had" (1:121). Even though Burton drops almost entirely the pose of Democritus Jr. after his satirical preface, he retains his position above criticism by speaking through others' voices. After condemning (while claiming not to) the "pride, envy, inconstancy, weakness, malice, self-will, lightness, insatiable lust, jealousy" (3:214) of women, he professes personally to honor them. For his tirade, "Let Simonides, Mantuan, Platina, Peter Aretine, and such women-haters bear the blame, if aught be said amiss; I have not writ a tenth of that which might be urged out of them and others" (3:216). Although apparently submerged in his satirical personae or the whole libraries of authorities he quotes, Burton finds a vantage from which to view human folly. So what if the voices he uses come from a melancholy scholar and a bunch of woman haters, men hopelessly mired in the melancholy world? The author is above the voice he adopts. Here Burton plays for defense.

Elsewhere, he plays for demonstration. By taking the role of the melancholiac seized by his madness, Burton portrays the symptoms of the disease he is anatomizing. At the end of the preface, anticipating readers' criticisms, he dismisses them petulantly: "I care not. I owe thee nothing (reader), I look for no favour at thy hands, I am independent, I fear not." Then immediately, he relents: "No, I recant, I will not, I care, I fear, I confess my fault, acknowledge a great offence. . . . I have overshot myself, I have spoken foolishly, rashly, unadvisedly, absurdly, I have anatomized mine own folly. . . . I have had a raving fit, a phantastical fit . . . I have insulted over most kind of men, abused some, offended others, wronged myself" (1:122). The touchiness, irascibility, vacillations, guilt, and self-absorption of the melancholiac are amply demonstrated in this performance. But so long as Burton plays the role of melancholy man, and so long as the reader plays along, neither will be overwhelmed by melancholy. A part of them stands outside of the roles they play.

Having dropped the mask of Democritus Jr. after the preface, Burton is free to play whatever role will demonstrate his point. One reason he so often contradicts himself is that he does not just discuss, for example, the merits of marriage or bachelorhood; he takes on each viewpoint as an absorbing role while he presents it. To consider the purgative powers of tobacco, he at first plays the advocate, then, within a sentence, becomes the righteous condemner.

> Tobacco, divine, rare, superexcellent tobacco, which goes far beyond all the panaceas, potable gold, and philosophers' stones, a sovereign remedy to all diseases. A good vomit, I confess, a virtuous herb, if it be well qualified, opportunely taken, and medicinally used; but as it is commonly abused by most men, which take it as tinkers do ale, 'tis a plague, a mischief, a violent purger of goods, land, health; hellish, devilish, and damned tobacco, the ruin and overthrow of body and soul. (2:228)

Burton does not merely make two points: that tobacco is a good purge, but addiction to it is expensive. He dramatizes two characters: the tobacco user, who extravagantly extolls its curative powers, and the Puritan, who rails against its use as sin. What appears at first to be a contradiction—"Tobacco, divine.... damned tobacco"—is just Burton at play.

Often, as in the following characterization of a jealous husband watching his wife and another man, Burton slides almost imperceptibly from third-person description to first-person enactment: "his eye is never off hers... accurately observing on whom she looks... still inquiring, maundering, gazing, listening, affrighted with every small object; why did she smile, why did she pity him, commend him? why did she drink twice to such a man? why did she offer to kiss, to dance? etc.; a whore, a whore, an arrant whore" (3:281). Burton moves from observing the jealous husband at a distance, to voicing as his own the questions that torment the husband, and finally to accusing the innocent wife with all the vehemence and irrationality of the sufferer of pathological jealousy.

The anatomy of love melancholy offers Burton his widest range of roles to play. Introducing this third partition, he promises to become a veritable one-man show: "I am resolved... boldly to show myself in this common stage, and in this tragi-comedy of love to act several parts, some satirically, some comically, some in a mixed tone, as the subject I have in hand gives occasion, and present scene shall require" (3:10). He is versatile enough to include in his repertoire not only the jealous husband, but also the doting lover who sees no beauty but his beloved's: "Diana was not to be compared to her... nor any goddess. Thetis' feet were as bright as silver... Minerva wise, Venus fair; but what of this? Dainty, come thou to me" (3:156). Burton's role play, however, goes beyond this trick of adopting the voice of the melancholy lover whom he sets out to describe.

In a member on "artificial allurements," for example, he becomes so engrossed in poetic descriptions of provocations to lust that he must pull himself up short: "But to leave all these phantastical raptures, I'll prosecute my intended theme" (3:92). Soon, however, he is beguiled again by quoted descriptions of kisses and foreplay; again, he must draw himself back to the work at hand: "But what have I to do with this? That which I aim at, is to show you the progress of this burning lust" (3:112). In these self-admonitions, Burton catches himself succumbing to the temptation to proliferate the poetry and anecdotes that ornament his treatise, just as the lover succumbs to the adornments of *femmes fatales*. Burton writes on "artificial allurements" in the role of his subject, the victim of artificial allurements. Playing a role that creates yet another self-referential paradox, Burton again offers his readers a vantage point for viewing the folly in which author and reader participate. He who plays at falling to temptation has not completely fallen.

As often as Burton plays a role, he plays a joke. Much of *The Anatomy* is written tongue-in-cheek, but the reader is sometimes unsure whether or not Burton is joking.[16] Are we supposed to laugh when we come to the last line of a preface of over one hundred pages and read, "I will begin" (1:123)? Are we supposed to be getting a joke when, after reading Burton's enormous list of foods that may cause melancholy, we discover there is little left to eat? Is Burton smiling ruefully at his daunting task when he lists, among examples of "superfluous industry" that cause melancholy, writing books of physic, and then wonders, "To what end are such great tomes? why do we spend so many years in their studies?" (1:366). Finally, in the following passage, do we not detect in his sly tone that Burton's primary goal is not to illustrate or even to elicit marvel at exotic ways, but to spark laughter (at the expense of the Other—orientals, blacks, women)?

> The Turks have I know not how many black, deformed eunuchs (for the white serve for other ministries) . . . sent commonly from Egypt, deprived in their childhood of all their privities, and brought up in the seraglio at Constantinople to keep their wives: which are so penned up they may not confer with any living man, or converse with younger women, have a cucumber or carrot sent into them for their diet, but sliced, for fear, etc., and so live and are left alone to their unchaste thoughts all the days of their lives. (3:284)

Even though we cannot be sure that such passages as these are intended to be funny, in other spots the context provides clues for interpreting Burton's play. The part of *The Anatomy* that seems to have engaged his imagination the least is the section on "Physic which cureth with Medicines." It consists mainly of recipes for cathartic simples, herbal alteratives, cordials, soporifics, and so forth. But toward the end of his tedious lists, Burton quotes the most comical remedies—bizarre even to the seventeenth-century mind: to induce sleep, "'anoint the soles of the feet with the fat of a dormouse, the teeth with ear-wax of a dog'" (2:252); to draw forth wind, "Put a pair of bellows' end into a clyster pipe, and applying it into the fundament, open the bowels" (2:260). As Burton approaches the end of his second partition, he seems to despair of evaluating the efficacy of these cures, and instead he begins to play with physic: he includes the bellows cure because it is "a strange remedy," and another peculiar recipe to cure dotage, containing spiced brains from a chaste ram, "for the rareness of it" (2:260, 248).[17] By ending a section devoted to earnest science on a playful note, Burton undermines or, at least, reframes what has gone before. Since he lists hundreds of remedies with little evaluation, each seems as useful as the next and all as curative as dormouse fat.

Burton uses a similar technique of deflation in the member on cures for love melancholy. After forty pages of dietary advice, instructions for curative slandering of the beloved, good counsel, and "Philters, Magical and Poetical Cures," Burton undercuts his own eloquent persuasions against love: "The last refuge and surest remedy . . . when no other means will take effect, is to let them go together, and enjoy one another" (3:228). This unexpected reversal recasts what has preceded it, and a puzzled reader thinks probable what he only intuited before: that Burton is joking in the immediately preceding subsection. There he records the curative value of "many magnetical medicines, as to piss through a ring," and of resort to "that renowned rock in Greece, of which Strabo writes . . . from which rock if any lover flung himself down headlong, he was instantly cured" (3:226–27)—some cure!

Clues of context are not always necessary to alert the reader that Burton is playing; sometimes he calls attention to it. After listing Jacobus de Voragine's twelve arguments in favor of marriage, he boasts, "how easy a matter is it to answer these motives, and to make an *antiparodia* quite opposite unto it! To exercise myself I will essay" (3:253). Then, in the midst of a subsection on letting lovers have their desire, he reverses each of the twelve arguments—merely to exercise his wit, certainly not to further the point at issue in the subsection.

The major clue that frames Burton's treatise as play is his style. Although *The Anatomy* is stuffed with Latin quotations from authorities, Burton occasionally uses Latin more as a puzzle for the learned than as a weighty authority. Only the educated reader (presumably male) could learn, for example, this scurrilous but, according to Burton, surefire method for curing a lovesick swain: *"Paretur aliqua vetula... et portet subtus gremium pannum menstrualem... subito extrahat pannum menstrualem, coram facie portando, exclamando, Talis est amica tua"* (3:201). Burton leaves his more salacious examples in untranslated Latin—both a diet for arousing lust and recipes for controlling it that include the right testicle of a wolf and a powder made from dried, beheaded frogs. Elsewhere, Burton provides rather loose translations of Latin phrases that amuse the educated male reader who can read the original.[18] One learned doctor's autobiographical musings, *"per multiplices amores discurrebam,"* become in Burton's words "I took a snatch where I could get it" (3:249).

Such spicy translations are just a special case of the piquant diction that peppers the whole book. In his playful imagination a beautiful, but empty-headed woman is "snout-fair alone" (3:271), and cuckolded husbands belong to a knightly order whose members wear "bull's feathers in their crests" (3:291). Nor is Burton ever at a loss for a comical, and lewd, comparison: an old man with a young wife is like the man "that had but a peck of corn weekly to grind, yet would needs build a new mill for it... either he must let his mill lie waste, pull it quite down, or let others grind at it" (3:301). In his witty comparisons, imaginative diction, linguistic puzzles, and sentences of interminable series, which one critic has likened to multiple-choice exams,[19] Burton has created a style that prepares the reader to expect jokes.

In addition to Burton's dramatic posturing and his jokes, much of the "science" and learning in *The Anatomy* is, he confesses, play. He undertakes to write a serious book of physic only, he says, "to exercise myself," to cure "idleness with idleness" (1:21). He writes a "Digression of Air," which, although it digresses from melancholy, poses most of the major scientific questions of his day, in order to "exercise myself for my recreation" (2:34). And he advises other melancholiacs like himself to pursue as a cure "exercises or recreations of the mind" (2:86). They might take up Italian or Dutch paintings, "neat architectures, devices, escutcheons, coats of arms . . . old coins . . . artificial works, perspective glasses. . . . Indian pictures made of feathers, China works, frames, thaumaturgical motions, exotic toys" (2:87). Or if these do not amuse, Burton suggests that the melancholy gentleman "find the philosopher's stone... invent impresses, emblems; make epithalamiums, epitaphs, elegies, epigrams . . . anagrams, chronograms, acrostics upon his friends' names; or write a comment on Martianus Capella... and rather than do nothing, vary a verse a thousand ways" (2:97–98). It is all one, so long as it busies the idle, and it is all play.

To Burton all study should be play. He makes little discrimination in his "Digression of Air" between finding at the Pole the true cause of the compass's magnetical attraction to the north, and finding in Madagascar "that great bird ruck, that can carry... an elephant," in Cuba spherical stones, in the mines of Switzerland fossils and archeological remains, and everywhere the "Many rare creatures and novelties each part of the world affords" (2:35–39). Burton loves the rare and marvelous, and he stuffs his treatise with oddities like those he advises his readers to peruse. As a result, *The Anatomy* resembles not so much the humanist's library as the virtuoso's cabinet, those collections belonging to the fashionable gentlemen scholars who rose to prominence in England in the first half of the seventeenth century.[20]

The virtuosi were not men like Boyle, Harvey, and Newton, who made scientific discoveries that changed the course of history. Nor were they all like the "dizzards" satirized in Shadwell's Gimcrack or in Swift's Laputans and Projectors at the Academy in Lagado. Rather, they were gentlemen of means and leisure who *delighted* in paintings, antiquities, and science—thus *dilettantes.* Although amateurs, some were intense and dedicated students who collected coins, pictures, shells, insects, and mechanical inventions merely because they inspired wonder and delight. Although not devoted to the Baconian goal of benefiting mankind by the advancement of learning, the virtuosi were not necessarily frivolous. Intensely devoted to entertaining themselves with learning, they were, in short, serious players.[21]

As such, Burton was a junior member of their ranks. Even though he offers his treatise "for the common good of all" (1:22), this offer is admittedly an afterthought to his primary goal of staving off his melancholy through recreation. On a scholar's wages he could not purchase statues, ostrich eggs, or mechanical flies, but he did collect books—a library ten times the size of the average don's, according to Michael O'Connell, including "jest books . . . cony-catching pamphlets, quartos of popular plays . . . , contemporary satires, pamphlets describing oddities and marvels. . . . just the sort of rubbish" excluded from Oxford's new Bodleian Library.[22] From these and his more orthodox reading, Burton gleaned curious anecdotes and oddments to delight both himself and the reader of *The Anatomy.*

By being an actor, playing jokes, writing wittily, and collecting rarities as a virtuoso, Burton frames his book as play, and play, he claims, can cure melancholy. Cataloguing virtually all the games and sports of his day as potential cures (2:69–126), he condemns the Puritans, who would have us "tyrannize over our brother's soul, lose the right use of many good gifts, honest sports, games and pleasant recreations" (3:375). He knows no more powerful remedy for care than "a cup of strong drink, mirth, music, and merry company" (2:115). So he becomes this much needed merry company for his reader, offering "these my writings . . . like gilded pills, which are so composed as well to tempt the appetite and deceive the palate, as to help and medicinally work upon the whole body; my lines shall not only recreate but rectify the mind" (3:7). Written as play to cure the author's melancholy, *The Anatomy* becomes play to cure the reader's melancholy.

In numerous self-justifications and parenthetical addresses, Burton attends to his reader, whom he engages not as a plaything, but as a playmate.[23] By remaining anonymous (in every edition after the first), all the while planting clues to his identity; by enticing his "Gentle Reader" in the first lines of the book to "be very inquisitive to know" who the author is, then chastizing that curiosity with "Seek not after that which is hid" (1:15)—Burton lures the reader to seek out the man behind the masks. Many biographical critics have taken the bait, speculating about his early childhood, his psychological make-up, and his rumored suicide.[24] That Burton has successfully engaged some readers in his hide-and-seek game may reveal more about his personality than what biographical researchers have found by playing the game. He even mentions, then withholds for enigmatic reasons, a "sovereign remedy" for jealousy, promising the reader, "if you be very desirous to know it, when I meet you next I will peradventure tell you what it is in your ear" (3:311). Burton teases the reader as if he were an intimate whom the author meets often.

Like one of the guys on the street corner, Burton also mocks, insults, and threatens his reader, accusing him in "The Argument of the Frontispiece" of being the model for the portrait of the silly "Inamorato" (1:7–8) and promising to pulverize critical readers with witticisms and to sacrifice them to the God of Mirth (1:124). The hostility that some critics have found in his mockery, insults, and delight in catalogues of invective is frequently, as in these examples, channeled into agonistic play with the reader.[25]

As often as he seeks a sparring partner, Burton draws the reader onto the stage of his book to become a fellow actor. Not only does he take the role of the jealous husband, but he offers it to his reader. After advising cuckolds, in the third person, to be patient, he admonishes the reader directly not to criticize his own wife's straying since "Thou rangest like a town bull." Soon he is giving the reader lines to speak ("Yea, but, thou repliest . . .") in a dialogue between a jealous husband and a wise counselor (3:291–92). At the end of the section on the cure of love-melancholy, he prays God "send us all good wives," then invites the reader to join in such nuptial festivities as end comedies, and finally sings an epithalamium to the couples assembled on stage (3:255). Since the world is folly and his book mirrors the world, Burton invites his reader to play the fool "in this common stage" of his book (3:10) and thereby comprehend the folly that comprehends him.

By teasing the reader, tweaking his nose, and casting him in a variety of roles, Burton has followed his own parting advice: "'Be not solitary, be not idle'" (3:432).[26] Playing with his book for over twenty years kept him from idleness. Although he claimed to have been "penned up most part in my study" (1:17) during these years, he was not solitary. Nor were his books and Oxford colleagues his only companions; he took his imagined reader for curative merry company.

III

The efficacy of this play therapy is not solely, as some have concluded, that it keeps reader and author busy, distracts them from their disease, or proves the skeptic's creed, that the search for truth is futile.[27] Burton's play gave seventeenth-century Englishmen a paradoxical stance outside of the mad world that contained them. It may also have prepared the ground for new formulations of truth to emerge from the debris of colliding viewpoints that were shaking the structures that had once defined identity.

Like so many of his peers, Burton was confused by the authorities proliferating in the print revolution, and caught between two ways of knowing.[28] Although impatient with the fruitless wrangling of philosophy and theology that led to no useful truths (1:35–36; 3:369), he follows the old methods by citing endless authorities, nor does he show any knowledge of Bacon's empirical methodology. Although the old-fashioned humoral physiology is responsible for much of the confusion he seeks to untangle, he does not incorporate Harvey's revolutionary discovery of the circulation of the blood (1628) into later editions of *The Anatomy.* Although he rails at superstition, dismisses most charms and magical cures, and generally attributes melancholy to "natural and inward causes" rather than to possession by devils (1:419), he nevertheless asserts, in a rare instance of deciding between opposed views, that tempests "are more often caused by those aerial devils" than by "natural causes" (1:191). Much like Donne and Marvell, Burton was a liminal man.

Not everyone registers the changes that rock a culture, and some, like the Stuarts and the Cavalier poets, hold all the more tenaciously to established ways. Marginal people seem to have the most sensitive antennae to these shifts—people who are somewhat outside the mainstream of everyday business or who fall between the categories of social stratification, people like fools, poets, madmen, and sometimes priests and university professors. As we have seen in the example of the Bedouin "fool" who played the American hippie, thereby discriminating himself and his friends from the polluting American influence, the marginal figure often interprets culture to itself. Burton was also such a marginal interpreter. Although unconscious of his role, he modeled for his changing culture the characteristic features of liminality: a sense of separation; association with symbols of effacement, ambiguity, and paradox; and the fragmentation and recombination of cultural elements in playful ways.

Frequently, Burton refers to himself as separate from the busy world—a spectator to mercantile affairs, domestic concerns, and the struggle for power. Once, he strove to make his mark on the world by seeking preferment, but as he was continually put off, he accepted his lot (2:188–89)—"a silent, sedentary, solitary, private life, *mihi et musis* . . . in the university" (1:17). Despite the "Misery of Scholars" and the indifference of the mighty to a scholar's advice, he admits, "I had as lief be still Democritus Junior, and *privus privatus*" (1:314), an obscure individual separated from the everyday go-around, who instead of acting in the world interprets it in his book.

Although resigned to his life as a university professor, Burton often denigrates that identity. In *The Anatomy* he uses the freedom guaranteed by his position on the margins of the busy world either to dissolve his identity into the myriad roles he plays or to split it into connected but contradictory parts. Thus one way he responds to the experience of liminality is by repeated self-effacement.[29] He derides himself (it does not matter whether seriously or playfully) as an idler, "a smatterer," whose life's work "'Tis not worth the reading" (1:33, 26). In addition to surrendering his self to each new role, he quotes almost obsessively, speaking in other men's words rather than his own. And he claims, "I dwell not in this study" (1:32), which is anyway "*neminis nihil*" [nothing by nobody] (1:122).[30]

Like Donne, Burton sometimes defines himself as a not-self, and sometimes as two selves. Thus a second way he responds to liminality is by creating an ambiguous and paradoxical voice for his treatise. In his reluctance to decide between opposed points of view and his delight in using the double stance of play to free him from a world of confusion, Burton, as we have seen, finds in ambiguity and paradox a way to live in that world.

The third way he responds to liminality is to play amid vast libraries containing the heritage of Western culture, fragmenting the elements of that heritage into anecdotes, snippets of poetry, and Latin tags, then recombining them to suit his fancy. Although he tries to divide his subject according to the Ramistic method for finding truth, he ends up not with dialectic, but with an inclusive collection of contradictory oddments. Less like a disciple of Ramus and more like the virtuoso who collects here a Raphael Madonna and there a bee in amber, Burton assembles bits of learning and lore into his cabinet, *The Anatomy,* for his own recreation. One might say that, since he quotes as often as he speaks, he has cobbled a self out of fragments from other men's selves, recombining them "in an extemporean style" (1:31).[31]

As a not-self, who cannot be censured, or a paradoxical self, who cannot be pinned down, on the margins of society without the power or prestige to be threatening, Burton plays freely with all the knowledge available to him. Like Donne's conceits, Burton's hodge-podge is a "hybridization," which detaches cultural elements from old structures of understanding and juxtaposes them in peculiar combinations. In this sense, *The Anatomy* also becomes an "anti-structure," a pool of latent alternatives, usually expressed in nonthreatening cultural genres, from which the possibility of new ways of thinking can arise.[32] For example, while exercising himself for his recreation in "A Digression of Air," Burton marvels that ships can be dug out of mountains in Switzerland; then in a flight of fancy he speculates on the causes:

> Came this from earthquakes, or from Noah's flood, as Christians suppose? or is there a vicissitude of sea and land, as Anaximenes held of old . . . ? The whole world belike should be new-moulded, when it seemed good to those all-commanding powers, and turned inside out, as we do hay-cocks in harvest, top to bottom, or bottom to top . . . or if the worlds be infinite, and every fixed star a sun, with his compassing planets (as Brunus and Campanella conclude), cast three or four worlds into one; or else of one world make three or four new, as it shall seem to them best. (2:40)

Out of a jumble of Biblical lore, pre-Socratic philosophy, farming techniques, the "new philosophy," and a willingness to play comes a premonition of geological evolution and of the astronomy of stellar evolution from contracting matter to novas that disperse matter for new stars. In liminal play Burton has come closer to present understandings of scientific truth than in all his attempts to bring order to Renaissance physiology.

So Burton's play both gives the reader a point of vantage in a "world turned upside downward" and scrambles old ideas and ways of thinking, thereby further loosening the structures of knowledge and perhaps preparing minds for new perspectives. Nevertheless, that new world just over the threshold would have appalled Burton, had he lived. There, physical data, not bookish authority, would constitute valid evidence, and the gap between knowledge about the body and knowledge about the soul would only widen.

8

Sir Thomas Browne Turning the World Around for Recreation

Toward the end of *Religio Medici,* Sir Thomas Browne claims, "The world that I regard is my selfe, it is the Microcosme of mine owne frame, that I cast mine eye on; for the other, I use it but like my Globe, and turne it round sometimes for my recreation."[1] Although a relatively young man when he wrote these words, the Norwich physician, moralist, and natural philosopher continued to play with the world throughout his long life. In dedicating *The Garden of Cyrus,* a treatise impossible to classify definitively as biology, botany, or mere fancy, he claims to expound on the quincunx because "bye and barren Themes are best fitted for invention" (86). His irrepressible "invention" seeks not "crambe verities and questions over-queried," those "Flat and flexible truths . . . beat out by every hammer," but "delightful Truths" (*G. of C.,* 173–74) found by comparing conical sections to vegetable seeds to cuttlefish eyes in one dizzying sentence (*G. of C.,* 170). Even in his scholarly attack on error, *Pseudodoxia Epidemica,* Browne approaches his subject playfully: he ridicules the same kinds of bizarre remedies that amused Burton ("the left stone of a Weesel, wrapt up in the skin of a she Mule . . . to secure incontinency from conception"), and he laughs at the story of a woman impregnated by merely swimming with a man ("'Tis a new and unseconded way in History to fornicate at a distance.")[2] A student of curious lore and collector of rarities, Browne takes the entire material world as his playground.

Although he claims to "regard" his self but play with the world, Browne also plays with his self. Despite his apologies in *Religio Medici* for his "extravagant" changeableness and "the humour of my irregular selfe," he exults in performing self-metamorphoses before his reader's eyes (*R.M.,* 7, 54). One moment he laments, "the man without a Navell yet lives in me; I feele that originall canker corrode and devoure me" (*R.M.,* 69); the next moment he basks in self-satisfaction: "I would not entertaine a base designe, or an action that should call mee villaine, for the Indies, and for this onely doe I . . . have mee thinkes, two armes too few to embrace my selfe" (*R.M.*, 73). Here and elsewhere, Browne is an actor striking a variety of poses, which prompted Coleridge to quip, "The Religio Medici . . . is a fine Portrait of a handsome man in his *best* Cloathes."[3]

Not limited to the macrocosm of the world or the microcosm of himself, Browne's play extends to the throne of God. Alluding to Wisdom's play before the Father in Proverbs 8:27–31 (Vulgate), he explains that the attribute of God "wherewith I recreate my devotion, is his wisedome, in which I am happy" (*R.M.*, 12). Musing on "those involved ænigma's and riddles of the Trinity . . . Incarnation and Resurrection" is the "solitary recreation" that puzzles his reason beyond itself to an *"oh altitudo"* (*R.M.*, 9). By Browne's own admission, studying the world, himself, or the Maker of both was recreation.

Readers may join the play by following the intricacies of his lively prose. A representative example is the conclusion to *The Garden of Cyrus*, where Browne entices readers to share his delight in tracing "the Labyrinth of Truth," which his book has just celebrated, by posing whole paragraphs of unanswered (and some unanswerable) questions about Benjamin's clothes, the five-act structure of comedy, sea stars, magnetism, chiromancy, and the cross-legged posture of goddesses. Each breathless section ends with a promise that whoever enters the labyrinth "may meet abstrusities of no ready resolution" or "shall not passe his hours in vulgar speculations" or "shall not fall on trite or triviall disquisitions" (172–74). In *Hydriotaphia* and *Pseudodoxia*, Browne plays the same trick of style, beginning series of sentences with substantive *whether, if, how,* or *why* questions that are left at the end of the sentence to the readers' "conjecture." Browne would have his readers' minds become as playful as his own in speculating beyond knowledge.

Not every reader, however, has accepted Browne's invitation to come out and play. Although most critics before and after Coleridge enjoy *Religio Medici*'s whimsicalities, many feel that they shouldn't: Browne is all style and no substance; he turns religion into metaphor, or toys with doubt and pain, or draws attention to his virtuoso performance instead of transforming his reader's soul.[4] Browne's defenders have answered these charges, praising his playful self-presentation and attitude toward both creature and Creator as a salutary corrective for an audience whose conflicts over science, faith, and the varieties of religious expression produced the persecution of Galileo, the Spanish Inquisition, and the English Civil War.[5] Still, after living through the war and outgrowing the youthful posing of *Religio Medici*, Browne continued to play. Some readers attribute the play spirit in later works to his desire to imitate the witty God of creation whose mystical hieroglyphics written, for example, in seaweed "plainly declareth ... how the needle of nature delighteth to work, even in low and doubtful vegetations" (*G. of C.*, 144).[6] This tradition of *Deus ludens* was, however, available to Donne, Herbert, Marvell, Burton, indeed to every educated seventeenth-century writer, and yet, as we shall later see, no one employed the doctrine of correspondences quite as Browne did. As each of these players created a ludic self out of available traditions to solve problems particular to his individual experience, so Browne's play, although rooted in a recognized tradition, gave his self its characteristic stance.

Despite variations of form and style, the literary play of these men serves two primary functions: defense and integration. For Hamlet and the voices of Donne, of Marvell sometimes, and of Burton, play affords an uneasy stance in the midst of contradictions. For the Hamlet of act 5, Herbert's voice throughout *The Temple,* and Marvell's voice in "The Garden" and "Upon Appleton House," play becomes a path toward integration by joining the self to an other—either divine providence, an internal Presence, or a nurturing pastoral retreat. In *Religio Medici* Browne's self may seem as elusive as Donne's or Marvell's, but in his whole canon Browne plays for integration, not defense—first by trying out a variety of selves, and then by expanding his flexible but stable self into a rich world of objects, the globe he turns around for his recreation.

I

Browne predicates his sense of self on the assumption that man can know nothing for certain. He knows neither himself nor others "truely" (*R.M.*, 61), and since "Many Positions seem quodlibetically constituted, and like a *Delphian* Blade will cut on both sides" (*C.M.*, 220), he joins "the wisest heads . . . , almost all Scepticks," who "stand like *Janus* in the field of knowledge" (*R.M.*, 66). If certain knowledge in this world is dubious, our prospects for knowledge beyond it are worse, comparable to "A Dialogue between two Infants in the womb concerning the state of this world" (*H.*, 116). But the consistent skepticism evident in these quotations from the early, middle, and late years of Browne's career never threatens his belief that he has a self.[7] Although he can never know himself fully, he believes that God knows him, "the substance without the ... accidents" (*R.M.*, 61).

He also believes that God is within him, sustaining his self—a belief not subject to his usual skepticism because he feels the divine presence intuitively. Whereas to Donne separation and alienation threaten to fragment his self, to Browne man can never be alone because he contains not only his thoughts, but also God and the devil (*R.M.*, 69). He is sure that "There is ... a peece of Divinity in us, something that was before the Elements, and owes no homage unto the Sun" (*R.M.*, 70); he is equally sure that "There is another man within mee that's angry with mee, rebukes, commands, and dastards mee" (*R.M.*, 64). The result, he confesses, is that "within the compasse of my selfe, I . . . find the battell of *Lepanto*" (*R.M.*, 64). Herbert, as we have seen, projects images of a sinful self, a confessing self, and the indwelling spirit of God, and then conducts playful agons between these opponents to feel the Presence that comes when one's competing selves reconcile. In these inner combats, Herbert finds himself, separate and whole. Writing in his early thirties, Browne describes a similar inner playground in *Religio Medici.* The Devil within plays "at Chesse" or "at sharpe" with him (*R.M.*, 20, 64), but because Satan's opponent is, he rejoices, "a common Spirit that playes within us . . . the Spirit of God, the fire and scintillation of that noble and mighty Essence" (*R.M.*, 31), there is no contest. Browne cannot lose his self in the game because his intuition of this inner Presence is so strong that he gives his will to it completely. Whereas Herbert's poetry dramatizes a self coming into being, Browne's prose reflects a self already assured of its integrity: his internal Battle of Lepanto was won before he turned thirty-three by that "peece of Divinity" within.

Nor does Browne fear the death of the self, despite his fascination with corporal dissolution evident in the grisly details of *Hydriotaphia,* in his discovery of adipocere (a fatty substance produced by decomposing bodies), and in his graphic record of a prolonged death in *A Letter to a Friend.* With fantastic and paradoxical rhapsodies, he conjures up visions of the self transcending time, either through metempsychosis (*R.M.*, 7) or through existence "in the Idea of God, and the decree of that Synod held from all Eternity." "I was not onely before my selfe, but *Adam,*" he marvels; "thus was I dead before I was alive, though my grave be *England,* my dying place was Paradise, and *Eve* miscarried of mee before she conceiv'd of *Cain*" (*R.M.*, 54). The self never disintegrates; it merely metamorphoses like the silkworm, which Browne claims "turn'd my Philosophy into Divinity" (*R.M.*, 38), or lies dormant like the seeds he "found in Wilde-Fowls Gizards [which] have sprouted in the earth" (*G. of C.*, 147). Death, then, is not self-loss, only another of nature's "strange and mysticall transmigrations" (*R.M.*, 38), which, despite the base uses to which we return, Browne is willing to experience—"Ready to be any thing, in the extasie of being ever" (*H.*, 125).

Browne often represents his sense of self—whole and eternal—in terms of the circle. It becomes his favorite image, giving form to his vision of his place in the world. Although it may be crossed by the right line of the body and the external world, the circle embraces the divisible and corporal line within its indivisible and divine arc (*G. of C.*, 168). No matter if a man and all he has made, subject as they are to the line of time, dissolve into atomies—a bone here, a comb there, a ring, a tooth; God's overarching providence nurtures and protects the soul, far better than the womblike urns that make "our last bed like our first" (*H.*, 102). Particularly in his twin meditations on entropy and order, *Hydriotaphia* and *The Garden of Cyrus,* the circle for Browne becomes something like a mandala, the circular images C. G. Jung discovered in the dreams and fantasies of people in the process of integrating the self. It is a talisman assuring Browne that "All things began in order, so shall they end, and so shall they begin again; according to the ordainer of order and mystical Mathematicks of the City of Heaven" (*G. of C.,* 174). He need never share Donne's fear of fragmentation or alienation because he feels the truth behind the paradoxical Hermetic definition: God is a circle whose center is everywhere and whose circumference is nowhere (*R.M.,* 10). Never beyond God's embrace and always assured of God's inner presence, Browne envisions himself as nurtured and centered.[8]

Yet this stable and whole self poses before the reader of *Religio Medici* as "extravagant" and "irregular." He claims to have once been tempted by heresies that his present self abjures (*R.M.,* 7–8); then in the preface to the authorized edition he warns that this work contains ideas that fit his "passed apprehension, which are not agreeable unto my present selfe" (*R.M.,* 1–2). His youthful self yields to the self at the time of writing, whom the self who has been forced to publish his earlier musings may in turn repudiate. Which self speaks any given part of the text is left ambiguous.[9] Whoever he is, sometimes he appears as the most melancholy of men, claiming that the world is a hospital, a place in which to die, not live (*R.M.,* 87); at other times, he practically sings a hymn to the order and beauty of nature, which produces nothing ugly, not even monsters (*R.M.,* 14–15).

This posturing differs from Donne's histrionics. The ambiguity of every Donne role prevents the reader from locating the voice with assurance; Donne plays to sustain a safe stance in between. While seducing the reader with its verve and power, Donne's voice holds him off with the hint that it has been joking all along. Browne, however, never teases the reader with his posing. Although he says his self changes, in truth, only his opinion on indifferent doctrines changes. And although he paints a variety of self-portraits, each is so obviously posed that the reader feels the constant presence of their one painter.[10] Whereas Donne's voice characterizes a self balancing precariously in between separation and union, the voice of *Religio Medici* characterizes a self safely sustained by its relation to the God within and without.

God knows the substance of Browne's self, but as a skeptic Browne realizes that he can only know its multiform accidents. So to discover these, he tries on various roles: the worldly wise melancholiac, the mystic in rapt contemplation of the Trinity, the rueful penitent, the man who seems proud that he lacks pride. In his role play, he resembles Shakespeare's comedic protagonists—Viola, Rosalind, or even Prince Hal—so sure of themselves in adversity, yet so willing to submerge their identities in disguise and acting in order to become more fully themselves. Browne in *Religio Medici* plays not to defend a threatened self, but to discover a self that he intuits as already whole but not yet wholly known.[11] The kind of integrative play evident in *Religio Medici,* as in *The Temple,* "The Garden," and "Upon Appleton House," requires a trusted playmate, whether a beneficent spirit within or a nurturing environment without, whose presence guarantees stability while Herbert, Marvell, and Browne play either to experience or to know their selves.

To Browne every man has a unique self: "so intrinsecal is every Man unto himself, that some doubt may be made, whether any would exchange his Being, or substantially become another Man" (*L. to F.,* 188). Nevertheless, seeing role play as a means toward self-knowledge, Browne willingly tries on other selves for a while. He desires to become one with his friends who, in truth, "are our selves" (*R.M.,* 63); he even becomes what might seem most alien—joining in an exaltation when he hears the *Ave Marie* Bell (*R.M.,* 4–5), wishing to imitate the heathens who "suck Divinity from the flowers of nature" (*R.M.,* 15), and because *"All flesh is grasse,"* identifying with cannibals, the *Anthropaphagi* whom all men abhor (*R.M.,* 36). This play with the self accounts for his unusual tolerance in an age of bitter sectarian controversy. Unlike many xenophobic and militantly Protestant Englishmen of his day, Browne's essential self was not threatened by the dissolution of social structures or the collision of competing values. Embracing difference, he allows the French to eat their frogs, the Jews to eat their locusts, and all men to follow their religious beliefs. Because his self is whole, without need of self-defense, he can extend it to others in empathy, tolerance, and charity.

He can also love himself, and he does—ardently. He admires the wonders in "the Cosmography of my selfe" (*R.M.,* 15), his life seems to him "a miracle of thirty yeares" (*R.M.,* 69), and he would hug himself if he could (*R.M.,* 73). Such loving attention to himself has for three centuries amused his fans and annoyed his detractors. His earliest critic wondered, "What should I say of his making so particular a narration of personall things, and private thoughts of his owne; the knowledge whereof cannot much conduce to any mans betterment."[12] Although more recent critics realize that many of Browne's references to himself are mere posing, those critics who want him to be a better physician of the soul find his apparent self-satisfaction dangerously complacent.[13] But Browne's assertions of self-love are often more complex than they seem. When he boasts that he has escaped the sin of pride (*R.M.,* 65) or that he has no bodily disfigurement, "whereby I might not call my selfe as wholesome a morsell for the wormes as any" (*R.M.,* 39), he acknowledges both the "peece of Divinity" within and the Lucifer who "keeps his court in my brest" (*R.M.,* 49). While confessing his moral excellence, he playfully displays pride in denying pride, and while admiring his physique, he comically images its assured corruption. In psychoanalytic terms, Browne's play demonstrates an integration of both good and bad internal objects. Because he has accepted himself as whole, if tainted and finite, he has no need to isolate evil and its consequences outside the self, or to project evil onto a bugbear, whether Puritanical zealotry or courtly dissolution. And because he acknowledges his own inner ambivalence and contradiction, he is not overwhelmed by the divisions that surround him.

In his willingness to play to find out who he is, warts and all, Browne creates an atmosphere in which readers can feel free to play along, temporarily suspending their identities and identifying with his whimsical persona.[14] Asking that his book "be taken in a soft and flexible sense, and not . . . called unto the rigid test of reason" (*R.M.*, 2), Browne fosters relaxation on the reader's part because the environment he creates is accepting, not punitive. He wins his reader's trust by not interjecting absolutes of belief into the text they share. Such an atmosphere of trust and acceptance invites the play that promotes psychological change. D. W. Winnicott has described the process of psychotherapy as taking place "in the overlap of two areas of playing, that of the patient and that of the therapist."[15] Although reading *Religio Medici* is not, any more than Marvell's poetic perambulation through gardens, an hour on the couch, it may have offered Browne's contemporaries a similar kind of healing experience. If only in the limited space of the text and in the limited time of reading, the reader can play at self-discovery with a model self who is whole, accepts its own contradicitons, and empathizes with those of alien nations and religions.

Such experiences were rare and much needed in Browne's troubled time. When the authorized edition of *Religio Medici* was published in 1643, the theatres had been closed, the Civil War had erupted, and pamphlets filled with grim controversy were flooding the presses. In this political context, according to Jonathan Post, Browne's "emphasis upon 'recreation'" may have been "an act of resistance against an increasingly powerful Parliament that under pressure from strict 'anti-theatre Puritan leaders' sought officially to outlaw all forms of playing."[16] On the other side, Browne's slender volume, which he had intended, he says, as "rather a memoriall unto me then an example or rule unto any other" (*R.M.*, 1), had occasioned a correspondence between two prominent noblemen. The Earl of Dorset stole some time from counseling King Charles to end the war and wrote to Sir Kenelm Digby, requesting his reaction to *Religio*. Digby, at the time in prison for his part in the skirmish at Acton, claimed to have sat up all night enthralled with the book and to have dashed off a set of critical *Observations*, which were soon published. This example indicates that Browne's embattled contemporaries were fascinated by *Religio Medici*, which soon became a best-seller in England and Europe and made the obscure provincial doctor quite a reputation for his wit and the sweetness of his temper.

The modest meditation did not, however, moderate zealotry, end religious schism, or stop the war. Few books ever do such things. (Neither *The Praise of Folly* nor *The Anatomy of Melancholy* could restrain man's unreason.) But Browne did give his contemporaries something they obviously needed—a place to communicate with a mind that did not advocate the *Plaine Mans Path-way to Heaven,* or preach *The Sovereign's Power and the Subject's Duty,* or animadvert upon anything. Browne played freely before his readers in *Religio Medici* and invited them to participate, for an all-too-brief moment, in an experience that could help them unite the scattered fragments of their own selves. In this sense, Sir Thomas Browne was, and is still, as good a physician of the soul as we have any right to expect.[17]

II

Browne plays not only to discover what can be known of the self, but also of God. Although he feels God's indwelling presence, he remains a skeptic about man's ability to know God or His ways through reason. He laughs himself out of trying to use ancient history to confirm Biblical story by remembering Justine's claim "that the children of *Israel* for being scabbed were banished out of Egypt" (*R.M.*, 29). Instead, he agrees to follow the fundamental rules laid down by God in the Bible as interpreted by men in the church. Minor Biblical inconsistencies are irrelevant because "The Foundations of Religion are already established, and the principles of Salvation subscribed unto by all" (*R.M.*, 59). Although in philosophy "truth seemes double-faced," in divinity he chooses to "follow the great wheele of the Church" (*R.M.*, 7), willingly observing "the civility of... knee,... hat, and hand" (*R.M.*, 4) and renouncing his youthful heresies.

Browne often images his faith as play by the rules of an exciting but nonagonistic game.[18] The divine enigmas of the Trinity, incarnation, and resurrection (*R.M.*, 9) and questions such as whether Judas hanged himself (*P.E.*, 512–13) are allowable for his "recreation" because church councils and decrees have left many points "untouch'd, unimagin'd, wherein the libertie of an honest reason may play and expatiate with security and farre without the circle of an heresie" (*R.M.*, 9). Once the rules of faith have been established, play with the details becomes free and safe. When the devil intrudes into the game (*R.M.*, 20), his strategy is to tempt Browne to cheat by renouncing the fundamental rule, faith. So long, however, as Browne plays by the rules, his game remains enthralling but risk free. Unlike Herbert, Browne does not dramatize redemptive agons with God in his works. Rather, he describes a game, delimited by Anglican doctrine and ritual, with the mysteries of faith, a game the object of which is to discover both himself and God.

Browne also sees Biblical history as a story or drama in which he has a part to play. Some modern theologians have argued that the proper response to the sacred is play. A holy player is an actor in a drama whose story is sufficient unto itself. S/he rejoices in the risk of living a narrative life and has no need to justify life's adventures to self or others: s/he simply lives the script and does not support it with arguments affirming belief.[19] Throughout *Religio Medici* Browne demonstrates this total surrender to the mythic story recorded in the Bible. Even though he finds "in Scripture stories that doe exceed the fables of Poets, and to a captious Reader sound like *Garagantua* or *Bevis,*" he can, he claims, "read the history of the Pigeon that was sent out of the Ark, and returned no more, yet not question how shee found out her mate that was left behind" (*R.M.*, 21–22). He revels in the riskiness of belief in the Biblical story. Thankful that he did not live in the days of miracles, Browne enjoys, he says, "that greater blessing pronounced to all that believe & saw not." But he envies most the "bold and noble faith" of those who lived before Christ's coming, "who upon obscure prophesies and mysticall Types could raise a beliefe, and expect apparent impossibilities" (*R.M.*, 9–10). Scripture has not, however, recorded all of God's story, and Browne feels he too has a role in its continual unfolding. He considers his life a miracle "which to relate, were not a History, but a peece of Poetry, and would sound to common eares like a fable" (*R.M.*, 69–70). In the all-seeing eye of God, Browne knows, his fable is contemporary to Adam's and Cain's, and will continue after his death (*R.M.*, 13–14, 54).

Donne and Herbert, indeed anyone in the seventeenth century who understood human history typologically, also envision their lives as part of God's story, but Browne is more self-conscious about the implications of his role within a narrative. Donne and Herbert play with God and enact His story in their lives, but they do not directly raise questions about the fictionality of their performances and beliefs. Browne does. As a young man in *Religio Medici* (32) and an old man in *Christian Morals* (229), he advises belief in guardian angels, even though he finds no reference in Scripture to such spirits, because belief in them can influence a man's life to good. Similarly, although he confesses that he would never give his life to defend a ceremony, he willingly kneels to exalt his devotion. In these examples, Browne knowingly believes a fiction and performs an act of worship as optional drama, not essential ritual. In other words, he is self-consciously playing.

Like Hamlet, however, Browne knows that, even though play may begin in fiction, it can bring reality into being: he can "weepe most seriously at a Play, and receive with a true passion, the counterfeit griefes of those knowne and professed impostures" (*R.M.*, 61). As in the players' tearful description of Hecuba's grief, Browne responds to the truth behind what he knows to be fiction. Indeed, the very doubleness of play belief can enable relations with God, about whom so little can be known for sure. Although faith, the felt presence of God, is a gift that Browne acknowledges, and the essential content of that faith is the rule of the church by which he agrees to play, Browne also plays to make divine transcendence imminent. Belief in fictions such as guardian angels, and dramatic gestures such as kneeling at appointed times, even though inessential and played, can bring man closer to God by reifying the divine mystery as someone who watches over man, someone to whom human marks of "civility" are due. Browne boldly acknowledges that some elements of religion may be fiction and drama, human creations through which we approach a transcendent reality that we will never fully comprehend. Nevertheless, this knowledge never undermines the felt presence of God that engenders his faith, nor tempts him to question the church doctrines that give content to that faith.

Some critics, however, mistrust the piety of a man who conceives of religion as play. Has he reduced religion to empty metaphor? they ask; can play be a valid response to the serious questions that skepticism poses for religion or that life poses for us all?[20] To Browne, metaphor is not empty; it is, as we shall explore further when discussing his scientific play, a way of knowing what can be known no other way. Furthermore, Browne's play is not a trivial response to skepticism; it affirms human life and reaches toward the transcendent despite what Browne has squarely faced, our limited knowledge and inevitable suffering.

III

Browne pursues another way to know God, seeking what can be known of His creation. This quest defines Browne's science as a form of worship. Not only does he read God's handwriting in the Book of Nature, finding, for example, in the growth of huge trees from tiny seeds an emblem of creation *ex nihilo* (*G. of C.*, 149), but he also glorifies God through objective observation and experiment. Men who write moral and mystical disquisitions on the lodestone's properties, argues Browne, "from postulated or precarious inferences, entreat a courteous assent" to God's glory, "yet do they most powerfully magnifie him . . . who demonstratively set forth its Magnalities; who . . . from experiments and undeniable effects, enforce the wonder of its Maker" (*P.E.*, 116–17). As a scientist, Browne feels that he owes to God, through "judicious enquiry into his acts, and deliberate research into his creatures, . . . the duty of a devout and learned admiration" (*R.M.*, 13). Repeatedly, he insists that the goal of science is wonder.

And wonder he does. *The Garden of Cyrus* is one long *"oh altitudo"* at God's "mystical Mathematicks," which have woven the quincunx and the number five into the fabric of the creation. His letters overflow with questions and recommendations about marvels not to be missed: ostriches from Morocco, stones near Baden imprinted with the shapes of frogs, and comets in the night sky in Norwich. He writes to thank donors of rare specimens and offers to send his own rarities to others. A tally of those collectibles mentioned in the extant letters alone conjures up visions of a house jam-packed with objects of wonder: the palm of a hand and the sole of a foot that a patient had sloughed off in a fever, a box of eggs within eggs, a lizard's skin, a hedgehog (until it escaped), a ball taken from an ox's stomach, several eyes (for experimental freezing in winter), a hurt stork, a big green spider, skulls of a polecat and a badger, a pelican strung up for a meteorological experiment, rare coins, rare fish, rare animals, and "pritty stones." (Dorothy Browne must have been an indulgent housekeeper.) John Evelyn, recording in his diary a visit to Browne, corroborates this partial picture of Browne's world: his "whole house & Garden being a Paradise & Cabinet of rarities, & that of the best collection, especially Medails, books, Plants, natural things, did exceedingly refresh me."[21] Presumably, they refreshed Browne too because they were specimens of the world he calls his "recreation."

The world Browne describes resembles a toy shop filled with curiosities bestowed on him by an indulgent father who is most honored by his son's play. My metaphor may be fanciful, but it matches Browne's representation of the world to his own son in letters that sparkle with enthusiasm in their torrent of advice: by all means see the famous cabinet of Clusius the botanist, don't miss the mines of Bohemia, gather plants from every region, and on and on. Experiencing his self as whole, centered, and nurtured, Browne joyously expands that self into the world. In his dealings with the world of people and things, he never seems to experience the fears of self-dispersal that surface in Donne's and Marvell's lyrics, or the anxiety over the proliferation of knowledge that impelled Burton toward futile attempts to order the chaos. He neither retreats from the object world as outside his magical control nor tries to contain or possess the other-than-self in order to stabilize the self or to fill an inner void. Never viewing his collections as private possessions, he would have donated forty rare animals to the Royal College of Physicians if he had not already been forced by a plague epidemic to dispose of them. As a player, Browne extends his self toward things in sheer wonder at their thingness (*R.M.*, 57), wonder that defines his brand of science.

Whether or not Browne's brand should be called science is a matter of debate. Some historians draw a distinction between the seventeenth-century scientist, who investigated nature to find useful truths, and the virtuoso, whose primary goal was delight. Others argue that writers of the period used the term *virtuoso* indiscriminately for a pioneering chemist like Robert Boyle and an antiquary and naturalist like Browne. On the one hand, Browne's interests and experiments, although seeming odd today, were comparable to the work discussed in the Royal Society. On the other hand, he remained uninfluenced by the increasingly popular mechanistic view of nature: he never turned his attention from questions about the ends of phenomena to questions about weight, mass, and time; from nature considered as part of the divine plan to parts of nature considered in isolation; from teleology to measurement. Contemporary opinion of his work further complicates the debate over Browne's science. A letter from a fellow physician treats Browne's most mystical and whimsical work, *The Garden of Cyrus,* not as a meditation on divine order but as a scientific account of truth that raises issues that the correspondent debates. Only five years after Browne's death, however, a pamphlet ridicules him as a doctor turned virtuoso, who stops on his way to a dying patient to chase butterflies.[22]

During the middle years of the seventeenth century, what constituted science was uncertain; neither the fields of inquiry nor proper methodologies had yet been established. Toward the end of the century, as empirical science became more sure of itself, terms like *dilettante* and *virtuoso* acquired connotations of triviality and silliness. If, however, we take these terms in their original sense to designate experts who delight in their studies, they can help distinguish between Browne's and many of his contemporaries' scientific aims. Whereas the Baconian pursues the advancement of learning to benefit mankind in practical ways, Browne pursues nature's truths to worship God through wonder. Since players seek wonder, novelty, and delight, whether or not their activities are useful, Browne belongs with those serious players, the virtuosi.[23]

The desire for novelty is a key motivation for play. Humans and animals seem to seek novelty in order to attain a state of ideal stimulation between anxiety, when the environment makes demands too great for comfort, and boredom, when the environment poses too few challenges. Because players can choose their modes of play, they generally select activities in which the environment's demands challenge but do not tax their abilities. Hence they escape the boredom and anxiety that rule the everyday world and experience exhilaration and a joyous loss of self-consciousness.[24] Certainly, Browne was such a novelty-seeking player. Although beset by a profound skepticism about reason's ability to comprehend the self, God, or the order of His universe, aggrieved by the deaths of his patients and eight of his twelve children, and confronted with the crises of a scientific revolution and the English Civil War, Browne seldom expresses the personal or metaphysical uneasiness of so many of his contemporaries. Assured of a self and cosmic order sustained by God's presence and might (beyond anxiety), Browne experiences the world as infinite variety and mystery (beyond boredom). His letters present a man who could never find life tedious; those to his traveling sons barrage them with questions and advice about new things they have seen or should seek out, like the properties of the "Jesuits powder" at Cales or the way the half-moon was set on St. Stephen's cathedral in Vienna (*Let-*

ters, 21, 39). His curiosity is omnivorous, but he delights most in the novel and the rare.

No fears of the new spoil the surprises Providence brings to Browne: unexpected emergencies, he rejoices, make "the World new unto us . . . whereby we pass not our days in the trite road of affairs affording no Novity; for the novellizing Spirit of Man lives by variety, and the new Faces of Things" (*C.M.,* 212). Discovering "the new Faces of Things" is also a major goal of his science: by joining "Sense unto Reason, and Experiment unto Speculation," he hopes to "give life unto Embryon Truths, and Verities yet in their Chaos." He prefers even the absurdities of Paracelsus to mere repetitions of stale truths (*C.M.,* 221). Browne's quest for novelty is not limited to discovery through experimentation. Because, as he explains in *The Garden of Cyrus,* "Subjects so often discoursed confine the Imagination, and fix our conceptions unto the notions of fore-writers," he chooses an odd and useless subject, the quincunx, to pursue his "novellizing" goal: "Of old things we write something new" (86). Instead of experimenting to discover eternal truths in nature that may be new to man, Browne's "invention" will create wholly new truths out of an apparent nothing, a "barren" theme, thereby imitating the Creator of that order that *The Garden of Cyrus* lauds.

Browne seeks novelty by rummaging through old lore more often than by experimenting to uncover hitherto unknown data. In his reading, he always ferrets out the exotic and novel details, such as (according to one scholar's catalogue) "the pensile tomb of Mahomet, the names of fish in the sea of Tiberias, lions in the Prince of Bavaria's court, talkative elephants, magnetical rocks, and vegetable horns."[25] Although in *Pseudodoxia Epidemica* Browne claims to "wander in the America and untravelled parts of Truth" (5), his treatise, like Burton's *Anatomy,* is as much a collection of odd, old stories as it is a scientific assault on error. While breakthroughs like Harvey's discovery of the circulation of the blood were revolutionizing medicine, Browne played with the novelty of marvelous lore. Paradoxically, he researches the old to find new puzzles for his curiosity.

Browne's penchant for the novel is largely responsible for his reputation among nineteenth-century literati as a quaint humorist. They admired him, but almost as if he were a rarity to be collected like one of his weird fish. To Coleridge, Browne "has brains in His head, which is all the more interesting for a little Twist in the Brains." To Melville, he was "a crack'd Archangel."[26] To be sure, their distance from seventeenth-century habits of mind accounts for much of what the nineteenth century saw as a "Twist" in Browne's seraphic but "crack'd" sensibility. But not all of it. Browne had a genuine hankering for the peculiar. In *Pseudodoxia,* while discussing errors in historical tenets, he wonders if the custom of popes changing their names comes from the time of *Bocca di Porco,* who thought it undignified for a pope to be named "swine face" (530). In *A Letter to a Friend* a consideration of the dying man's consumption leads Browne to wonder if crocodiles cough (186). And at the end of an inconclusive analysis "Of the Fishes eaten by our Saviour with his Disciples after his Resurrection from the Dead," he poses a question for his correspondent: what was the species of fish in the story about the murderer who was served a fish resembling his victim? Browne's mind seldom stays on the path of his argument, wandering off to chase the odd butterfly here and there. Aware of his own extravagance, he prefers "such Discourses [as] allow excursions, and venially admit of collaterall truths, though at some distance from their principals" (*G. of C.*, 86). While chasing novelty, he believes, one may net truth.

And if not truth, delight—Browne's primary goal in spinning the world around as a toy globe. Whereas the heirs of Bacon sought truth for medicine and technology, Browne saw truth as a labyrinth or an unexplored continent (*P.E.*, 5) affording adventure and "delight" to the investigator (*G. of C.*, 172, 174). A letter to his son about selecting material for a narrative of the son's travels illustrates Browne's hierarchy of values. He advises Edward to include in the section on the baths at Baden "the story of the man that putt a snakes head into his mouth in the bath, & of the Hussar wch bathd in a frost at midnight" (*Letters*, 55), but to exclude from the section on the mines of Bohemia details on how metals are prepared. He would add the piquant story, and excise the useful but dull information. Although *Pseudodoxia*'s address to the reader echoes Bacon and proclaims a practical goal—to increase truth by clearing away much of what man once thought he knew—the body of the treatise undermines its stated intent. Critics have noted that Browne's digressiveness, his confession to being an amateur, and his constant authorial presence make *Pseudodoxia* resemble a series of essays more than a scientific treatise.[27] He also indulges in catalogues of peculiar questions, like those at the end of the unscientific *Garden of Cyrus,* questions that sound more like puzzles for the mind than inquiries leading to practical truths (see especially the ends of Books 3 and 6 of *Pseudodoxia*). To end what began as an attempt to sweep out error to make room for truth, Browne chooses to list not propositions whose truth he doubts, but exotic and sensational facts and occurrences that he claims to wish were not true. His delight in curiosities has supplanted his original Baconian purpose.

In his correspondence, in *Hydriotaphia* and *The Garden of Cyrus,* and in *Pseudodoxia,* Browne addresses the "ingenuous Gentry" (*P.E.*, 4), among whom were the virtuosi and dilettanti who would share his delight in ancient urns and burial customs, in botany and Pythagorean numerology, and in curious lore to be collected like rare and archaic treasures.[28] His works are often just such collections of oddities, all jumbled together without apparent order. *Pseudodoxia* asks on the same page whether or not worms have blood and why bees hum (*P.E.*, 260). *The Garden of Cyrus* considers the superiority of animal to vegetable musk after describing the seminal powers of carcasses and before wondering about eggs with two yolks (*G. of C.*, 149). Browne's mind, like Burton's, resembles a virtuoso's cabinet of rarities more than a Baconian instrument for measuring data. But, unlike Burton, he did not feel impelled to try to order the collection. His posthumously published *Miscellany Tracts* reveal his disinclination to organize knowledge into separate disciplines each requiring specialization. He writes as a historian and botanist on garlands and plants in Scripture, as an amateur poet playing with anagrams and ropalic verses (poems of five words, each increasing by one syllable), as an anthropologist on artificial hills and burrows, as a physician on the plague, as a literary critic on *Hudibras*, and as a linguist comparing passages of Anglo-Saxon to contemporary English.

Content in his belief that the "ordainer of order" (*G. of C.*, 174) has unified all knowledge, Browne does not isolate one aspect of nature to search out its underlying laws. Rather, like a virtuoso in prose, he collects everything "rich and strange." Perhaps his propensity to play with polysyllabic and Latinate coinages is another manifestation of his instinct for collecting. His works are museums of exotic words, as in his admonition to "forget not how assuefaction unto any thing minorates the passion from it, how constant Objects loose their hints, and steal an inadvertisement upon us" (*C.M.*, 234).[29] Whether gathering odd specimens, odd stories, or odd words, Browne seeks evidence of the variety and plenitude of God's creation, which, although concealing from him its ordering principles, becomes an infinite source of novelty, delight, and wonder.

IV

Browne is as self-conscious about his scientific play as about his religious play. He mocks his own endeavors. Although his works, like his house, are a "Paradise & Cabinet of rarities," he parodies the virtuoso's passion for the rare and odd. Like an earlier physician of body and soul, Rabelais, who included in his imaginary Library of Saint Victor's *The Art of Farting Decently in Public* and three volumes on bacon eating, Browne catalogues the contents of an imaginary cabinet. In "Musaeum Clausum, or Bibliotheca Abscondita: Containing some remarkable books, antiquities, pictures & rarities of several kinds, scarce or never seen by any man now living," he includes a hitherto undiscovered work by Epicurus, *de Pietate;* Seneca's Epistles to St. Paul; the skin of a snake bred out of human spinal marrow; and "*Batrachomyomachia*, or the Homerican Battel between Frogs and Mice, neatly described upon the Chizel Bone of a large Pike's Jaw" (*Miscellany Tracts*, 119).[30] Some of the contents of this fabulous cabinet are comically absurd, but others are not far removed from Browne's own prizes: even though it did not come from a snake bred in a human spine, Browne admires his reptile skin greatly (*Letters*, 85), and he believes that bodies may breed insects or worms (*G. of C.*, 148–49). Here and perhaps even in his treatises—ostensibly more serious but no less jumbled and peculiar—Browne plays with the world, knows that he is playing, and plays with his own play in order to laugh himself and his fellow virtuosi out of taking their researches too seriously.

Humor becomes one of his most valuable weapons in the wars of truth. It dispels error and promotes the complex vision necessary to see truth whole, if not the precision of mind necessary to measure bits of data. Frequently *Pseudodoxia* laughs a vulgar error to scorn in snippy asides: that moles "have eyes in their head," scoffs Browne, "is manifest unto any, that wants them not in his own" (219). Sometimes, a witticism prepares the reader for disbelief, as in the opening of the section on beavers: "That a Bever to escape the Hunter, bites off his testicles or stones, is a Tenet very ancient; and hath had thereby advantage of propagation" (*P.E.*, 167). The double entendre in the final word alerts the reader to the absurdity of the beaver sacrificing his progeny on the dubious hope of diverting hunters from him to the musk supposedly contained in his testicles.[31] Other times Browne's humor accentuates the error of collapsing categories. If everyone understood the difference between seminal and corruptive generation—between propagation of a species by the union of seed and egg, and generation of another species, usually vermin, from a corrupting body—then "The problem might have been spared, Why we love not our lice as well as our children?" (*P.E.*, 197). Here the confusion of (supposed) error becomes comic incongruity, and Browne makes what he believes to be an important distinction. Such witticisms can wither error and promote belief in experience over authority.[32]

By requiring the reader to understand a word in two senses—one metaphorical, one literal—Browne also provides a model for multilevel thinking that does not oversimplify. In some ways *Pseudodoxia* is a treatise on the use and abuse of metaphor.[33] Again and again, Browne traces errors to ignorant literalizations of metaphors or to amphibology or equivocation. For example, Pythagoras enjoined his disciples to avoid beans, a metaphor for elections in which votes were cast by beans. But later followers righteously fasted from pulse (32–33). Patiently, Browne disentangles the literal from the metaphorical meanings that have produced vulgar errors. The mild dove lacks gall only metaphorically, not anatomically (166). The griffin is a fine hieroglyph for a guardian with the sight and speed of an eagle and the courage of a lion; nevertheless, no such creature exists (191).

But Browne's wordplay clarifies the distinction more forcefully than his patient explanations. Sharply and suddenly, in the moment necessary to get the joke, a pun thrusts upon the readers' attention the levels of meaning so often conflated. Repeatedly, while arguing a point on a literal level, Browne uses a word requiring metaphorical understanding. While discussing the possibility of silent gunpowder, Browne notes, "Of white powder and such as is discharged without report, there is no small *noise* in the World" (129). He dismisses the story that the Basilisk comes from a cock's egg hatched by a toad or serpent as "a conceit as *monstrous* as the brood it self" (177). And when introducing speculation "Of the Blackness of Negroes," he laments, "Which whoever strictly enquires, shall find no less of *darkness* in the cause, than blackness in the effect it self" (461). (Emphases mine.) In these examples, the witticism forces the reader to think on two levels at once: the literal noise of gunpowder and the figurative noise of rumor; the literal monstrousness of the Basilisk and the figurative monstrousness of asserting that cocks lay eggs and that serpents or toads hatch them; the literal darkness of skin color and the figurative darkness of obscure causes. The reader who can appreciate the comic incongruity in conflating levels of meaning is one who can actually keep them apart in his mind. In other words, the reader who gets Browne's jokes is less likely to fall into the vulgar error of taking metaphors literally.

In comic incongruity and wordplay used deliberately to deflate error, Browne demonstrates that he comprehends the basic principle that underlies hybridization, the ludicrous juncture that distinguishes and clarifies. Thus, the same structure that animates the play of Donne's conceits, Marvell's conflations, Burton's catalogues, and Browne's own proliferating questions and digressions also underlies the play of *Pseudodoxia*. Each isolates snippets of cultural knowledge, rejoins them in startling ways, and thereby both loosens an obsolescent cultural framework and prepares minds for a new one. Whereas Donne, Marvell, and Burton were probably unconscious of the complex effects of their wit on the future of knowledge, Browne self-consciously uses puns, metaphor, and odd juxtapositions in order to dismantle a moribund worldview.

At times, however, he seems to carry on the Royal Society's war against metaphor as the enemy obscuring the truth of fact. He warns that, by drawing moral examples from such fables as the phoenix's rebirth from its own flames or the pelican feeding its young with its blood, preachers may mislead the vulgar, and teachers, their students (*P.E.*, 60, 62). Yet he spices his most scientific work with metaphor and elucidates as often as he demythologizes hieroglyphs. The Egyptians, he explains, "to express complexed significations . . . took a liberty to compound and piece together creatures of allowable forms into mixtures inexistent." Although misleading the vulgar, hieroglyphs are to the knowing reader "commendable inventions . . . of laudable significations" (*P.E.*, 380). Browne believes that another kind of truth coexists with the truth of fact, one requiring a "soft and flexible sense" for understanding metaphors (*R.M.*, 2) and the "loose and popular delivery" suited to "Divinity" (*P.E.*, 60). Indeed, the highest truth can be expressed by finite man in no other way. Browne scorns those who take literally paintings of God as an old greybeard, for "he that challenged the boldest hand unto the picture of an Echo, must laugh at this attempt, not only in the description of invisibility, but circumscription of Ubiquity, and fetching under lines incomprehensible circularity" (*P.E.*, 389). Faced with the task of representing omnipresence and infinity, Browne chooses the Hermetic metaphor comparing God to a circle, not the "strict and definitive expressions . . . always required in Philosophy" (*P.E.*, 60) but of little use in worship.

To Browne, man's inability to describe or measure accurately a phenomenon does not preclude its existence, but he does want readers to recognize the difference between two ways of knowing, "strict and definitive" description and "soft and flexible" metaphor. He knows in both ways: *The Garden of Cyrus* represents nature as a metaphor for divine truth, but *Pseudodoxia* requires accurate descriptions of natural facts. Both kinds of truth are valid, and the wordplay of *Pseudodoxia,* which asks readers to hold in their minds simultaneously literal and figurative meanings, not only attunes readers to the error of equivocation, but also fosters the complex seeing necessary to those who embrace both reason and faith. Play becomes Browne's mode of vision to comprehend Truth, always multiple and elusive—so different from the scientific method of gathering data, single and clear.

Centuries of writers before Browne had read nature as God's book. But Browne's play with the ways of knowing truth makes his use of the doctrine of correspondences significantly different from his predecessors'. Although in *The Garden of Cyrus* he wonders at the sacramental presence of God's handwriting in nature, in *Pseudodoxia* he identifies the hieroglyphs as metaphors for what man cannot know with certainty, not as traces of the divine presence. And, he knows another, more certain way to describe nature. Browne's greater self-consciousness about man's metaphor-making powers does not diminish his faith.[34] It does, however, evince the shift from an older sacramental vision toward a consciousness founded in play. Seeing nature as knowable only through God, the authors of medieval bestiaries used the metaphors of correspondence to figure forth God's truth. As the correspondences came under increasingly serious attack, Donne, Herbert, and Marvell played with them. Browne both plays with them and calls them play, all the while believing in their efficacy to represent fundamentally unknowable truths.

V

Readers of Browne frequently locate him on the verge of an era, as an amphibium whose allegiance was divided between the medieval synthesis of all knowledge into a hierarchical order predicated on the truths of faith, and modern empiricism and rationalism.[35] His mind does seem to span these worldviews: in *Pseudodoxia,* for example, he proves that ice coagulates from the surface downwards by citing his experiments and a passage from Job (85). He still adduces Biblical authority in scientific inquiry. Nevertheless, Browne was not a liminal man in the same radical way that Donne, Marvell, and Burton were. In *rites de passage,* Turner's paradigm for liminality, contradictions, ambiguities, and confusing mixtures of cultural symbols barrage the novice, erasing his old identity in preparation for his new one. In between, the liminal figure sustains assaults upon his self and stability not unlike the contradictory fears and desires, the dilemmas that threaten self-annihilation, and the paradoxes of self-referentiality that Donne, Marvell, and Burton dramatize. Despite his position in between the medieval and the modern worlds, Browne never describes himself as menaced in these ways. Like Herbert, he is confident that God knows and upholds the substance of his self, but he plays to know its accidents, to know this unknowable God, to extend his self into God's world of novel and delightful objects, and to approach God's truth in all its complexity.

All these men wrote as basic frameworks for thought collided in the seventeenth century, and they responded to conflict and contradiction with play—each in his own style. What precedent did they have for this peculiar response? And what followed their experiments? These questions lead us now to the antecedent tradition for the ludic self and to a preview of new kinds of play that evolved in the following century.

9

Before and After: Folly and Leisure

Prior to the Renaissance and Reformation, European social structures allowed a periodic release of energy in festive folly. Most English women and men followed a rhythm of communal duties; obligatory work alternated with obligatory holidays, and the modern distinction between work time and leisure time was unknown. Work was often ritualized and celebratory, as in the ceremonialism of craft guilds in control of "mysteries"; games and sports, such as archery or hunting, prepared men for war or work; and the Church periodically suspended labor so that men and women could fulfill their obligations of religious celebration, which frequently included riotous festivities. Work could be played, and play could be required—all within a stratified society sustained, in part, by a periodic dialectic between order and playful disorder.[1]

In the late seventeenth and early eighteenth centuries, the increasingly urban, mercantile, and individualized society of England began to alter the pattern of cyclical agrarian time. The concentration of capital began to free some women and men from daily labor (while increasing the drudgery of others). More and more workers toiled outside the home during hours defined by employers. As a result, the rhythm of seasonal work and church holiday no longer regulated everyone's life. During time set apart from work—a new kind of time, spare time—some could choose their recreation. Public pleasure gardens, spas, and the bourgeois vacation gained popularity in the eighteenth century, evidence of an evolving conception of leisure.[2] As play and work became more distinct, new genres of recreation arose on the margins of a society increasingly dominated by production. These new pastimes, such as reading novels or frequenting coffee houses and gambling clubs, were, in contrast to medieval festive play, less obligatory, more individualized, and less directly bound to the maintenance of social order.[3]

Before the sixteenth- and seventeenth-century crises, folly erupted during transitions in the liturgical year to conduct a dialogue with the ruling social structures. At the interstices of a temporal cycle governing the culture, revellers could invert, travesty, and juggle all values and norms. After the Renaissance crises, increasingly more women and men could choose leisure activities for their off-hours. Although a separate kind of time, not a gap in the orderly progress of time, leisure could also provide a margin for rethinking cultural codes. These two recreative modes frame the historical moment of the ludic self, a time when, for a few key figures, play moved from the interstices and borders of social order to the center of consciousness. Literary representations of folly in the Renaissance anticipate the play of Donne, Herbert, Marvell, Burton, and Browne, while a contemporary fishing manual anticipates the new concept of leisure.

I

The medieval and Renaissance fool was an odd figure. He indulged every appetite, yet inspired awe as one touched by God; enjoyed access to the great, but remained a social nullity; inverted the social structure, and received rewards for causing havoc. In short, he embodied ambiguity and paradox. His play on the margins of society had helped generate an anti-structure to the medieval order, but that way of allowing for innovation was insufficient to accommodate revolutionary change. Nevertheless, the fool became a powerful symbol in the Renaissance mind. He moved from communal festivals and noble courts onto the popular stage and into the pages of widely available books because he represented pure potential: he was untrammeled by absolutes, agile enough to size up any situation and make a winning response, and free from responsibility for his shocking quips and antics. Those sensitive to the magnitude of the changes transforming Europe —men like Rabelais, Erasmus, More, Shakespeare, and Cervantes—needed this potential, freedom, and flexibility.

Rabelais seems to have been always on the move: becoming a Franciscan, a Benedictine, a secular priest, a physician, a member of an abbot's, a bishop's, a cardinal's, a seigneur's retinues; and travelling to the centers of intellectual and political controversy, Paris, Montpellier, Rome, and all points in between. Despite high-placed patrons, his satire that spared no one embroiled him in these controversies, forcing him once into hiding and perhaps to prison. Erasmus—born on the fringes of society, a priest's bastard—also rejected the rigors of monastic life and, like Rabelais, became a vagabond. His detachment from the social hierarchy and from any fixed place turned into a frame of mind, making him a peripatetic scholar, eventually Christendom's foremost humanist, and the lone voice for compromise in

Luther's war with Rome. Although More arose from bourgeois origins to become chancellor of England, he retained an Erasmian detachment from court life. When his wit so charmed Henry VIII that the king began to summon him for after-dinner entertainment, as kings summoned their fools, More curbed his natural merriness. But his later attempt to detach himself by silence from Henry's and the Pope's contradictory demands could not save him from martyrdom. From obscurity in a rural backwater, Shakespeare rose to become one of London's favorite entertainers, a position that brought him both financial success and the dubious privilege of hanging around the fringes of courtly society. And although Cervantes fought off the poverty to which he was born by becoming a soldier of fortune (wounded at the Battle of Lepanto, captured by pirates, and sold into slavery), then an author, he died a poor man, despite having written Spain's all-time best-seller.

These men witnessed and suffered the changes that altered Europe: the continental Reformation, France's quarrels and England's break with Rome, England's growing discontent with monarch and church, and the precipitous decline of Spain. They moved freely among the levels of social hierarchy but remained detached, living always on the edge or in between. In spirit they shared the marginality of the fool. In their works, they translated the fool from the margins of society, where he had played out alternatives to a social structure that evolved slowly, into an interior orientation that gave them a perspective on a culture in transition.[4]

According to Mikhail Bakhtin, Rabelais used the folly released in folk carnival to liberate minds from the Middle Ages' "narrow, vertical, extratemporal model of the world, with its absolute top and bottom, its system of ascents and descents," and to prepare minds for "a new model . . . in which the leading role was transferred to the historical lines, to the movement forward in real space and in historic time." Bakhtin's analysis demonstrates well how Rabelais anticipates Donne and Marvell in loosening objects and symbols from the medieval synthesis in which they were embedded. A prime example is young Gargantua's experimentation with various "Arse-wipes":

> Once I wiped myself on a lady's velvet mask, and I found it good. For the softness of the silk was most voluptuous to my fundament. Another time on one of their hoods, and I found it just as good. Another time on a lady's neckerchief; another time on some ear-flaps of crimson satin. But there were a lot of turdy gilt spangles on them, and they took all the skin off my bottom. . . . Then I wiped myself with a hen, a cock, and a chicken, with a calf's skin, a hare, a pigeon, and a cormorant, with a lawyer's bag, with a penitent's hood, with a coif, with an otter. But to conclude, I say and maintain that there is no arse-wiper like a well-downed goose. (66, 69)

Like Donne's conceits and Marvell's play with the myths of the old vision, this hodge-podge initiates a rethinking of all objects, uncrowning and renewing them by a different standard of value. In foolery like this and in Rabelais's pervasive wordplay, Bakhtin sees a carnivalization of the object world and of speech that frees readers from "official philosophy . . . from truisms and commonplace ideas," breaking the "century-old chains of medieval philosophy."[5]

Although Bakhtin's conception of carnivalization supports my contention that adopting the fool's stance previews the ludic self, his claims for the self embodied in carnival seem questionable, and his description of the effects of carnivalization, partial. There are no selves, argues Bakhtin, in carnival, only "the material bodily principle . . . contained not in the biological individual, not in the bourgeois ego, but in the people, a people who are continually growing and renewed" (19). The self is a later product of an economics of possession. Although Bakhtin represents "the people," imaged in the grotesque body, as a universal, deeply positive principle, he also describes Spanish Corpus Christi Day parades in which "negroes and moors" were paraded as "a grotesque deviation from the bodily norm" (230). This example exposes the darker side of carnival: its frequent aggression against those deemed alien in order to assert self-definition by group solidarity.[6]

Much of this aggression is directed against women. Bakhtin accounts for Rabelais's anti-feminism with reference to a prebourgeois "popular tradition . . . in no way hostile to woman. . . . Woman is essentially related to the material bodily lower stratum . . . that degrades and regenerates simultaneously" (240). Rabelais's version of the carnival spirit, however, includes the right of male access to the female body. Because an elegant lady refuses to "be covered and breed from" the importunate Panurge, he sprinkles her with a canine aphrodisiac that draws 600,014 dogs to sniff, slobber, and piss on her finery (239–44). Likewise, when Panurge offers to rebuild the walls of Paris with "the thing-o'-my-bobs of the ladies," which are "cheaper than stone," Rabelais does not emphasize, as Bakhtin claims, "the material bodily procreative principle" against which "military power and strength are helpless" (314). Rather, he graphically describes these vaginas as distilling "that blessed fruit of the great pox, as small as rain, but devilish dry," as attracting flies that "leave their excretions there," and as thus requiring swats "with fine fox-tails, or good ass-pizzles from Provence" (219). Although the first example intends to mock the pride of those who would possess their bodies as separate from all that farts and pisses, lives and dies, it also asserts man's right to possess the female body. The second example does not image the female body to deflate pretention, but to degrade that very body, asserting male separateness from his source.

Perhaps, then, the grotesque body of carnival represents not the precapitalist, universal principle of "the people," but the maternal body, with which revellers can merge in periodic indulgence and which they can debase to counter fears of engulfment. If so, then carnival and the literature that internalizes its spirit reenacts the conflicts attendant on the earliest stages of self-formation. As we have seen, preoccupations of the nascent self resurface when social structures come under attack, at carnival time as well as in periods of radical historical change.

Another criticism leveled at Bakhtin, specifically at his claims for the transformational powers of carnival, argues that carnival is licenced and contained by the power structure, and that its social effects are negligible.[7] When, however, the stance of folly, not necessarily traditional carnival themes, is internalized, then its paradoxes, reversals, inversions, and hybridizations of cultural codes escape containment in periodic festival to become a new way to orient the self. Rabelais shared this new mode of vision with his contemporary Erasmus.

In *Encomium Moriae* Erasmus speaks through not just any fool, but Folly herself. When she sets out to prove that, because all are fools, she is the universal monarch, she creates a classic self-referential paradox: if her claim is true, then what she, also a fool, says must be foolish and, therefore, not true. If she speaks truth, then she speaks folly. Thus, because her biting satire of contemporary life may be simultaneously truth and folly, Erasmus safely distances himself from the whole tangle. From the start he passes his book off as mere play, ambiguously entitling it as a praise either of folly or of his witty but wise friend More, and dismissing it in the preface as "some sport" (1).[8] By playing the fool in a world of fools, Erasmus can detach himself from the universal confusion and explore both sides of every question—that flattery is foolish deception, that flattery insures concord among friends and mates (25–28), that the Church has fallen to the folly of greed, that the Church preaches the holy folly of the cross (97–100, 116). By thinking the way the fool acts, Erasmus learned to live within, while observing from without, an era of competing worldviews.

More kept a household fool, and, by all reports, knew how to play the fool. Erasmus claimed that "jesting was the main object of his life," and other friends less attuned to More's wit complained, "Ye use . . . to look so sadly when ye mean merrily that many times men doubt whether ye speak in sport when ye mean good earnest."[9] In *Utopia* More used his wit to give unwanted counsel in a dangerous time. He places his description of a "no place" (or "good place"?) in the mouth of an idealistic traveler, Raphael Hythloday, whose name means "nonsense-peddler" (or "God heals through nonsense"?); he assumes for himself the safe role of the dubious interlocutor; and he casts his book as a hoax for the amusement of humanist friends who would get the etymological jokes (3, n.; 6, n. 9). By framing the whole enterprise as play, he can satirize English pride and greed while playing with the possibilities of a community without private property—with ideals, such as universal disdain for self-display, and with more questionable practices, such as state-sanctioned pressure on the terminally ill to commit suicide. Using dialogue form and portraying Utopia as sometimes ideal, sometimes flawed, and often ludicrous, More turns the questions of good government around for his reader to examine from a variety of angles. Unlike Hythloday, who refuses to serve as counselor to a king, More in writing the *Utopia* tries to do what the character "More" claims is the job of a good counselor: to "influence policy indirectly, handle the situation tactfully, and thus what you cannot turn to good, you may at least make less bad" (29). In a work of fiction, a joke, mere "nonsense" about "nowhere," More gives honest, if indirect, counsel on how to think complexly about the complexities of governance, all the while remaining detached and uncommitted.[10] Through fool's play, he gains this advantageous double stance.

Shakespeare embodies the Protean nature of the fool in Feste, Touchstone, Lear's fool, and Hamlet's "antic disposition." More generally, Shakespeare's way of seeing the world shares much with Erasmus's vision in *Encomium Moriae*. Standing apart, Shakespeare sets characters, each as compelling as the next, in motion to play out insoluble dilemmas. Typically, he presents oppositions, each of which seems desirable and destructive, so that readers and viewers face impossible choices.[11] In *Henry IV, part I,* Falstaff so full of life charms us, but his callousness toward his ragged charge of foot is deplorable. Hotspur's vigor and feistiness are winning, but his egotism is brattish. And lest we think too simply of Hal as the ideal of princely honor, his first soliloquy reveals the calculating politician beneath the armor and plumes of the last act. Similarly, Kate the shrew and Shylock the Jew must in the end convert to the ruling orthodoxy, but their lively characterizations produce critiques at least as compelling as their conversions. Shakespeare's dramas entice the audience into a world that questions values and absolutes, the world of inversions and ambiguities to which medieval folly once reduced society. Now, however, theatre plays the role of the fool.

Sancho Panza and Don Quixote also originated in medieval folly, Sancho as the "natural" ruled by appetite and Don Quixote as the foolish madman. But Cervantes reverses the tradition: instead of opposing the materialistic fool to mock the reigning ideals of society, Cervantes makes Sancho's realism the reigning worldview, and Don Quixote's idealism aberrant folly.[12] Playing with the tradition of folly, Cervantes reverses its reversals, asking his reader whether the "real" world of Spain in decline—peopled by dirty muleteers, greedy innkeepers, and peasant sluts—calls Don Quixote's chivalric ideals into question, or vice versa. Since Cervantes attributes *Don Quixote* to the Moor, Cide Hamete Benengeli, but pointedly reminds us that infidels are liars, can we assume that Cervantes shares Benengeli's stated goal, to destroy the illusion of knight errantry (75–78, 940)? If not, can we assume that Cervantes laments the passing of a noble ideal?

Don Quixote's knightly vigil, his exaltation of the wench Aldonza to the lady Dulcinea, and his ineffectual vow to right wrongs are obviously ludicrous; nevertheless, genuine acts of chivalry do occur in the novel. After being rescued from servants who try to wash his beard with dishwater, Sancho kneels to the Duchess, his protectress, and offers to serve her as a loyal knight (684–85). If even the novel's reality principle converts to Don Quixote's ideal, which "reality" should the reader credit? Furthermore, after the novel has established the grimy world of inns and travelers as the reality against which to judge Don Quixote's fantastic visions, the mad Don meets the wanderer Cardenio, a youth driven mad by love, who pens Petrarchan sonnets and whose story includes all the conventions of romance fiction. Now the reader's "reality" seems as fantastic as Don Quixote's hilarious attempt to enact the love madness of Orlando or Amadis de Gaul (183–217). And when Quixote encounters on the dusty roads characters out of fiction —like Gines da Pasamonte, a self-confessed picaresque hero (176–77), and Don Alvaro Tarfe, a character from the spurious part 2 of *Don Quixote* (926–29)—Cervantes explodes the readers' smug assurance of what is real and what fiction. Like the fool who gleefully turns the world upside down, Cervantes dissolves the distinctions by which the reader defines reality, detaching him from a worldview too long taken for granted and offering a new perspective on the values colliding at the end of an era in Spain.

By the Renaissance, the fool had moved from the margins of society into literary consciousness, metamorphosing from an antic figure in motley into a mode of vision. Using the flexibility and freedom of fool's play to interpret a world in crisis, Rabelais, Erasmus, More, Shakespeare, and Cervantes form a significant literary context for the evolution of the ludic self.

Although the play of Donne, Herbert, Marvell, Burton, and Browne structurally resembles the fool's stance, they seldom revert to the traditional carnival themes of the grotesque body so prominent in Rabelais and echoed in Erasmus, Shakespeare, and Cervantes. A different set of cultural codes was beginning to construct the self in the seventeenth century, codes disciplining the body's smells and orifices of interchange, increasing the distance between separate bodies and thus separate selves. This change, evident in prologues to plays chastizing rowdy audiences and in the dwindling of the great hall in country house architecture, was part of the larger shift that separated objects and selves from the residual monolithic system of hierarchies.[13] Although the seventeenth-century players considered here register both changes in their texts, they do not project alienated selves. Instead, they fill the new space opened up between self and other, between self and system, with play.

II

Unlike his contemporaries, Izaak Walton plays without adopting play as a stance for the self. *The Compleat Angler* is a puzzling book. It is part fishing manual (detailing, for example, the feeding habits of the "Tyrant" Pike, the correct methods for scouring "gentles," and the best recipe for removing the "waterish" taste of the Chub), part meditation on the quiet life (including both a sermon on thankfulness and the "Come live with me" lyrics of Marlowe, Raleigh, and Donne), and part fictional account of a fishing trip (describing a May Day morning on which a fisherman, Piscator, sets out from London; his meeting with a huntsman, Venator; their five days of angling; and return to Tottenham High-Cross).[14] *The Compleat Angler* seems to be neither fish nor fowl. What is its intent?

Walton and his contemporaries valued the book as a how-to manual. Charles Cotton, styling himself "Piscator Junior" and lavishly praising "Father Izaak," composed a sequel on fly fishing, and Robert Venables added another to make up a three-part volume, *The Universal Angler,* published in 1676. Still, this fishing book has charmed readers like Sir Leslie Stephen, to whom "fishing is an abomination."[15] In *The Sketch Book,* Washington Irving tells of being "completely bitten with the angling mania" from reading "the seductive pages of honest Izaak Walton." But when he took to the streams, "as stark mad as was ever Don Quixote from reading books of chivalry," he confesses, "I hooked myself instead of the fish; tangled my line in every tree; lost my bait; broke my rod; until I gave up the attempt in despair, and passed the day under the trees, reading old Izaak."[16] The oddity is that a book devoted largely to the minutest details of fishing fascinates readers who are no more than armchair anglers.

Although readers classify *The Compleat Angler* variously, Walton tells us in the opening epistle what his book is, how he wrote it, and how we should read it: *"I wish the* Reader *. . . to take notice, that in writing of it I have made my self a* recreation *of a* recreation; *and that it might prove so to him, and not read* dull *and* tediously, *I have in several places mixt (not any scurrility, but) some innocent, harmless mirth"* (169). *The Compleat Angler* is a reenactment (re-creation) of play (recreation) and, as such, becomes recreation for the reader as well as the author.[17] Walton leads the reader into the play of angling through the fictional situation. He conveys his practical and moral instruction by taking the role of Piscator, the experienced fisherman, and offering the role of Venator, the huntsman ignorant of angling, to his reader. Like author and reader, Piscator meets Venator on the first page, parts with him on the last, and instructs him on all the pages in between. As the dubious Venator converts to the joys of fishing and joins "the Brotherhood of the angle," so does the reader, who imaginatively accompanies Piscator to Trout Hall, becomes his diligent "scholar" during the day, and shares the angler's mirth, songs, and fish dinners in the evenings. Hence Walton allows readers like Irving and Stephen to play at fishing—to let the recreation of reading a re-creation of angling substitute for the thing itself. He is angling not merely to catch future anglers, but to recruit converts to the angler's cast of mind.

Like his contemporaries, Walton frames his book as play, but his goal is not finding a way to live with the dilemmas of seventeenth-century life. Unlike Hamlet, Donne, Herbert, Marvell, Burton, and Browne, who play amidst treacherous villains, the splendor and terror of Omnipotence, the perils of history, and hundreds of unanswered questions of science, Walton plays with fish. Fishing and writing about fishing are a temporary retreat from conflict, not a way to live within it. In phrases that betoken the growing separation of work from play, Walton contrasts the joyful fisherman to "the *Lawyer* . . . swallowed up with business" and "the *States-man* . . . preventing or contriving plots" (261). In fishing, Piscator promises Venator "a contentedness above the reach of" "money-getting-men . . . that spend all their time first in getting, and next in anxious care to keep it" (177). Whether Walton is fishing or the armchair angler is reading about fishing, the goal is escape from labor in order to recreate the spirit.

Walton's anglers rejuvenate themselves through what Mihaly Csikszentmihalyi calls "flow." When an actor's field of action is delimited in time and space, when clearly defined actions produce unambiguous results, and when the actor has sufficient skill to meet the demands of the environment, then s/he may experience the exhilarating tension, feeling of competence, loss of self-consciousness, and merger with the environment that constitute flow.[18] Csikszentmihalyi's informants experienced flow while dancing, rock climbing, and playing chess; apparently, Walton flowed while fishing.

This resonant interchange with the environment and consequent experience of wholeness are what Piscator offers Venator in the recreation of angling and what Walton offers the reader in the recreative re-creation of angling. The sportsmen leave the busy city, setting themselves apart from the confusing world of business, law, and politics. That world is a bewildering "Hodg-poch of business, and mony, and care, / And care, and mony and trouble" (335)—where "pertinacious Schismatick[s]" wrangle fruitlessly over absurd points like "whether it was easiest to rip a Cloak, or to unrip a Cloak" (264) and where the owner of a pleasant meadow had so "many Law-suits depending . . . that they both damp'd his mirth, and took up so much of his time and thoughts, that he himself had not leisure to take the sweet content" offered by his own fields (333–34). Leaving all controversy, whether theological or legal, behind, the angler delimits his field of action to exclude the unpredictable world of humans and to include only the predictable habits of fish.

Walton praises the simple life of the fisherman while at the same time instructing Venator in the myriad details of extremely complex fishing techniques: tying artificial flies, knotting a line, painting a pole, securing the right bait for the right fish, finding each breed's hiding place, determining what fish bites when, and so forth. The angler's life is simple, but only insofar as he narrows his focus to comprehensible (although complicated) actions that achieve clear results: the angler knows that he has used the right tackle, secured the right bait, found the right spot, and fished at the right time when he catches a fish. If he fails, there are a finite number of snags to untangle. Consequently, fishing can generate the resonant relation with the environment that characterizes flow. Piscator experiences this sense of wholeness, rejoicing that he can match his mind to nature: "No life," he tells Venator, "so happy and so pleasant, as the life of a well governed *Angler;*... we sit on *Cowslip-banks,* hear the birds sing, and possess our selves in as much quietness as these silent silver streams, which we now see glide so quietly by us" (261). In angling he matches his actions to the environment's demands, and his quiet mind becomes a mirror of the quiet stream.

Turning from the baffling complexity of theology, politics, and business, which can overwhelm the wisest, both angler and reader enjoy the fascinating complexity of angling, which can challenge the real and the vicarious sportsman. Instead of playing to live amidst unpredictable confusion and conflict, Walton plays to reduce the unmanageable to manageable proportions, thereby regaining a sense of competence.[19]

In some ways *The Compleat Angler* (published in five editions between 1653 and 1676) seems old-fashioned. It advocates what appears to be a pastoral retreat from the religious and political turmoil of the Commonwealth and Protectorate, and perhaps also from the immorality of the Restoration.[20] In his praise of the calm, simple life of the angler and of several noted Anglican fishermen, Walton may have intended to associate "angling" with "Anglican" (an etymology acceptable to the seventeenth-century mind), thus with men of the good old days before the war.[21] But the world to which Walton retreats is not a golden age in a *locus amoenus* or an unfallen Eden; it is a state of mind in which the intricacies of sport engross the player. So long as the angler is coordinating three poles simultaneously to catch a bream, anointing worms with ivy berry oil to give them an irresistable smell, recounting "fish tales" about pikes blinded by malicious frogs and choked by a necklace of tadpoles, or sharing the "secret" recipe for pike, his mind is free from the complexity of the work-a-day world. While seeking in the ancient tradition of the pastoral a mode for expressing his response to seventeenth-century life, Walton turns the pastoral impulse into something new.

The Compleat Angler anticipates the new concept of leisure, which evolved throughout the eighteenth and nineteenth centuries. The obligatory communal holidays of the Middle Ages sanctioned play, at liminal times in marginal places among fringe people, that challenged and renewed the social order. By contrast, leisure was free time, set apart from obligatory labor for society, in which the individual selected an activity for recreation. Before and after the Renaissance, play (whether it be the fool's inversions of social norms or the sportsman's reduction of social complexity to a manageable scale) maintained a dialogue with the prevailing social structure from its margins. For a brief moment in between, a few literary players changed the way we can think about who we are by transforming play from a marginal indulgence into a stance for the self.

Men like Rabelais, Erasmus, More, Shakespeare, and Cervantes, who witnessed first-hand the Renaissance revolutions in states and minds, came to see in new ways by internalizing folly. Later, as England sped through a century of economic dislocation, theological wrangling, and intellectual ferment toward political upheaval in civil war and regicide, Donne, Herbert, Marvell, Burton, and Browne redefined the self, threatened by these shocks to the cultural structures that had once formed and sustained it. They all in characteristic ways imaged the contradictions of seventeenth-century life as they experienced them—the poets, as conflicts that assault the nascent self; the prose writers, as competing ways of knowing the self (both body and soul), nature, and God. They all in characteristic ways also played to survive these clashes, to loosen the old structures that had once defined the self, and to scramble the pieces, experimenting with what new stances and structures might arise.

Although crafting the ludic self may have been serious business, the results are no less delightful. For sheer dash and verve, these literary players remain unsurpassed even by postmodern sleight-of-hand.

Notes

Chapter 1

1. William Shakespeare, *Hamlet,* in *The Complete Works of Shakespeare,* ed. Hardin Craig and David Bevington, rev. ed. (Glenview, Illinois: Scott, Foresman, 1973), 1.5.172. Subsequent quotations from Shakespeare will follow this edition. Robert Burton, *The Anatomy of Melancholy,* ed. Holbrook Jackson (1932; reprint, New York: Vintage Books, 1977), 1:20. Sir Thomas Browne, *Religio Medici and Other Works,* ed. L. C. Martin (Oxford: Clarendon Press, 1964), 70. Izaak Walton, *The Compleat Angler 1653–1676,* ed. Jonquil Bevan (Oxford: Clarendon Press, 1983), 169.

2. Sir John Harington, "A Treatise on Playe," in *Nugae Antiquae,* ed. Thomas Park (London: Vernor and Hood, Poultry, and Cuthell and Martin, 1804), 1:188–89. See 2 Sam. 6:21–22 in the King James Version. All Biblical quotations follow the King James Version unless otherwise noted.

3. See Barbara K. Lewalski, *Protestant Poetics and the Seventeenth-Century Religious Lyric* (Princeton: Princeton Univ. Press, 1979), 190. Although Lewalski sees the association in emblem books of the religious life with play as inadvertent, Leah Sinanoglou Marcus has described the revival in the seventeenth century of a long tradition connecting child's play to Christian humility. The most prominent representatives of this tradition are perhaps the thirteenth-century Franciscans; see Marcus, *Childhood and Cultural Despair: A Theme and Variations in Seventeenth-Century Literature* (Pittsburgh: Univ. of Pittsburgh Press, 1978), 16, 76–79.

4. "To My Worthy Friend Master Geo. Sands, on his Translation of the Psalmes," in *The Poems of Thomas Carew,* ed. Rhodes Dunlap (Oxford: Clarendon Press, 1949), 93–94, ll. 13–16.

5. Daniel Featley, *Ancilla Pietatis,* quoted in Lewalski, *Protestant Poetics,* 223.

6. *John Donne: The Complete English Poems,* ed. A. J. Smith (1971; reprint, New York: Penguin Books, 1980), 319, ll. 71–72; 323, ll. 188–89. Subsequent quotations from Donne's poetry will follow this edition and will be cited parenthetically in the text.

7. Mikhail Bakhtin, *Rabelais and His World,* trans. Helene Iswolsky (Cambridge: MIT Press, 1968). Richard A. Lanham, *The Motives of Eloquence: Literary*

Rhetoric in the Renaissance (New Haven: Yale Univ. Press, 1976), 1–35. Richard Helgerson, *Self-Crowned Laureates: Spenser, Jonson, Milton, and the Literary System* (Berkeley: Univ. of California Press, 1983). Marcus, *Childhood and Cultural Despair,* and *The Politics of Mirth: Jonson, Herrick, Milton, Marvell, and the Defense of Old Holiday Pastimes* (Chicago: Univ. of Chicago Press, 1986). Frank J. Warnke, *Versions of Baroque: European Literature in the Seventeenth Century* (New Haven: Yale Univ. Press, 1972), 66–129; quote taken from "Sacred Play: Baroque Poetic Style," *Journal of Aesthetics and Art Criticism* 22 (1964): 463. See also Thomas Greene, "The Flexibility of the Self in Renaissance Literature," in *The Disciplines of Criticism: Essays in Literary Theory, Interpretation, and History,* ed. Peter Demetz, Thomas Greene, and Lowry Nelson, Jr. (New Haven: Yale Univ. Press, 1968), 241–64.

8. Jacques Lacan, *The Language of the Self: The Function of Language in Psychoanalysis,* trans. Anthony Wilden (Baltimore: The Johns Hopkins Press, 1968); "The Mirror-phase as Formative of the Function of the I," *New Left Review* 51 (Sept.–Oct. 1968): 71–77.

9. Lacan, "Mirror-phase," 72–74. Wilden, Introduction to Lacan, *Language of the Self,* xiii.

10. D. W. Winnicott, "Ego Distortion in Terms of True and False Self," in *The Maturational Processes and the Facilitating Environment: Studies in the Theory of Emotional Development* (New York: International Universities Press, 1965), 140–52.

11. Michel Foucault, "What is an Author?" in *Textual Strategies: Perspectives in Post-Structuralist Criticism,* ed. Josué V. Harari (Ithaca: Cornell Univ. Press, 1979), 153. Jonathan Goldberg, *Voice Terminal Echo: Postmodernism and English Renaissance Texts* (New York: Methuen, 1986), 20.

12. Julia Kristeva has described a subject on trial and in process: Toril Moi, Introduction to *The Kristeva Reader,* ed. Toril Moi (New York: Columbia Univ. Press, 1986), 13–15; and Kristeva, "The System and the Speaking Subject," in *Kristeva Reader,* 27–30.

13. Fred Weinstein and Gerald M. Platt, *Psychoanalytic Sociology: An Essay on the Interpretation of Historical Data and the Phenomena of Collective Behavior* (Baltimore: The Johns Hopkins Press, 1973), 69, n. 15.

14. D. W. Winnicott, *Playing and Reality* (New York: Basic Books, 1971), 38–52, 95–103.

15. Sigmund Freud, *Beyond the Pleasure Principle,* vol. 18 of *The Standard Edition of the Complete Psychological Works of Sigmund Freud,* trans. James Strachey (London: Hogarth Press, 1953–74), 14–17. Anthony Wilden, "Lacan and the Discourse of the Other," in Lacan, *Language of the Self,* 191.

16. Kristeva, "Speaking Subject," in *Kristeva Reader,* 26; *Revolution in Poetic Language,* trans. Margaret Waller (New York: Columbia Univ. Press, 1984).

17. Among the many surveys of play theory, I have found the following ones most useful. For animal play and the social science perspectives on human play, see Jerome S. Bruner, Alison Jolly, and Kathy Sylva, eds., *Play: Its Role in Development and Evolution* (New York: Basic Books, 1976), and Susanna Millar, *The Psychology of Play* (1968; reprint, New York: Jason Aronson, 1974). Millar discusses the Nyansongo children on 209–11. For children's play, see Helen B. Schwartzman, *Transformations: The Anthropology of Children's Play* (New York: Plenum Press, 1978). For the uses of play among modern philosophers and scientists as well as social scientists, see Mihai I. Spariosu, *Literature, Mimesis and Play: Essays in Literary Theory* (Tübingen: Gunter Narr Verlag,1982), 13–52, and *Dionysus Reborn: Play and the Aesthetic Dimension in Modern Philosophical and Scientific Discourse* (Ithaca: Cornell Univ. Press, 1989). For theologians on play, see Harvey Cox, *The Feast of Fools: A Theological Essay on Festivity and Fantasy* (Cambridge: Harvard Univ. Press, 1969); Robert E. Neale, *In Praise of Play: Toward a Psychology of Religion* (New York: Harper and Row, 1969); David L. Miller, *Gods and Games: Toward a Theology of Play* (New York: World Publishing Company, 1970); Jürgen Moltmann, *Theology of Play*, trans. Reinhard Ulrich (New York: Harper, 1972); and Hugo Rahner, *Man at Play* (New York: Herder and Herder, 1972).

18. See James A. G. Marino, "An Annotated Bibliography of Play and Literature," *Canadian Review of Comparative Literature* 12 (June 1985): 306–53.

19. Johan Huizinga, *Homo Ludens: A Study of the Play-Element in Culture*, trans. Karl Mannheim (1949; reprint, Boston: Beacon Press, 1955), 132, 129, 119.

20. Jacques Derrida, "Structure, Sign, and Play in the Discourse of the Human Sciences," in *The Structuralist Controversy: The Languages of Criticism and the Sciences of Man*, ed. Richard Macksey and Eugenio Donato (Baltimore: The Johns Hopkins Press, 1970), 247–65.

21. Spariosu, *Dionysus Reborn*, 65–124, 153–63; Heraclitus's fragment 52 is quoted on 13. For more expert expositions and criticisms of Derrida's position than this study can offer, see M. H. Abrams, "The Deconstructive Angel," *Critical Inquiry* 3 (1977): 425–38; and Frank Lentricchia, *After the New Criticism* (Chicago: Univ. of Chicago Press, 1980), 164–89, 208–10. In response to questions, Derrida has claimed that American critics have overestimated the importance of "free play" in his *oeuvre*, "Afterward: Toward an Ethic of Discussion," in *Limited Inc*, trans. Samuel Weber and Jeffry Mehlman (Evanston, Illinois: Northwestern Univ. Press, 1988), 115–16. I would like to thank Bainard Cowan for calling my attention to this discussion.

22. Much of Fink's work remains untranslated. See, however, Chap. 2, n. 11. For surveys of his views, see Spariosu, *Dionysus Reborn*, 125–33, and David Farrell Krell, "Towards an Ontology of Play: Eugen Fink's Notion of *Spiel*," *Research in Phenomenology* 2 (1972): 63–93.

23. Schwartzman, *Transformations*, 330. Susanna Millar notes, "Perhaps play is best used as an adverb; not as a name of a class of activities, nor as distinguished by the accompanying mood, but to describe how and under what conditions an action is performed," *Psychology of Play*, 21.

24. Gregory Bateson, "The Message 'This is play,'" in *Group Processes: Transactions of the Second Conference,* ed. Bertram Schaffner (New York: Josiah Macy, Jr. Foundation, 1956), 145–242; "Metalogue: Why a Swan?" and "A Theory of Play and Fantasy," in *Steps to an Ecology of Mind* (New York: Ballantine Books, 1972), 33–37, 177–93.

25. Fulke Greville, *Life of Sir Philip Sidney,* ed. Nowell Smith (Oxford: Clarendon Press, 1907), 153–54. Annabel Patterson also adduces Greville's phrase in her exposition of the deliberate and functional ambiguity of Renaissance texts, *Censorship and Interpretation: The Conditions of Writing and Reading in Early Modern England* (Madison: Univ. of Wisconsin Press, 1984), 42–43.

26. Erving Goffman, *Frame Analysis: An Essay on the Organization of Experience* (New York: Harper and Row, 1974), 40–58. Goffman describes a third transformational frame, "ceremonials" or rituals: "On the occasion of these 'performative displays' something gets accomplished once and for all which has important connections and ramifications in [the participants'] wider world" (58). Since Huizinga (*Homo Ludens,* 14–27), many play theorists have considered ritual to be a kind of play. Because both have paradoxical frames, play and ritual have similar logical structures: they are activities that redefine themselves. For example, in the Catholic mass, actions that allude to and purport to imitate preparing and eating a meal transform themselves into a bloodless sacrifice and communal merger with the divine. Despite close structural parallels, ritual differs from play experientially because the participants believe the efficacy of the ritual transformation to be a matter of high seriousness and to extend well beyond the action itself. Because nonbelievers might make the same claim for the transforming power of play, game, sport, or drama, the dividing line between play and ritual is often difficult to maintain.

In a fourth category of paradoxical and transforming frames called "technical redoings," Goffman includes experiment. Also structurally similar to play, experimentation frames a context in which actions (such as Francis Bacon freezing a chicken) redefine themselves as a means of gathering information (a scientific procedure to determine the principles of refrigeration). As in make-believe, contests, and ceremonials, these actions are not what they are (73–74).

27. Sigmund Freud, "Creative Writers and Day-Dreaming," in *Standard Edition,* 9:143–53.

28. *Milton's Sonnets,* ed. E. A. J. Honigmann (New York: St. Martins Press, 1966), Sonnet 19, p. 22.

29. David J. Leigh, S. J., "Donne's 'A Hymne to God the Father': New Dimensions," *Studies in Philology* 75 (1978): 84–92; and David Novarr, "Donne and the 'Undeterminable Desire of More'" (paper delivered at a conference entitled "The Eagle and the Dove: Reassessing John Donne," Univ. of Michigan-Dearborn, 15–16 October 1982).

30. Thomas O. Sloane makes a similar distinction in his contrast between Donne's and Milton's use of humanist rhetoric: *Donne, Milton, and the End of Humanist Rhetoric* (Berkeley: Univ. of California Press, 1985).

31. For distinguishing playful from nonplayful literature, see Peter Hutchinson, *Games Authors Play* (London: Methuen, 1983), 13–14. For the playful self projected from a literary text, see Lanham, *Motives of Eloquence*. For the roles that authors offer to readers, see Walter J. Ong, S. J., "The Writer's Audience Is Always a Fiction," *PMLA* 90 (1975): 9–21.

Chapter 2

1. Tony Manocchio and William Petitt use *Hamlet* to illustrate the double bind theory in *Families Under Stress: A Psychological Interpretation* (London: Routledge and Kegan Paul, 1975), 56–101. David Leverenz uses R. D. Laing's term *knots* to describe some of the familial binds in *Hamlet;* see "The Woman in *Hamlet*: An Interpersonal View," *Signs* 4 (1978): 291–308. For the distinctions between my perspective and other psychological readings of the play based on the theories of Freud, Erikson, Laing, and Lacan, see my "*Hamlet*, 'A Man to Double Business Bound,'" *Shakespeare Quarterly* 34 (1983):181–99.

2. John H. Weakland, "The 'Double Bind' Hypothesis of Schizophrenia and Three-Party Interaction (1960)," in *Double Bind: The Foundation of the Communicational Approach to the Family,* ed. Carlos E. Sluki and Donald C. Ransom (New York: Grune and Stratten, 1976), 24. See also Milton M. Berger, ed., *Beyond the Double Bind: Communication and Family Systems, Theories, and Techniques with Schizophrenics* (New York: Brunner/Mazel, 1978). Both of these collections of essays contain the original 1956 paper "Toward a Theory of Schizophrenia," by Gregory Bateson, Don D. Jackson, Jay Haley, and John Weakland, plus numerous articles expanding, modifying, and revising the theory.

3. Bateson et al., "Toward a Theory of Schizophrenia," in Sluki and Ransom, *Double Bind,* 14–15.

4. *Ibid.*, 17. Many revisions of the original double bind theory emphasize that an observer ought not to isolate a "binder" and a "victim" in families where double bind patterns of communication predominate. Generally, the binds are mutually imposed, and assigning blame to one family member for beginning the pattern has little relevance to the present situation. Whereas the complexity of living beings in human families may make it difficult to assign blame, families portrayed in art may more clearly reveal the source of the double bind.

5. *Ibid.*, p. 18. While describing the genesis of culture in human sacrifice that ends reciprocal violence, René Girard relates the double bind theory and *Hamlet*, each separately, to his theories about revenge. He argues that the double bind, as defined here, is merely one instance of "mimetic desire" that forms the basis of all human interaction: for example, fathers always tell sons, "Imitate me, but don't imitate me by appropriating my prerogatives." So sons become their fathers' rivals, and violent conflict is inevitable. (See *Violence and the Sacred,* trans. Patrick Gregory [Baltimore: The Johns Hopkins Press, 1977], 143–92; *Things Hidden Since the Foundation of the*

World, trans. Stephen Bann and Michael Metteer [Stanford: Stanford Univ. Press, 1987], 291–94). To Girard, *Hamlet* dramatizes, in its protagonist's disgust and delay, Shakespeare's own weariness with the circular violence of the revenge play genre. Although Girard interprets Hamlet's delay as reluctance to "enter the circle of mimetic desire and rivalry" (289), Girard does not discuss the specific double binds confronting Hamlet (see "Hamlet's Dull Revenge," in *Literary Theory/Renaissance Texts*, ed. Patricia Parker and David Quint [Baltimore: The Johns Hopkins Press, 1986], 280–302).

6. Critics have described the play's paradoxes variously. For the interrogative mode of the play, see C. S. Lewis, "Hamlet: The Prince or the Poem?" in *Modern Shakespearean Criticism: Essays on Style, Dramaturgy, and the Major Plays*, ed. Alvin B. Kernan (New York: Harcourt, Brace and World, 1970), 301–11; and Maynard Mack, "The World of *Hamlet*," *Yale Review* 41 (1952): 502–23. For irony, see Harry Levin, *The Question of Hamlet* (1959; reprint, New York: Viking Press, 1964), and Thomas F. Van Laan, "Ironic Reversal in *Hamlet*," *Studies in English Literature* 6 (1966): 247–62. For irreconcilable oppositions, see John Lawlor, *The Tragic Sense in Shakespeare* (New York: Harcourt Brace, 1960), 9–16, 45–73; Norman Rabkin, *Shakespeare and the Common Understanding* (New York: The Free Press, 1967), 1–13; Nicholas Brooke, *Shakespeare's Early Tragedies* (London: Methuen, 1968), 163–206; Nigel Alexander, *Poison, Play, and Duel: A Study in Hamlet* (Lincoln: Univ. of Nebraska Press, 1971), 8–9, 14; and Bernard McElroy, *Shakespeare's Mature Tragedies* (Princeton: Princeton Univ. Press, 1973), 29–88. For verbal mystification, see Paul A. Jorgensen, *Redeeming Shakespeare's Words* (Berkeley: Univ. of California Press, 1962), 100–20; Maurice Charney, *Style in Hamlet* (Princeton: Princeton Univ. Press, 1969); and Lawrence Danson, *Tragic Alphabet: Shakespeare's Drama of Language* (New Haven: Yale Univ. Press, 1974), 22–49.

7. Although some critics have argued that *adulterate* did not have such a specific meaning, the ghost's word, at least, implies that Gertrude may have been an adulteress—an implication sufficient to taint Hamlet's mind. In documenting Elizabethan revulsion at marriages between brothers- and sisters-in-law, Roland M. Frye mentions preachers who labeled such marriages "adultery"; see *The Renaissance Hamlet: Issues and Responses in 1600* (Princeton: Princeton Univ. Press, 1984), 79. For opposing views, see John Dover Wilson, *What Happens in Hamlet* (London: Cambridge Univ. Press, 1935), 292–94, and McElroy, *Shakespeare's Mature Tragedies*, 53.

8. Wilson, *What Happens in Hamlet*, 44–50; M. M. Mahood, *Shakespeare's Wordplay* (London: Methuen, 1957), 17–18; Irving Ribner, *Patterns in Shakespearean Tragedy* (London: Methuen, 1960), 72–73; and Alexander, *Poison, Play, and Duel*, 45–46.

9. Eleanor Prosser, *Hamlet and Revenge*, 2nd ed. rev. (Stanford: Stanford Univ. Press, 1971), 5–10, 135–37. Frye (*Renaissance Hamlet*, 22–75) outlines the contemporary contexts that made Hamlet's dilemma "intensely challenging, and perhaps even insoluble": the condemnations of private revenge but the duty of magistrates to revenge and punish; the condemnations of rebellion against a crowned king but the justifications for tyrannicide.

10. Although he attributes Hamlet's confusion to unstated scruples about taking revenge, John Lawlor (*The Tragic Sense,* 45, 66, 72) agrees that *Hamlet* does not understand himself and that this lack of self-knowledge is what makes his soliloquies pose unanswerable questions.

11. Eugen Fink, "The Oasis of Happiness: Toward an Ontology of Play," trans. from *Oase des Glücks* by Ute and Thomas Saine. In *Games, Play, Literature: Yale French Studies* 41 (1968): 23–24.

12. For similar views, see Brents Stirling, *Unity in Shakespearian Tragedy: The Interplay of Theme and Character* (New York: Columbia Univ. Press, 1956), 86–110; and McElroy, *Shakespeare's Mature Tragedies,* 61.

13. See Roy W. Battenhouse, *Shakespearean Tragedy: Its Art and Its Christian Premises* (Bloomington: Indiana Univ. Press, 1969), 236; and McElroy, *Shakespeare's Mature Tragedies,* 63–64. For the traditional Freudian interpretations of the poisoning and Hamlet's "oral aggression," see Norman Holland, *Psychoanalysis and Shakespeare* (New York: McGraw-Hill, 1964), 193–94; and Melvin D. Faber, "*Hamlet*, Sarcasm and Psychoanalysis," *Psychoanalytic Review* 55 (1968): 79–90.

14. To Eileen Jorge Allman, these forces prevent *Hamlet* from maturing into a true "Player-King" who eventually redeems his society through play; see *Player-King and Adversary: Two Faces of Play in Shakespeare* (Baton Rouge: Louisiana State Univ. Press, 1980), 211–54. For less positive approaches to the motivations for Hamlet's playing, see Lanham, *Motives of Eloquence,* 129–43; and Battenhouse, *Shakespearean Tragedy,* 255– 58.

15. Nigel Alexander analyzes *duel* as one of the three crucial symbolic actions in the play in *Poison, Play, and Duel.*

16. Similarly, a schizophrenic will often try to escape from double bind interactions by insisting that either s/he or the other person is really someone else or is not really present. See Bateson et al., "Toward a Theory of Schizophrenia," in *Double Bind,* 9. Eleanor Prosser argues that the ghost is, in fact, a "goblin damned" who urges Hamlet to commit the mortal sin of murder (*Hamlet and Revenge,* 108–22).

17. Although the Craig-Bevington edition prefers the reading "Tropically," the Q_1 reading is "Trapically."

18. See Simon O. Lesser, *Fiction and the Unconscious* (Boston: Beacon Press, 1957), 135, 262; and Jay Haley, "Paradoxes in Play, Fantasy, and Psychotherapy," *Psychiatric Research Reports* 2 (1955): 52–58.

19. Nigel Alexander discusses Hamlet's failure to love Ophelia in *Poison, Play, and Duel,* 119–52.

20. Prosser, *Hamlet and Revenge,* 213. Frye (*Renaissance Hamlet,* 151–64) defends Hamlet's chiding of Gertrude, citing Protestant theologians' conception of shriving, of amending one's neighbor's sin. But Hamlet's language reveals a passion and revulsion beyond the requirements of persuasion.

21. For discussions of Hamlet's playing avenger, see Prosser, *Hamlet and Revenge,* 192; Charney, *Style in Hamlet,* 318, and *Hamlet's Fictions* (New York: Routledge, 1988), 77–87; Battenhouse, *Shakespearean Tragedy,* 255–56; Danson, *Tragic Alphabet,* 44–45; and Lanham, *Motives of Eloquence,* 134–36.

22. Charney agrees that Providence releases Hamlet from the trap of "infinite regress patterns of revenge and sexuality," *Hamlet's Fictions,* 61–76. William B. Warner, however, denies that Providence concludes the play's action and describes Hamlet's agreeing to the duel as the play of sport, the zestful confrontation with chance of a Nietzschean tragic hero; see *Chance and the Text of Experience: Freud, Nietzsche, and Shakespeare's Hamlet* (Ithaca: Cornell Univ. Press, 1986), 260–76.

23. Prosser, *Hamlet and Revenge,* 111–12. Walter N. King, in *Hamlet's Search for Meaning* (Athens: Univ. of Georgia Press, 1982), 22–40, and Frye, in *Renaissance Hamlet,* 14–22, also emphasize the ambiguity of the ghost throughout the play.

24. Although, as Frye shows, Ophelia is legally entitled to full burial rites, the play devotes two dialogues to the doubtfulness of her death; see *Renaissance Hamlet,* 150, 298–99.

25. See 3.4.175. Fredson Bowers argues that the two terms *scourge* and *minister* had these distinct meanings in sixteenth-century England; see "Hamlet as Minister and Scourge," *PMLA* 70 (1955): 740–49. R. W. Dent, however, cites contemporary evidence of *scourge* bearing no implication of taint or need for eventual punishment, "Hamlet: Scourge and Minister," *Shakespeare Quarterly* 29 (1978): 82–84.

26. Critics have gathered into opposing camps on the issue of Hamlet's regeneration or degradation. S. F. Johnson, of the former camp, rehearses the debate up to 1952, in "The Regeneration of *Hamlet,*" *Shakespeare Quarterly* 3 (1952): 187–207. Since then, the most prominent supporters of the view that Hamlet becomes God's redeemed agent of revenge are Maynard Mack, "The World of *Hamlet,*" 520–23; Bowers, "Hamlet as Minister and Scourge," 748–49, and "The Death of Hamlet: A Study in Plot and Character," in *Studies in the English Renaissance Drama,* ed. Josephine W. Bennett, Oscar Cargill, and Vernon Hall (New York: New York Univ. Press, 1959), 28–43; Ribner, *Patterns in Shakespearean Tragedy,* 80–83; Sr. Miriam Joseph, C. S. C., "*Hamlet,* a Christian Tragedy," *Studies in Philology* 59 (1962): 119–40; B. L. Reid, "The Last Act and the Action of *Hamlet,*" *Yale Review,* 54 (1964): 59–80; Prosser, *Hamlet and Revenge,* 219–40; David Bevington, Introduction to *Hamlet,* in *The Complete Works,* 899–903; and Frye, *Renaissance Hamlet*, 254–80. Of those who maintain that Hamlet is tainted in his revenge, the most prominent are Battenhouse, *Shakespearean Tragedy,* 152–55, 250–65; Alan C. Dessen, "Hamlet's Poisoned Sword: A Study in Dramatic Imagery," *Shakespeare Studies* 5 (1969): 53–69; and John F. Andrews, "'Dearly Bought Revenge': *Samson Agonistes, Hamlet,* and Elizabethan Revenge Tragedy," *Milton Studies* 13 (1979): 81–107.

27. Walter King explores the paradox of how Hamlet gains freedom within a providential universe, and emphasizes that the ending solves but also sustains the play's ambiguity, in *Hamlet's Search for Meaning,* 1, 14–21, 147–65. Ruth M. Levit-

sky, in "Rightly to Be Great," *Shakespeare Studies* 1 (1965): 142–67, and Frye, in *Renaissance Hamlet,* 167–204, detail the philosophical and religious contexts that would have made it as hard for a contemporary audience as for Hamlet to determine what constituted honorable action in his situation.

28. See Gregory Bateson, "Double Bind (1969)"; Lyman C. Wynne, "On the Anguish, and Creative Passions, of Not Escaping Double Binds"; and Richard Rabkin, "Critique of the Clinical Use of the Double Bind Hypothesis," in Sluki, *Double Bind,* 237–50, 287–306. Bateson (241– 42) describes an experiment with a porpoise that, as odd as it seems, may illuminate Hamlet's transformation in act 5. The female porpoise had been trained to expect a whistle followed by food when she raised her head above the water. She had learned a *context* for behavior. But her trainer wanted her to present a new piece of behavior each time she entered the tank. Thus she must learn the *context of the first context.* Naturally, on her second entrance into the tank, she futilely raised her head above the water. Only by accident did she produce a new piece of behavior, a tail flap, and receive a reward. For fourteen sessions the confused porpoise continued to perform the most recently rewarded behavior, producing new behaviors only by accident. Before the fifteenth session, however, she was visibly excited, and when let into the tank, "she put on an elaborate performance including eight conspicuous pieces of behavior of which four were entirely new—never before observed in this species of animal." Like the porpoise who learned how to learn, Hamlet transcends double binds by leaping to a higher level of insight.

Chapter 3

1. Sylvia L. Thrupp, ed., *Change in Medieval Society: Europe North of the Alps, 1050–1500* (New York: Appleton-Century Crofts, 1964), vi–vii.

2. Anton C. Zijderveld, *Reality in a Looking-Glass: Rationality Through an Analysis of Traditional Folly* (London: Routledge and Kegan Paul, 1982), 18–19.

3. For complete studies of the fool, see Enid Welsford, *The Fool: His Social and Literary History* (London: Faber and Faber, 1935); William Willeford, *The Fool and His Scepter: A Study in Clowns and Jesters and Their Audience* (Evanston, Illinois: Northwestern Univ. Press, 1969); Zijderveld, *Reality in a Looking-Glass;* and Sandra Billington, *A Social History of the Fool* (New York: St. Martin's Press, 1984). Mikhail Bakhtin, in *Rabelais and His World,* argues that folk carnival, by inverting all social norms, flaunting the grotesque body, and mocking anything fixed or serious, represents the second life and universal body of the people, beyond the strictures of power. For a critique of this position, see Chapter 9.

4. Zijderveld, *Reality in a Looking-Glass,* 4–5, 147–48. Jonathan Dollimore and Alan Sinfield, eds., *Political Shakespeare: New Essays in Cultural Materialism* (Ithaca: Cornell Univ. Press, 1985), 18–47, 109–28. Peter Stallybrass and Allon White, *The Politics and Poetics of Transgression* (London: Methuen, 1986), 1–26.

5. Victor Turner, "Liminal to Liminoid, in Play, Flow, and Ritual: An Essay in

Comparative Symbology," in *The Anthropological Study of Human Play,* ed. Edward Norbeck, *Rice University Studies* 60 (1974): 59–61. Barbara Babcock, ed., *The Reversible World: Symbolic Inversion in Art and Society,* (Ithaca: Cornell Univ. Press, 1978), 13–36.

6. Natalie Zemon Davis, "Women on Top: Symbolic Sexual Inversion and Political Disorder in Early Modern Europe," in *The Reversible World,* 178–82. See also Zijderveld, *Reality in a Looking-Glass,* 76.

7. Stephen Greenblatt, *Renaissance Self-Fashioning: From More to Shakespeare* (Chicago: Univ. of Chicago Press, 1980). Hugh M. Richmond has argued that the politico-religious controversies of the Renaissance and Reformation produced rich self-characterizations and a new sense of personal identity, in "Personal Identity and Literary Personae: A Study in Historical Psychology," *PMLA* 90 (1975): 209–21.

8. For summary discussions of how children's play relates to adaptation to complex adult societies, see Brian Sutton-Smith, "Play as Adaptive Potentiation," in *Studies in the Anthropology of Play: Papers in Memory of B. Allan Tindall,* ed. Phillips Stevens, Jr. (Westpoint, New York: Leisure Press, 1977), 232–37; and Schwartzman, *Transformations,* 124–26, 196–99. For the concept of mobile self in both modernity and the Renaissance, see Greenblatt, *Renaissance Self-Fashioning,* 224–31.

9. Households usually consisted of a nuclear family of four to six members —parents, children, and possibly servants. See Jean-Louis Flandrin, *Families in Former Times: Kinship, Household and Sexuality,* trans. Richard Southern (Cambridge: Cambridge Univ. Press, 1979), 50–57; Lawrence Stone, *The Family, Sex and Marriage in England 1500–1800* (London: Weidenfeld and Nicolson, 1977), 23–25; and Richard Wall, "The Household: Demographic and Economic Change in England, 1650–1970," in *Family Forms in Historic Europe,* ed. Richard Wall (Cambridge: Cambridge Univ. Press, 1983), 493. For the use of wet nurses, see David Hunt, *Parents and Children in History: The Psychology of Family Life in Early Modern France* (New York: Basic Books, 1970), 106–108, 177; Alan Macfarlane, *The Family Life of Ralph Josselin, a Seventeenth-Century Clergyman* (Cambridge: Cambridge Univ. Press, 1970), 81–88; Joseph E. Illick, "Child-Rearing in Seventeenth-Century England and America," in *The History of Childhood,* ed. Lloyd deMause (New York: The Psychohistory Press, 1974), 308; Flandrin, *Families in Former Times,* 203–209; Stone, *Family . . . in England,* 6, 99–100, 107, 159; Keith Wrightson, *English Society 1580–1680* (New Brunswick, New Jersey: Rutgers Univ. Press, 1982), 108; and Steven Ozment, *When Fathers Ruled: Family Life in Reformation Europe* (Cambridge: Harvard Univ. Press, 1983), 118–19.

10. For this vicious cycle, see Illick, "Child-Rearing in Seventeenth-Century England," in deMause, *History of Childhood,* 310–11; Stone, *Family . . . in England,* 81; and Randolph Trumbach, *The Rise of the Egalitarian Family: Aristocratic Kinship and Domestic Relations in Eighteenth-Century England* (New York: Academic Press, 1978), 188. For greater domesticity in the eighteenth century, see Trumbach, *Rise of the Egalitarian Family,* 191–98. For lack of intimacy, see Philippe Ariès,

Centuries of Childhood, trans. Robert Baldick (London: Jonathan Cape, 1962), 38–40; Flandrin, *Families in Former Times*, 92, 205; and Stone, *Family . . . in England*, 5–6, 27, 70, 99–101, 105, 117, 194. The Josselins, however, seem to have valued their children and to have remained in close contact with them throughout their adult lives; see Macfarlane, *Family Life of Ralph Josselin*, 82, 110–25. The case notes of the seventeenth-century physician Richard Napier, recorded from lower- as well as middle- and upper-class patients, indicate greater family intimacy than Ariès, Stone, and their followers have assumed; see Michael MacDonald, *Mystical Bedlam: Madness, Anxiety, and Healing in Seventeenth-Century England* (Cambridge: Cambridge Univ. Press, 1981), 80–85. See also Wrightson's critique of the theory of parental indifference in *English Society*, 104–18, and Stone's qualification in *Family . . . in England*, 114. MacDonald suspects that historians often record the results of male, not female, attitudes.

11. Alice Judson Ryerson, "Medical Advice on Child Rearing, 1550–1900," *Harvard Educational Review* 31 (1961): 305, 312–13; Hunt, *Parents and Children in History*, 127; Illick, "Child-Rearing in Seventeenth-Century England," in deMause, *History of Childhood*, 307–309, 311; and Stone, *Family . . . in England*, 99, 101, 159–61.

12. For sending children away, see Ivy Pinchbeck and Margaret Hewitt, *From Tudor Times to the Eighteenth Century*, vol. 1 of *Children in English Society* (London: Routledge and Kegan Paul, 1969), 224, 232, 281; Macfarlane, *Family Life of Ralph Josselin*, 89–91; Hunt, *Parents and Children in History*, 180, 184; M. J. Tucker, "The Child as Beginning and End: Fifteenth and Sixteenth Century English Childhood," in deMause, *History of Childhood*, 246, 250; Flandrin, *Families in Former Times*, 95; Stone, *Family . . . in England*, 6, 106–107; and Trumbach, *Rise of the Egalitarian Family*, 251. For reports of English cruelty, see Tucker, "The Child as Beginning and End," in deMause, *History of Childhood*, 250–51; and Flandrin, *Families in Former Times*, 241. Boyle's reason is quoted in Illick, "Child-Rearing in Seventeenth-Century England," in deMause, *History of Childhood*, 343, n. 81. For breaking children's wills, see Hunt, *Parents and Children in History*, 139; Stone, *Family . . . in England*, 162; and Trumbach, *Rise of the Egalitarian Family*, 244.

13. On toys, see Antonia Fraser, *A History of Toys* (New York: Delacorte Press, 1966), 72–89. On Bruegel's "Children's Games," see Iona and Peter Opie, "Games (Young) People Play," *Horizon* 13 (1971): 16–19. Puritan preacher's warning quoted in Pinchbeck and Hewitt, *Children in English Society*, 266. More's poem quoted in Tucker, "The Child as Beginning and End," in deMause, *History of Childhood*, 251–52. For physician's tolerance of play, see Illick, "Child-Rearing in Seventeenth-Century England," in deMause, *History of Childhood*, 342, n. 72. Chesterfield's letter quoted in Pinchbeck and Hewitt, *Children in English Society*, 298.

14. Grammar school students were at their desks from 6:00 to 11:00 a.m. and from 1:00 to 5:30 p.m. See Illick, "Child-Rearing in Seventeenth-Century England," in deMause, *History of Childhood*, 322–23. For separation from women and for corporal punishment, see Walter J. Ong, S. J., "Latin Language Study as a Renaissance Puberty Rite," in *Rhetoric, Romance, and Technology: Studies in the Interaction of*

Expression and Culture (Ithaca: Cornell Univ. Press, 1971), 113–41, and *Fighting for Life: Contest, Sexuality, and Consciousness* (Ithaca: Cornell Univ. Press, 1981), 119–48; and Stone, *Family... in England,* 163–66.

15. Pinchbeck and Hewitt, *Children in English Society,* 232–33, 259; and Illick, "Child-Rearing in Seventeenth-Century England," in deMause, *History of Childhood,* 323.

16. For conformity to an absolute, see Hunt, *Parents and Children in History,* 49–50, 157; Stone, *Family... in England,* 5, 151–55, 216–17, 643; and Wrightson, *English Society,* 115. Even the self-fashioning that Greenblatt discusses always takes place in relation to an absolute; see *Renaissance Self-Fashioning,* 9. Lady Jane Grey's description quoted in Tucker, "The Child as Beginning and End," in deMause, *History of Childhood,* 248.

17. Lanham, *Motives of Eloquence,* 1–35; Greenblatt, *Renaissance Self-Fashioning,* 230–31; and William Kerrigan, "The Articulation of the Ego in the English Renaissance," in *The Literary Freud: Mechanisms of Defense and the Poetic Will,* ed. Joseph H. Smith, vol. 4 of *Psychiatry and the Humanities* (New Haven: Yale Univ. Press, 1980), 267–77.

18. For parallels to English child-rearing practices found in early New England settlements, see Edmund S. Morgan, *The Puritan Family: Religion and Domestic Relations in Seventeenth-Century New England,* rev. ed. (New York: Harper and Row, 1966), 65–108; and John Demos, *A Little Commonwealth: Family Life in Plymouth Colony* (Oxford: Oxford Univ. Press, 1970), 100–106, 131–44.

19. Wrightson, *English Society,* 121–82.

20. *Ibid.,* 183–221.

21. Lionel Arthur Govett, *The King's Book of Sports: A History of the Declarations of King James I. and King Charles I. as to the Use of Lawful Sports on Sundays* (London: Eliot Stock, 1890), 38–40.

22. Marcia Vale, *The Gentleman's Recreations: Accomplishments and Pastimes of the English Gentleman 1580–1630* (Totowa, New Jersey: Rowman and Littlefield, 1977), 5.

23. James I, *Basilikon Doron,* in *A Miscellany* (London: George Routledge and Sons, 1888), 124.

24. Christopher Whitfield, *A History of Chipping Campden and Captain Robert Dover's Olympick Games* (Eton: Shakespeare Head Press, 1958), 91ff.

25. Govett, *King's Book of Sports,* 116–31.

26. *Annalia Dubrensia: Upon the Yeerely Celebration of Mr. Robert Dovers Olimpick Games upon Cotswold-Hills* (London, 1636).

27. Christina Hole, *English Sports and Pastimes* (London: B. T. Batsford,

1949), 97–98. The following poem, modernized from E. L. Guilford, *Select Extracts Illustrating Sports and Pastimes in the Middle Ages* (New York: Macmillan, 1920), 14–15, illustrates traditional yearly festivals:

> At Yule we wonten gambol, dance, to carol and to sing,
> To have good spiced sewe [ale] and roast and plum-pie for a king;
> At Easter-eve pain-puffes; Gangtide [Rogationtide] Gates did holy messes
> bring;
> At Pasque [Easter] began our Morris, and ere Pentecost our May,
> Though Robin Hood, Lyle John, Friar Tuck and Marian deftly play,
> And Lord and Lady gang til kirk with lads and lasses gay
> Fra mass and e'ensong so good cheer and glee on every green,
> As save our walles, 'twixt Eames and Sibbes [friends and relations], like game
> was neere seen.
> At Baptist Day [June 24, Midsummer Day], with ale and cakes, 'mid bonfires
> neighbours stood;
> At Martinmas [Nov. 11] we turned a crab, then told of Robin Hood,
> Till after long time merk, when blest were windows, doors, and lights,
> And pails were filled and hearths were swept 'gainst fairy elves and sprites;
> Rock and Plough Monday [after Christmas] games shall gang with Saint feasts
> and kirk sights.

For studies of Herrick's use of traditional sports and festivals in his poetry, see Leah Sinanoglou Marcus, "Herrick's *Noble Numbers* and the Politics of Playfulness," *English Literary Renaissance* 7 (1977): 108–26; and "Herrick's *Hesperides* and the 'Proclamation made for May,'" *Studies in Philology* 76 (1979): 49–74.

28. Marcus, *Politics of Mirth.*

29. For Cavalier retreat, see Earl Miner, *The Cavalier Mode from Jonson to Cotton* (Princeton: Princeton Univ. Press, 1971). For retreat into childhood, see Marcus, *Childhood and Cultural Despair.*

30. Victor Turner, *Dramas, Fields, and Metaphors: Symbolic Action in Human Society* (Ithaca : Cornell Univ. Press, 1974).

31. For King Charles's dramatization of his execution, see C. V. Wedgwood, *A Coffin for King Charles: The Trial and Execution of Charles I* (1964; reprint, New York: Time Incorporated, 1966). For the sacrifice of scapegoats, see Girard, *Violence and the Sacred.* For sword dancing and mummers' plays, see Welsford, *Fool,* 70 71; and Guilford, *Select Extracts,* 18.

32. For psychic disturbance in Renaissance Europe, see Lynn White, Jr., "Death and the Devil," in *The Darker Vision of the Renaissance: Beyond the Fields of Reason,* ed. Robert S. Kinsman (Berkeley: Univ. of California Press, 1974), 25–46. For a summary of other historical arguments, see MacDonald, *Mystical Bedlam,* 72, 263–64, nn. 1, 2. For fascination with madness, see MacDonald, *Mystical Bedlam,* 121–22.

33. MacDonald, *Mystical Bedlam,* 16, 26, 31, 61, 66–69.

34. According to Spariosu, literary play arises in periods, like the Renaissance, of "cognitive nihilism" and "axiological relativism." Such play proposes and tests alternative models while simultaneously sustaining the ruling mechanisms of power; see *Literature, Mimesis and Play,* 10, 40–41; *Dionysus Reborn,* x, 11, 24–27. See also Hutchinson, *Games Authors Play,* 87–89.

35. Weinstein and Platt, *Psychoanalytic Sociology.*

Chapter 4

1. The comparison has been made before by Theodore Spencer, "Donne and his Age," in *A Garland for John Donne: 1631–1931,* ed. Theodore Spencer (1931; reprint, Gloucester, Massachusetts: Peter Smith, 1958), 187–96; and Evelyn Hardy, *Donne: A Spirit in Conflict* (London: Constable, 1942), 240–43.

2. Gerald Guinness has classified the forms of Donne's poetic play using the categories of Roger Caillois: *agon, alea* (chance), *ilinx* (vertigo), and *mimicry.* See "Playing for Life in Donne's Elegies, Songs and Sonnets," in *Auctor Ludens: Essays on Play in Literature,* ed. Gerald Guinness and Andrew Hurley (Philadelphia: John Benjamins, 1986), 137–55. Some critics merely note, without evaluation, that Donne plays: T. S. Eliot, "Donne in Our Time," in Spencer, *Garland,* 2; Paul N. Siegel, "Donne's *Paradoxes and Problems,*" *Philological Quarterly* 28 (1949): 511; and Evelyn M. Simpson, *The Sermons of John Donne,* ed. George R. Potter and Evelyn M. Simpson (Berkeley: Univ. of California Press, 1953–62), 10:3. All quotations from Donne's sermons will follow this edition and will be cited in the text parenthetically by volume, sermon, and page numbers.

3. Pierre Legouis, *Donne the Craftsman: An Essay upon the Structure of the Songs and Sonnets* (1928; reprint, New York: Russell and Russell, 1962), 29, 37, 68–69; J. B. Leishman, *The Monarch of Wit: An Analytical and Comparative Study of the Poetry of John Donne* (1951; reprint, London: Hutchinson, 1969), 96; Clay Hunt, *Donne's Poetry: Essays in Literary Analysis* (New Haven: Yale Univ. Press, 1954), 88, 135; Richard E. Hughes, *The Progress of the Soul: The Interior Career of John Donne* (New York: William Morrow, 1968), 37, 49.

4. Charles Monroe Coffin, *John Donne and the New Philosophy* (Morningside Heights, New York: Columbia Univ. Press, 1937), 114, 294; A. Alvarez, *The School of Donne* (1961; reprint, New York: New American Library, 1967), 26; Arnold Stein, *John Donne's Lyrics: The Eloquence of Action* (1962; reprint, New York: Octagon Books, 1980), 90, 101; Joan Webber, *Contrary Music: The Prose Style of John Donne* (Madison: Univ. of Wisconsin Press, 1963), 131; Michael McCanles, "Paradox in Donne," *Studies in the Renaissance* 13 (1966): 266–87; N. J. C. Andreasen, *John Donne: Conservative Revolutionary* (Princeton: Princeton Univ. Press, 1967), 7–14; Murray Roston, *The Soul of Wit: A Study of John Donne* (London: Clarendon Press, 1974), 74, 80, 95; John S. Chamberlin, *Increase and Multiply: Arts-of-Discourse Pro-*

cedure in the Preaching of Donne (Chapel Hill: Univ. of North Carolina Press, 1976), 28, 33–34, 158; Patricia Garland Pinka, *This Dialogue of One: The Songs and Sonnets of John Donne* (Tuscaloosa: Univ. of Alabama Press, 1982), 24–25.

5. A. J. Smith, *John Donne: The Songs and Sonets* (London: Edward Arnold, 1964), 35; Wilbur Sanders, *John Donne's Poetry* (Cambridge: Cambridge Univ. Press, 1971), 23, 33, 45, 48, 55.

6. Letter [to Sir Henry Wotton? 1600?], in *John Donne: Selected Prose*, ed. Helen Gardner and Timothy Healy (Oxford: Clarendon Press, 1967), 111.

7. Fear of separation: Hardy, *Donne: A Spirit in Conflict*, 244; D. W. Harding, "Coherence of Theme in Donne's Poetry," *Kenyon Review* 13 (1951): 431–32; John Carey, *John Donne: Life, Mind and Art* (New York: Oxford Univ. Press, 1981), 37–38, 59, 61–62. Fear of being possessed: Hughes, *Progress of the Soul*, 44.

8. For the concept of "voice," see Sanders, *John Donne's Poetry*, 8; and Walter J. Ong, S. J., "Voice as Summons for Belief: Literature, Faith, and the Divided Self," in *The Barbarian Within and Other Fugitive Essays and Studies* (New York: Macmillan, 1962), 49–67.

9. For valedictions, see Richard W. Bollman, S. J., "Saying Goodbye: Essays on Donne's Poetics of Departure," (Ph.D. diss., SUNY Buffalo, 1975), 5, 8. Thomas Docherty, in *John Donne, Undone* (London: Methuen, 1986), 51–71, argues from a deconstructionist perspective that female changeability and promiscuity in the love poems threaten to destabilize masculine identity.

10. Hardy, *Donne: A Spirit in Conflict*, 235; Harding, "Coherence of Theme in Donne's Poetry," 432; Carey, *John Donne*, 20–21, 38, 268–69.

11. David Aers and Gunther Kress, "'Darke Texts Need Notes': Versions of Self in Donne's Verse Epistles," and "Vexatious Contraries: A Reading of Donne's Poetry," in David Aers, Bob Hodge, and Gunther Kress, *Literature, Language and Society in England 1580–1680* (Totowa, New Jersey: Barnes and Noble, 1981), 23–74. Arthur F. Marotti, *John Donne, Coterie Poet* (Madison: Univ. of Wisconsin Press, 1986). Jonathan Goldberg, *James I and the Politics of Literature: Jonson, Shakespeare, Donne, and Their Contemporaries* (Baltimore: The Johns Hopkins Press, 1983).

12. *The Complete Poetry of Ben Jonson*, ed. William B. Hunter, Jr. (New York: Norton, 1963), 32.

13. See Aers's and Kress's analysis of "You have refined me . . ." in "Versions of Self."

14. Erik Erikson, *Young Man Luther: A Study in Psychoanalysis and History* (New York: Norton, 1958), 115–19. See also Sanders, *John Donne's Poetry*, 67.

15. Erik Erikson, *Childhood and Society*, rev. ed. (New York: Norton, 1963), pp. 72–85.

16. See Ronald J. Corthell, "Style and Self in Donne's Satires," *Texas Studies in Literature and Language* 24 (1982): 155–84.

17. Bollman, "Saying Goodbye," 12–13, 24, 33, n. 36.

18. Marotti, *Coterie Poet,* 51–52. A typical example is a sonnet sequence, *La Tersicore* (1637), in which the Italian academician Alessandro Adimari paradoxically praises fifty varieties of unattractive women (the hunchback, the squit-eyed, etc.) for the amusement of his fellows.

19. Carey, *John Donne,* 45; Stein, *John Donne's Lyrics,* 167; Sanders, *John Donne's Poetry,* 45, 144. See also Pinka, *Dialogue of One,* 17–18, 39; and Tilottama Rajan, "'Nothing Sooner Broke': Donne's *Songs and Sonets* as Self-Consuming Artifact," *ELH* 49 (1982): 805–28.

20. Sanders calls for some way around this "crude dichotomy" in *John Donne's Poetry,* 21.

21. Smith, *John Donne,* 66. For readings emphasizing irony, see Aers and Kress, "Vexatious Contraries," 57–65; and Marotti, *Coterie Poet,* 157–65.

22. Edward LeComte, *Grace to a Witty Sinner: A Life of Donne* (New York: Walker, 1965), 45; Samuel Johnson, from "The Life of Cowley," in *Discussions of John Donne,* ed. Frank Kermode (Boston: D. C. Heath, 1962), 7; T. S. Eliot, "The Metaphysical Poets," in Kermode, *Discussions,* 45; Dwight Cathcart, *Doubting Conscience: Donne and the Poetry of Moral Argument* (Ann Arbor: Univ. of Michigan Press, 1975), 12, 65, 86, 121; Robert S. Jackson, *John Donne's Christian Vocation* (Evanston, Illinois: Northwestern Univ. Press, 1970), 43; Odette de Mourgues, *Metaphysical, Baroque, and Précieux Poetry* (Oxford : Clarendon Press, 1953), 7, 74.

23. Frank J. Warnke, "Baroque Poetry and the Experience of Contradiction," *Colloquia Germanica* 1 (1967): 44.

24. C. D. Johnson, "Bedroom and Landscape in Donne's *The Songs and Sonnets,*" *The Cresset* 37 (1974): 6–9. All quotations of the *Devotions* are from *John Donne: Devotions Upon Emergent Occasions together with Death's Duel* (Ann Arbor: Univ. of Michigan Press, 1959).

25. For the critical debate on the tone of "The Ecstasy," see Legouis, *Donne the Craftsman,* 61–70; Merritt Y. Hughes, "The Lineage of 'The Exstasie,'" *Modern Language Review* 27 (1932): 1–5, "Kidnapping Donne," *Essays in Criticism* (1934; reprint, Freeport, New York: Books for Libraries Press, 1966), 61–89, and "Some of Donne's 'Ecstasies,'" *PMLA* 75 (1960): 509–18; G. R. Potter, "Donne's *Exstasie,* Contra Legouis," *Philological Quarterly* 15 (1936): 247–53; A. J. Smith, "The Metaphysic of Love," *Review of English Studies* 9 (1958): 362–75; Helen Gardner, "The Argument about 'The Ecstasy,'" in *Elizabethan and Jacobean Studies Presented to Frank Percy Wilson* (Oxford: Clarendon Press, 1959), 279–306; and David Novarr "'The Exstasie': Donne's Address on the States of Union," in *Just So Much Honor: Essays Commemorating the Four-Hundredth Anniversary of the Birth of John Donne,* ed. Peter Amadeus Fiore (University Park: Pennsylvania State Univ. Press, 1972), 219–43.

26. John Dryden, from "A Discourse concerning the Original and Progress of Satire," in Kermode, *Discussions,* 5.

27. For another discussion of the "marginality" of Donne's sick bed, see Bollman, "Saying Goodbye," 105–12.

28. According to the *Oxford English Dictionary, deep,* "said of things involving heavy expenditure or liability," was current in the early seventeenth century, and *deep* was used to describe "drinking, gaming, or other practices" as early as 1577. Although the term *deep play* is found in Boswell's *Life of Johnson* and Gay's *Beggar's Opera,* its most frequently noted use is in Jeremy Bentham's *The Theory of Legislation,* ed. C. K. Ogden (New York: Harcourt, Brace, 1931), 106, n.

29. Lewalski, *Protestant Poetics,* 147–78.

30. Webber, *Contrary Music,* 125, 137; Lewalski, *Protestant Poetics,* 150.

31. Stanley E. Fish condemns such wit as not "self-consuming": *Self-Consuming Artifacts: The Experience of Seventeenth-Century Literature* (Berkeley: Univ. of California Press, 1972), 1–77, 353–73.

32. Winfried Schleiner has argued that the images and themes in Donne's sermons are rooted in Christian tradition and therefore can tell us little about Donne's frame of mind; see *The Imagery of John Donne's Sermons* (Providence: Brown Univ. Press, 1970), 65–66. Carey, however, has pointed out that Donne's principle of selection from among the great varieties of traditional themes and images is revealing; see *John Donne,* 219.

33. For the importance of suffering in Donne's work, see Terry G. Sherwood, *Fulfilling the Circle: A Study of John Donne's Thought* (Toronto: Univ. of Toronto Press, 1984), 102–30.

34. For the importance of the Body of Christ in Donne's thinking, see *ibid.,* 63–101.

35. Chamberlin, *Increase and Multiply,* 28. For Donne's reaction against Ramistic preaching and his return to the older Augustinian tradition, see Chamberlin, *Increase and Multiply,* 95–108. See also Dennis Quinn, "Donne's Christian Eloquence," in *Seventeenth-Century Prose: Modern Essays in Criticism,* ed. Stanley E. Fish (New York: Oxford Univ. Press, 1971), 353–74.

36. Chamberlin, *Increase and Multiply,* 34; and Achsah Guibbory, "John Donne and Memory as 'the Art of *Salvation,*'" *Huntington Library Quarterly* 43 (1979/80): 261–74.

37. "Outlandish Proverbs, selected," in *The Works of George Herbert,* ed. F. E. Hutchinson (1941; reprint, Oxford: Clarendon Press, 1978), number 234.

38. See also 5:1, 36–37, and 10:6, 146–48.

39. Izaak Walton, *The Life of Dr. John Donne,* in *John Donne: Devotions,* xxi; Jasper Mayne, "On Dr. Donnes death," in *Donne: Poetical Works,* ed. Herbert J. C. Grierson (1929; reprint, London: Oxford Univ. Press, 1971), 353, ll. 57–64; T. S.

Eliot, "Lancelot Andrewes," *Essays Ancient and Modern* (New York: Harcourt, Brace, 1932), 9–10, 20–21.

40. Hardy, *Donne: A Spirit of Conflict*, 229, 231. Legouis calls Donne's fanciful expositions of barren texts making something out of nothing and hairsplitting for its own sake: *Donne the Craftsman*, 36.

41. Dennis Quinn, "Donne and the Wane of Wonder," *ELH* 36 (1969): 626–47.

42. Gale H. Carrithers, *Donne at Sermons: A Christian Existential World* (Albany: State Univ. of New York Press, 1972), 8–17.

43. R. C. Bald, *John Donne: A Life* (New York: Oxford Univ. Press, 1970), 450.

44. Edmund Gosse, *The Life and Letters of John Donne* (London: William Heinemann, 1899), 2:268.

45. Bald, *John Donne*, 22–25. Carey, among others, has emphasized the fascination with martyrdom as central to Donne's life: *John Donne*, 19, 48–49, 205.

46. Donne confesses his own inclinations to suicide in the preface to *Biathanatos* (composed in 1609); see Gardner and Healy, *Selected Prose*, 26–27. Bald observes how, in *Pseudo-Martyr*, Donne takes for granted that all men desire self-destruction, 223.

47. Gosse, *Life and Letters*, 1:195, 171.

48. Bald, *John Donne*, 238, 271.

49. Carey emphasizes Donne's poor choice of patrons: *John Donne*, 83–88.

50. An engraving of this image (from the midchest up) became the frontispiece for "Death's Duel" (1632). The statue carved by Nicholas Stone of the entire body and urn survived the 1666 fire and still stands in St. Paul's. See Derek Parker, *John Donne and His World* (London: Thames and Hudson, 1975), 110–11. See also Bollman, "Saying Goodbye," 147.

51. Louis I. Bredvold, "The Naturalism of Donne in Relation to Some Renaissance Traditions," *Journal of English and German Philology* 22 (1923): 471–502; Carey, *John Donne*, 232–35; Coffin, *John Donne*, 264–67; Judah Stampfer, *John Donne and the Metaphysical Gesture* (New York: Funk and Wagnalls, 1970), 24; Michael Francis Maloney, *John Donne, His Flight from Medievalism* (1944; reprint, New York: Russell and Russell, 1965), 139, 143; Patrick Cruttwell, *The Shakespearean Moment and its Place in the Poetry of the Seventeenth Century* (London: Chatto and Windus, 1954), 39–72; William Zunder, *The Poetry of John Donne: Literature and Culture in the Elizabethan and Jacobean Period* (Totowa, New Jersey: Barnes and Noble Books, 1982); Docherty, *John Donne, Undone*, 17–50.

52. Victor Turner, *The Ritual Process: Structure and Anti-Structure* (Ithaca: Cornell Univ. Press, 1969), 94–130; and "Liminal to Liminoid," 56–59.

53. Turner, "Liminal to Liminoid," 60–61.

54. Turner, "Betwixt and Between: The Liminal Period in *Rites de Passage*," in *The Forest of Symbols: Aspects of Ndembu Ritual* (Ithaca: Cornell Univ. Press, 1967), 105–106.

55. Turner, "Liminal to Liminoid," 60–61.

56. Brian Sutton-Smith, "Games of Order and Disorder," *The Association for the Anthropological Study of Play Newsletter* 4 (1977): 25. Robert Fagen has surveyed the considerable evidence that animal play increases behavioral flexibility in *Animal Play Behavior* (Oxford: Oxford Univ. Press, 1981), vii, 260–66, 271, 321, 331–32, 351–52, 379, 450, 469.

57. Stallybrass and White, *Politics . . . of Transgression*, 13–16.

58. Goldberg, *James I*, 65–67, 107–112.

59. Stallybrass and White, *Politics . . . of Transgression*, 56–58.

60. Rosalie L. Colie, *Paradoxia Epidemica: The Renaissance Tradition of Paradox* (Princeton: Princeton Univ. Press, 1966). See also Cleanth Brooks, *The Well Wrought Urn: Studies in the Structure of Poetry* (New York: Harcourt, Brace, 1947), 3–20; and McCanles, "Paradox in Donne."

61. Siegel, "Donne's *Paradoxes and Problems*," 507–11; Helen Peters, ed., *John Donne: Paradoxes and Problems* (Oxford: Clarendon Press, 1980), xxiv; Carey, *John Donne*, 236.

62. Peters, *Paradoxes*, 40–42.

63. Johnson, "The Life of Cowley," in Kermode, *Discussions*, 8.

64. T. S. Eliot, "Donne in Our Time," in Spencer, *Garland*, 8. See also Coffin, *John Donne*, 294.

65. Legouis, *Donne the Craftsman*, 71; Eliot, "Donne in Our Time," in Spencer, *Garland*, 8–11; Coffin, *John Donne*, 52–53, 56–57, 231, 284; Maloney, *John Donne*, 62, 210; Alvarez, *The School of Donne*, xix; Carey, *John Donne*, 250.

66. For standard theories of the conceit, see Rosemond Tuve, *Elizabethan and Metaphysical Imagery: Renaissance Poetic and Twentieth-Century Critics* (Chicago: Univ. of Chicago Press, 1947), 130–37, 163, 170, 203; and Joseph A. Mazzeo, "Modern Theories of Metaphysical Poetry," in Kermode, *Discussions*, 118–25. Tuve minimizes the difference between Elizabethan and metaphysical conceits, claiming that the latter merely became sharper and more condensed to match the decorum of the meditative lyric, epigram, and satire—the fashionable genres of the day. Mazzeo finds the origin of conceits in the medieval theory of correspondences. Neither of these theories, however, explains either why Donne and his followers chose these genres or why their conceits became so much more startling than those in medieval or Elizabethan poetry.

67. See Schwartzman, *Transformations*, 1, 7–8.

68. Hunt, *Donne's Poetry*, 152–53; Roston, *The Soul of Wit*, 18; Carey, *John Donne*, 248.

69. Letter [to Sir Henry Wotton? 1600?], in Gardner and Healy, *Selected Prose*, 111.

70. Spencer, "Donne and his Age," in Spencer, *Garland*, 195–96; Maloney, *John Donne*, 143; Marjorie Hope Nicolson, *The Breaking of the Circle: Studies in the Effect of the "New Science" upon Seventeenth-Century Poetry*, rev. ed. (New York: Columbia Univ. Press, 1960), 155–56.

71. Mayne, "On Dr. Donnes death," in *Donne: Poetical Works*, ed. Grierson, 351, ll. 7–8.

72. Goffman, *Frame Analysis*, 440–44.

73. Carrithers, *Donne at Sermons*, 8–17. See Bald for the story about Donne's having one offender arrested: *John Donne*, 402–405.

74. Webber, *Contrary Music*, 147, 165, 181–82.

Chapter 5

1. *The Works of George Herbert*, ed. F. E. Hutchinson (1941; reprint, Oxford: Clarendon Press, 1978), ll. 80, 203, 89. All subsequent quotations from Herbert's works will be cited parenthetically in the text.

2. See *King Lear*, 2.4.79–86.

3. Robert B. Hinman emphasizes play in "The 'Verser' at *The Temple* Door: Herbert's 'The Church Porch,'" in Claude J. Summers and Ted-Larry Pebworth, eds., *"Too Rich to Clothe the Sunne": Essays on George Herbert* (Pittsburgh: Univ. of Pittsburgh Press, 1980), 55–75.

4. Izaak Walton, "The Life of Mr. George Herbert," in *The Lives of Dr. John Donne, Sir Henry Wooton, Mr. Richard Hooker, Mr. George Herbert, and Dr. Robert Sanderson* (New York: George P. Putnam, 1850), 303.

5. The tradition begins with Baxter's famous remark in *Poetical Fragments* (1681) that "*Herbert* speaks *to God* like one that *really believeth a God*" (in Hutchinson, xliii–xliv) and continues with Herbert J. C. Grierson, *Cross Currents in English Literature of the Seventeenth Century* (London, 1929; reprint, Baltimore: Penguin Books, 1966), 206; Joseph H. Summers, *George Herbert: His Religion and Art* (Cambridge: Harvard Univ. Press, 1954), 61–62, 69; Margaret M. Blanchard, "The Leap into Darkness: Donne, Herbert, and God," *Renascence* 17 (1964): 38–50; Alicia Ostriker, "Song and Speech in the Metrics of George Herbert," in *Essential Articles for the Study of George Herbert's Poetry*, ed. John R. Roberts (Hamden, Connecticut:

Archon Books, 1979), 298–310; Mary Ellen Rickey, *Utmost Art: Complexity in the Verse of George Herbert* (Lexington: Univ. of Kentucky Press, 1966), 128, 168–69; Valerie Carnes, "The Unity of George Herbert's *The Temple:* A Reconsideration," in Roberts, *Essential Articles,* 374–92; Harold E. Toliver, "Poetry as Sacred Conveyance in Herbert and Marvell," in *Pastoral Forms and Attitudes* (Berkeley: Univ. of California Press, 1971), 116–37; and Lewalski, *Protestant Poetics,* 293–300.

6. Helen C. White, *The Metaphysical Poets: A Study in Religious Experience* (1936; reprint, New York: Collier Books, 1966), 170–73; Louis L. Martz, *The Poetry of Meditation: A Study in English Religious Literature of the Seventeenth Century,* rev. ed. (New Haven: Yale Univ. Press, 1962), 306–309; Rosalie L. Colie, "Logos in *The Temple:* George Herbert and the Shape of Content," in *Paradoxia Epidemica,* 190–215; Arnold Stein, *George Herbert's Lyrics* (Baltimore: The Johns Hopkins Press, 1968), 103–104, 123; Diana Benet, *Secretary of Praise: The Poetic Vocation of George Herbert* (Columbia: Univ. of Missouri Press, 1984), 48, 54–55.

7. Aldous Huxley describes Herbert's God as "a projection of his most real, his essential self" (quoted in White, *Metaphysical Poets,* 144), and others have expanded this insight in historical and psychological terms: Heather A. R. Asals identifies all the voices of "The Church" as one because Christ and His body are one in the voice of the Psalmist Everyman ("The Voice of George Herbert's 'The Church,'" in Roberts, *Essential Articles,* 393–407, and *Equivocal Predication: George Herbert's Way to God* [Toronto: Univ. of Toronto Press, 1981], 38–56); Lewalski emphasizes Herbert's imitation of God (*Protestant Poetics,* 245–47); Helen Vendler believes that Herbert invented God in the image of his mother (*The Poetry of George Herbert* [Cambridge: Harvard Univ. Press, 1975], 55); Stanley Fish accuses Herbert of "the sin of playing God" (*The Living Temple: George Herbert and Catechizing* [Berkeley: Univ. of California Press, 1978], 166); and A. D. Nuttall analyzes what he sees as the impropriety from a Calvinist point of view of Herbert's imitating God (*Overheard by God: Fiction and Prayer in Herbert, Milton, Dante and St. John* [London: Methuen, 1980], 1–82).

8. For arguments stressing the distance between Herbert and his persona, see Margaret Carpenter, "From Herbert to Marvell: Poetics in 'A Wreath' and 'The Coronet,'" *Journal of English and German Philology* 69 (1970): 50–62; John R. Mulder, "*The Temple* as Picture," and Ilona Bell, "The Double Pleasures of Herbert's '*Collar,*'" in Summers and Pebworth, *Too Rich,* 3–14, 77–78; Marion Meilaender, "Speakers and Hearers in *The Temple,*" *The George Herbert Journal* 5 (1981–82): 31–44; and Benet, *Secretary of Praise,* 99–100. Fish objects that the separation of Herbert from his speaker makes him an unserious posturer and role player (*Living Temple,* 6).

9. A list of sources would be impractical; interested readers may refer to John R. Roberts, *George Herbert: An Annotated Bibliography of Modern Criticism 1905–1974* (Columbia: Univ. of Missouri Press, 1978).

10. For struggle, see White, *Metaphysical Poets,* 165; Margaret Bottrall, *George Herbert* (London: John Murray, 1954), 98; Stein, *George Herbert's Lyrics,* 96–101, 186; Stanley Stewart, "Time and *The Temple,*" in Roberts, *Essential Articles,*

365; and Garret Keizer, "George Herbert and the Tradition of Jacob," *Cithara* 18 (1978): 18–26. Perhaps the fullest treatment of struggle, as a process of sanctification, is Gene Edward Veith, Jr., *Reformation Spirituality: The Religion of George Herbert* (Lewisburg, Pennsylvania: Bucknell Univ. Press, 1985), 133–76. For play, see Louis Untermeyer, *Play in Poetry* (New York: Harcourt, Brace, 1938), 51; M. M. Mahood, *Poetry and Humanism* (1949; reprint, New York: Norton, 1970), 27–28; and Rickey, *Utmost Art*, 153, 157–58.

11. A. J. Clements has traced the concept of the two selves, the ego and the image of God, through the Bible, the church fathers, and the medieval English mystics who might have influenced Herbert. Although Clements discusses the combats between the two selves in Herbert's poetry, he does not describe fully the results produced by games between aspects of the self. See "Theme, Tone, and Tradition in George Herbert's Poetry," in Roberts, *Essential Articles*, 33–51.

12. Elliott M. Avedon and Brian Sutton-Smith, *The Study of Games* (New York: John Wiley, 1971), 7. Bernard Suits, *The Grasshopper: Games, Life, and Utopia* (Toronto: Univ. of Toronto Press, 1978), 34, 130–38.

13. *The Life of Edward, First Lord Herbert of Cherbury written by himself*, ed. J. M. Shuttleworth (London: Oxford Univ. Press, 1976), 2–6, 8–10.

14. Amy M. Charles, *A Life of George Herbert* (Ithaca: Cornell Univ. Press, 1977), 28–33, 42–44; Marchette Chute, *Two Gentle Men: The Lives of George Herbert and Robert Herrick* (New York: E. P. Dutton, 1959), 23–25. See also William Blackburn, "Lady Magdalen Herbert and Her Son George," *South Atlantic Quarterly* 50 (1951): 378–88; and Aubrey Noakes, "The Mother of George Herbert," *Contemporary Review* 183 (1953): 39–45.

15. Charles, *Life*, 48–49; Hutchinson, Letters 3 (364–65) and 7 (369–70).

16. Walton, *Lives*, 271, 274; Charles, *Life*, 90.

17. For a discussion of the agonistic structure of the Western educational establishment and the connection between academic debate and male self-definition, see Ong, "Latin Language Study ," 113–41, and *Fighting for Life*, 119–48; and Kerrigan, "Articulation of the Ego," 268–73.

18. Charles, *Life*, 104–106; Chute, *Two Gentle Men*, 83–84. For the relevant parts of the Latin oration, see Hutchinson, 447–49.

19. *The Latin Poetry of George Herbert: A Bilingual Edition*, trans. Mark McCloskey and Paul R. Murphy (Athens: Ohio Univ. Press, 1965), 108–17; Chute, *Two Gentle Men*, 89–93.

20. For aggression, see Anthony Storr, *Human Aggression* (New York: Atheneum, 1968), 38–48; Margaret S. Mahler and Manuel Furer, "Certain Aspects of the Separation-Individuation Phase," *Psychoanalytic Quarterly* 32 (1963): 1–14; Mahler, "On the Significance of the Normal Separation-Individuation Phase," in vol. 2 of *Drives, Affects, Behavior*, ed. Max Schur (New York: International Universities

Press, 1965), 161–69; and Mahler, "A Study of the Separation-Individuation Process," *The Psychanalytic Study of the Child* 26 (1971): 403–24. Much of Mahler's work is synthesized in *The Psychological Birth of the Human Infant: Symbiosis and Individuation* (New York: Basic Books, 1975). For competition, the process of separation, and verbal combat, see Ong, *Fighting for Life*, 51–115; and Roger D. Abrahams, "Playing the Dozens," *Journal of American Folklore* 75 (1962): 209–20, and "The Training of the Man of Words in Talking Sweet," *Language in Society*, 1 (1972): 15–29. For examples from *Romeo and Juliet*, see 1.4.11–52; 2.4.38–97.

21. George H. Mead, *Mind, Self, and Society from the Standpoint of a Social Behaviorist* (Chicago: Univ. of Chicago Press, 1934), 150–63; Abrahams, "Playing the Dozens"; Ong, *Fighting for Life*, 193–207; D. W. Winnicott, "The Capacity to be Alone," in *The Maturational Processes*, 29–36.

22. Carl Francis Keppler defines this second self as a logically impossible but no less real figure who seems separate from the self, and therefore "second," but simultaneously united to one's identity, and therefore "self." S/he is always out there, a being in his or her own right, not a mere figment of the imagination, yet s/he is also always in here, a psyche intergrown to the self: *The Literature of the Second Self* (Tucson: Univ. of Arizona Press, 1972), 9–10.

23. Clements, "Theme, Tone, and Tradition," in Roberts, *Essential Articles*, 41–43.

24. Keppler, *Second Self*, 202–206; Carl Gustav Jung, "Conscious, Unconscious, and Individuation," in *The Archetypes of the Collective Unconscious*, vol. 9, pt. 1 of *The Collected Works of C. G. Jung*, ed. Sir Herbert Read, Michael Fordham, Gerhard Adler (New York: Pantheon Books, 1959), 275–89; Jung, "The Self" and "Christ, a Symbol of the Self," in *Aion: Researches into the Phenomenology of the Self*, vol. 9, pt. 2 of *Collected Works*, 23–71; and Martin Buber, *I and Thou*, trans. Ronald Gregor Smith (Edinburgh: T. and T. Clark, 1953).

25. Mihaly Csikszentmihalyi and Stith Bennett, "An Exploratory Model of Play," *American Anthropologist* 73 (1971): 45–58; Csikszentmihalyi, *Beyond Boredom and Anxiety: The Experience of Play in Work and Games* (San Francisco: Jossey-Bass, 1975), and *Flow: The Psychology of Optimal Experience* (New York: Harper and Row, 1990). Sigmund Freud, *Jokes and Their Relation to the Unconscious*, vol. 8 of *Standard Edition*.

26. Herbert believed that festival play promotes unity and summons Presence. He goes beyond canon law in *The Country Parson* to praise such ancient customs as Rogation Day processions to beat the bounds of the parish. All parishioners should attend, he says, because "absence breedes strangeness, but presence love. Now Love is [the parson's] business, and aime" (283–84). For his use of contest to meet the divine, see Bottrall, *George Herbert*, 107, and Ilona Bell, "'Setting Foot into Divinity': George Herbert and the English Reformation," in Roberts, *Essential Articles*, 63–83. Barbara Leah Harman, however, describes literary representation as a substitute for, not a summoning of, Presence, "George Herbert's 'Affliction (I)': The Limits

of Representation," in Roberts, *Essential Articles*, 508–24, and *Costly Monuments: Representations of the Self in George Herbert's Poetry* (Cambridge: Harvard Univ. Press, 1982), 41–169.

27. Stanley Fish, "Letting Go: The Dialectic of the Self in Herbert's Poetry," in *Self-Consuming Artifacts*, 156–223; Barbara Leah Harman, "Herbert, Coleridge and the Vexed Work of Narration," *Modern Language Notes* 93 (1978): 888–911, and *Costly Monuments*, 41–169. For other cogent arguments against this position, see Chana Bloch, *Spelling the Word: George Herbert and the Bible* (Berkeley: Univ. of California Press, 1985), 27–45; and Donald R. Dickson, *The Fountain of Living Waters: The Typology of the Waters of Life in Herbert, Vaughan, and Traherne* (Columbia: Univ. of Missouri Press, 1987), 82–87.

28. See Hermine Van Nuis, "Sincerity of Being and Simplicity of Expression: George Herbert's Ethics and Aesthetics," *Christianity and Literature* 27 (1977): 17; and Mulder, "*The Temple* as Picture," in Summers and Pebworth, *Too Rich*, 11–12.

29. See also L. C. Knights, *Explorations: Essays in Criticism Mainly on the Literature of the Seventeenth Century* (London: Chatto and Windus, 1946), 121–23; Robert Ellrodt, "George Herbert and the Religious Lyric," in Roberts, *Essential Articles*, 3–32.

30. These poems are frequently discussed as a sequence. Bart Westerweel reviews the criticism in *Patterns and Patterning: A Study of Four Poems by George Herbert* (Amsterdam: Rodopi, 1984), 63–64. See also Veith, *Reformation Spirituality*, 64–74; and Dickson, *Fountain of Living Waters*, 94–95.

31. Simon O. Lesser, in *Fiction and the Unconscious*, describes how a sense of wholeness can be achieved by splitting the self into competing forces—such as id, super-ego, and ego—and allowing each of these forces its place in a fiction.

32. Walton, *Lives*, 266.

33. See Fish, *Self-Consuming Artifacts*, 183–89.

34. Chana Bloch, "Spelling the Word: Herbert's Reading of the Bible," in Summers and Pebworth, *Too Rich*, 15–31, and *Spelling the Word*, 113–69; Harman, *Costly Monuments*, 170–96.

35. Knights, *Explorations*, 116; Ellrodt, "Herbert and the Religious Lyric," in Roberts, *Essential Articles*, 14.

36. *Match* may have the secondary meaning here of "a matrimonial compact" (*OED*, *match* sb,[1] II, 10). See *wooe* in l. 10.

37. For a history and description of Primero, see J. S. McTear, "Primero," *Notes and Queries*, series 11, 7 (1913): 1–3, 23–24, 41–43. For the proverbial use of "Most take all," see F. P. Wilson, "A Note on George Herbert's 'The Quidditie,'" *Review of English Studies* 19 (1943): 398–99; A. D., "Five Notes on George Herbert," *Notes and Queries* 197 (1952): 421–22; and Jess Cloud, "Herbert's 'The Quidditie,'" *Explicator* 34 (1975): item 32. For Herbert's use of Primero, see Melissa C.

Wanamaker, *Discordia Concors: The Wit of Metaphysical Poetry* (Port Washington, New York: Kennikat Press, 1975), 46–47, 51; and Michael Clifton, "Staking his Heart: Herbert's Use of Gambling Imagery in *The Temple*," *The George Herbert Journal* 8 (1984): 43–55.

38. For Herbert's use of laminar imagery, see Rickey, *Utmost Art*, 61ff; and John Hollander, *The Untuning of the Sky: Ideas of Music in English Poetry 1500–1700* (Princeton: Princeton Univ. Press, 1961), 288–94. For examples of subliminal allusions to other games or contests, see "The Foil" (fencing), and "Affliction I" and "The Method" (bowling). "Mattens," another game poem in which God and man "make a match," resembles "The Pulley" in its figures of God's "Powring" blessings on man and of man's learning not to rest in nature but to rise to nature's God.

39. Rickey quotes Thomas Nashe's use of *pulley* as a verbal form of *pull: Utmost Art*, 98–99. For the multiple meanings of *rest* in "The Pulley," see Michael Routh, "A Crux of 'The Pulley,'" *Seventeenth-Century News* 40 (1982): 44–45.

40. See Charles, *A Life*, 79–87, for a discussion of the two manuscripts of *The Temple*.

41. For discussions of the final lines of "The Quidditie," see Rickey, *Utmost Art*, 76, 117; Coburn Freer, *Music for a King: George Herbert's Style and the Metrical Psalms* (Baltimore: The Johns Hopkins Press, 1972), 230–31; Mark Taylor, *The Soul in Paraphrase: George Herbert's Poetics* (The Hague: Mouton, 1974), 47; and Bloch, "Spelling the Word," in Summers and Pebworth, *Too Rich*, 30, n. 14.

42. Stein, *George Herbert's Lyrics*, 194.

43. As a eucharistic poem, "Love III" prefigures the final marriage feast. Of course, as an Anglican, Herbert did not insist on the physical merger of God and man in the eucharist; Anglicans shunned disputes about the precise mechanism of God's presence in the sacrament.

44. Hutchinson glosses the lines as a reference to measuring sword lengths before a duel (494). To Fredson Bowers (in "Herbert's Sequential Imagery: 'The Temper,'" in Roberts, *Essential Articles*, 236–37), they refer to a contest of measuring arm lengths between tiny man and infinite God. See also Clements, "Theme, Tone, and Tradition," in Roberts, *Essential Articles*, 47; and Warnke, *Versions of Baroque*, 131–32.

45. Keizer, "George Herbert and the Tradition of Jacob," 23.

46. For a different view of spiritual conflict in "Artillerie," see Clements, "Theme, Tone, and Tradition," in Roberts, *Essential Articles*, 34–39. For spiritual combat in other poems by Herbert, see Ira Clark, "'Lord, in Thee the *Beauty* Lies in the *Discovery*': 'Love Unknown' and Reading Herbert," in Roberts, *Essential Articles*, 473–93.

47. Jeffrey Hart, "Herbert's *'The Collar'* Re-read," in Roberts, *Essential Articles*, 453–60; Barbara Leah Harman, "The Fiction of Coherence: George Herbert's

'The Collar,'" *PMLA* 93 (1978): 865–77; Ilona Bell, "The Double Pleasures of Herbert's '*Collar,*'" in Summers and Pebworth, *Too Rich,* 77–88.

48. Moltmann, *Theology of Play,* 15–45; Rahner, *Man at Play,* 5–25.

49. Colie, *Paradoxia Epidemica,* 199; Taylor, *The Soul in Paraphrase,* 82.

50. See Judy Z. Kronenfeld, "Herbert's 'A Wreath' and Devotional Aesthetics: Imperfect Efforts Redeemed by Grace," *ELH* 48 (1981): 290–309.

51. William Kerrigan, "Ritual Man: On the Outside of Herbert's Poetry," *Psychiatry* 48 (1985): 68–82.

52. William H. Pahlka argues that when Herbert brings his sinful will to metrical language, a reflection, according to Augustine, of the divine order of the universe, then Herbert invites God's participation in his speech. In recording his unstable experiences, he discovers in the ratios of verse, which mirror the ratios of nature and its informing Logos, the presence of a second hand in his work: *Saint Augustine's Meter and George Herbert's Will* (Kent, Ohio: Kent State Univ. Pres, 1987).

53. Goldberg, *Voice Terminal Echo,* 108.

54. Veith, *Reformation Spirituality,* 191–97.

55. See annotations on Genesis 32: 27–28 in *The New Oxford Annotated Bible,* ed. Herbert G. May and Bruce M. Metzger (New York: Oxford Univ. Press, 1977), 41. Keizer, "George Herbert and the Tradition of Jacob," 18–26.

56. Fish, *Self-Consuming Artifacts,* 189–215.

57. Using the Augustinian theory of signs, Richard Todd compares the human need to read God's opaque signs to the interpretive work of the reader confronted with Herbert's artful poems: *The Opacity of Signs: Acts of Interpretation in George Herbert's The Temple* (Columbia: Univ. of Missouri Press, 1986).

58. George Wither, "To the Reader," in *A Collection of Emblemes, Ancient and Moderne* (1635; reprint, Columbia: Univ. of South Carolina Press, 1975). Westerweel, *Patterns and Patterning,* 43.

59. Nuttall, *Overheard by God,* 9–19.

60. Fish argues that Herbert's poems lead the reader by stages to self-discovery through a series of chained questions, "overt or implied" (*Living Temple,* 35). Poems like "Jesu," "Trinity Sunday," and "A Wreath" do not, however, pose or imply questions; they present puzzles and invite the reader to discover solutions.

61. See, for example, Rosemond Tuve, *A Reading of George Herbert* (Chicago: Univ. of Chicago Press, 1952); Lewalski, *Protestant Poetics,* 283–316; and Bloch, *Spelling the Word.*

62. See, for example, Thomas A. Burns, "Fifty Seconds of Play: Expressive Interaction in Context," *Western Folklore* 37 (1978): 1–29.

63. For various solutions to the puzzle of *The Temple*'s unity, see Roberts, *Essential Articles,* 328–432; and Jerry Leath Mills, "Recent Studies in Herbert," *English Literary Renaissance* 6 (1976): 111–13. For more recent theories, see Stanley Stewart, *George Herbert* (Boston: Twayne, 1986), 83–89, who emphasizes the believer's temporal life in the church beginning in baptism, and Veith, *Reformation Spirituality,* 134, who emphasizes the sequential processes of justification and sanctification in forms of reformation spirituality.

64. Ivan Earle Taylor, "Cavalier Sophistication in the Poetry of George Herbert," *Anglican Theological Review* 39 (1957): 229–43; Martz, *Poetry of Meditation,* 268.

65. Marion White Singleton, *God's Courtier: Configuring a Different Grace in George Herbert's Temple* (Cambridge: Cambridge Univ. Press, 1987).

Chapter 6

1. Barbara Everett, "The Shooting of the Bears: Poetry and Politics in Andrew Marvell," in *Andrew Marvell: Essays on the Tercentenary of his Death,* ed. R. L. Brett (London: Oxford Univ. Press, 1979), 68. Robert Ellrodt, "Marvell's Mind and Mystery," in *Approaches to Marvell: The York Tercentenary Lectures,* ed. C. A. Patrides (London: Routledge and Kegan Paul, 1978), 216.

2. For the facts of Marvell's biography, see Pierre Legouis, *Andrew Marvell: Poet, Puritan, Patriot,* rev. ed. (London: Oxford at the Clarendon Press, 1970), and John Dixon Hunt, *Andrew Marvell: His Life and Writings* (Ithaca: Cornell Univ. Press, 1978). Annabel M. Patterson, *Marvell and the Civic Crown* (Princeton: Princeton Univ. Press, 1978), 11, 48. *The Poems and Letters of Andrew Marvell,* ed. H. M. Margoliouth, 3rd ed. rev. by Pierre Legouis and E. E. Duncan-Jones (Oxford: Clarendon Press, 1971), vol. 2, Letters, 166. All quotations from Marvell's English poetry are taken from volume 1 of this edition. Parenthetical references to stanzas are in Roman numerals; to lines, in Arabic numerals. All references to his Latin poetry are to the following edition: William A. McQueen and Kiffin A. Rockwell, *The Latin Poetry of Andrew Marvell* (Chapel Hill: Univ. of North Carolina Press, 1964).

3. Frank Kermode, "The Argument of Marvell's 'Garden,'" in *Marvell: Modern Judgements,* ed. Michael Wilding (London: Macmillan, 1969), 126. Rosalie L. Colie, *"My Ecchoing Song": Andrew Marvell's Poetry of Criticism* (Princeton: Princeton Univ. Press, 1970), 124–26.

4. Joseph H. Summers, "The Alchemical Ventriloquist: Andrew Marvell," *The Heirs of Donne and Jonson* (New York: Oxford Univ. Press, 1970), 133. Ong, "Voice as Summons for Belief," in *The Barbarian Within,* 49–67.

5. Some have noted the self-absorption or self-reflexiveness of his lyrics, but have not labeled it narcissism: Anne Ferry, *All in War with Time: Love Poetry of Shakespeare, Donne, Jonson, Marvell* (Cambridge: Harvard Univ. Press, 1975),

233–34; Patterson, *The Civic Crown,* 105–106; Christopher Ricks, "'Its own resemblance,'" and Ellrodt, "Mind and Mystery," in Patrides, *Approaches to Marvell,* 108–35, 228. Others have used the term *narcissism,* untechnically in describing aspects of Marvell's lyrics: George deF. Lord, "From Contemplation to Action: Marvell's Poetical Career," in *Andrew Marvell: A Collection of Critical Essays,* ed. George deF. Lord (Englewood Cliffs, New Jersey: Prentice-Hall, 1968), 64; M. J. K. O'Loughlin, "This Sober Frame: A Reading of 'Upon Appleton House,'" in Lord, *Collection of Critical Essays,* 137; Harold E. Toliver, *Marvell's Ironic Vision* (New Haven: Yale Univ. Press, 1965), 65; and Michael McCanles, *Dialectical Criticism and Renaissance Literature* (Berkeley: Univ. of California Press, 1975), 114.

6. For a detailed survey of Marvell's reputation, see Wilding, "Introduction," *Modern Judgements,* 10–39.

7. T. S. Eliot, "Andrew Marvell," in Lord, *Collection of Critical Essays,* 21–22; George Williamson, *The Donne Tradition: A Study of English Poetry from Donne to the Death of Cowley,* (Cambridge: Harvard Univ. Press, 1930), 150–61; Muriel C. Bradbrook and M. G. Lloyd Thomas, *Andrew Marvell* (London: Cambridge Univ. Press, 1940), 39–40; J. B. Leishman, *The Art of Marvell's Poetry* (London: Hutchinson, 1966), 23, 56, 307–308; Winifred Nowottny, sel. from *The Language Poets Use,* in *Andrew Marvell: A Critical Anthology,* ed. John Carey (Baltimore: Penguin, 1969), 315; A. J. Smith, "Marvell's Metaphysical Wit," in Patrides, *Approaches to Marvell,* 56–86.

8. Robin Grove, sel. from "Marvell," and J. B. Broadbent, sel. from "The Metaphysical Decadence," in Carey, *Critical Anthology,* 295–301, 155–60.

9. Ruth Wallerstein, *Studies in Seventeenth-Century Poetic* (New York: Univ. of Wisconsin Press, 1950), 168–74. Critics still occasionally see Marvell's play as incompatible with a serious intent: John Klause, *The Unfortunate Fall: Theodicy and the Moral Imagination of Andrew Marvell* (Hamden, Connecticut: Archon Books, 1983), 3, 84.

10. Summers, *Heirs,* 138–42; Ellrodt, "Mind and Mystery," in Patrides, *Approaches to Marvell,* 222–23.

11. Frank J. Warnke, "Sacred Play," 455–64, "Play and Metamorphosis in Marvell's Poetry," *Studies in English Literature* 5 (1965): 23–30; Louis L. Martz, "Andrew Marvell: The Mind's Happiness," *The Wit of Love: Donne, Carew, Crashaw, Marvell* (Notre Dame, Indiana: Univ. of Notre Dame Press, 1969), 151–90; Kermode, "The Argument of Marvell's 'Garden,'" in Wilding, *Modern Judgements,* 125–40; Colie, *"My Ecchoing Song,"* 75, 144, 260.

12. Warnke's work depends heavily on the play theories of Johan Huizinga, which have been extensively revised by recent theorists. O'Loughlin claims that "Upon Appleton House" is play imitating General Fairfax's play in retirement ("This Sober Frame," in Lord, *Collection of Critical Essays,* 120–42). Jim Swan uses psychoanalyst D. W. Winnicott's theories of mother-child interactions in a "play space" to illuminate "The Garden" ("At Play in the Garden of Ambivalence: Andrew Mar-

vell and the Green World," *Criticism* 17 [1975]: 295–307). In *Childhood and Cultural Despair,* 201–41, Marcus focuses on the child at play in Marvell's lyrics, and in *Politics of Mirth,* 213–18, 233–63, on Marvell's distancing of himself from the Stuarts' political use of rural play.

13. Skeptics have criticized the use of psychoanalytic theory to interpret Marvell's lyrics because tradition and genre, not psychic configurations, are the immediate source of many literary details adduced as evidence in psychoanalytic readings. (See Wallerstein, *Studies,* 168–78; and Colie, *"My Ecchoing Song,"* 13.) But the traditions and genres available to any Renaissance poet are legion, and consequently the principle of selection among traditions and genres, and the variations played on the era's loose system of decorum can yield valuable evidence about an author's preoccupations. (See Rosalie L. Colie, *The Resources of Kind: Genre-Theory in the Renaissance,* ed. Barbara K. Lewalski [Berkeley: Univ. of California Press, 1973], and Kenneth Burke, "On Covery, Re- and Dis-," *Accent* 13 [1953]: 226.) Furthermore, whether one explains an image by reference to tradition or to psychoanalytic theory depends on the level of generality preferred. For example, the speaker's retreat in "The Garden" to the happiness of "The Mind, that Ocean where each kind / Does streight its own resemblance find," from which he creates worlds and seas, has been explained as an allusion to the Hermetic doctrine of creation, which influenced Italian and English Neoplatonists: man's pure mind fell in love with its own reflection in the earth's waters, and their union produced man's body. (Maren-Sofie Røstvig, "Upon Appleton House," in Wilding, *Modern Judgements,* 228–29; Donald M. Friedman, *Marvell's Pastoral Art* [Berkeley: Univ. of California Press, 1970], 22.) The mental retreat may also recapitulate an infant's omnipotent fantasy that the world mirrors its desires with gratifications that it creates. Both viewpoints account for the image; the former generalizes to the level of historical tradition, and the latter generalizes to the universal experience rendered not only in Hermetic traditions, but also in myths from many cultures and eras. Whether or not psychoanalytic theory is actually a modern mythology is debatable. Nevertheless, its findings are based on data and can unite many details in Marvell's lyrics into a picture as coherent and relevant as those pictures offered in reconstructions of the manifold traditions available to the well-educated Renaissance poet. For a more speculative psychoanalytic reading than mine, see William Kerrigan, "Marvell and Nymphets," *Greyfriar: Siena Studies in Literature* 27 (1986): 3–21.

14. This brief summary of the genesis of the human self is indebted primarily to Heinz Kohut, *The Analysis of the Self: A Systematic Approach to the Psychoanalytic Treatment of Narcissistic Personality Disorders* (New York: International Universities Press, 1971), and *The Restoration of the Self* (New York: International Universities Press, 1977).

15. Norman O. Brown, *Love's Body* (New York: Random House, 1966), 166–67.

16. Wallerstein (*Studies,* 276) attributes Marvellian dialectic to philosophical debates about the relation of soul to body. Martz (*Wit of Love,* 170, 190) attributes it to the mannerist sensibility. McCanles (*Dialectical Criticism,* 95–117) and R. I. V.

Hodge (*Foreshortened Time: Andrew Marvell and Seventeenth Century Revolutions* [Cambridge, England: D. S. Brewer, 1978], 7–26) claim the influence of dialectical logic in the seventeenth century. Patterson (*Civic Crown*, 26–27) emphasizes the political choices facing Marvell. Smith ("Marvell's Metaphysical Wit," in Patrides, *Approaches to Marvell*, 56–86) discusses Marvell's metaphysical exploration of man's double nature. Perhaps the most complete analysis of Marvell's "thwarting reversals," although not fully accounting for them, is John Carey's "Reversals Transposed: An Aspect of Marvell's Imagination," in Patrides, *Approaches to Marvell*, 136–54. Those critics contrasting Marvell's use of antithesis to paradox are George Williamson, *Proper Wit of Poetry* (London: Faber and Faber, 1961), 95; Leishman, *Art of Marvell's Poetry*, 172; and Toliver, *Marvell's Ironic Vision*, 2–3.

17. Lawrence W. Hyman, *Andrew Marvell* (New York: Twayne Publishers, 1964), 52–59; Toliver, *Marvell's Ironic Vision*, 44–52; Ann E. Berthoff, *The Resolved Soul: A Study of Marvell's Major Poems* (Princeton: Princeton Univ. Press, 1970), 88–110; Smith, "Marvell's Metaphysical Wit," in Patrides, *Approaches to Marvell*, 60–61.

18. Berthoff, *Resolved Soul*, 75–88.

19. H. R. Swardson (*Poetry and the Fountain of Light: Observations on the Conflict Between Christian and Classical Traditions in Seventeenth-Century Poetry* [Columbia: Univ. of Missouri Press, 1962], 96–98) notes Marvell's placement of the Golden Age farther back than innocent sexuality, in a garden of presexual innocence. For the second birth of separation, see Mahler, *Psychological Birth*.

20. Ferry, *All in War*, 233–34.

21. E. W. Tayler, "Marvell's Garden of the Mind," in Wilding, *Modern Judgements*, 259; Friedman, *Marvell's Pastoral Art*, 10–14; Isabel G. MacCaffrey, "The Scope of Imagination in 'Upon Appleton House,'" in *Tercentenary Essays in Honor of Andrew Marvell*, ed. Kenneth Friedenreich (Hamden, Connecticut: Archon, 1977), 225.

22. Ricks, "'Its own resemblance,'" in Patrides, *Approaches to Marvell*, 108–35; McQueen and Rockwell, *The Latin Poetry*, 12.

23. Toliver (*Marvell's Ironic Vision*, 153) and Berthoff (*The Resolved Soul*, 132–33) discuss Marvell's view of heterosexual love as a threat to the soul's autonomy.

24. Jim Swan, "History, Pastoral and Desire: Andrew Marvell's Mower Poems," *International Review of Psychoanalysis* 3 (1976): 196–97. Swan's psychoanalytic reading of the Mower poems anticipates mine in some details.

25. For a discussion of narcissistic rage, see Arnold Rothstein, *The Narcissistic Pursuit of Perfection* (New York: International Universities Press, 1980), 56–57, 79–81.

26. Marion Meilaender, "Marvell's Pastoral Poetry: Fulfillment of a Tradition," *Genre* 12 (1979): 188–89.

27. In a different context, Don Parry Norford notes the merger between nymph and fawn: "Marvell and the Arts of Contemplation and Action," *ELH* 41 (1974): 57–58.

28. Kohut, *Analysis of the Self,* 16–17, and *Restoration of the Self,* 197 n. 11.

29. For discussions of the allusions, see Bradbrook and Thomas, *Andrew Marvell,* 47–48; Karina Williamson, "Marvell's 'The Nymph Complaining': A Reply," in Carey, *Critical Anthology,* 281–87; Ruth Nevo, "Marvell's 'Songs of Innocence and Experience,'" *Studies in English Literature* 5 (1965): 5–15; Leishman, *Art of Marvell's Poetry,* 156; Don Cameron Allen, *Image and Meaning: Metaphoric Traditions in Renaissance Poetry,* rev. ed. (Baltimore: The Johns Hopkins Press, 1968), 165–86; Geoffrey H. Hartman, "'The Nymph Complaining for the Death of Her Faun': A Brief Allegory," in *Beyond Formalism: Literary Essays 1958–70* (New Haven: Yale Univ. Press, 1970), 173–92; and Martz, *Wit of Love,* 181. For the characterization of the nymph, see Edward S. LeComte, "Marvell's 'The Nymph Complaining for the Death of Her Faun,'" in Carey, *Critical Anthology,* 274–81; Leo Spitzer, "Marvell's 'Nymph Complaining for the Death of Her Faun': Sources versus Meaning," in *Seventeenth-Century English Poetry: Modern Essays in Criticism,* ed. William R. Keast, rev. ed. (London: Oxford Univ. Press, 1971), 372–87; and Colie, *"My Ecchoing Song,"* 88–90, 130–32. Arguing that "The Nymph" is about its own status as a text, Jonathan Goldberg emphasizes the emptiness at the end of the poem, as the voice, which has been a substitute for presence, dies: "Marvell's Nymph and the Echo of Voice," *Glyph* 8 (1981): 19–39, and *Voice Terminal Echo,* 14–37.

30. Lucy Gent ("Marvell's Games with Teleology," *Renaissance Quarterly* 32 [1979]: 514–28) and Michael Long (*Marvell, Nabokov: Childhood and Arcadia* [Oxford: Clarendon Press, 1984], x–xi) emphasize Marvell's distancing of himself by play from speakers who interpret Providence in a man-centered way and who yearn for a childhood Arcadia.

31. Colie, *"My Ecchoing Song,"* plate 2.

32. *Ibid.,* 49–51, 110–13, 127.

33. The *recreate/re-create* pun is a favorite formulation of Rosalie Colie and Joan Webber to describe seventeenth-century literary play, but neither explains how play can help restructure the self. Colie, *Paradoxia Epidemica,* 190–215; Joan Webber, *The Eloquent "I": Style and Self in Seventeenth-Century Prose* (Madison: Univ. of Wisconsin Press, 1968), 151, 178–79.

34. Legouis, *Poet, Puritan, Patriot,* 19–20, 27–28.

35. Although not describing this double process in psychoanalytic terms, several critics have intuited its efficacy for self-formation: S. L. Goldberg, "Marvell: Self and Art," in Carey, *Critical Anthology,* 160–75; Toliver, *Marvell's Ironic Vision,* 88–95; Martz, *Wit of Love,* 169; Colie, *"My Ecchoing Song,"* 263, 293; Balachandra Rajan, "Andrew Marvell: The Aesthetics of Inconclusiveness," in Patrides, *Approaches to Marvell,* 161, 166–68. Martz (162–69), Colie (90, 132), and Ferry (*All in War,* 210–212) have especially emphasized Marvell's detachment from himself.

36. For representative versions of these views, see Leishman, *Art of Marvell's Poetry,* 292–318; Wallerstein, *Studies,* 151–342; Maren-Sofie Røstvig, "Andrew Marvell's 'The Garden': A Hermetic Poem," *English Studies* 40 (1959): 65–76; Kermode, "The Argument of Marvell's 'Garden,'" in Wilding, *Modern Judgements,* 125–40; and Stanley Stewart, *The Enclosed Garden: The Tradition and the Image in Seventeenth-Century Poetry* (Madison: Univ. of Wisconsin Press, 1966), 152–83.

37. My own reading is indebted primarily to Toliver, *Marvell's Ironic Vision,* 139–49; Summers, *Heirs,* 130–55; and Colie, *"My Ecchoing Song,"* 141–77.

38. See Rosemary Freeman, *English Emblem Books* (London: Chatto and Windus, 1948), 174–95; Toliver, *Marvell's Ironic Vision,* 143; and Jeffry B. Spencer, *Heroic Nature: Ideal Landscape in English Poetry from Marvell to Thomson* (Evanston, Illinois: Northwestern Univ. Press, 1973), 4–5. For archetypal symbolism, see Freud, *Introductory Lectures on Psycho-analysis,* vol. 15 of *Standard Edition,* 156, 158, 162.

39. For the symbolic meaning of green, see Don Cameron Allen, "Symbolic Color in the Literature of the English Renaissance," *Philological Quarterly* 15 (1936): 85–86.

40. Kohut, *Analysis of the Self,* 50–52.

41. Hyman (*Andrew Marvell,* 23–36) discusses Marvell's frequent isolation of sexuality from innocence in characterizing females. Norford ("Arts of Contemplation and Action," 61, 67–70) claims that, for Marvell, love of woman and love of nature are incompatible.

42. Freud, *Jokes and Their Relation to the Unconscious,* vol. 8 of *Standard Edition,* 117–39, 166–71. Of course, the similes, metaphors, symbols, and wit found in all literature have their roots in the unconscious. But Marvell's puns and incongruous juxtapositions of levels of reality, often resembling the nonsense of Lewis Carroll, have escaped much of the censorship that usually disguises archaic thought processes. We can detect more of what Freud described as a child's pleasurable play with words, without regard for meaning or coherence, which is the genesis of wit.

43. These and other puns have been most notably analyzed by A. H. King, "Some Notes on Andrew Marvell's 'Garden,'" *English Studies* 20 (1938): 118–21; and Colie, *"My Ecchoing Song,"* 147–52.

44. Colie, *"My Ecchoing Song,"* 79, 84, 158–60.

45. Kermode, "The Argument of Marvell's 'Garden,'" in Wilding, *Modern Judgements,* 125–40.

46. Hyman, *Andrew Marvell,* 64–66.

47. There is a debate about whether Marvell envisioned a garden laid out in the shape of a sundial or whether the "Dial" is a metaphor for the garden's participation in nature's temporal cycle or in the new order of Grace. See Bradbrook and

Thomas, *Andrew Marvell,* frontispiece, 63; Stewart, *Enclosed Garden,* 180; Patrick Cullen, *Spenser, Marvell, and Renaissance Pastoral* (Cambridge: Harvard Univ. Press, 1970), 161; and Berthoff, *Resolved Soul,* 11–13. In line 69, *it* may refer to *Dial,* which precedes the pronoun, or *Bee,* which follows it. Both the floral clock and the bee work; in fact, the bee may compute the clock's as well as its own time (*its,* l. 70). See Harry Berger, Jr., "Marvell's 'Garden': Still Another Interpretation," *Modern Language Quarterly* 28 (1967): 302, n.18.

48. Bateson, "A Theory of Play and Fantasy," in *Steps to an Ecology of Mind,* 191–93; Haley, "Paradoxes in Play, Fantasy, and Psychotherapy," 52–58; Winnicott, *Playing and Reality,* 38, 54; Kohut, *Analysis of the Self,* 210–11.

49. Kohut, *Analysis of the Self,* 13, 196–97, 207.

50. Whether or not the analyst can dispense with making interpretations and be merely a fallible mirror and focus for the analysand's idealization is a matter of debate. Kohut warns against overinterpreting. Meredith Anne Skura (*The Literary Use of the Psychoanalytic Process* [New Haven: Yale Univ. Press, 1981], 172ff) has described the interchange between reader and author, through the medium of a literary text, as transference.

51. For Marvell's use of literary and philosophical traditions, see Røstvig, "Upon Appleton House," in Wilding, *Modern Judgements,* 215–32; Kitty W. Scoular, *Natural Magic: Studies in the Presentation of Nature in English Poetry from Spenser to Marvell* (London: Oxford at the Clarendon Press, 1965), 164–70; and Leishman, *Art of Marvell's Poetry,* 250–73. For Marvell's use of historical events, see Allen, *Image,* 187–225. For how Marvell manipulates tradition and history, see Colie, *"My Ecchoing Song,"* 181–294.

52. Critics have noted the peculiar, metamorphic quality of Marvell's conceits, comparing them even to Clevelandisms. See Leishman, *Art of Marvell's Poetry,* 270; Smith, "Marvell's Metaphysical Wit," in Patrides, *Approaches to Marvell,* 76–77; Allan Gray, "The Surface of Marvell's 'Upon Appleton House,'" *English Literary Renaissance* 9 (1979): 178–81; and Long, *Marvell, Nabokov,* 202. Peter Schwenger sees these metamorphic images as manifestations of deceit: "'To Make His Saying True': Deceit in *Appleton House,*" *Studies in Philology* 77 (1980): 84–104.

53. Some critics have noted the disturbing, nightmarish, even anarchic quality of the meadow and flood sequences. See Grove, sel. from "Marvell," in Carey, *Critical Anthology,* 300; William A. McClung, *The Country House Poem in English Renaissance Poetry* (Berkeley: Univ. of California Press, 1977), 168–69; and Hodge, *Foreshortened Time,* 151, 158. Others have alluded to the primitive mental functioning evident here. See William Empson, *Some Versions of Pastoral* (1935; reprint, London: Chatto and Windus, 1968), 135–36; and Colie, *"My Ecchoing Song,"* 263, 266.

54. Several critics have emphasized the speaker's playfulness and the containment of his chaotic vision. See Bradbrook and Thomas, *Andrew Marvell,* 36–37;

Wallerstein, *Studies,* 300–318; John M. Wallace, *Destiny His Choice: The Loyalism of Andrew Marvell* (Cambridge: Cambridge Univ. Press, 1968), 233–36, 246–48; Martz, *Wit of Love,* 182–87; and Harold Skulsky, "*Upon Appleton House:* Marvell's Comedy of Discourse," *ELH* 52 (1985): 591–620.

55. Colie (*"My Ecchoing Song,"* 247–49) and Long (*Marvell, Nabokov,* 211) have noted the predominance in the poem of images of nurture.

56. Scoular, *Natural Magic,* 171; Colie, *"My Ecchoing Song,"* 209; and Long, *Marvell, Nabokov,* 195. Although this passage resembles Fairfax's translation from Saint-Amant's poem, *La Solitude,* as Bradbrook and Thomas have noted (*Andrew Marvell,* 24), what Marvell includes adds to the narcissistic quality of the passage: the direct reference to Narcissus and the reflected world's doubts about being in or out of the river. See Patterson, *Civic Crown,* 105–106.

57. For a discussion of this sudden fixity of objects, see Scoular, *Natural Magic,* 174–76. Ellrodt ("Mind and Mystery," in Patrides, *Approaches to Marvell,* 221–22, n. 26) has noted Marvell's fascination with cold, congealed objects.

58. For discussions of Marvell's ambivalent attitude toward Fairfax, see Hodge, *Foreshortened Time,* 150; and Patterson, *Civic Crown,* 95–97.

59. Rajan, "Andrew Marvell: The Aesthetics of Inconclusiveness," in Patrides, *Approaches to Marvell,* 161–63.

60. See Hodge, *Foreshortened Time,* 125, 130–31.

61. Kohut, *Analysis of the Self,* 191–92. To define the state of the healthy self, whole but doomed to death, Kohut has coined the term *Tragic Man,* in contrast to the Freudian *Guilty Man* (*Restoration of the Self,* 133). Klause (*Unfortunate Fall*) examines Marvell's lifelong conflict between two philosophical positions: that which values escape to a realm of pure perfection and that which values the triumph over evil by struggle.

62. See Christopher Hill, "Society and Andrew Marvell," in Wilding, *Modern Judgements,* 74; and Toliver, *Marvell's Ironic Vision,* 154–61.

63. Colie (*"My Ecchoing Song,"* 67–69) has noted the allusions to "the formal aspects of a game" in "An Horatian Ode"; and Christopher Clausen ("Games for Death and Two Maidens," in Guinness, *Auctor Ludens,* 171–81) discusses the "sport" proposed at the end of "To His Coy Mistress."

64. Robert Wilcher, *Andrew Marvell* (Cambridge: Cambridge Univ. Press, 1985), 7, 105, 125.

65. Smadar Lavie, "The Fool and the Hippies: Ritual/Play and Social Inconsistencies Among the Mzeina Bedouin of the Sinai," in *The Masks of Play,* ed. Brian Sutton-Smith and Diana Kelly-Byrne (New York: Leisure Press, 1984), 63–70. For an extensive discussion of the function of play in culture, see Clifford Geertz, "Deep Play: Notes on the Balinese Cockfight," *Daedalus* 101 (1972): 1–37.

66. According to Kohut, "The work of the great artist . . . reflects the dominant psychological issue of his era. The artist stands, as it were, in proxy for his generation" (*Restoration of the Self,* 285–86). Colie (*"My Ecchoing Song,"* 153) has analyzed Marvell's lyrics as "metapoetic."

67. See Wallerstein, *Studies,* 248–51, 340–42.

68. See, for example, Bradbrook and Thomas, *Andrew Marvell,* 26, 55; Hill, "Society and Andrew Marvell," in Wilding, *Modern Judgements,* 68, 87; F. W. Bateson, sel. from *English Poetry: A Critical Introduction,* in Carey, *Critical Anthology,* 102–106; Toliver, *Marvell's Ironic Vision,* 5–6; Legouis, *Poet, Puritan, Patriot,* 223; Hodge, *Foreshortened Time,* 2–3, 158; and Roger Sharrock, "Marvell's Poetry of Evasion and Marvell's Times," *English* 28 (1979): 3–40.

69. Warren L. Chernaik, *The Poet's Time: Politics and Religion in the Work of Andrew Marvell* (Cambridge: Cambridge Univ. Press, 1983), 5.

70. *The Rehearsal Transpros'd and The Rehearsal Transpros'd: The Second Part,* ed. D. I. B. Smith (London: Oxford at the Clarendon Press, 1971), 147.

Chapter 7

1. Donne's *Devotions Upon Emergent Occasions,* which he prepared for publication, were equally popular, but as meditations they are more personal and particular than, for example, Browne's reflections on the religion of a doctor.

2. Ong, "The Writer's Audience," 9–21.

3. Robert Burton, *The Anatomy of Melancholy: What it is, with all the kinds, causes, symptomes, prognostickes and severall cures of it,* ed. Holbrook Jackson (1932; reprint, New York: Vintage Books, 1977), 1:68. All subsequent references will be cited parenthetically in the text by volume and page numbers. For the widespread use of the "world turned upside down" trope, see David Kunzle, "World Upside Down: The Iconography of a European Broadsheet Type," in Babcock, *Reversible World,* 39–94.

4. For praise and blame, see James Roy King, *Studies in Six Seventeenth Century Writers* (Athens: Ohio Univ. Press, 1966), 60–64, 83; and Ruth A. Fox, *The Tangled Chain: The Structure of Disorder in the Anatomy of Melancholy* (Berkeley: Univ. of California Press, 1976), 13. For defining *The Anatomy* as a scientific treatise or an anatomy of society, see Lawrence Babb, *Sanity in Bedlam: A Study of Robert Burton's Anatomy of Melancholy* (East Lansing: Michigan State Univ. Press, 1959); Bergan Evans, *The Psychiatry of Robert Burton* (New York: Columbia Univ. Press, 1944); and William R. Mueller, *The Anatomy of Robert Burton's England* (Berkeley: Univ. of California Press, 1952). For deliberate confusion, see Bridget Gellert Lyons, *Voices of Melancholy: Studies in Literary Treatments of Melancholy in Renaissance England* (New York: Norton, 1971), 124; and Fish, "Thou Thyself Art the Subject of My Discourse: Democritus Junior to the Reader," in *Self-Consuming Artifacts,*

303–52. For heterogeneity, see Colie, "Burton's *Anatomy of Melancholy* and the Structure of Paradox," in *Paradoxia Epidemica*, 430–60; Michael O'Connell, *Robert Burton* (Boston: Twayne, 1986), 48–49; and Webber, "Robert Burton: The Anatomy of Democritus Junior," in *Eloquent "I,"* 80–114.

5. O'Connell, *Robert Burton*, 41–46. Spariosu, *Literature, Mimesis and Play*, 10, and *Dionysus Reborn*, 24.

6. T. E. Brown, "Robert Burton," *New Review* 13 (September, 1895): 257–66; Charles Whibley, *Literary Portraits* (London: Archibald Constable, 1904), 264–66; Siegbert Prawer, "Burton's 'Anatomy of Melancholy,'" *The Cambridge Journal* 1 (1948): 688; Fish, *Self-Consuming Artifacts*, 322.

7. *The Life of Milton*, in *Samuel Johnson: Selected Prose and Poetry*, ed. Bertrand H. Bronson (New York: Rinehart, 1952), 464.

8. David Renaker, "Robert Burton and Ramist Method," *Renaissance Quarterly* 24 (1971): 210–20; King, *Studies*, 79–83.

9. Critics have recognized Burton's unwillingness to decide most issues: Prawer, "Burton's Anatomy," 679. Some see his indecision as a symptom of his own or his affected melancholy: Evans, *Psychiatry*, 19; Lyons, *Voices*, 131–33. Others attribute it to his goal of inclusiveness—to include old knowledge with new regardless of the contradictions (Babb, *Sanity*, 42, 70; O'Connell, *Robert Burton*, 44–45), to sustain a speculative attitude toward all knowledge (Webber, *Eloquent "I,"* 86), or merely to order man's understanding of disorder (Fox, *Tangled Chain*, 36–39).

10. Babb, *Sanity*, 63.

11. Fox, *Tangled Chain*, 227–35; Colie, *Pseudodoxia*, 455–59. Devon L. Hodges, in *Renaissance Fictions of Anatomy* (Amherst: Univ. of Massachusetts Press, 1985), 1–19, 107–23, analyzes how Renaissance anatomists, including Burton, try and fail to stand outside the subject they study.

12. Burton occasionally makes a distinction between metaphorical and actual melancholy, but in the treatise as a whole he insists that "melancholy in what sense you will, properly or improperly . . . truly or metaphorically, 'tis all one" (1:40).

13. Burton's use of self-referential paradoxes has been a common, if unacknowledged, theme in what several astute readers have said about *The Anatomy*. Ruth Fox (*Tangled Chain*, 252, 257–58) sees Burton turning the causes of his melancholy, overmuch study and idleness, into its cure by engaging in the scholarship, which Burton calls mere idling, necessary to write a book on melancholy. Bridget Lyons (*Voices*, 114, 124) sees Burton as modeling in his writing the symptoms of the disease about which he writes. And James S. Tillman has demonstrated how Burton used the classical trope of the satirist satirized: "The Satirist Satirized: Burton's Democritus Jr.," *Studies in the Literary Imagination* 10 (1977): 89–96. None of these readers, however, has noted how Burton gets outside the crippling paradoxes of his world by framing himself inside paradoxes of his own making. See, however, Fox, *Tangled Chain*, 101, 113, for the function of digression.

14. Mueller, *Anatomy,* 26–27.

15. Most critics agree that Democritus Jr. is not a consistent persona in the modern sense, but is more often than not Burton's mouthpiece: Babb, *Sanity,* 37; Richard L. Nochimson, "Burton's *Anatomy:* The Author's Purposes and the Reader's Response," *Forum for Modern Language Studies* 13 (1977): 265–84. Reinhard H. Friederich has compared Burton's shifting roles to the composite forms of mannerist style: "Training His Melancholy Spaniel: Persona and Structure in Robert Burton's 'Democritus Junior to the Reader,'" *Philological Quarterly* 55 (1976): 198. Lyons and Tillman have emphasized the relation between the character of Burton's persona and the subject of his anatomy (see note 13).

16. Jean Robert Simon, *Robert Burton (1577–1640) et L' Anatomie de la Mélancolie* (Paris: Didier, 1964), 478–90. O'Connell thinks that most often Burton is not joking: *Robert Burton,* 39–40.

17. Bakhtin describes the mock prescription as a widely recognized genre of "grotesque realism": *Rabelais,* 161.

18. Babb, *Sanity,* 54; Evans, *Psychiatry,* 37; O'Connell, *Robert Burton,* 79–85.

19. Webber, *Eloquent "I,"* 101.

20. John Middleton Murry, *Countries of the Mind: Essays in Literary Criticism* (London: W. Collins Sons, 1922), 35, 63; Prawer, "Burton's Anatomy," 685–86.

21. Walter E. Houghton, Jr., "The English Virtuoso in the Seventeenth Century," *Journal of the History of Ideas* 3 (1942): 51–73, 190–219.

22. O'Connell, *Robert Burton,* 15–17.

23. Evans, *Psychiatry,* 35; Fish, *Self-Consuming Artifacts,* 305–306, 309; Nochimson, "Burton's *Anatomy,*" 265–84.

24. Murry, *Countries,* 63–73; Evans, *Psychiatry,* passim; Simon, *Robert Burton,* 491–516.

25. Evans, *Psychiatry,* 17, 22–24. For studies of male agonistic play, especially verbal combat, see Abrahams, "Playing the Dozens," 209–20, "Training of the Man of Words," 15–29; and Ong, *Fighting for Life,* 51–115.

26. Webber, *Eloquent "I,"* 100; Fish, *Self-Consuming Artifacts,* 346–49; O'Connell, *Robert Burton,* 73–74.

27. Fox, *Tangled Chain,* 142; Fish, *Self-Consuming Artifacts,* 346–47; Lyons, *Voices,* 129–30.

28. Murry, *Countries,* 56; King, *Studies,* 91; Lyons, *Voices,* viii–ix.

29. Evans, *Psychiatry,* 16; Nochimson, "Burton's *Anatomy,*" 279–80.

30. Fox, *Tangled Chain,* 231, 234.

31. Evans, *Psychiatry,* 25–31.

32. See also Webber, *Eloquent "I,"* 102; Fox, *Tangled Chain,* 152. In arguing that the Renaissance imperialist spirit appropriated alien cultures just as the virtuosi collected rarities, Steven Mullaney takes the Marxist stance that the margins seldom offer a culture the potential for change. Instead, the marginal is the Other against which power defines and solidifies itself: "Strange Things, Gross Terms, Curious Customs: The Rehearsal of Cultures in the Late Renaissance," *Representations* 1 (1983): 40–67.

Chapter 8

1. Sir Thomas Browne, *Religio Medici and Other Works,* ed. L. C. Martin (Oxford: Clarendon Press, 1964), 70. All quotations from *Religio Medici, Hydriotaphia, The Garden of Cyrus, A Letter to a Friend,* and *Christian Morals* will be taken from this edition and will be noted parenthetically by abbreviations in the text.

2. *The Works of Sir Thomas Browne,* ed. Geoffrey Keynes (London: Faber and Faber, 1964), 2:51, 527. All quotations from *Pseudodoxia Epidemica* (vol.2), *Miscellany Tracts,* etc. (vol. 3), and *Letters* (vol. 4) will be taken from this edition and noted parenthetically by abbreviations in the text. Browne's extant medicinal prescriptions, which Keynes collected as miscellaneous writings, are all simple herbal compositions, in marked contrast to the bizarre concoctions he ridicules (3:463–65).

3. *Coleridge on the Seventeenth Century,* ed. Roberta Florence Brinkley (Durham, North Carolina: Duke Univ. Press, 1955), 438–39.

4. For summaries of the objections of Browne's earliest critics, Sir Kenelm Digby and Alexander Ross, see Frank Livingstone Huntley, "The Publication and Immediate Reception of *Religio Medici,*" *The Library Quarterly* 25 (1955): 203–18; and James N. Wise, *Sir Thomas Browne's Religio Medici and Two Seventeenth-Century Critics* (Columbia: Univ. of Missouri Press, 1973). On Browne's lack of substance, see Edmund Gosse, *Sir Thomas Browne* (London: Macmillan, 1905), 190–203; and T. S. Eliot, "Prose and Verse," *Chapbook* 22 (1921): 3–10. On religion as metaphor, see Dewey Kiper Ziegler, *In Divided and Distinguished Worlds: Religion and Rhetoric in the Writings of Sir Thomas Browne* (Cambridge: Harvard Univ. Printing Office, 1943). On toying with doubt, see Webber, *Eloquent "I,"* 180–83. On Browne drawing attention to his virtuosity, see Fish, *Self-Consuming Artifacts,* 353–73.

5. Joseph H. Summers, "Stanley Fish's Reading of Seventeenth-Century Literature," *Modern Language Quarterly* 35 (1974): 403–17; Frank J. Warnke, "A Hook for Amphibium: Some Reflections on Fish," in *Approaches to Sir Thomas Browne: The Ann Arbor Tercentenary Lectures and Essays,* ed. C. A. Patrides (Columbia: Univ. of Missouri Press, 1982), 49–59.

6. C. A. Patrides, "'Above Atlas His Shoulders': An Introduction to Sir Thomas Browne," in *Sir Thomas Browne: The Major Works,* ed. C. A. Patrides (Har-

mondsworth, England: Penguin Books, 1977), 41–42; "'The Best Part of Nothing': Sir Thomas Browne and the Strategy of Indirection," in Patrides, *Approaches to Sir Thomas Browne*, 31–48.

7. Louis I. Bredvold, *The Intellectual Milieu of John Dryden: Studies in Some Aspects of Seventeenth-Century Thought* (Ann Arbor: Univ. of Michigan Press, 1934), 40–46. Balachandra Rajan, "Browne and Milton: The Divided and the Distinguished," in Patrides, *Approaches to Sir Thomas Browne*, 1–11.

8. Frank Livingstone Huntley, "Sir Thomas Browne and the Metaphor of the Circle," *Journal of the History of Ideas* 14 (1953): 353–64. Laurence A. Breiner, "The Generation of Metaphor in Thomas Browne," *Modern Language Quarterly* 38 (1977): 261–75. For a concise statement of Jung's views on mandalas, see *The Essential Jung*, selected by Anthony Storr (Princeton: Princeton Univ. Press, 1983), 229–38.

9. J. R. Mulryne, "The Play of Mind: Self and Audience in *Religio Medici*," in Patrides, *Approaches to Sir Thomas Browne*, 60–68.

10. Webber, *Eloquent "I,"* 156.

11. Later, at an age when self-assurance and sententiousness had replaced the self-testing and whimsicalities of *Religio Medici*, Browne warned the reader, "Though the World be Histrionical, and most Men live Ironically, yet be thou what thou singly art, and personate only thy self.... He who counterfeiteth, acts a part, and is as it were out of himself" (*C.M.*, 240).

12. Quoted in Joan Bennett, "A Note on *Religio Medici* and Some of its Critics," *Studies in the Renaissance* 3 (1956): 183; discussed in Wise, *Religio Medici and Two Seventeenth-Century Critics*, 117–18. Wise (179) justifies, and Webber (*Eloquent "I,"* 158, 168) excuses Browne's apparent egotism.

13. Ziegler, *In Divided and Distinguished Worlds*, 93–95; Fish, *Self-Consuming Artifacts*, 366, 371–73.

14. On reader identification, see Gosse, *Sir Thomas Browne*, 49–50.

15. Winnicott, *Playing and Reality*, 38.

16. Jonathan F. S. Post, *Sir Thomas Browne* (Boston: Twayne, 1987), 90.

17. In his story "The Celestial Omnibus," E. M. Forster has Browne, the bus driver, confess that he did not heal bodies very well, "But as a healer of the spirit I have succeeded beyond my hopes and my deserts. For though my draughts were not better nor subtler than those of other men, yet, by reason of the cunning goblets wherein I offered them, the queasy soul was ofttimes tempted to sip and be refreshed": *The Collected Tales of E. M. Forster* (New York: Alfred A. Knopf, 1947), 58–59.

18. Webber, *Eloquent "I,"* 179.

19. Robert E. Neale, "Play and the Sacred," in *Motivations in Play, Games, and Sports*, ed. Ralph Slovenko and James A. Knight (Springfield, Illinois: Charles C.

Thomas, 1967), 148–57; and Neale, *In Praise of Play.* See also Cox, *Feast of Fools.*

20. Ziegler, *In Divided and Distinguished Worlds,* 47–48. Webber, *Eloquent "I,"* 182–83. For Xenophanes's similar use of "the 'as if' mode of being" to make inaccessible truth partly accessible, see Spariosu, *Literature, Mimesis and Play,* 16–17.

21. *The Diary of John Evelyn,* ed. E. S. de Beer (Oxford: Clarendon Press, 1955), 3:594.

22. For the debate about the meaning of the term *virtuoso,* see Houghton, "The English Virtuoso," 51–58; and Richard S. Westfall, *Science and Religion in Seventeenth-Century England* (New Haven: Yale Univ. Press, 1958), 10–25. For arguments that Browne was comparable to the scientists of his day, see Almonte C. Howell, "Sir Thomas Browne and Seventeenth-Century Scientific Thought," *Studies in Philology* 22 (1925): 61–80; and Robert Ralston Cawley, "The Timelessness of *Pseudodoxia Epidemica,*" in *Studies in Sir Thomas Browne,* ed. Robert Ralston Cawley and George Yost (Eugene: Univ. of Oregon Books, 1965), 1–40. For opposing arguments, see *Seventeenth-Century Verse and Prose,* ed. Helen C. White, Ruth C. Wallerstein, and Richard Quintana (New York: Macmillan, 1951), 1:314; and Marie Boas Hall, "Thomas Browne Naturalist," in Patrides, *Approaches to Sir Thomas Browne,* 178–87. For the letter responding to *The Garden of Cyrus* as a work of science, see *Letters,* 4:265–67. For the pamphlet ridiculing Browne as a virtuoso, see Gideon Harvey, *The Conclave of Physicians, Detecting Their Intrigues, Frauds, and Plots, Against Their Patients* (London, 1683), 59–61.

23. Johan Huizinga's often quoted definition of play emphasizes its delight ("The play-mood is one of rapture and enthusiasm") and its separation from "the sphere of necessity or material utility": *Homo Ludens,* 132. More recent studies, however, have demonstrated that activities performed in the practical sphere of work are frequently played: Helen B. Schwartzman, "Towards a Theory of Everyday Play" (paper delivered at Conference on Forms of Play in the Early Modern Period, Univ. of Maryland, 22–23 March 1984).

24. Fagen, *Animal Play Behavior,* 450–76; Millar, *The Psychology of Play,* 43–47, 114–25; Csikszentmihalyi, *Beyond Boredom and Anxiety,* 33–36, 80–81, and *Flow,* 48–77.

25. Cawley, "Sir Thomas Browne and his Reading," in Cawley, *Studies in Sir Thomas Browne,* 114.

26. *Coleridge on the Seventeenth Century,* 448. Jan Leyda, *The Melville Log: A Documentary Life of Herman Melville 1819–1891* (New York: Harcourt Brace, 1951), 1:273.

27. For science as delight, see Leonard Nathanson, *The Strategy of Truth: A Study of Sir Thomas Browne* (Chicago: Univ. of Chicago Press, 1967), 4. For *Pseudodoxia* as essays, see Ted-Larry Pebworth, "Wandering in the America of Truth: *Pseudodoxia Epidemica* and the Essay Tradition," in Patrides, *Approaches to Sir Thomas Browne,* 166–77.

28. Browne addressed *Hydriotaphia* and *The Garden of Cyrus* to Thomas Le Gros and Nicholas Bacon, local men of learning. *Pseudodoxia* (2:104–105, 239) and the extant letters (4:8, 39, 42) contain references to virtuosi's cabinets, both English and European, that Browne had seen or would have liked to see.

29. Gosse notes Browne's enjoyment of such odd words as *mascles, fusils,* and *saltyres: Sir Thomas Browne,* 127.

30. Patrides, "The Strategy of Indirection," in Patrides, *Approaches to Sir Thomas Browne,* 32–33.

31. Browne enjoys this kind of double entendre and can sustain the joke through a lengthy argument. In *Pseudodoxia,* while considering joint male and female emission in copulation, and Satan's theft of semen to impregnate his votaries, Browne plays the literal against the sexual meanings of "cut off... conceive... introduced... husbanded... conception" (2:527–28).

32. In response to the Romantics' judgment that Browne was a quaint humorist, critics such as Edmund Gosse (*Sir Thomas Browne,* 183–84) and Mario Praz ("Sir Thomas Browne," *English Studies* 11 [1929]: 168) have gone to the other extreme to assert that there is no humor in Browne. More recent critics have righted the balance, finding *Pseudodoxia* Browne's most humorous work: Almonte C. Howell, "Sir Thomas Browne as Wit and Humorist," *Studies in Philology* 42 (1945): 564–77; Egon Stephen Merton, *Science and Imagination in Sir Thomas Browne* (New York: King's Crown Press, 1949), 111–12; Joan Bennett, *Sir Thomas Browne: "A Man of Achievement in Literature"* (Cambridge: Cambridge Univ. Press, 1962), 175–82; and Frank Livingstone Huntley, *Sir Thomas Browne: A Biographical and Critical Study* (Ann Arbor: Univ. of Michigan Press, 1962), 170–72. While describing Browne's vision as "broadly comic," Post, however, reads the tone of Book 1 of *Pseudodoxia* as "high seriousness": *Sir Thomas Browne,* xii, 97.

33. Mario Praz, *Studies in Seventeenth-Century Imagery* (London: Warburg Institute, 1939), 1:204–205; Huntley, *Sir Thomas Browne,* 160–62.

34. For criticism of Browne's self-conscious use of metaphor in religion, see Ziegler, *In Divided and Distinguished Worlds.*

35. For a representative statement of this view, see Basil Willey, *The Seventeenth Century Background: Studies in the Thought of the Age in Relation to Poetry and Religion* (1934; reprint, Garden City, New York: Doubleday, 1953), 49–50, 60.

Chapter 9

1. Keith Thomas, "Work and Leisure in Pre-Industrial Society," *Past and Present* 29 (1964): 50–66; Turner, "Liminal to Liminoid," 62–76; Stanley Parker, *The Sociology of Leisure* (New York: International Publications Service, 1976), 20–25.

2. Hole, *English Sports and Pastimes,* 4–5, 90, 95, 146–57, 162–70.

3. *Ibid.*, 93, 170–71; Turner, "Liminal to Liminoid," 84–86.

4. Billington, *Social History of the Fool*, 27–31. Similarly, Stallybrass and White discuss the internalization in eighteenth-century literature of the carnivalesque body as a mode to think with: *Politics of Transgression*, 104ff.

5. Bakhtin, *Rabelais*, 403, 426. Further quotations will be cited parenthetically. Francois Rabelais, *The Histories of Gargantua and Pantagruel*, trans. J. M. Cohen (1955; reprint, Harmondsworth, England: Penguin Books, 1986). Quotations are cited parenthetically.

6. Stallybrass and White, *Politics of Transgression*, 19.

7. *Ibid.*, 13–19.

8. All quotations are taken from the following edition and are cited parenthetically in the text: *The Praise of Folly by Desiderius Erasmus*, trans. Hoyt Hopewell Hudson (1941; reprint, Princeton: Princeton Univ. Press, 1969). For Erasmus's play with paradox, see Walter Kaiser, *Praisers of Folly: Erasmus, Rabelais, Shakespeare* (Cambridge: Harvard Univ. Press, 1963), 19–100; and Colie, *Paradoxia Epidemica*, 15–22.

9. Letter from Erasmus to Ulrich von Hutten, quoted in *Sir Thomas More: Utopia*, ed. and trans. Robert M. Adams (New York: Norton, 1975), 130. All quotations are from this edition and will be cited parenthetically in the text. *Encyclopaedia Britannica* (Chicago: Enlclyclopaedia Britannica, Inc., 1969), 15:833.

10. Greenblatt, *Renaissance Self-Fashioning*, 31.

11. Rabkin, *Shakespeare and the Common Understanding*, 12; Goldberg, *James I*, 230.

12. Kaiser, *Praisers of Folly*, 277–96. For a discussion of the levels of play in *Don Quixote*, see Spariosu, "Enactment of Fiction in 'Don Quijote,'" in *Literature, Mimesis and Play*, 74–91. All quotations are taken from the following edition and are cited parenthetically in the text: Miguel de Cervantes Saavedra, *The Adventures of Don Quixote*, trans. J. M. Cohen (1950; reprint, Baltimore: Penguin, 1975).

13. Stallybrass and White, *Politics of Transgression*, 90–94. Mark Girouard, *Life in the English Country House: A Social and Architectural History* (1978; reprint, Harmondsworth, England: Penguin Books, 1980), 94, 104, 110, 120–28.

14. All quotations will be taken from the following edition and will be cited parenthetically in the text: Izaak Walton, *The Compleat Angler: 1653–1676*, ed. Jonquil Bevan (Oxford: Clarendon Press, 1983).

15. Leslie Stephen, "Country Books," in *Hours in a Library* (London: Smith, Elder, and Co., 1899), 3:185.

16. Washington Irving, *The Sketch Book of Geoffrey Crayon, Gent.* (New York: New American Library, 1961), 320–21.

17. For the seventeenth-century usage of *recreation* in both senses, see *The Oxford English Dictionary,* recreation[1] 3, and recreation[2].

18. Csikszentmihalyi and Bennett, "An Exploratory Model of Play," 45; Csikszentmihalyi, *Beyond Boredom and Anxiety,* 36, and *Flow,* 48–67.

19. Freud argued that attaining mastery of potentially overwhelming situations is a primary motivation in play: *Beyond the Pleasure Principle*, vol. 18 of *Standard Edition*, 14–17.

20. John R. Cooper has analyzed Walton's use of the pastoral genre: *The Art of The Compleat Angler* (Durham, North Carolina: Duke Univ. Press, 1968), 52.

21. B. D. Greenslade, "*The Compleat Angler* and the Sequestered Clergy," *Review of English Studies*, n.s., 5 (1954): 361–66. For etymology, see Douglas Bush, *English Literature in the Earlier Seventeenth Century: 1600–1660* (New York: Oxford Univ. Press, 1945), 225.

Bibliography

Abrahams, Roger D. "Playing the Dozens." *Journal of American Folklore* 75 (1962): 209–20.

———. "The Training of the Man of Words in Talking Sweet." *Language in Society* 1 (1972): 15–29.

Abrams, M. H. "The Deconstructive Angel." *Critical Inquiry* 3 (1977): 425–38.

Aers, David, Bob Hodge, and Gunther Kress. *Literature, Language and Society in England 1580–1680*. Totowa, New Jersey: Barnes and Noble, 1981.

Alexander, Nigel. *Poison, Play, and Duel: A Study in Hamlet*. Lincoln: Univ. of Nebraska Press, 1971.

Allen, Don Cameron. *Image and Meaning: Metaphoric Traditions in Renaissance Poetry*. Rev. ed. Baltimore: The Johns Hopkins Press, 1968.

———. "Symbolic Color in the Literature of the English Renaissance." *Philological Quarterly* 15 (1936): 81–92.

Allman, Eileen Jorge. *Player-King and Adversary: Two Faces of Play in Shakespeare*. Baton Rouge: Louisiana State Univ. Press, 1980.

Alvarez, A. *The School of Donne*. 1961. Reprint. New York: New American Library, 1967.

Andreasen, N. J. C. *John Donne: Conservative Revolutionary*. Princeton: Princeton Univ. Press, 1967.

Andrews, John F. "'Dearly Bought Revenge': *Samson Agonistes, Hamlet*, and Elizabethan Revenge Tragedy." *Milton Studies* 13 (1979): 81–107.

Annalia Dubrensia: Upon the Yeerely Celebration of Mr. Robert Dovers Olimpick Games upon Cotswold-Hills. London, 1636.

Ariès, Philippe. *Centuries of Childhood: A Social History of Family Life*. Trans. Robert Baldick. London: Jonathan Cape, 1962.

Asals, Heather A. R. *Equivocal Predication: George Herbert's Way to God*. Toronto: Univ. of Toronto Press, 1981.

Avedon, Elliott M., and Brian Sutton-Smith. *The Study of Games*. New York: John Wiley, 1971.

Babb, Lawrence. *Sanity in Bedlam: A Study of Robert Burton's Anatomy of Melancholy.* East Lansing: Michigan State Univ. Press, 1959.

Babcock, Barbara, ed. *The Reversible World: Symbolic Inversion in Art and Society.* Ithaca: Cornell Univ. Press, 1978.

Bakhtin, Mikhail. *Rabelais and His World.* Trans. Helene Iswolsky. Cambridge: MIT Press, 1968.

Bald, R. C. *John Donne: A Life*. New York: Oxford Univ. Press, 1970.

Bateson, Gregory. "The Message 'This is play.'" In *Group Processes: Transactions of the Second Conference,* ed. Bertram Schaffner, 145–242. New York: Josiah Macy, Jr. Foundation, 1956.

———. *Steps to an Ecology of Mind.* New York: Ballantine Books, 1972.

Battenhouse, Roy W. *Shakespearean Tragedy: Its Art and Its Christian Premises.* Bloomington: Indiana Univ. Press, 1969.

Benet, Diana. *Secretary of Praise: The Poetic Vocation of George Herbert.* Columbia: Univ. of Missouri Press, 1984.

Bennett, Joan. "A Note on *Religio Medici* and Some of its Critics." *Studies in the Renaissance* 3 (1956): 175–84.

———. *Sir Thomas Browne: "A Man of Achievement in Literature."* Cambridge: Cambridge Univ. Press, 1962.

Bentham, Jeremy. *The Theory of Legislation.* Ed. C. K. Ogden. New York: Harcourt, Brace, 1931.

Berger, Harry, Jr. "Marvell's 'Garden': Still Another Interpretation." *Modern Language Quarterly* 28 (1967): 285–304.

Berger, Milton M., ed. *Beyond the Double Bind: Communication and Family Systems, Theories, and Techniques with Schizophrenics.* New York: Brunner/Mazel, 1978.

Berthoff, Ann E. *The Resolved Soul: A Study of Marvell's Major Poems.* Princeton: Princeton Univ. Press, 1970.

Billington, Sandra. *A Social History of the Fool.* New York: St. Martin's Press, 1984.

Blackburn, William. "Lady Magdalen Herbert and Her Son George." *South Atlantic Quarterly* 50 (1951): 378–88.

Blanchard, Margaret M. "The Leap into Darkness: Donne, Herbert, and God." *Renascence* 17 (1964): 38–50.

Bloch, Chana. *Spelling the Word: George Herbert and the Bible.* Berkeley: Univ. of California Press, 1985.

Bollman, Richard W., S. J. "Saying Goodbye: Essays on Donne's Poetics of Departure." Ph. D. diss., State Univ. of New York, Buffalo, 1975.

Bottrall, Margaret. *George Herbert*. London: John Murray, 1954.

Bowers, Fredson. "The Death of Hamlet: A Study in Plot and Character." In *Studies in the English Renaissance Drama,* ed. Josephine W. Bennett, Oscar Cargill, and Vernon Hall, 28–43. New York: New York Univ. Press, 1959.

———. "Hamlet as Minister and Scourge." *PMLA* 70 (1955): 740–49.

Bradbrook, Muriel C., and M. G. Lloyd Thomas. *Andrew Marvell*. London: Cambridge Univ. Press, 1940.

Bredvold, Louis I. *The Intellectual Milieu of John Dryden: Studies in Some Aspects of Seventeenth-Century Thought*. Ann Arbor: Univ. of Michigan Press, 1934.

———. "The Naturalism of Donne in Relation to Some Renaissance Traditions." *Journal of English and German Philology* 22 (1923): 471–502.

Breiner, Laurence A. "The Generation of Metaphor in Thomas Browne." *Modern Language Quarterly* 38 (1977): 261–75.

Brooke, Nicholas. *Shakespeare's Early Tragedies*. London: Methuen, 1968.

Brooks, Cleanth. *The Well Wrought Urn: Studies in the Structure of Poetry*. New York: Harcourt, Brace, 1947.

Brown, Norman O. *Love's Body*. New York: Random House, 1966.

Brown, T. E. "Robert Burton." *New Review* 13 (September, 1895): 257–66.

Browne, Sir Thomas. *Religio Medici and Other Works*. Ed. L. C. Martin. Oxford: Clarendon Press, 1964.

———. *The Works of Sir Thomas Browne*. Ed. Geoffrey Keynes. 4 vols. London: Faber and Faber, 1964.

Bruner, Jerome S., Alison Jolly, and Kathy Sylva, eds. *Play: Its Role in Development and Evolution*. New York: Basic Books, 1976.

Buber, Martin. *I and Thou*. Trans. Ronald Gregor Smith. Edinburgh: T. and T. Clark, 1953.

Burke, Kenneth. "On Covery, Re- and Dis-." *Accent* 13 (1953): 218–26.

Burns, Thomas A. "Fifty Seconds of Play: Expressive Interaction in Context." *Western Folklore* 37 (1978): 1–29.

Burton, Robert. *The Anatomy of Melancholy: What it is, with all the kinds, causes, symptomes, prognostickes and severall cures of it*. Ed. Holbrook Jackson. 1932. Reprint. New York: Vintage Books, 1977.

Bush, Douglas. *English Literature in the Earlier Seventeenth Century: 1600–1660*. New York: Oxford Univ. Press, 1945.

Carew, Thomas. *The Poems of Thomas Carew*. Ed. Rhodes Dunlap. Oxford: Clarendon Press, 1949.

Carey, John, ed. *Andrew Marvell: A Critical Anthology*. Baltimore: Penguin, 1969.

———. *John Donne: Life, Mind and Art*. New York: Oxford Univ. Press, 1981.

Carpenter, Margaret. "From Herbert to Marvell: Poetics in 'A Wreath' and 'The Coronet.'" *Journal of English and German Philology* 69 (1970): 50–62.

Carrithers, Gale H. *Donne at Sermons: A Christian Existential World*. Albany: State Univ. of New York Press, 1972.

Cathcart, Dwight. *Doubting Conscience: Donne and the Poetry of Moral Argument*. Ann Arbor: Univ. of Michigan Press, 1975.

Cawley, Robert Ralston, and George Yost, eds. *Studies in Sir Thomas Browne*. Eugene: Univ. of Oregon Books, 1965.

Cervantes. See Saavedra, Miguel de Cervantes.

Chamberlin, John S. *Increase and Multiply: Arts-of-Discourse Procedure in the Preaching of Donne*. Chapel Hill: Univ. of North Carolina Press, 1976.

Charles, Amy M. *A Life of George Herbert*. Ithaca: Cornell Univ. Press, 1977.

Charney, Maurice. *Hamlet's Fictions*. New York: Routledge, 1988.

———. *Style in Hamlet*. Princeton: Princeton Univ. Press, 1969.

Chernaik, Warren L. *The Poet's Time: Politics and Religion in the Work of Andrew Marvell*. Cambridge: Cambridge Univ. Press, 1983.

Chute, Marchette. *Two Gentle Men: The Lives of George Herbert and Robert Herrick*. New York: E. P. Dutton, 1959.

Clifton, Michael. "Staking his Heart: Herbert's Use of Gambling Imagery in *The Temple*." *The George Herbert Journal* 8 (1984): 43–55.

Cloud, Jess. "Herbert's 'The Quidditie.'" *Explicator* 34 (1975): item 32.

Coffin, Charles Monroe. *John Donne and the New Philosophy*. Morningside Heights, New York: Columbia Univ. Press, 1937.

Coleridge, Samuel Taylor. *Coleridge on the Seventeenth Century*. Ed. Roberta Florence Brinkley. Durham, North Carolina: Duke Univ. Press, 1955.

Colie, Rosalie L. *"My Ecchoing Song": Andrew Marvell's Poetry of Criticism*. Princeton: Princeton Univ. Press, 1970.

———. *Paradoxia Epidemica: The Renaissance Tradition of Paradox*. Princeton: Princeton Univ. Press, 1966.

———. *The Resources of Kind: Genre-Theory in the Renaissance*. Ed. Barbara K. Lewalski. Berkeley: Univ. of California Press, 1973.

Cooper, John R. *The Art of The Compleat Angler.* Durham, North Carolina: Duke Univ. Press, 1968.

Corthell, Ronald J. "Style and Self in Donne's Satires." *Texas Studies in Literature and Language* 24 (1982): 155–84.

Cox, Harvey. *The Feast of Fools: A Theological Essay on Festivity and Fantasy.* Cambridge: Harvard Univ. Press, 1969.

Cruttwell, Patrick. *The Shakespearean Moment and its Place in the Poetry of the Seventeenth Century.* London: Chatto and Windus, 1954.

Csikszentmihalyi, Mihaly. *Beyond Boredom and Anxiety: The Experience of Play in Work and Games.* San Francisco: Jossey-Bass, 1975.

———. *Flow: The Psychology of Optimal Experience.* New York: Harper and Row, 1990.

Csikszentmihalyi, Mihaly, and Stith Bennett. "An Exploratory Model of Play." *American Anthropologist* 73 (1971): 45–58.

Cullen, Patrick. *Spenser, Marvell, and Renaissance Pastoral.* Cambridge: Harvard Univ. Press, 1970.

D., A. "Five Notes on George Herbert." *Notes and Queries* 197 (1952): 420–22.

Danson, Lawrence. *Tragic Alphabet: Shakespeare's Drama of Language.* New Haven: Yale Univ. Press, 1974.

deMause, Lloyd, ed. *The History of Childhood.* New York: The Psychohistory Press, 1974.

Demos, John. *A Little Commonwealth: Family Life in Plymouth Colony.* London: Oxford Univ. Press, 1970.

Dent, R. W. "Hamlet: Scourge and Minister." *Shakespeare Quarterly* 29 (1978): 82–84.

Derrida, Jacques. "Afterward: Toward an Ethic of Discussion." In *Limited Inc,* trans. Samuel Weber and Jeffrey Mehlman. Evanston, Illinois: Northwestern Univ. Press, 1988.

———. "Structure, Sign, and Play in the Discourse of the Human Sciences." In *The Structuralist Controversy: The Languages of Criticism and the Sciences of Man,* ed. Richard Macksey and Eugenio Donato, 247–65. Baltimore: The Johns Hopkins Press,1970.

Dessen, Alan C. "Hamlet's Poisoned Sword: A Study in Dramatic Imagery." *Shakespeare Studies* 5 (1969): 53–69.

Dickson, Donald R. *The Fountain of Living Waters: The Typology of the Waters of Life in Herbert, Vaughan, and Traherne.* Columbia: Univ. of Missouri Press, 1987.

Docherty, Thomas. *John Donne, Undone*. London: Methuen, 1986.

Dollimore, Jonathan, and Alan Sinfield, eds. *Political Shakespeare: New Essays in Cultural Materialism*. Ithaca: Cornell Univ. Press, 1985.

Donne, John. *Donne: Poetical Works*. Ed. Herbert J. C. Grierson. 1929. Reprint. London: Oxford Univ. Press, 1971.

———. *John Donne: The Complete English Poems*. Ed. A. J. Smith. 1971. Reprint. New York: Penguin Books, 1980.

———. *John Donne: Devotions Upon Emergent Occasions together with Death's Duel*. Ann Arbor: Univ. of Michigan Press, 1959.

———. *John Donne: Paradoxes and Problems*. Ed. Helen Peters. Oxford: Clarendon Press, 1980.

———. *John Donne: Selected Prose*. Ed. Helen Gardner and Timothy Healy. London: Clarendon Press, 1967.

———. *The Sermons of John Donne*. Ed. George R. Potter and Evelyn M. Simpson. 10 vols. Berkeley: Univ. of California Press, 1953–62.

Eliot, T. S. "Lancelot Andrewes." In *Essays Ancient and Modern*, 3–23. New York: Harcourt, Brace, 1932.

———. "Prose and Verse." *Chapbook* 22 (1921): 3–10.

Empson, William. *Some Versions of Pastoral*. 1935. Reprint. London: Chatto and Windus, 1968.

Erasmus, Desiderius. *The Praise of Folly by Desiderius Erasmus*. Trans. Hoyt Hopewell Hudson. 1941. Reprint. Princeton: Princeton Univ. Press, 1969.

Erikson, Erik. *Childhood and Society*. Rev. ed. New York: Norton, 1963.

———. *Young Man Luther: A Study in Psychoanalysis and History*. New York: Norton, 1958.

Evans, Bergan. *The Psychiatry of Robert Burton*. New York: Columbia Univ. Press, 1944.

Evelyn, John. *The Diary of John Evelyn*. Vol. 3. Ed. E. S. de Beer. Oxford: Clarendon Press, 1955.

Everett, Barbara. "The Shooting of the Bears: Poetry and Politics in Andrew Marvell." In *Andrew Marvell: Essays on the Tercentenary of his Death*, ed. R. L. Brett, 62–103. London: Oxford Univ. Press, 1979.

Faber, Melvin D. "Hamlet, Sarcasm and Psychoanalysis." *Psychoanalytic Review* 55 (1968): 79–90.

Fagen, Robert. *Animal Play Behavior*. Oxford: Oxford Univ. Press, 1981.

Ferry, Anne. *All in War with Time: Love Poetry of Shakespeare, Donne, Jonson, Marvell.* Cambridge: Harvard Univ. Press, 1975.

Fink, Eugen. "The Oasis of Happiness: Toward an Ontology of Play." Trans. from *Oase des Glücks* by Ute and Thomas Saine. In *Games, Play, Literature: Yale French Studies* 41 (1968): 19–30.

Fish, Stanley E. *The Living Temple: George Herbert and Catechizing*. Berkeley: Univ. of California Press, 1978.

———. *Self-Consuming Artifacts: The Experience of Seventeenth-Century Literature*. Berkeley: Univ. of California Press, 1972.

Flandrin, Jean-Louis. *Families in Former Times: Kinship, Household and Sexuality.* Trans. Richard Southern. Cambridge: Cambridge Univ. Press, 1979.

Forster, E. M. "The Celestial Omnibus." In *The Collected Tales of E. M. Forster.* New York: Alfred A. Knopf, 1947.

Foucault, Michel. "What is an Author?" In *Textual Strategies: Perspectives in Post-Structuralist Criticism,* ed. Josué V. Harari, 141–60. Ithaca: Cornell Univ. Press, 1979.

Fox, Ruth A. *The Tangled Chain: The Structure of Disorder in the Anatomy of Melancholy.* Berkeley: Univ. of California Press, 1976.

Fraser, Antonia. *A History of Toys*. New York: Delacorte Press, 1966.

Freeman, Rosemary. *English Emblem Books*. London: Chatto and Windus, 1948.

Freer, Coburn. *Music for a King: George Herbert's Style and the Metrical Psalms.* Baltimore: The Johns Hopkins Press, 1972.

Freud, Sigmund. *The Standard Edition of the Complete Psychological Works of Sigmund Freud.* Trans. James Strachey. 24 vols. London: Hogarth Press, 1953–1974.

Friederich, Reinhard H. "Training His Melancholy Spaniel: Persona and Structure in Robert Burton's 'Democritus Junior to the Reader.'" *Philological Quarterly* 55 (1976): 195–210.

Friedman, Donald M. *Marvell's Pastoral Art*. Berkeley: Univ. of California Press, 1970.

Frye, Roland M. *The Renaissance Hamlet: Issues and Responses in 1600*. Princeton: Princeton Univ. Press, 1984.

Gardner, Helen. "The Argument about 'The Ecstasy.'" In *Elizabethan and Jacobean Studies Presented to Frank Percy Wilson,* 279–306. Oxford: Clarendon Press, 1959.

Geertz, Clifford. "Deep Play: Notes on the Balinese Cockfight." *Daedalus* 101 (1972): 1–37.

Gent, Lucy. "Marvell's Games with Teleology." *Renaissance Quarterly* 32 (1979): 514–28.

Girard, René. "Hamlet's Dull Revenge." In *Literary Theory/Renaissance Texts*, ed. Patricia Parker and David Quint, 280–302. Baltimore: The Johns Hopkins Press, 1986.

———. *Things Hidden since the Foundation of the World*. Trans. Stephen Bann and Michael Meteer. Stanford: Stanford Univ. Press, 1987.

———. *Violence and the Sacred*. Trans. Patrick Gregory. Baltimore: The Johns Hopkins Press, 1977.

Girouard, Mark. *Life in the English Country House: A Social and Architectural History*. 1978. Reprint. Harmondsworth, England: Penguin Books, 1980.

Goffman, Erving. *Frame Analysis: An Essay on the Organization of Experience*. New York: Harper and Row, 1974.

Goldberg, Jonathan. *James I and the Politics of Literature: Jonson, Shakespeare, Donne, and their Contemporaries*. Baltimore: The Johns Hopkins Press, 1983.

———. "Marvell's Nymph and the Echo of Voice." *Glyph* 8 (1981): 19–39.

———. *Voice Terminal Echo: Postmodernism and English Renaissance Texts*. New York: Methuen, 1986.

Gosse, Edmund. *The Life and Letters of John Donne*. 2 vols. London: William Heinemann, 1899.

———. *Sir Thomas Browne*. London: Macmillan, 1905.

Govett, Lionel Arthur. *The King's Book of Sports: A History of the Declarations of King James I. and King Charles I. as to the Use of Lawful Sports on Sundays*. London: Eliot Stock, 1890.

Gray, Allan. "The Surface of Marvell's 'Upon Appleton House.'" *English Literary Renaissance* 9 (1979): 169–82.

Greenblatt, Stephen. *Renaissance Self-Fashioning: From More to Shakespeare*. Chicago: Univ. of Chicago Press, 1980.

Greene, Thomas. "The Flexibility of the Self in Renaissance Literature." In *The Disciplines of Criticism: Essays in Literary Theory, Interpretation, and History*, ed. Peter Demetz, Thomas Greene, and Lowry Nelson, Jr., 241-64. New Haven: Yale Univ. Press, 1968.

Greenslade, B. D. "*The Compleat Angler* and the Sequestered Clergy." *Review of English Studies*, n.s. 5 (1954): 361-66.

Greville, Fulke. *Life of Sir Philip Sidney*. Ed. Nowell Smith. Oxford: Clarendon Press, 1907.

Grierson, Herbert J. C. *Cross Currents in English Literature of the Seventeenth Century*. London, 1929. Reprint. Baltimore: Penguin Books, 1966.

Guibbory, Achsah. "John Donne and Memory as 'the Art of *Salvation*.'" *Huntington Library Quarterly* 43 (1979/80): 261–74.

Guilford, E. L. *Select Extracts Illustrating Sports and Pastimes in the Middle Ages*. New York: Macmillan, 1920.

Guinness, Gerald, and Andrew Hurley, eds. *Auctor Ludens: Essays on Play in Literature*. Philadelphia: John Benjamins, 1986.

Haley, Jay. "Paradoxes in Play, Fantasy, and Psychotherapy." *Psychiatric Research Reports* 2 (1955): 52–58.

Harding, D. W. "Coherence of Theme in Donne's Poetry." *Kenyon Review* 13 (1951): 427–44.

Hardy, Evelyn. *Donne: A Spirit in Conflict*. London: Constable, 1942.

Harington, Sir John. "A Treatise on Playe." In vol. 1 of *Nugae Antiquae*, ed. Thomas Park, 186–232. London: Vernor and Hood, Poultry, and Cuthell and Martin, 1804.

Harman, Barbara Leah. *Costly Monuments: Representations of the Self in George Herbert's Poetry*. Cambridge: Harvard Univ. Press, 1982.

———. "The Fiction of Coherence: George Herbert's 'The Collar.'" *PMLA* 93 (1978): 865–77.

———. "Herbert, Coleridge and the Vexed Work of Narration." *Modern Language Notes* 93 (1978): 888–911.

Hartman, Geoffrey H. "'The Nymph Complaining for the Death of Her Faun': A Brief Allegory." In *Beyond Formalism: Literary Essays 1958–70*, 173–92. New Haven: Yale Univ. Press, 1970.

Harvey, Gideon. *The Conclave of Physicians, Detecting Their Intrigues, Frauds, and Plots, Against Their Patients*. London, 1683.

Helgerson, Richard. *Self-Crowned Laureates: Spenser, Jonson, Milton, and the Literary System*. Berkeley: Univ. of California Press, 1983.

Herbert, George. *The Latin Poetry of George Herbert: A Bilingual Edition*. Trans. Mark McCloskey and Paul R. Murphy. Athens: Ohio Univ. Press, 1965.

———. *The Works of George Herbert*. Ed. F. E. Hutchinson. 1941. Reprint. Oxford: Clarendon Press, 1978.

Hodge, R. I. V. *Foreshortened Time: Andrew Marvell and Seventeenth Century Revolutions*. Cambridge, England: D. S. Brewer, 1978.

Hodges, Devon L. *Renaissance Fictions of Anatomy*. Amherst: Univ. of Massachusetts Press, 1985.

Hole, Christina. *English Sports and Pastimes*. London: B. T. Batsford, 1949.

Holland, Norman. *Psychoanalysis and Shakespeare*. New York: McGraw-Hill, 1964.

Hollander, John. *The Untuning of the Sky: Ideas of Music in English Poetry 1500–1700*. Princeton: Princeton Univ. Press, 1961.

Honigmann, E. A. J., ed. *Milton's Sonnets*. New York: St. Martin's Press, 1966.

Houghton, Walter E., Jr. "The English Virtuoso in the Seventeenth Century." *Journal of the History of Ideas* 3 (1942): 51–73, 190–219.

Howell, Almonte C. "Sir Thomas Browne and Seventeenth-Century Scientific Thought." *Studies in Philology* 22 (1925): 61–80.

———. "Sir Thomas Browne as Wit and Humorist." *Studies in Philology* 42 (1945): 564–77.

Hughes, Merritt Y. "Kidnapping Donne." In *Essays in Criticism*, 61–93. 1934. Reprint. Freeport, New York: Books for Libraries Press, 1966.

———. "The Lineage of 'The Exstasie.'" *Modern Language Review* 27 (1932): 1–5.

———. "Some of Donne's 'Ecstasies.'" *PMLA* 75 (1960): 509–18.

Hughes, Richard E. *The Progress of the Soul: The Interior Career of John Donne*. New York: William Morrow, 1968.

Huizinga, Johan. *Homo Ludens: A Study of the Play-Element in Culture*. Trans. Karl Mannheim. 1949. Reprint. Boston: Beacon Press, 1955.

Hunt, Clay. *Donne's Poetry: Essays in Literary Analysis*. New Haven: Yale Univ. Press, 1954.

Hunt, David. *Parents and Children in History: The Psychology of Family Life in Early Modern France*. New York: Basic Books, 1970.

Hunt, John Dixon. *Andrew Marvell: His Life and Writings*. Ithaca: Cornell Univ. Press, 1978.

Huntley, Frank Livingstone. "The Publication and Immediate Reception of *Religio Medici*." *The Library Quarterly* 25 (1955): 203–18.

———. *Sir Thomas Browne: A Biographical and Critical Study*. Ann Arbor: Univ. of Michigan Press, 1962.

———. "Sir Thomas Browne and the Metaphor of the Circle." *Journal of the History of Ideas* 14 (1953): 353–64.

Hutchinson, Peter. *Games Authors Play*. London: Methuen, 1983.

Hyman, Lawrence W. *Andrew Marvell*. New York: Twayne, 1964.

Irving, Washington. *The Sketch Book of Geoffrey Crayon, Gent*. New York: New American Library, 1961.

Jackson, Robert S. *John Donne's Christian Vocation*. Evanston, Illinois: Northwestern Univ. Press, 1970.

James I. *Basilikon Doron*. In *A Miscellany*. London: George Routledge and Sons, 1888.

Johnson, C. D. "Bedroom and Landscape in Donne's *The Songs and Sonnets*." *The Cresset* 37 (1974): 6–9.

Johnson, S. F. "The Regeneration of Hamlet." *Shakespeare Quarterly* 3 (1952): 187–207.

Johnson, Samuel. *The Life of Milton*. In *Samuel Johnson: Selected Prose and Poetry*, ed. Bertrand H. Bronson, 446–69. New York: Rinehart, 1952.

Jonson, Ben. *The Complete Poetry of Ben Jonson*. Ed. William B. Hunter, Jr. New York: Norton, 1963.

Jorgensen, Paul A. *Redeeming Shakespeare's Words*. Berkeley: Univ. of California Press, 1962.

Joseph, Miriam, C. S. C. "*Hamlet*, a Christian Tragedy." *Studies in Philology* 59 (1962): 119–40.

Jung, Carl Gustav. *The Archetypes of the Collective Unconscious* and *Aion: Researches into the Phenomenology of the Self*. Vol. 9, pts. 1 and 2 of *The Collected Works of C. G. Jung*. Ed. Sir Herbert Read, Michael Fordham, Gerhard Adler. New York: Pantheon Books, 1959.

———. *The Essential Jung*. Ed. Anthony Storr. Princeton: Princeton Univ. Press, 1983.

Kaiser, Walter. *Praisers of Folly: Erasmus, Rabelais, Shakespeare*. Cambridge: Harvard Univ. Press, 1963.

Keizer, Garret. "George Herbert and the Tradition of Jacob." *Cithara* 18 (1978): 18–26.

Keppler, Carl Francis. *The Literature of the Second Self*. Tucson: Univ. of Arizona Press, 1972.

Kermode, Frank, ed. *Discussions of John Donne*. Boston: D. C. Heath, 1962.

Kerrigan, William. "The Articulation of the Ego in the English Renaissance." In *The Literary Freud: Mechanisms of Defense and the Poetic Will*, ed. Joseph H. Smith, 261–308. Vol. 4 of *Psychiatry and the Humanities*. New Haven: Yale Univ. Press, 1980.

———. "Marvell and Nymphets." *Greyfriar: Siena Studies in Literature* 27 (1986): 3–21.

———. "Ritual Man: On the Outside of Herbert's Poetry." *Psychiatry* 48 (1985): 68–82.

King, A. H. "Some Notes on Andrew Marvell's 'Garden.'" *English Studies* 20 (1938): 118–21.

King, James Roy. *Studies in Six Seventeenth Century Writers*. Athens: Ohio Univ. Press, 1966.

King, Walter N. *Hamlet's Search for Meaning*. Athens: Univ. of Georgia Press, 1982.

Klause, John. *The Unfortunate Fall: Theodicy and the Moral Imagination of Andrew Marvell*. Hamden, Connecticut: Archon Books, 1983.

Knights, L. C. *Explorations: Essays in Criticism Mainly on the Literature of the Seventeenth Century*. London: Chatto and Windus, 1946.

Kohut, Heinz. *The Analysis of the Self: A Systematic Approach to the Psychoanalytic Treatment of Narcissistic Personality Disorders*. New York: International Universities Press, 1971.

———. *The Restoration of the Self*. New York: International Universities Press, 1977.

Krell, David Farrell. "Towards an Ontology of Play: Eugen Fink's Notion of *Spiel*." *Research in Phenomenology* 2 (1972): 63–93.

Kristeva, Julia. *The Kristeva Reader*. Ed. Toril Moi. New York: Columbia Univ. Press, 1986.

———. *Revolution in Poetic Language*. Trans. Margaret Waller. New York: Columbia Univ. Press, 1984.

Kronenfeld, Judy Z. "Herbert's 'A Wreath' and Devotional Aesthetics: Imperfect Efforts Redeemed by Grace." *ELH* 48 (1981): 290–309.

Lacan, Jacques. *The Language of the Self: The Function of Language in Psychoanalysis*. Trans. Anthony Wilden. Baltimore: The Johns Hopkins Press, 1968.

———. "The Mirror-phase as Formative of the Function of the I." *New Left Review* 51 (Sept.–Oct. 1968): 71–77.

Lanham, Richard A. *The Motives of Eloquence: Literary Rhetoric in the Renaissance*. New Haven: Yale Univ. Press, 1976.

Lavie, Smadar. "The Fool and the Hippies: Ritual/Play and Social Inconsistencies Among the Mzeina Bedouin of the Sinai." In *The Masks of Play*, ed. Brian Sutton-Smith and Diana Kelly-Byrne, 63–70. New York: Leisure Press, 1984.

Lawlor, John. *The Tragic Sense in Shakespeare*. New York: Harcourt Brace, 1960.

LeComte, Edward. *Grace to a Witty Sinner: A Life of Donne*. New York: Walker, 1965.

Legouis, Pierre. *Andrew Marvell: Poet, Puritan, Patriot*. Rev. ed. London: Oxford at the Clarendon Press, 1970.

———. *Donne the Craftsman: An Essay upon the Structure of the Songs and Sonnets.* 1928. Reprint. New York: Russell and Russell, 1962.

Leigh, David J., S. J. "Donne's 'A Hymne to God the Father': New Dimensions." *Studies in Philology* 75 (1978): 84–92.

Leishman, J. B. *The Art of Marvell's Poetry.* London: Hutchinson, 1966.

———. *The Monarch of Wit: An Analytical and Comparative Study of the Poetry of John Donne.* 1951. Reprint. London: Hutchinson, 1969.

Lentricchia, Frank. *After the New Criticism.* Chicago: Univ. of Chicago Press, 1980.

Lesser, Simon O. *Fiction and the Unconscious.* Boston: Beacon Press, 1957.

Leverenz, David. "The Woman in Hamlet: An Interpersonal View." *Signs* 4 (1978): 291–308.

Levin, Harry. *The Question of Hamlet.* 1959. Reprint. New York: Viking Press, 1964.

Levitsky, Ruth M. "Rightly to be Great." *Shakespeare Studies* 1 (1965): 142–67.

Lewalski, Barbara K. *Protestant Poetics and the Seventeenth-Century Religious Lyric.* Princeton: Princeton Univ. Press, 1979.

Lewis, C. S. "Hamlet: The Prince or the Poem?" In *Modern Shakespearean Criticism: Essays on Style, Dramaturgy, and the Major Plays,* ed. Alvin B. Kernan, 301–11. New York: Harcourt, Brace and World, 1970.

Leyda, Jan. Vol. 1 of *The Melville Log: A Documentary Life of Herman Melville 1819–1891.* New York: Harcourt Brace, 1951.

Long, Michael. *Marvell, Nabokov: Childhood and Arcadia.* Oxford: Clarendon Press, 1984.

Lord, George deF., ed. *Andrew Marvell: A Collection of Critical Essays.* Englewood Cliffs, New Jersey: Prentice-Hall, 1968.

Lyons, Bridget Gellert. *Voices of Melancholy: Studies in Literary Treatments of Melancholy in Renaissance England.* New York: Norton, 1971.

MacCaffrey, Isabel G. "The Scope of Imagination in 'Upon Appleton House.'" In *Tercentenary Essays in Honor of Andrew Marvell,* ed. Kenneth Friedenreich, 224–44. Hamden, Connecticut: Archon, 1977.

McCanles, Michael. *Dialectical Criticism and Renaissance Literature.* Berkeley: Univ. of California Press, 1975.

———. "Paradox in Donne." *Studies in the Renaissance* 13 (1966): 266–87.

McClung, William A. *The Country House Poem in English Renaissance Poetry.* Berkeley: Univ. of California Press, 1977.

MacDonald, Michael. *Mystical Bedlam: Madness, Anxiety, and Healing in Seventeenth-Century England*. Cambridge: Cambridge Univ. Press, 1981.

McElroy, Bernard. *Shakespeare's Mature Tragedies*. Princeton: Princeton Univ. Press, 1973.

Macfarlane, Alan. *The Family Life of Ralph Josselin, a Seventeenth-Century Clergyman*. Cambridge: Cambridge Univ. Press, 1970.

McTear, J. S. "Primero." *Notes and Queries*, series 11, 7 (1913): 1–3, 23–24, 41–43.

Mack, Maynard. "The World of *Hamlet*." *Yale Review* 41 (1952): 502–23.

Mahler, Margaret S. "On the Significance of the Normal Separation-Individuation Phase." In vol. 2 of *Drives, Affects, Behavior*, ed. Max Schur, 161–69. New York: International Universities Press, 1965.

———. *The Psychological Birth of the Human Infant: Symbiosis and Individuation*. New York: Basic Books, 1975.

———. "A Study of the Separation-Individuation Process." *The Psychanalytic Study of the Child* 26 (1971): 403–24.

Mahler, Margaret S., and Manuel Furer. "Certain Aspects of the Separation-Individuation Phase." *Psychoanalytic Quarterly* 32 (1963): 1-14.

Mahood, M. M. *Poetry and Humanism*. 1949. Reprint. New York: Norton, 1970.

———. *Shakespeare's Wordplay*. London: Methuen, 1957.

Maloney, Michael Francis. *John Donne, His Flight from Medievalism*. 1944. Reprint. New York: Russell and Russell, 1965.

Manocchio, Tony, and William Petitt. *Families Under Stress: A Psychological Interpretation*. London: Routledge and Kegan Paul, 1975.

Marcus, Leah Sinanoglou. *Childhood and Cultural Despair: A Theme and Variations in Seventeenth-Century Literature*. Pittsburgh: Univ. of Pittsburgh Press, 1978.

———. "Herrick's *Hesperides* and the 'Proclamation made for May.'" *Studies in Philology* 76 (1979): 49–74.

———. "Herrick's *Noble Numbers* and the Politics of Playfulness." *English Literary Renaissance* 7 (1977): 108–26.

———. *The Politics of Mirth: Jonson, Herrick, Milton, Marvell, and the Defense of Old Holiday Pastimes*. Chicago: Univ. of Chicago Press, 1986.

Marino, James A. G. "An Annotated Bibliography of Play and Literature." *Canadian Review of Comparative Literature* 12 (June 1985): 306–53.

Marotti, Arthur F. *John Donne, Coterie Poet*. Madison: Univ. of Wisconsin Press, 1986.

Martz, Louis L. *The Poetry of Meditation: A Study in English Religious Literature of the Seventeenth Century*. Rev. ed. New Haven: Yale Univ. Press, 1962.

———. *The Wit of Love: Donne, Carew, Crashaw, Marvell*. Notre Dame, Indiana: Univ. of Notre Dame Press, 1969.

Marvell, Andrew. *The Latin Poetry of Andrew Marvell*. Ed. William A. McQueen and Kiffin A. Rockwell. Chapel Hill: Univ. of North Carolina Press, 1964.

———. *The Poems and Letters of Andrew Marvell*. Ed. H. M. Margoliouth. 2 vols. 3rd ed. rev. by Pierre Legouis and E. E. Duncan-Jones. Oxford: Clarendon Press, 1971.

———. *The Rehearsal Transpros'd and The Rehearsal Transpros'd: The Second Part*. Ed. D. I. B. Smith. London: Oxford at the Clarendon Press, 1971.

Mead, George H. *Mind, Self, and Society from the Standpoint of a Social Behaviorist*. Chicago: Univ. of Chicago Press, 1934.

Meilaender, Marion. "Marvell's Pastoral Poetry: Fulfillment of a Tradition." *Genre* 12 (1979): 181–201.

———. "Speakers and Hearers in *The Temple*." *The George Herbert Journal* 5 (1981–82): 31–44.

Merton, Egon Stephen. *Science and Imagination in Sir Thomas Browne*. New York: King's Crown Press, 1949.

Millar, Susanna. *The Psychology of Play*. 1968. Reprint. New York: Jason Aronson, 1974.

Miller, David L. *Gods and Games: Toward a Theology of Play*. New York: World Publishing Company, 1970.

Mills, Jerry Leath. "Recent Studies in Herbert." *English Literary Renaissance* 6 (1976): 105–118.

Miner, Earl. *The Cavalier Mode from Jonson to Cotton*. Princeton: Princeton Univ. Press, 1971.

Moltmann, Jürgen. *Theology of Play*. Trans. Reinhard Ulrich. New York: Harper, 1972.

More, Thomas. *Sir Thomas More: Utopia*. Ed. and trans. Robert M. Adams. New York: Norton, 1975.

Morgan, Edmund S. *The Puritan Family: Religion and Domestic Relations in Seventeenth-Century New England*. Rev. ed. New York: Harper and Row, 1966.

Mourgues, Odette de. *Metaphysical, Baroque, and Précieux Poetry*. Oxford : Clarendon Press, 1953.

Mueller, William R. *The Anatomy of Robert Burton's England.* Berkeley: Univ. of California Press, 1952.

Mullaney, Steven. "Strange Things, Gross Terms, Curious Customs: The Rehearsal of Cultures in the Late Renaissance." *Representations* 1 (1983): 40–67.

Murry, John Middleton. *Countries of the Mind: Essays in Literary Criticism.* London: W. Collins Sons, 1922.

Nardo, Anna K. "Hamlet, 'A Man to Double Business Bound.'" *Shakespeare Quarterly* 34 (1983): 181–99.

Nathanson, Leonard. *The Strategy of Truth: A Study of Sir Thomas Browne.* Chicago: Univ. of Chicago Press, 1967.

Neale, Robert E. *In Praise of Play: Toward a Psychology of Religion.* New York: Harper and Row, 1969.

———. "Play and the Sacred." In *Motivations in Play, Games, and Sports,* ed. Ralph Slovenko and James A. Knight, 148–57. Springfield, Illinois: Charles C. Thomas, 1967.

Nevo, Ruth. "Marvell's 'Songs of Innocence and Experience.'" *Studies in English Literature* 5 (1965): 1–21.

Nicolson, Marjorie Hope. *The Breaking of the Circle: Studies in the Effect of the "New Science" upon Seventeenth-Century Poetry.* Rev. ed. New York: Columbia Univ. Press, 1960.

Noakes, Aubrey. "The Mother of George Herbert." *Contemporary Review* 183 (1953): 39–45.

Nochimson, Richard L. "Burton's *Anatomy:* The Author's Purposes and the Reader's Response." *Forum for Modern Language Studies* 13 (1977): 265–84.

Norford, Don Parry. "Marvell and the Arts of Contemplation and Action." *ELH* 41 (1974): 50–73.

Novarr, David. "Donne and the 'Undeterminable Desire of More.'" Paper presented at Biennial Renaissance Conference, The Eagle and the Dove: Reassessing John Donne, Univ. of Michigan-Dearborn, 15-16 October 1982.

———. "'The Exstasie': Donne's Address on the States of Union." In *Just So Much Honor: Essays Commemorating the Four-Hundredth Anniversary of the Birth of John Donne,* ed. Peter Amadeus Fiore, 219–43. University Park: Pennsylvania State Univ. Press, 1972.

Nuttall, A. D. *Overheard by God: Fiction and Prayer in Herbert, Milton, Dante and St. John.* London: Methuen, 1980.

O'Connell, Michael. *Robert Burton.* Boston: Twayne, 1986.

Ong, Walter J., S. J. *Fighting for Life: Contest, Sexuality, and Consciousness*. Ithaca: Cornell Univ. Press, 1981.

———. "Latin Language Study as a Renaissance Puberty Rite." In *Rhetoric, Romance, and Technology: Studies in the Interaction of Expression and Culture*, 113–41. Ithaca: Cornell Univ. Press, 1971.

———. "Voice as Summons for Belief: Literature, Faith, and the Divided Self." In *The Barbarian Within and Other Fugitive Essays and Studies*, 49–67. New York: Macmillan, 1962.

———. "The Writer's Audience Is Always a Fiction." *PMLA* 90 (1975): 9–21.

Opie, Iona and Peter. "Games (Young) People Play." *Horizon* 13 (1971): 16–19.

Ozment, Steven. *When Fathers Ruled: Family Life in Reformation Europe*. Cambridge: Harvard Univ. Press, 1983.

Pahlka, William H. *Saint Augustine's Meter and George Herbert's Will*. Kent, Ohio: Kent State Univ. Press, 1987.

Parker, Derek. *John Donne and His World*. London: Thames and Hudson, 1975.

Parker, Stanley. *The Sociology of Leisure*. New York: International Publications Service, 1976.

Patrides, C. A., "'Above Atlas His Shoulders': An Introduction to Sir Thomas Browne." In *Sir Thomas Browne: The Major Works*, ed. C. A. Patrides, 21–52. Harmondsworth, England: Penguin Books, 1977.

———, ed. *Approaches to Marvell: The York Tercentenary Lectures*. London: Routledge and Kegan Paul, 1978.

———, ed. *Approaches to Sir Thomas Browne: The Ann Arbor Tercentenary Lectures and Essays*. Columbia: Univ. of Missouri Press, 1982.

Patterson, Annabel M. *Censorship and Interpretation: The Conditions of Writing and Reading in Early Modern England*. Madison: Univ. of Wisconsin Press, 1984.

———. *Marvell and the Civic Crown*. Princeton: Princeton Univ. Press, 1978.

Pinchbeck, Ivy and Margaret Hewitt. *From Tudor Times to the Eighteenth Century*. Vol. 1 of *Children in English Society*. London: Routledge and Kegan Paul, 1969.

Pinka, Patricia Garland. *This Dialogue of One: The Songs and Sonnets of John Donne*. Tuscaloosa: Univ. of Alabama Press, 1982.

Post, Jonathan F. S. *Sir Thomas Browne*. Boston: Twayne, 1987.

Potter, George R. "Donne's *Exstasie*, Contra Legouis." *Philological Quarterly* 15 (1936): 247–53.

Prawer, Siegbert. "Burton's 'Anatomy of Melancholy.'" *The Cambridge Journal* 1 (1948): 671–88.

Praz, Mario. "Sir Thomas Browne." *English Studies* 11 (1929): 161–71.

———. *Studies in Seventeenth-Century Imagery.* 2 vols. London: Warburg Institute, 1939.

Prosser, Eleanor. *Hamlet and Revenge.* 2nd ed. rev. Stanford: Stanford Univ. Press, 1971.

Quinn, Dennis. "Donne and the Wane of Wonder." *ELH* 36 (1969): 626–47.

———. "Donne's Christian Eloquence." In *Seventeenth-Century Prose: Modern Essays in Criticism,* ed. Stanley E. Fish, 353–74. New York: Oxford Univ. Press, 1971.

Rabelais, Francois. *The Histories of Gargantua and Pantagruel.* Trans. J. M. Cohen. 1955. Reprint. Harmondsworth, England: Penguin Books, 1986.

Rabkin, Norman. *Shakespeare and the Common Understanding.* New York: The Free Press, 1967.

Rahner, Hugo. *Man at Play.* New York: Herder and Herder, 1972.

Rajan, Tilottama. "'Nothing Sooner Broke': Donne's *Songs and Sonets* as Self-Consuming Artifact." *ELH* 49 (1982): 805–28.

Reid, B. L. "The Last Act and the Action of *Hamlet.*" *Yale Review* 54 (1964): 59–80.

Renaker, David. "Robert Burton and Ramist Method." *Renaissance Quarterly* 24 (1971): 210–20.

Ribner, Irving. *Patterns in Shakespearean Tragedy.* London: Methuen, 1960.

Richmond, Hugh M. "Personal Identity and Literary Personae: A Study in Historical Psychology." *PMLA* 90 (1975): 209–21.

Rickey, Mary Ellen. *Utmost Art: Complexity in the Verse of George Herbert.* Lexington: Univ. of Kentucky Press, 1966.

Roberts, John R. *George Herbert: An Annotated Bibliography of Modern Criticism 1905–1974.* Columbia: Univ. of Missouri Press, 1978.

———, ed. *Essential Articles for the Study of George Herbert's Poetry.* Hamden, Connecticut: Archon Books, 1979.

Roston, Murray. *The Soul of Wit: A Study of John Donne.* London: Clarendon Press, 1974.

Røstvig, Maren-Sofie. "Andrew Marvell's 'The Garden': A Hermetic Poem." *English Studies* 40 (1959): 65–76.

Rothstein, Arnold. *The Narcissistic Pursuit of Perfection.* New York: International Universities Press, 1980.

Routh, Michael. "A Crux of 'The Pulley.'" *Seventeenth Century News* 40 (1982): 44–45.

Ryerson, Alice Judson. "Medical Advice on Child Rearing, 1550–1900." *Harvard Educational Review* 31 (1961): 305, 312–13.

Saavedra, Miguel de Cervantes. *The Adventures of Don Quixote*. Trans. J. M. Cohen. 1950. Reprint. Baltimore: Penguin, 1975.

Sanders, Wilbur. *John Donne's Poetry*. Cambridge: Cambridge Univ. Press, 1971.

Schleiner, Winfried. *The Imagery of John Donne's Sermons*. Providence, Rhode Island: Brown Univ. Press, 1970.

Schwartzman, Helen B. "Towards a Theory of Everyday Play." Paper delivered at Conference on Forms of Play in the Early Modern Period, Univ. of Maryland, 22–23 March 1984.

———. *Transformations: The Anthropology of Children's Play*. New York: Plenum Press, 1978.

Schwenger, Peter. "'To Make His Saying True': Deceit in *Appleton House*." *Studies in Philology* 77 (1980): 84–104.

Scoular, Kitty W. *Natural Magic: Studies in the Presentation of Nature in English Poetry from Spenser to Marvell*. London: Oxford at the Clarendon Press, 1965.

Shakespeare, William. *The Complete Works of Shakespeare*. Ed. Hardin Craig and David Bevington. Rev. ed. Glenview, Illinois: Scott, Foresman and Company, 1973.

Sharrock, Roger. "Marvell's Poetry of Evasion and Marvell's Times." *English* 28 (1979): 3–40.

Sherwood, Terry G. *Fulfilling the Circle: A Study of John Donne's Thought*. Toronto: Univ. of Toronto Press, 1984.

Shuttleworth, J. M., ed. *The Life of Edward, First Lord Herbert of Cherbury written by himself*. London: Oxford Univ. Press, 1976.

Siegel, Paul N. "Donne's *Paradoxes and Problems*." *Philological Quarterly* 28 (1949): 507–11.

Simon, Jean Robert. *Robert Burton (1577–1640) et L' Anatomie de la Mélancolie*. Paris: Didier, 1964.

Simpson, Evelyn M. *A Study of the Prose Works of John Donne*. Oxford: Clarendon Press, 1924.

Singleton, Marion White. *God's Courtier: Configuring a Different Grace in George Herbert's Temple*. Cambridge: Cambridge Univ. Press, 1987.

Skulsky, Harold. "*Upon Appleton House:* Marvell's Comedy of Discourse." *ELH* 52 (1985): 591–620.

Skura, Meredith Anne. *The Literary Use of the Psychoanalytic Process*. New Haven: Yale Univ. Press, 1981.

Sloane, Thomas O. *Donne, Milton, and the End of Humanist Rhetoric*. Berkeley: Univ. of California Press, 1985.

Sluki, Carlos E., and Donald C. Ransom, eds. *Double Bind: The Foundation of the Communicational Approach to the Family.* New York: Grune and Stratten, 1976.

Smith, A. J. *John Donne: The Songs and Sonets*. London: Edward Arnold, 1964.

———. "The Metaphysic of Love." *Review of English Studies* 9 (1958): 362–75.

Spariosu, Mihai I. *Dionysus Reborn: Play and the Aesthetic Dimension in Modern Philosophical and Scientific Discourse*. Ithaca: Cornell Univ. Press, 1989.

———. *Literature, Mimesis and Play: Essays in Literary Theory.* Tübingen: Gunter Narr Verlag, 1982.

Spencer, Jeffry B. *Heroic Nature: Ideal Landscape in English Poetry from Marvell to Thomson*. Evanston, Illinois: Northwestern Univ. Press, 1973.

Spencer, Theodore, ed. *A Garland for John Donne: 1631–1931*. 1931. Reprint. Gloucester, Massachusetts: Peter Smith, 1958.

Spitzer, Leo. "Marvell's 'Nymph Complaining for the Death of Her Faun': Sources versus Meaning." In *Seventeenth-Century English Poetry: Modern Essays in Criticism,* ed. William R. Keast, 372–87. Rev. ed. London: Oxford Univ. Press, 1971.

Stallybrass, Peter, and Allon White. *The Politics and Poetics of Transgression*. London: Methuen, 1986.

Stampfer, Judah. *John Donne and the Metaphysical Gesture*. New York: Funk and Wagnalls, 1970.

Stein, Arnold. *George Herbert's Lyrics*. Baltimore: The Johns Hopkins Press, 1968.

———. *John Donne's Lyrics: The Eloquence of Action*. 1962. Reprint. New York: Octagon Books, 1980.

Stephen, Leslie. "Country Books." In vol. 3 of *Hours in a Library,* 175–206. London: Smith, Elder, and Co., 1899.

Stewart, Stanley. *The Enclosed Garden: The Tradition and the Image in Seventeenth-Century Poetry.* Madison: Univ. of Wisconsin Press, 1966.

———. *George Herbert*. Boston: Twayne, 1986.

Stirling, Brents. *Unity in Shakespearian Tragedy: The Interplay of Theme and Character.* New York: Columbia Univ. Press, 1956.

Stone, Lawrence. *The Family, Sex and Marriage in England 1500–1800*. London: Weidenfeld and Nicolson, 1977.

Storr, Anthony. *Human Aggression*. New York: Atheneum, 1968.

Suits, Bernard. *The Grasshopper: Games, Life and Utopia*. Toronto: Univ. of Toronto Press, 1978.

Summers, Claude J., and Ted-Larry Pebworth, eds. *"Too Rich to Clothe the Sunne": Essays on George Herbert.* Pittsburgh: Univ. of Pittsburgh Press, 1980.

Summers, Joseph H. *George Herbert: His Religion and Art.* Cambridge: Harvard Univ. Press, 1954.

———. *The Heirs of Donne and Jonson.* New York: Oxford Univ. Press, 1970.

———. "Stanley Fish's Reading of Seventeenth-Century Literature." *Modern Language Quarterly* 35 (1974): 403–17.

Sutton-Smith, Brian. "Games of Order and Disorder." *The Association for the Anthropological Study of Play Newsletter* 4 (1977): 19–26.

———. "Play as Adaptive Potentiation." *Studies in the Anthropology of Play: Papers in Memory of B. Allan Tindall,* ed. Phillips Stevens, Jr., 232–37. Westpoint, New York: Leisure Press, 1977.

Swan, Jim. "At Play in the Garden of Ambivalence: Andrew Marvell and the Green World." *Criticism* 17 (1975): 295–307.

———. "History, Pastoral and Desire: Andrew Marvell's Mower Poems." *International Review of Psychoanalysis* 3 (1976): 193–202.

Swardson, H. R. *Poetry and the Fountain of Light: Observations on the Conflict Between Christian and Classical Traditions in Seventeenth-Century Poetry.* Columbia: Univ. of Missouri Press, 1962.

Taylor, Ivan Earle. "Cavalier Sophistication in the Poetry of George Herbert." *Anglican Theological Review* 39 (1957): 229–43.

Taylor, Mark. *The Soul in Paraphrase: George Herbert's Poetics.* The Hague: Mouton, 1974.

Thomas, Keith. "Work and Leisure in Pre-Industrial Society." *Past and Present* 29 (1964): 50–66.

Thrupp, Sylvia L., ed. *Change in Medieval Society: Europe North of the Alps, 1050–1500.* New York: Appleton-Century Crofts, 1964.

Tillman, James S. "The Satirist Satirized: Burton's Democritus Jr." *Studies in the Literary Imagination* 10 (1977): 89–96.

Todd, Richard. *The Opacity of Signs: Acts of Interpretation in George Herbert's The Temple.* Columbia: Univ. of Missouri Press, 1986.

Toliver, Harold E. *Marvell's Ironic Vision.* New Haven: Yale Univ. Press, 1965.

———. "Poetry as Sacred Conveyance in Herbert and Marvell." In *Pastoral Forms and Attitudes,* 116–37. Berkeley: Univ. of California Press, 1971.

Trumbach, Randolph. *The Rise of the Egalitarian Family: Aristocratic Kinship and*

Domestic Relations in Eighteenth-Century England. New York: Academic Press, 1978.

Turner, Victor. "Betwixt and Between: The Liminal Period in *Rites de Passage*." In *The Forest of Symbols: Aspects of Ndembu Ritual*, 93–111. Ithaca: Cornell Univ. Press, 1967.

———. *Dramas, Fields, and Metaphors: Symbolic Action in Human Society*. Ithaca: Cornell Univ. Press, 1974.

———. "Liminal to Liminoid, in Play, Flow, and Ritual: An Essay in Comparative Symbology." In *The Anthropological Study of Human Play*, ed. Edward Norbeck. *Rice University Studies* 60 (1974): 53–92.

———. *The Ritual Process: Structure and Anti-Structure*. Ithaca: Cornell Univ. Press, 1969.

Tuve, Rosemond. *Elizabethan and Metaphysical Imagery: Renaissance Poetic and Twentieth-Century Critics*. Chicago: Univ. of Chicago Press, 1947.

———. *A Reading of George Herbert*. Chicago: Univ. of Chicago Press, 1952.

Untermeyer, Louis. *Play in Poetry*. New York: Harcourt, Brace, 1938.

Vale, Marcia. *The Gentleman's Recreations: Accomplishments and Pastimes of the English Gentleman 1580–1630*. Totowa, New Jersey: Rowman and Littlefield, 1977.

Van Laan, Thomas F. "Ironic Reversal in *Hamlet*." *Studies in English Literature* 6 (1966): 247–62.

Van Nuis, Hermine. "Sincerity of Being and Simplicity of Expression: George Herbert's Ethics and Aesthetics." *Christianity and Literature* 27 (1977): 11–21.

Veith, Gene Edward, Jr. *Reformation Spirituality: The Religion of George Herbert*. Lewisburg, Pennsylvania: Bucknell Univ. Press, 1985.

Vendler, Helen. *The Poetry of George Herbert*. Cambridge: Harvard Univ. Press, 1975.

Wall, Richard. "The Household: Demographic and Economic Change in England, 1650–1970." In *Family Forms in Historic Europe*, ed. Richard Wall, 493–512. Cambridge: Cambridge Univ. Press, 1983.

Wallace, John M. *Destiny His Choice: The Loyalism of Andrew Marvell*. Cambridge: Cambridge Univ. Press, 1968.

Wallerstein, Ruth. *Studies in Seventeenth-Century Poetic*. New York: Univ. of Wisconsin Press, 1950.

Walton, Izaak. *The Compleat Angler 1653–1676*. Ed. Jonquil Bevan. Oxford: Clarendon Press, 1983.

———. "The Life of Mr. George Herbert." In *The Lives of Dr. John Donne, Sir*

Henry Wooton, Mr. Richard Hooker, Mr. George Herbert, and Dr. Robert Sanderson. New York: George P. Putnam, 1850.

Wanamaker, Melissa C. *Discordia Concors: The Wit of Metaphysical Poetry*. Port Washington, New York: Kennikat Press, 1975.

Warner, William B. *Chance and the Text of Experience: Freud, Nietzsche, and Shakespeare's Hamlet*. Ithaca: Cornell Univ. Press, 1986.

Warnke, Frank J. "Baroque Poetry and the Experience of Contradiction." *Colloquia Germanica* 1 (1967): 38–48.

———. "Play and Metamorphosis in Marvell's Poetry." *Studies in English Literature* 5 (1965): 23–30.

———. "Sacred Play: Baroque Poetic Style." *Journal of Aesthetics and Art Criticism* 22 (1964): 455–64.

———. *Versions of Baroque: European Literature in the Seventeenth Century*. New Haven: Yale Univ. Press, 1972.

Webber, Joan. *Contrary Music: The Prose Style of John Donne*. Madison: Univ. of Wisconsin Press, 1963.

———. *The Eloquent "I": Style and Self in Seventeenth-Century Prose*. Madison: Univ. of Wisconsin Press, 1968.

Wedgwood, C. V. *A Coffin for King Charles: The Trial and Execution of Charles I*. 1964. Reprint. New York: Time Incorporated, 1966.

Weinstein, Fred, and Gerald M. Platt. *Psychoanalytic Sociology: An Essay on the Interpretation of Historical Data and the Phenomena of Collective Behavior*. Baltimore: The Johns Hopkins Press, 1973.

Welsford, Enid. *The Fool: His Social and Literary History*. London: Faber and Faber, 1935.

Westerweel, Bart. *Patterns and Patterning: A Study of Four Poems by George Herbert*. Amsterdam: Rodopi, 1984.

Westfall, Richard S. *Science and Religion in Seventeenth-Century England*. New Haven: Yale Univ. Press, 1958.

Whibley, Charles. *Literary Portraits*. London: Archibald Constable, 1904.

White, Helen C. *The Metaphysical Poets: A Study in Religious Experience*. 1936. Reprint. New York: Collier Books, 1966.

White, Helen C., Ruth C. Wallerstein, and Richard Quintana, eds. *Seventeenth-Century Verse and Prose*. Vol. I, 1600–1660. New York: Macmillan, 1951.

White, Lynn, Jr. "Death and the Devil." In *The Darker Vision of the Renaissance: Beyond the Fields of Reason*, ed. Robert S. Kinsman, 25–46. Berkeley: Univ. of California Press, 1974.

Whitfield, Christopher. *A History of Chipping Campden and Captain Robert Dover's Olympick Games*. Eton: Shakespeare Head Press, 1958.

Wilcher, Robert. *Andrew Marvell*. Cambridge: Cambridge Univ. Press, 1985.

Wilden, Anthony. "Lacan and the Discourse of the Other." In Lacan, *Language of the Self*, 159–311. See Lacan.

Wilding, Michael, ed. *Marvell: Modern Judgements*. London: Macmillan, 1969.

Willeford, William. *The Fool and His Sceptre: A Study in Clowns Jesters and Their Audience*. Evanston, Illinois: Northwestern Univ. Press, 1969.

Willey, Basil. *The Seventeenth Century Background: Studies in the Thought of the Age in Relation to Poetry and Religion*. 1934. Reprint. Garden City, New York: Doubleday, 1953.

Williamson, George. *The Donne Tradition: A Study in English Poetry from Donne to the Death of Cowley*. Cambridge: Harvard Univ. Press, 1930.

———. *The Proper Wit of Poetry*. London: Faber and Faber, 1961.

Wilson, F. P. "A Note on George Herbert's 'The Quidditie.'" *Review of English Studies* 19 (1943): 398–99.

Wilson, John Dover. *What Happens in Hamlet*. London: Cambridge Univ. Press, 1935.

Winnicott, Donald Woods. *The Maturational Processes and the Facilitating Environment*. New York: International Universities Press, 1965.

———. *Playing and Reality*. New York: Basic Books, 1971.

Wise, James N. *Sir Thomas Browne's Religio Medici and Two Seventeenth-Century Critics*. Columbia: Univ. of Missouri Press, 1973.

Wither, George. *A Collection of Emblemes, Ancient and Moderne*, 1635. Reprint. Columbia: Univ. of South Carolina Press, 1975.

Wrightson, Keith. *English Society 1580–1680*. New Brunswick, New Jersey: Rutgers Univ. Press,1982.

Ziegler, Dewey Kiper. *In Divided and Distinguished Worlds: Religion and Rhetoric in the Writings of Sir Thomas Browne*. Cambridge: Harvard Univ. Printing Office, 1943.

Zijderveld, Anton C. *Reality in a Looking-Glass: Rationality Through an Analysis of Traditional Folly*. London: Routledge and Kegan Paul, 1982.

Zunder, William. *The Poetry of John Donne: Literature and Culture in the Elizabethan and Jacobean Period*. Totowa, New Jersey: Barnes and Noble Books, 1982.

Index